THE ISLAND THAT DISAPPEARED

THE ISLAND THAT DISAPPEARED

OLD PROVIDENCE AND THE MAKING OF THE WESTERN WORLD

TOM FEILING

First published in 2017 by

EXPLORE BOOKS

www.exploretravelwriting.com
email: explorebooks@outlook.com

For bulk and special sales please contact explorebooks@outlook.com

A catalogue record for this book is available
from the British Library

ISBNs: 978-1-911184-04-1 (paperback)
978-1-911184-05-8 (ePub)
978-1-911184-06-5 (mobi)

Typeset by Josh Bryson
Maps by Simonetta Giori
Cover design by Dan Mogford
Cover image of Lord Saye and Sele (detail from),
© National Portrait Gallery, London

Printed and bound in Great Britain
Distributed by Turnaround Publisher Services, UK

CONTENTS

PART FOUR

INTRODUCTION

> What should we do but sing his praise
> That led us through the watery maze
> Unto an isle so long unknown,
> And yet far kinder than our own?
> – *Bermudas*, Andrew Marvell, 1654

> Now that bird ... is maybe two hundred years old, Hawkins – they lives for
> ever mostly; and if anybody's seen more wickedness, it must be the devil him-
> self. She's sailed with England, the great Cap'n England, the pirate. She's been
> at Madagascar, and at Malabar, the Surinam, and Providence and Portobello.
> –'Long' John Silver, talking of his parrot, Captain Flint,
> in Robert Louis Stevenson's *Treasure Island*, 1883

This book began with a conversation I had with my editor at Penguin,
a few weeks after publication of my last book, *Short Walks from Bogotá:
Journeys in the New Colombia*. In the course of my research, I had travelled the length and breadth of Colombia, and spoken to a lot of Colombians about their country's history, politics and culture. 'How about
writing something similar about the UK?' she suggested. She received a
lot of pitches from British writers proposing to write books about far-
flung parts of the world, but few of them seemed interested in reporting
on the state of their own country. This suited me fine; after spending
several years in far-flung places, I was keen to know more about my own
country. In the spring of 2012, I bought a camper van, and spent the
next six months travelling around the country, navigating by a self-im-
posed rule that I would avoid all towns and cities, and stick to B roads,
guided only by a compass. I wanted to stop thinking about the land in
terms of A to B and attune myself to the natural boundaries of cliffs,
rivers and hills.

I didn't know what I was looking for. I ploughed through several
books that purported to capture the essence of England (and even one
or two that claimed to do the same for the other home nations). I started
with Kate Fox's *Watching the English*, which I read on Brighton Beach;
graduated to *The English* by Jeremy Paxman and Peter Ackroyd's *Albion:
The Origins of the English Imagination*; and by the time I had finished

George Orwell's *The Lion and the Unicorn* I was at the Kyle of Tongue in the furthest reaches of Scotland where the van was being rocked on its axles by a storm coming in from the North Atlantic. I had strayed a long way off the beaten track.

The problem with writing books – as well as with sightseeing – is that everyone wants to visit the best bits. The English think they have their history sewn up. There are thousands of newspaper columnists and TV producers who take it upon themselves to distil the essence of the national character, as revealed in a series of cherry-picked favourite episodes. They seem content to pore over a tide of books, films, and documentaries that largely rehash what we already know. In order of immediacy, the cherries are deemed to be the Second World War (reduced to a simple struggle of good over evil), the First World War (patriotic sacrifice), the Victorians (enterprise, industry and sexual repression), Elizabeth I (a secular Virgin Mother) and Henry VIII (the original macho brute).

A few weeks later, I parked up for the night outside a small, isolated church near Stokesay in Shropshire. I was too cut off from everything to know it, but that night, Danny Boyle was presenting his take on the meaning of Britain's history at the opening ceremony of the Olympic Games in London. While he was transmogrifying England's dark Satanic Mills to become the National Health Service, I was reading about the English Civil War in the van.

Somewhere beyond the church, there was a party going on; perhaps, I told myself, in a marquee erected on the lawn of a prosperous farmer's house, thrown by his son to celebrate the opening of the Games. By the time the church bell tolled midnight, he and his friends were in full song. I was too far away to make out the words, but they were clearly having trouble keeping up with the techno soundtrack. As the sound of their slurred and straining voices ebbed over the wheat fields, I found past and present melting into one another. The unseen marquee became a cave, the song a chant, and its singers Neanderthals back from a successful hunting trip.

That's what I want, I said to myself – something that connects the present to the distant past; a crack through which I might find something overlooked but essential about England's history. Why did I know so little about the Civil War, England's last and greatest domestic conflagration, I wondered? I had picked up the bare bones of the plot somewhere along the way: how the roundheads had fought the cavaliers, and

Charles I ended up losing his head. But the hours I had spent watching history documentaries on BBC2 had given me next to no understanding of a war that had raged for over ten years, and killed 250,000 Britons. I suppose the religious dispute at the heart of the conflict can mean little to modern, secular Britain. The victory of Parliament is no longer the landmark it once was, and its Puritan champion, Oliver Cromwell, has been written off for the wanton slaughter he unleashed on the people of Wexford and Drogheda. 'Puritan' has become a term of abuse, 'republican' an anachronism. And then there is the little matter of regicide, a last resort that set royalist nerves on edge forever after. Yet the recession and austerity that precipitated the Civil War, the migrant crisis that coincided with it, and the religious fundamentalism that drove it suggested that the time was ripe for a fresh look.

As I read more about the Civil War, I was struck by mention of the Providence Island Company. It was not often mentioned, but among its members were most of the Puritan nobles who led Parliament into war against the king. I recognised the name from my time in Colombia. The congressman who represents the department of San Andrés and Providencia is the only native English-speaker in the chamber. Since the islands are 500 miles north of the mainland, most Colombians don't pay them much attention. Like them, I had wondered about tiny Providence, cut adrift 150 miles off the Miskito coast of Nicaragua, but not enough to visit.

Guided by an inkling that the island had something new and original to tell me about the UK, I trawled the internet, and ordered the only three books to have been written about the place. I discovered that the Providence Island Company's records had been lost for 250 years. Only in 1876 did the archivists at the Public Record Office realise that they had been mistakenly filed under New Providence, the first English settlement on the Bahamas. In fact, Old Providence predates both New Providence and Providence, Rhode Island.

No one I spoke to in London had even heard of the island. Yet it had once been hugely important to England, for it was the site of one of its first, and most ambitious colonies. The first settlers arrived on the *Seaflower* in 1631, ten years after its sister ship, the *Mayflower*, landed at Plymouth, Massachusetts. Unlike New England, the colony had a short life – it was wiped out by the Spanish in 1641 – but the more I read about it, and what followed it, the more convinced I became that I had hit upon a neat précis of the story of how Britain became a world power.

We live in an era of globalisation in which nations are becoming less important. But globalisation is not a new idea. Like Puritanism, it is a utopian project, and the post-national, post-racial ideal at its core is part of England's contribution to world culture. Arguably, globalisation began with Oliver Cromwell, the religious fundamentalist who led a Protestant crusade, killed the king, and laid the foundations for what would become the largest empire the world has ever known. For a time, Providence had been 'the Lord Protector's darling,' and the beacon guiding God's chosen people into the wilderness. But Cromwell's Commonwealth died with him, to be replaced by the refinement and corruption of the Restoration era. Providence went the same way: the model godly society was over-run by pirates, the Spanish drove them both away, and the island was eventually abandoned.

Then I met a Colombian artist at a gallery opening who had spent several summers on Providence when he was growing up. What was it like, I asked him? Well, the islanders were nothing like the archetypal villagers that Gabriel García Márquez described in *One Hundred Years of Solitude*, he told me. Most of them were Baptists for a start, and although they understood Spanish, most of them refused to speak it. But they had been hospitable enough, at least to begin with, and the older islanders were noticeably pious and well educated. Crime was practically unheard of, and usually involved nothing more serious than the theft of coconuts. But his memories of the island had been tainted by an acrimonious dispute between his parents and the island's mayor, which only ended when they sold up and returned to the mainland. In spite of their outward show of piety, there were still a lot of pirates on Providence, he concluded.

I wanted to see what had happened to Providence since it sailed off the edge of the world stage; to listen for echoes of the dramatic confrontation between Puritans and pirates that took place there 380 years ago. I had reasons of my own for going there too: a desire for a refuge from the world. I certainly wasn't being driven into exile, as the Puritan settlers were, but the desire for 'purification' from the 'contaminants' of the modern world has not gone away, and neither has the instinct that told me I would find it on a faraway tropical island.

I spent four wonderful months on Providence, an earthly paradise that may well be the last vestige of the Caribbean as it was before the drug trade, corruption and mass tourism became facts of life. It was not easy to piece together the story of what happened following the resettlement of the island. There is no Public Record Office on Providence, and what passes for truth may well be closer to myth. I had to become a very local historian, which meant ditching the history books for the Dictaphone, and listening to the stories told by the 5,000 people who live on the island today.

One of the supposedly quintessential English traits that Peter Ackroyd mentions in *Albion: the Origins of the English Imagination* is the love of the miniature. Some of the most memorable landscapes I had seen travelling around the UK in 2012 were the tiny tableaux of gorse, wildflowers and toadstools on the cliffs of north Devon. I found the diminutive story of Providence no less enchanting, as if the very act of looking at a microcosm reminds us that there are epic dramas being played out on stages large and small. There are still Puritans and pirates on Providence, and they have a lot to tell us about the legacy of the early colonial period, not just for the Caribbean, but for modern Britain. So while the story you're about to read might be set on a tiny island, at its heart is a story about England, and how its people have been shaped by their country's imperial past.

Part One covers the rise and fall of the original Puritan colony on Providence. Part Two covers Henry Morgan and the Brethren of the Coast who took the Puritans' place. This takes us up to the interval: the century after 1680 when the island was abandoned. Part Three opens with my arrival on the island, and goes on to explore how Britain grew rich on the back of a very different kind of colony – Jamaica – and how the Puritans and pirates of the Caribbean were mythologised by the empire builders of the Victorian era. This is where I look into the fascinating story of what happened after Francis Archbold resettled the island in 1789. Finally, Part Four looks at the legacy of Puritanism and piracy, and the challenges the islanders face today, as their isolation comes to an end.

A few words on the text: in colonial times, the English called the island 'Providence', while the Spanish called it 'Santa Catalina'. After gaining independence from Spain, the Colombians called it 'Providencia de Santa Catalina', but these days, they just call it 'Providencia', while

English speakers call it 'Old Providence'. I have chosen to use all these names, depending on the period, and whose point of view I am trying to convey.

The neighbouring island has also been through several monikers: the first English settlers called it 'Henrietta', after King Charles' French wife, but the island was largely ignored until 1785, when the Spanish crown reasserted its claim to what it called 'San Andrés'. The islanders preferred to call it 'St Andrew's', but these days, most of them use the Spanish name, and I have done the same. The Mosquito Coast is not what it was either. The name has nothing to do with flying insects, and everything to do with the tribe the English settlers encountered when they first ventured from Providence to the coast of Central America. In modern times, it became known as the 'Misquito coast', then the 'Miskito Coast', and now there is talk of it becoming the 'Miskitu coast'. I have opted to use the second, most common, name.

I have amended citations from the original sources to conform to modern English spelling, but left them otherwise unchanged. In most instances, I have converted seventeenth-century prices into their modern-day equivalent with the help of several handy online currency converters.[i]

---

[i]   The National Archive's currency converter can be accessed at: http://www.nationalarchives.gov.uk/currency/results.asp. Francis Turner's article, *Money and Exchange Rates in 1632*, can be found at: http://projects.exeter.ac.uk/RDavies/arian/current/howmuch.html. *Pirate Money* can be found at: http://pirates.hegewisch.net/money.html. To calculate the present day purchasing power of Dutch guilders, I used: http://www.iisg.nl/hpw/calculate2.php.

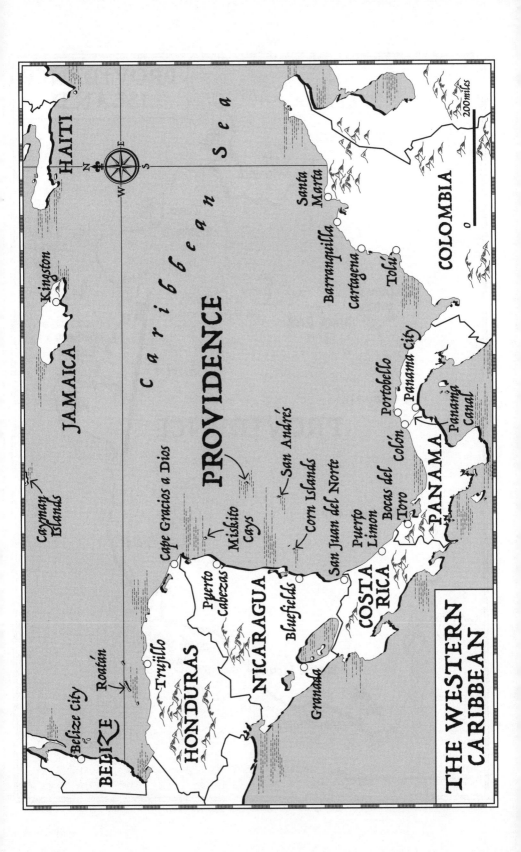

THE WESTERN CARIBBEAN

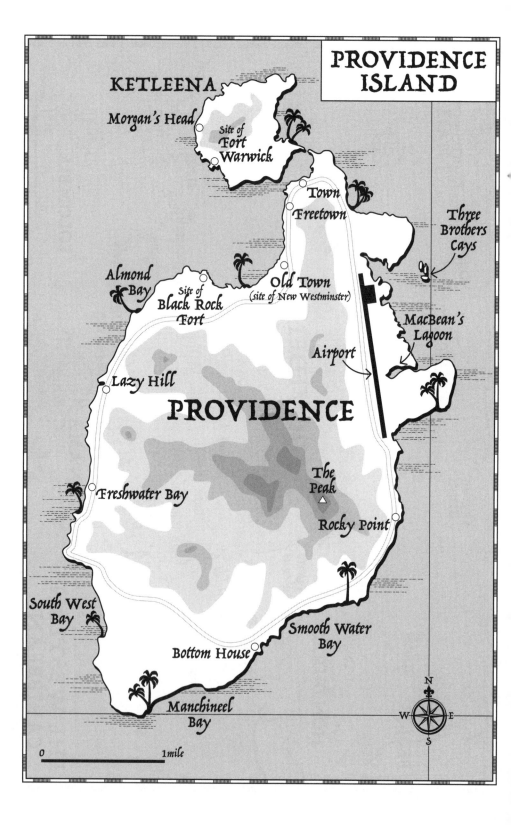

PART ONE

1

BUILDING NEW WESTMINSTER

1629: emerging from a sea that shimmered near silver in the light of mid-morning, the island looked like a black peaked hat. As the *Robert* drew closer, its flanks turned dark green, suggestive of rich, fertile soils, and the seabed rose steeply from the depths, turning the water a brilliant turquoise. Captain Daniel Elfrith dropped anchor at the edge of the coral reef that runs down the eastern side of the island, and had his men row him ashore in a longboat. He stepped onto a beach of fine, white sand that rose steeply into deep forest. Ahead of them, the sunlight was playing on the fronds of tall palm trees that marked the watershed of a lush valley. They made their way to the fast-running stream, which gave them their first taste of fresh water since leaving the Somers Isles, 1,800 miles to the northeast.[i]

Captain Elfrith resolved to explore his discovery. The undergrowth was dense, and they had to clamber over the roots of huge cotton trees, so they stuck to the course of the stream. As they climbed higher, the trees thinned out. Emerging onto flatter ground, they found wild orange and lemon trees growing in abundance. They also found trees bearing fruit that none of them had seen before: papaya, guava and soursop.

It took them several hours to reach the summit of the island's highest peak, but once there, the lie of the island became clear to them. Freshwater streams coursed through steep-sided valleys that branched out in every direction, levelling out as they approached the shore, 1,000 feet below, where they could see the *Robert* riding at anchor. They could see

---

[i] The Somers Isles are today known as Bermuda. The first settlement was established in 1609, but only lasted for ten months. The isles were resettled in 1612, and the Somers Isles Company was founded in 1615. The saga of the *Sea Venture*, which was shipwrecked on the Somers Isles while en route to Virginia in 1609, supplied William Shakespeare with the idea for *The Tempest*.

1

shades of brilliant aquamarine around the coral reef, which stretched out of sight to the north.

There were also masses of birds, which chattered over their heads as they passed under the boughs of the cotton trees. Through his spyglass, Captain Elfrith watched a pelican scoop plump fish from the glittering sea; a solitary heron standing sentinel in the mangroves; man-of-war birds (or frigatebirds) nesting on the rocky offshore cays. He didn't know it, but many of the birds he saw had come to the island to escape the winters of New England, where another band of English pioneers was struggling to keep from freezing to death.

The island was full of promise: it was well watered, its soils were rich and there was plenty of flat land close to the shore where a community of settlers could raise all manner of crops. The natural harbour in the northwest was to leeward, and the hills surrounding it would protect it from the storms that swept across the western Caribbean in the autumn. Captain Elfrith was coming to the end of a fruitless cruise in the far west of the Caribbean Sea. The day before, he had landed at another island, 40 miles due south. It too had been small – just twelve miles long – and while its sandy soils were fertile and it appeared to be uninhabited, he had searched in vain for a supply of fresh water. It was also low-lying, and he had been concerned that the lack of a vantage point would make it hard to defend from attack.

Elfrith was a privateer, and he had come looking for prizes. He was carrying letters of marque – a license authorising him to attack and rob Spanish merchant ships, granted by the state in times of war to any citizen with the means and intent to deprive King Philip IV of his ill-gotten gains. After his accession to the throne in 1625, King Charles had wasted no time in declaring war on Spain. By extension, this meant royal authorisation for a privateering war against Spanish shipping.

Among the English ship owners to recognise the extraordinary opportunity this posed, none had been quicker on the uptake than the Earl of Warwick. Warwick had first issued commissions to corsairs in the Caribbean in 1618. Of all the privateering ships that had set sail between 1626 and 1630, half had sailed for him. Elfrith was one of the Earl's most experienced privateers, a headstrong and argumentative man who liked nothing better than picking off a lone Spanish ship and then boasting of what he had done back in port. He had grown up listening to stories of Sir Francis Drake's audacious raid of Cartagena in 1586, and considered himself heir to the noble tradition of robbing the Spanish established by Queen Elizabeth I.

Until Elizabeth came to the throne, England had had no colonies, nor was it allowed any. Pope Alexander VI had confirmed Spain's dominion over the vast continent on the other side of the Atlantic in 1493, when he issued the *Inter caetera*. By this papal bull, a line was drawn north to south through the Atlantic Ocean; beyond the line only the soldiers and priests of the King of Spain were allowed to pass. English, Dutch and French ships had no business crossing the line, and foreign sailors found cruising American waters were liable to be killed on sight.

In the eyes of Catholic Spain, the New World was God's reward to the Spanish king for the *reconquista* of the Iberian peninsula. The long struggle to expel the Moors had been completed in 1492, the same year that Christopher Columbus first sailed to the Americas. As the historian Francisco López de Gómara told Emperor Charles V, after the Creation and the coming of Jesus Christ, the discovery of the Americas was the most important episode in the history of the world.

Good Queen Bess had not been deterred by Iberian claims to exclusivity in the Americas. In 1592, a squadron of English men-of-war seized the *Madre de Deus*, an enormous Portuguese galleon returning from India with a cargo of gold, silver, pearls, diamonds, amber, musk, tapestries and ebony. Sale of the cargo had raised £500,000, half the net value of the entire English Exchequer. Under Elizabeth's rule, privateering (licensed piracy) became a mainstay of English moneymaking. The Queen grew to depend on her sea robbers: without them, and the money they made from privateering, England would not have defeated the Spanish Armada in 1588.

Of course, were it not for the sea robbers, King Philip II would not have felt the need to launch an armada in the first place, but that would be to overlook the religious dimension of the conflict. The typical privateer saw himself as a combination of loyal knight, dutiful public servant and devout man of God – and saw no contradiction between the three. Sir Francis Drake had sailed with a sword in one hand, and a copy of John Foxe's *Book of Martyrs* in the other. The *Book of Martyrs* didn't just record the suffering of the Protestant martyrs; it related their deaths to the wider war between Protestant and Catholic, Christ and Antichrist, whose climax was fast approaching.

Ever since Tyndale's English translation of the New Testament in 1526, Protestant merchants had looked for a chance to combine their love of God with their hunger for riches. Their sponsorship of the privateers' voyages into distant seas gave them a chance to line their pockets, and to hasten the fall of the Catholic Church – the Whore of Babylon mentioned in the Book of Revelation in the Scriptures. The Elizabethan privateering tradition gave them a divinely ordained sense of purpose, and a generation of seafaring heroes that the entire country could celebrate.

Yet by 1627 those glory days seemed long gone. Following her death in 1603, Elizabeth was succeeded by James Stuart, who showed little interest in taking the fight to the Spanish. The country's privateers were called back to their home ports, and its merchant adventurers were encouraged to divert their efforts into the more prosaic task of building colonies in North America. By 1629, James' son, Charles I, had been on the throne for four years, and had already earned a reputation for incompetence and duplicity. Shortly after his accession to the throne, he declared war on Spain, but he was notoriously fickle, and easily swayed by the pro-Spanish faction at court, which argued for a less belligerent stance towards England's traditional foe.

Such were the thoughts ebbing and flowing through Captain Elfrith's mind as he surveyed the island through his spyglass. Then he caught sight of something unwelcome: a little ship riding at anchor in the harbour. Scanning east, he spotted a narrow sandbar, framed by mangroves, which led to another, much smaller, but equally green island, where a small band of men were cleaning their weapons. On a rocky promontory beyond the sandbar was a stockade, armed with two cannon. Elfrith and his men drew their cutlasses: if the men on the beach were Spanish, they were unlikely to welcome the arrival of foreign interlopers.

It took them the best part of the afternoon to reach the sandbar. The descent was steep at times, and they had to use their weapons to cut a path through the ferns and bromeliads underfoot, and the lianas hanging from the boughs overhead. On more than one occasion their progress was interrupted by a steep cliff, and they had to clamber down slopes of soft, black stone to the flatter land below.

Emerging from the woods, they walked along the sandy shore towards the men on the spit. 'We come in peace,' they shouted, as they drew their cutlasses. 'We are Dutch,' the strangers' leader replied in English. This made them fellow interlopers in the King of Spain's western lands.

4

Stuffing his clay pipe with roughly shredded tobacco, William Blauveldt invited Daniel Elfrith to join him for a smoke. He and his men were hoping to capture one of the Spanish merchant ships that regularly ran supplies to the coastal towns, he told the Englishman. They had arrived on the island a few days before to take on fresh water and hunt the wild pigs and pigeons that lived in the woods. They had built the armed stockade that Elfrith had spied from the peak to guard against any Spanish vessel that might come looking for them.

There is no record of the first European to land on the island the Spanish called 'Santa Catalina.' Nor is there any account of the first sailor to reach San Andrés, the low-lying island that Daniel Elfrith had sailed from the previous day. Both islands appear on the *Carta Universal*, which was the most authoritative map of the known world when it was published in 1527. Christopher Columbus likely passed them in 1502, when he was probing the coastline of Central America in his misguided search for a westward passage to the Indian Ocean, but he makes no mention of either of them. Until Elfrith's arrival, the only recorded visitor was Sir Francis Drake, who took on fresh water at Santa Catalina on his way to the Spanish port of Nombre de Dios, whose storehouses of gold and silver bullion he raided in 1572.

The Spanish customarily named unknown islands after the day on which they were discovered. Every day of the year corresponds to the name of a Catholic saint: 25th November is St Catherine's Day, and 30th November is St Andrew's Day, which suggests that whoever discovered Santa Catalina reached the island five days before reaching San Andrés. But aside from naming them, the Spanish paid no heed to either island for they were too small and too isolated to hold any promise for a conquistador. The English settlers scratching a living from the soils of New England were committed smallholders, but even the lowliest Spanish soldier regarded the prospect of tilling the land with disdain. He had come west looking for gold, and he left the mining of it to enslaved Indian labour.

In the 134 years that had passed since Pope Alexander VI sanctified the Spanish king's dominion over the New World, an army of soldiers, priests and royal officials had taken possession of mainland America. But

Daniel Elfrith and William Blauveldt were not the first infidels to spot an opening. In 1620, the Conde de la Gomara, president of the *audiencia* of Guatemala, noted that the western Caribbean had become infested with foreign adventurers, pirates, escaped slaves and indomitable Indian tribes, 'each more ferocious than the next.'[1] He advised the king to send an expedition to Santa Catalina, so as to deny the intruders a foothold. But Philip IV chose to ignore the Conde's advice. *Los piratas ingleses* were of less concern to the king than the nearby shallow reefs of Roncador, Quitasueño, Serrana and Serranilla, which had already been the cause of many a shipwreck. The royal maps used by ships' captains plying *la carrera de Indias* drew their attention to the reefs, not the islands. Santa Catalina was deemed an irrelevance.

Returning to the Somers Isles, Daniel Elfrith rushed to tell the islands' governor about his exciting discovery. Philip Bell welcomed his father-in-law's return, and listened to his account with great interest. Their patron, the Earl of Warwick, had been looking for a location in which to build a new colony, as the Somers Isles' experiment was close to collapse. Most of the seedlings the settlers had brought out from England had withered in the sun, the few that had taken root were buffeted by the high winds that blew in off the Atlantic, and much of their meagre harvest had been eaten by rats.

While Elfrith went to check on the state of his fields, Philip Bell wrote a letter to the Earl of Warwick's agent and closest business partner, his cousin, the MP Sir Nathaniel Rich. If his father-in-law's description of the lush island was accurate, the proceeds made from crops grown on Santa Catalina would surely 'double or treble any man's estate in all England,' he wrote. The island also offered great opportunities to privateers, for it lay 'in the heart of the Indies, and the mouth of the Spanish,' just three days' sailing from the ports at Portobello and Cartagena. It was already blessed with excellent natural defences; once fortified, he felt sure that it would be 'invincible.'[2]

Sir Nathaniel Rich received Bell's letter at the end of April 1629, and immediately sent word to the Earl of Warwick. The Earl was one of the wealthiest men in England, and the single biggest sponsor of its fledgling trade and colonisation projects. He had been running the Somers Isles

Company for over a decade, and had invested large sums of money in colonies and trading missions in Massachusetts, Virginia, Guyana and the East Indies.

The first meeting to discuss the colonisation of Santa Catalina was held on 19 November 1630 at Lord Brooke's house in Holborn, though only 'when the plague then raging in London had abated sufficiently for members to assemble together.'[3] The 20-strong gathering included some of the most powerful men in England. Among them were leading members of the House of Lords like the Earl of Warwick, Lord Brooke and Lord Saye and Sele, and several of the commoners that they sponsored in the Lower House: ambitious, talented men like John Pym, Sir Thomas Barrington, Oliver St John and Sir Benjamin Rudyerd.

What marked these men out from their peers was not their wealth or power, but their devotion to God. The 'Puritan' wing of the Church of England had been around since the days when Queen Elizabeth was on the throne, though most of those so labelled considered it 'an odious name,' used only by the 'lewd and profane of life.' They preferred to call one another 'loving friend.' Although most Puritans considered themselves loyal members of the Church of England, the most powerful of them undoubtedly formed a class within a class. The defenders of 'the true religion' needed one another, for the road to salvation was riddled with pitfalls, and those intent on walking it needed guidance, as well as protection from their foes.

When etiquette allowed, it was only natural that they should marry their brethren's sisters, nieces and cousins. Most of the men who gathered at Brooke House that day were related to someone in the room. Oliver St John was married to a cousin of Sir Thomas Barrington, who was in turn the brother-in-law of Sir Gilbert Gerard. Barrington was also a cousin of other prominent Puritans in the House of Commons, like Oliver Cromwell and John Hampden.

The men who gathered at Brooke House were rooted in the local government of rural England, but they were anything but parochial. Their religion was under threat from enemies at home and abroad, and this gave them an international outlook. They had been raised on a diet of anti-Catholic, anti-Spanish rhetoric, which conflated the superstition and idolatry that they regarded as inherent in Catholicism with the sloth, tyranny, and cruelty that they associated with the Spanish.

But they also wanted to emulate Spain, for since discovering the gold and silver mines of Mexico and Peru, it had enjoyed a golden age the likes of which had never been seen before. By 1629, however, King Philip IV's empire was overextended and ripe for collapse. Two years before, the Dutch admiral Piet Hein had captured his annual treasure fleet off the coast of Cuba. The 100 tons of silver that Hein brought back to Holland was valued at more than 11 million guilders (£89 million in today's money) and funded the Dutch army for the next eight months. Why shouldn't England repeat Hein's success, and deprive the followers of the Antichrist of their ill-gotten gains into the bargain?

In addition to licensed piracy, Protestant Holland had also shown the riches to be made by legal trade. Having secured control over herring fishing in the North Sea, the Dutch had become 'waggoners of all seas,' carrying goods to and from ports all over Europe. The Continent's commercial and financial development was no longer directed from Paris, but Amsterdam and Rotterdam, and now the Dutch had colonies of their own at New Amsterdam and Curaçao.

A strong sea breeze from Holland blew through the City of London, and Dutch Protestants' spirited defence of the true religion was taken as an example to all patriotic Englishmen. The 20 adventurers gathered at Brooke House had all enjoyed the benefits of having such a wealthy neighbour on the other side of the English Channel. Flemish weavers paid good prices for English wool, which accounted for 90 per cent of the country's exports. The wool trade had brought great wealth to many of England's landowners, who had rebuilt their houses in the latest styles, and furnished them with fine silks and tapestries from Holland and Italy. Their tables were laden with Spanish and French wines, and their dishes enlivened by exotic spices, currants, and citrus fruits imported from Venice and the Levant. As one observer wrote in 1587, 'It is a world to see how many strange herbs, plants and unusual fruits are daily brought unto us from the Indies, Americas, Taprobane, Canary Isles and all parts of the world.'[4] That year, luxury goods made up two thirds of England's imports; many of them were imported from distant colonies and trading stations run by England's Spanish and Dutch rivals. Such conspicuous consumption of foreign goods undermined England's merchants and weighed heavy on its balance of trade.

It might have been an inequitable state of affairs, but it was perfectly sustainable, and it took a war to bring matters to a head. The Protestant Reformation, based on the printed word and the spread of literacy

8

among a minority of the population, had unleashed a furious reaction from the Catholic Church. This Counter-Reformation was punitive as well as defensive, and particularly in its early stages, it was incredibly violent. In 1618, the Catholic and Protestant powers of Europe had taken up arms to fight what would become known as the Thirty Years' War. As the conflict intensified, European waters became infested with pirates, and English wool merchants found themselves cut off from their markets on the Continent. By the mid-1620s, England's cloth trade had collapsed, and the country had fallen into a terrible recession. Many of those gathered at Brooke House came from textile towns, and had seen for themselves the poverty and hopelessness that prevailed among their tenants and servants. It was said that the last ten years had been the worst the country had ever lived through. When the plague swept the country in 1625 and again in 1630, many took it as a sign of divine wrath at the benighted state of Englishmen's souls. The ranks of the jobless swelled, and wages fell to their lowest ever point. This was compounded by a series of poor harvests, which brought many villages in the north of England to the brink of starvation.

God, they told themselves, was urging the country towards a coordinated programme of imperial expansion. This would foster production of the cotton, dyes, oils and fixatives that the English cloth trade needed, shift the balance of trade, and give productive employment to the idle hands milling in the squares of England's market towns. It would also glorify 'the true religion' at the expense of Catholic Spain.

Yet the Stuart kings showed no interest in emulating the belligerent expansionism of Queen Elizabeth. Charles had shown himself eager to make his name as a warrior, and declared war on both Spain and France, but both campaigns were fiascos: Edward Cecil so mismanaged the attack on Cádiz that he entirely missed the Spanish galleons he planned to rob. He was unable to feed his own soldiers, many of whom died of malnutrition and disease, let alone defeat the armies of Catholic Europe. King Charles would play no further role in the Thirty Years' War, and showed no interest in pursuing the aggressive foreign policy urged on him by the Earl of Warwick. Instead, he fell back on the Crown's longstanding policy of moralising, exhortation and false promises.

While Charles would have made a bad king under the best of circumstances, few of his subjects appreciated that he simply didn't have the money to match the belligerence of continental monarchs like Louis

XIII of France, whose annual income was ten times larger than Charles'. The royal finances had been tending towards collapse since 1500 – the Dissolution of the Monasteries was a windfall that only delayed the day of reckoning. Over the course of the sixteenth century, royal income had doubled, but prices had risen fivefold.[5] If the king's finances were to be put on a sound footing, Parliament would have to grant him the right to increase existing taxes, and impose new ones.

The English still had little to show for their efforts in the New World in 1629. Thomas Warner had tried to build a settlement at Oyapoc in present day Guyana; when that failed, he went looking for a place where he and his men might 'be quiet among themselves,' and founded the first permanent English colony in the Caribbean on St Kitts in 1622.[6] He returned to London, where he secured the backing of City merchant Maurice Thompson. His investment brought quick returns: in 1627, the *Hopewell* returned from St Kitts with 30,000 pounds of tobacco. Encouraged by Warner's success, the Earl of Carlisle built a colony on Barbados in 1629.

The English also moved into North America. In 1630, King Charles granted a patent to the Massachusetts Bay Company. But the early settlers of New England had limited aspirations, and little in common with the soaring ambitions of the men gathered at Brooke House. John Winthrop, the future governor of Massachusetts, was driven to leave England not by the promise of a new life in a new land, but the threat of impending doom. In 1629, he wrote a letter to his wife, in which he confessed, 'I am verily persuaded God will bring some heavy affliction upon this land … If the Lord sees it will be good for us, he will provide shelter and a hiding place for us and others.'[7] The Puritan grandees in London did not consider the first settlers of the Massachusetts Bay colony to be born leaders. John Winthrop came from the lower gentry, as did most of those who followed him on his 'errand into the wilderness.' The 'middling sort' made good settlers, but they lacked the ambition that marked out the true colonialist.

In economic terms too, the barren shores of New England looked far less promising than the verdant islands of the Caribbean. Neither Virginia nor Massachusetts could produce cotton or dyewoods, let alone the grapevines and mulberry bushes the new company's shareholders coveted. The Earl of Warwick was happy to sponsor their narrow, self-serving little settlements on the shores of New England, but there was no way of knowing how long their precarious grip would hold.

If England was to build a mighty empire, the defenders of 'the true religion' would first have to cut off the flow of American gold to the King of Spain's coffers. Robbery and righteousness, greed and godliness, were bound together in the imperial venture. The early English merchant adventurers saw no contradiction in the forces propelling them towards the Americas. As the Pilgrim Edward Winslow wrote in 1624, 'In America, religion and profit jump together.'[8] In the face of the pacifism and incompetence of their king, and the tepid ambitions of the typical lowborn Puritan, the grandees gathered at Brooke House would throw down the gauntlet to the Spanish. God would protect those who took up His call, and reward those who stayed the course.

Building a colony on Santa Catalina would be a costly venture, but it was too important to trust to the vagaries of the market. There could be no place for the rapacious, short-term thinking of the typical City of London merchant in the grandees' scheme. Instead, they would form a private company, and limit shares to those 20 men sitting around the table.[ii] This meant that each of them would have to invest a much larger sum than they had in any previous colonial venture. The largest contributions were made by the Earl of Warwick, Lord Saye and Sele, and the wealthiest man in the room, 22-year-old Robert Greville, Lord Brooke, a man of 'all-daring and undaunted spirit.'[9]

John Pym was appointed company treasurer. A 'pudgy little man' of 'rough and shaggy appearance,'[10] Pym had made a name for himself as a fierce critic of the overweening King Charles, and a champion of Parliament's rights. He would be assisted by his principal allies in the House of Commons, Oliver St John, Sir Gilbert Gerard and Sir Benjamin Rudyerd, each of whom had experience of high office in various branches of government.

A week after their first meeting, company secretary William Jessop drafted a petition to the king, requesting permission to colonise Santa Catalina. Securing Charles' consent would be a delicate process, and one best left to the man who had been invited to become the company's gov-

---

ii   The number of shareholders reached 34 by the mid-1630s.

ernor, the Earl of Warwick's brother, Henry Rich. Henry had no Puritan leanings, was not invited to invest in the company, and attended just one meeting of the board during his eleven-year stint as governor. But none of this mattered, for his role was simply to be the company's friend at court. In return, he could expect a healthy cut of the vast profits the new colony was expected to make.

King Charles was not an easy person to get on with. 'His deportment was very majestic,' wrote the courtier Sir Philip Warwick, 'for he would not let fall his dignity, no, not to the greatest foreigners that came to visit him at his court.' Mild and sweet by temperament, he seemed convinced that his divine right to rule put him beyond the laws of the land. The future Archbishop of Canterbury, William Laud, called him 'a mild and gracious prince who knew not how to be, or how to be made, great.'[11]

Charles was all too familiar with the Puritan grandees, for they had been making problems for him in Parliament within months of his accession to the throne. Lord Saye and Sele had opposed his attempts to raise new taxes, and John Pym had followed the same line in the House of Commons. Charles had faced strong and united opposition when Parliament met again in March 1628, and when this was followed by a ream of additional demands in June, he suspended Parliament and dismissed the Puritan MPs from his government. He recalled Parliament in the autumn, hoping it would approve his latest money-raising schemes, but securing the assent of such hard-headed opponents was beyond him. In exasperation, he dissolved Parliament in March 1629, and for the next eleven years he governed the country without consulting Parliament.

Yet the king's interest was piqued by the petition that Henry Rich brought before him for it informed him of the discovery of an island ideally situated 'to annoy the King of Spain in the Indies, and convenient to receive a fleet that has a design on any leeward part of the Indies, or Cartagena, Portobello, the Bay of Honduras, Hispaniola, Cuba or Jamaica.' Although Charles was pursuing a policy of peace with Spain, it looked unlikely to last, and while he didn't want to invest the little money he had in colony building, he could see the benefit of keeping his most troublesome opponents occupied. On 4 December 1630, he granted a patent for the incorporation of 'the Company of Adventurers of the City of Westminster for the Plantation of the Islands of Providence or Catalina, Henrietta or Andrea, and the adjacent islands lying upon the

coast of America."[iii]

The choice of names was significant. The company's Puritan grandees had renamed Santa Catalina Providence by way of thanks to God, whose watchful guidance had led Daniel Elfrith to the western Caribbean. San Andrés was renamed for Charles' wife, Queen Henrietta Maria, in a careful attempt to placate him. It seems to have worked, for Charles went a step further, granting the company the right to settle any island between latitude 10 and 20 degrees north 'not in the actual possession of any other Christian prince.' He even issued letters of marque, which gave the Earl of Warwick permission to plunder any Spanish ships he might encounter in the Caribbean. In return for his munificence, Charles wanted a fifth of any gold, silver or precious stones that came into the company's possession. If Parliament wouldn't allow him to tax his subjects, he would tax its wealthiest members' ventures in the New World instead.

In considering the constitution by which Providence would be run, the need for discipline and hierarchy was uppermost in the shareholders' minds. Philip Bell, the governor of the Somers Isles, was appointed governor of the Providence Island Company's new colony. He would take his instructions from London, although he was expected to consult a six-man island council of prominent soldiers and civilians over the day-to-day running of the colony. Most of the council's members were in the advance party that gathered on the company dock in Deptford in October 1630. Experienced army officers and ships' captains, many of them were relatives of company shareholders. Daniel Elfrith would return to the island he had discovered as its admiral. Captain William Rudyerd, younger brother of MP Sir Benjamin Rudyerd, was appointed commander of the settlers, the first contingent of whom would be dispatched early the following year. His second-in-command was John Pym's nephew, Lieutenant William Rous. Since the threat of Spanish attack was never far from the shareholders' minds, they appointed an English veteran of the Dutch war against the Spanish, Captain Samuel Axe, to oversee military affairs. Aside from the island council and a

---

[iii] These days, 'Catalina' is used to refer to the small island off the northern tip of Providencia, although some English speakers still call it 'Ketleena'.

detachment of soldiers, the advance party also included a contingent of 'artificers' – carpenters, sawyers, masons, shipwrights and coopers – who would build the first settlement on the island.

Among other things, the colony on Providence was an audacious experiment in how to build a modern community. The objectives of the Providence Island Company were likely inspired by Francis Bacon's *New Atlantis*, which had become hugely influential among England's promoters of overseas expansion since its publication in 1627.[12] A utopian fragment about a godly, hierarchical, and scientific community set on an island 'off the coast of America,' it too begins with a wandering European stumbling upon an unknown island. Among the scientific wonders the narrator finds in New Atlantis are water desalination plants, refrigeration plants and flying machines. But Bacon's book looked backwards as often as it did forwards. *New Atlantis* was grounded in the belief that the Americas were a lost Paradise, the wilderness that God had promised to transform into Eden in the Book of Isaiah. But Bacon also promoted the idea that the wealth and power of the state should be harnessed to advance man's knowledge of the natural world. While knowledge was the key to improving the material conditions of life, it was being held back by England's education system, which prized ancient, redundant philosophy over empirical evidence and scientific enquiry.

From Deptford, Captain Elfrith sailed down the Thames, past the Downs and into the English Channel. His first port of call was the Somers Isles, where they were joined by Philip Bell and a band of discontented settlers. Bell had been governor of the Isles for the past three years, and was relieved to see them sink over the horizon: in a letter home written shortly before leaving, he admitted that he could no longer 'live in such a slavish subjection to such mean and base minded men as the citizen part of the company are.'[13] He was a serious and devout man, and the utopian mission of the new colony appealed.

The *Robert* reached Providence on Christmas Eve 1630. Wading ashore from a longboat, Philip Bell led the advance party in a prayer service, in which he thanked God for watching over their voyage and for delivering them from the enemy. In the days that followed, the new governor was delighted to find that Providence surpassed his father-in-law's ebullient description. The island covered just eight square miles, but its mild climate and fertile soils convinced him that it was the best

14

in the Caribbean. A light, near-constant breeze from the northeast kept temperatures in the low 80s, and while the hills were covered with dense woods, they harboured few insects and no dangerous animals. Nor was there was there any sign of a native population to contend with. In his first letter to the company in London, Bell wrote, 'by anyone's standards, Providence must be accounted utterly beautiful.'[14]

The only sticking point was William Blauveldt and the other Dutch buccaneers, who were still living on the little island off the northern tip of Providence. The company was concerned that they might betray the English presence to the Spanish, so Captain Axe was instructed to confine them to the island until he had completed the fortifications the island needed to withstand an attack. Blauveldt and his friends should be 'so respected that they have no cause of complaint,' but reminded that they could only ever be 'occupiers and manuerers' of the company's island.[15]

Over the days that followed, the members of the island council surveyed the low-lying land that ringed the island for a suitable site for a settlement. They chose a spot where the island's principal stream opened onto a broad plain between the western shore and the hills. Captain Axe had his men clear the dense scrub, while the carpenters and sawyers cut a track into the hills, and set about felling cedar and ironwood trees. They were accustomed to fashioning planking from cedar, but the ironwood trees were the hardest any of them had ever come across. They could only be felled with axes, but made excellent foundation posts.

By the end of January 1631, they had built a row of simple, well-built huts for themselves. The bricks that had served as ballast in the hull of the *Robert* were brought ashore to serve as the foundations of the church and the governor's house. When the masons had laid the last English brick, they dug clay from the flatter ground, and fired bricks of their own in a kiln. By the summer, they had built a church and the house for the governor. They called their little settlement 'New Westminster.'

Next, they turned their attention to the farm buildings that the first settlers would need. Behind each hut they built a pen for the pigs, chickens and cattle they had brought out from London. The carpenters built sheds for their crops, and the cooper a forge, where he hammered iron into ploughs, hoes, spades, nails and hooks. The masons built a horse-powered mill to grind the settlers' harvest of 'Indian corn' into flour, and ovens in which to bake cornbread.

Fields were marked out and corn, yucca and potatoes planted. But little rain fell in April, and they watched with growing concern as the hills surrounding their settlement turned the colour of straw. Until they brought in the first harvest, the advance party had to live off the hard-tack and salted meat they had brought out from London. In the first months of the year, they cleared several acres of land around New Westminster for food crops. Yet the island offered plentiful supplements: the wooded hills abounded with strange fruit, and the coral that grew on the offshore reef attracted shoals of exotic fish. Only in May did the rains come – terrific downpours that lasted for days on end and turned the stream running through New Westminster into a raging torrent.

When the rainclouds finally passed, the fields were illuminated by dazzling sunlight, and the first seedlings appeared. At night, when the members of the island council gathered in the governor's house to toast their good fortune, the soldiers, sailors and artificers gathered around the fire to puff on their clay pipes with the Dutchmen, and listen to William Blauveldt's tales of buccaneering around the Caribbean. When the moon was bright, they watched huge green turtles struggle up the beach to lay their eggs in the warm sand. Blauveldt showed them that these eggs were good to eat, and that by flipping the mother onto her back, they could cut her underbelly open with a cutlass. The meat of the green turtle, cooked over an open fire, became a cherished staple of their diet. In the winter months, the island also abounded with monk seals, which became a great source of fuel as well as food, as once their molten blubber was turned into tallow, it could supply their lamps.[16] These hulking creatures were so passive that they could be caught and bludgeoned with barely a struggle. Wasn't their meek self-sacrifice another sign of the provision God had made for his most daring followers, they asked one another?

At the end of their first year on the island, Philip Bell prepared a report for the company in London. The colony had met with God's favour, he assured the shareholders. 'You would most willingly spend an age in this same Eden,' he wrote. 'This, your little spot of land, will grow one of the gardens of the world.'[17] Bell felt confident that the island could sustain the first party of settlers, who were due to arrive in the New Year. The day was surely at hand when the merchants of the City of London would import tropical produce from an English colony, instead of feeding the coffers of the country's enemies.

In February 1632, the Providence Island Company's 20 shareholders met at Brooke House to consider Philip Bell's report. How stark was the contrast with the first report from the new colony at Massachusetts Bay, which the Earl of Warwick received around the same time. Its governor, John Winthrop, could only lament the death, disease and general hardship his settlers had had to endure during their first twelve months in New England. Philip Bell's report carried no such ill omens: there had been no outbreaks of fever among the advance party, and few deaths.

Admittedly, the immediate future was not without problems. Many of the seedlings the advance party had planted on arrival had died during the long drought of the first half of 1631. In the months since, they had harvested three crops of corn; nevertheless Bell asked that they be permitted to grow tobacco until they had a better understanding of the island's climate and the crops best suited to it. Tobacco was the first profitable crop to be grown in North America. By 1619, it was selling for three shillings per pound in London, and the average annual income of a Virginian tobacco farmer was soon running at seven times that of an English tenant farmer. Stories abounded of Englishmen who had arrived as servants rising into the ranks of Virginia's planter elite. Suitably encouraged, a generation of young men headed for the Americas to make their fortunes.

But tobacco had powerful detractors. 'Surely smoke becomes a kitchen far better than a dining chamber?' King James asked in his *A Counterblast to Tobacco*, written in 1604. 'And yet it makes a kitchen oftentimes in the inward parts of men, soiling and infecting them with an unctuous, oily kind of soot, as has been found in some great tobacco takers, that after their death were opened.' James hated tobacco with a vengeance. He considered it 'loathsome to the eye, hateful to the nose, harmful to the brain, dangerous to the lungs, and in the black stinking fume thereof, nearest resembling the horrible Stygian smoke of the pit that is bottomless.'[18]

Several of the shareholders shared his vehement anti-tabagism. Aside from the physical harm it caused, tobacco farming was an unreliable base on which to build a successful colony. Thanks to their dependence on tobacco, planters in Virginia and the Somers Isles had neglected their food crops, and faced starvation within a few years of their arrival. Tobacco might have made fortunes for the first settlers of Virginia, but by 1630,

English marketplaces were flooded with the stuff. The Providence Island Company's shareholders were determined to avoid the short-sighted greed that had stunted the growth of the American colonies. In their reply to Bell's report, they reminded him that farmers were making just a groat on every pound of tobacco sold, 'which may justly slack your pace in the pursuit of that commodity.'[19]

Governor Bell read the company's response with no little concern. He and the other former Somers Islanders were the only members of the advance party with any experience of raising tropical crops. They had planted tobacco confident that it would fetch a good price in the markets of London; the measly return they could now expect forced them to confront their no less measly understanding of the island's soil and climate.

2
EDUCATING ESSEX

At the company's foundation, each of its shareholders had agreed to 'harken out' for the 100 upstanding men and boys who would make up the first party of settlers on Providence. They would have to have farming, craft and carpentry skills, for most of the island had yet to be cleared or planted. They were also expected to be God-fearing, for the colony would flourish only with His blessing, and sinful behaviour was sure to invite His wrath. The following description of a seventeenth-century manor in Buckinghamshire gives some idea of the hardworking, plain-living ideal that the company wanted to replicate on Providence.

> The household represented all that was best in the puritan way of life. The inhabitants brewed and baked, they churned and ground their meal, they bred up, fed and slew their beeves and sheep, and brought up their pigeons and poultry at their own doors. Their horses were shod at home, their planks were sawn, [and] their rough ironwork was forged and mended.[1]

The ideal manor was one in which everyone knew his place. It was also practically self-sufficient, which ensured that members of the household had few distractions, and few sources of temptation.

John Pym returned to his Tavistock constituency to put the word out in the villages of south Devon, while Lord Brooke went recruiting among his tenants in Warwickshire and Staffordshire, and Lord Saye and Sele did the same in north Oxfordshire. Robert Rich Earl of Warwick, assisted by his cousin Sir Nathaniel Rich and his neighbour Sir Thomas Barrington, went looking for settlers in their home county of Essex. In a county dominated by a handful of wealthy families, none was wealthier than Robert Rich, who was said to be worth £15,000 a year (equivalent to £1.3 million in today's money). His grandfather, Richard Rich, had been one of Henry VIII's most rapacious servants. Following the Dissolution of the Monasteries, the King had given him swathes of land in the county. Robert's father, also called Robert, had invested the money he made from his tenants in a fleet of ships, and went on to become one of England's leading privateers.

For a religious man like Robert Rich Snr, robbing Spanish ships was more than a way of making money; it was his duty as a good Christian. King James I, who was no Puritan, disagreed. He never believed that the King of Spain was an agent of the Whore of Babylon mentioned in the Bible, or that the Pope was the Antichrist, and thought the best way to pacify the Christian world was by making peace with Spain. But the Spanish king showed little interest in signing a peace treaty, and in the face of his indifference, James found the money to be made from privateering too tempting to resist. Not only did he grant Robert Rich letters of marque authorising him to attack the Spanish king's ships, he happily accepted the £10,000 (£960,000 in today's money) that Rich offered him for the earldom.

When Robert Rich died in 1618, his title passed to Robert the younger, who became the biggest landowner in one of England's most prosperous counties. The young earl's steward recalled that while young Henry Rich chose to pursue a career at the court of King Charles, his brother Robert had always been more concerned with 'planting colonies in the New World, than himself in the king's favour.'[2] Robert was wealthy, but he was also devout, and his faith gave him an unwavering sense of purpose. After graduating from Emmanuel College, Cambridge, which had been established as a training college for Puritan preachers in 1584, he went on to sponsor the careers of some of England's most uncompromising preachers, who believed that their faith impelled them to do all they could to undermine Catholic Spain. The young earl was also very much a man of action: in 1627, he had sailed for the Azores, where he planned to capture the Spanish treasure fleet as it made its way back to Cádiz. Although he failed to take the galleons, he was said to have been 'as active and as open to danger as any man there,' and could 'as nimbly climb up to top and yard as any common mariner in the ship.'[3]

Riding northeast from London to his family seat at Leez Priory near Felsted, the earl and his companions found the roads in a parlous state. Much of Essex was still marshland, and the cottagers who lived on its fringes were often laid low with ague – malaria – carried by the mosquitoes that thrived on the stagnant water.[4] The cottagers' hovels seemed more overcrowded than ever, and they passed many hungry wanderers. As far as the county's property owners were concerned, cottagers were synonymous with the 'rascality,' whose viciousness only seemed to increase in proportion to their rising numbers. So widespread was poaching from the earl's game reserves that sausages made from poached Essex venison were a well-known delicacy on the streets of east London.

Husbandmen and cottagers had few opportunities to rise up through the ranks of Essex society, but rising prosperity kept most of them reasonably content. At the turn of the seventeenth century, half the population ate meat daily, the rest ate it at least twice a week, and until the recession hit in the late 1620s, even the earl's oldest tenants could remember only rising prosperity.

The recession could not have come at a worse time. The last 50 years had seen rapid population growth in England. It was also a time of land hunger, for many landlords were keen to move into sheep farming, which meant planting hedges and building fences to create enclosures in which their sheep could graze. As land that had once been planted with wheat and barley was given over to sheep, the common land that cottagers depended on became the target of land grabs by unscrupulous landowners.

It was a time when 'sheep ate men.' Many husbandmen were no longer able to raise food crops for themselves, and had to find work on neighbouring manors. For many of them, it was their first taste of working for a wage. From the Black Death until well into the reign of Queen Elizabeth, England's yeomen had worried about the cost and scarcity of labour – so much so that the government even introduced a maximum wage for labourers. But with so many landless cottagers forced to look for paid work, the labour shortage became a glut. Wages fell, families went hungry and those unable to find work had no choice but become squatters on land they had once held in common with their neighbours. The entire county was said to be 'filling up at the bottom.'[5]

Under normal circumstances, the county's cottagers and husbandmen had better prospects than most, for they lived within a few days' walk of prosperous towns like Braintree, Chelmsford and Colchester, where wool gathered from sheep raised on enclosed land was brought to be washed, spun and woven. But with Europe consumed by the Wars of Religion, seaborne trade was at risk of attack by pirates, and the wool trade was thrown into a terrible recession.

Directly or otherwise, half the population of Essex depended on the trade for a living. In 1629, the county's cloth workers saw their wages cut by over a third. Many were forced to sell their beds to buy food, and employers kept to their houses for fear of running into their poverty-stricken workers in the street. Robert Hammond, an unemployed wool comber from Braintree, had resisted the temptation to rob, riot or turn vagrant, but his patience was wearing thin. 'It is hard to starve,' he lamented,

> I took no lewd course to wrong any man, nor yet to run about the country as others have done. I never stirred, but kept my work, and it is nothing else which now I crave: to maintain my charge, that I may take no unlawful course.[6]

According to the town corporation of Colchester, wandering paupers were 'the principal cause of the great poverty within this town.'[7] Yet the jobless were not allowed to leave their home county. If a jobless man like Robert Hammond wanted to look for work beyond the borders of Essex, he had to apply for a pass from the local magistrate; anyone caught on the road without one could expect to have his ears bored. Fortunately, he wouldn't have found it hard to come by a skilled counterfeiter like Davy Bennett, a pockmarked young man known to drift the county's back roads. For a fee, Davy would forge a pass and even carried a bag of counterfeit magistrates' seals under his cloak. Armed with a forged pass, a jobless man could make his way to London. By the middle of the century, one in six Englishmen had done just that.

Rising numbers of poachers, jobless cloth workers and hungry migrants - 'sturdy rogues' in the parlance of the day - made the property owners of Essex anxious. In better days, those unable to support themselves could count on the benevolence of their neighbours, for Christian charity was the bedrock on which the village hierarchy stood. But with so many new faces tramping the county's roads, the 'middling sort' was feeling less generous. In the words of a popular ballad of the day, 'Neighbourhood nor love is none / True dealing now is fled and gone.'[8]

Those sent away empty-handed from a yeoman's door were often heard to utter 'the beggar's curse.' This made the householder feel guilty, but it also induced fear, for only the Devil could fulfil the beggar's curse (God only came to the aid of the submissive poor). If a yeoman's milk curdled or his hens failed to lay in the days following the beggar's visit, the blame would fall on the Devil, and the poor wretches he had tempted to do his bidding. Prosecutions for witchcraft had peaked at the end of Elizabeth's reign, but the 1630s saw another flurry of witch baiting.

Not everyone succumbed to the hysteria: William Laud, the future Archbishop of Canterbury, blamed the recession not on witches or divine wrath, but grain speculators. But Laud's rational scepticism was thin on the ground in a county as stagnant and God-fearing as the Essex of 1630.

Prior to the dissolution of Parliament in 1628, Puritan MPs like the Earl of Warwick's cousin, Sir Nathaniel Rich, had raged at the sloth of the poor in the House, but also at the avarice of the rich: Sir Nathaniel believed that the root cause of England's misfortunes was the terrible sinfulness of its people, for unchristian behaviour provoked God's anger. Not for the first time, Puritan MPs called for the punishment of blasphemy to be made more severe, and urged that 'excess in apparel' be made illegal.[9]

Instead, the king's Poor Law made a multitude of provisions for the poor: the rates were increased, workhouses were restocked and the laws governing apprenticeships tightened up. Thereafter, the poor were better treated, grain stocks better administered, and local government improved. Charles also established a Commission for Depopulation, with powers to impose fines on landowners whose enclosures had led to the loss of land previously dedicated to food crops. Unfortunately, the commission's work was undermined by the dire state of the king's finances. Anxious to raise money without recalling Parliament, Charles began selling exemptions to the law, which boosted his coffers, but did nothing to stem the tide of landless labourers pouring into English towns and cities.

With central government stymied by a lack of resources, and local government in the pocket of the local landowner, it fell to the parish to come up with an effective response to the crisis. The stipend offered the typical church minister was pitifully small, and consequently the clergy attracted few learned men. Most church ministers were what Puritans called 'dumb dogs' – incapable of preaching. But in the parishes where the Earl of Warwick held sway, the minister was sure to be a Puritan, and he knew very well what was required if England was to pull itself out of the mire. Casting a critical eye over his congregation, he could only wonder at how far they had strayed from the Gospel. For many churchgoers, and especially the poor, God was simply a talisman: a lucky charm to be wielded as protection from the slings and arrows of outrageous fortune. For a minister, however, Sunday service was more than a weekly ritual of mumbling one's way through the catechism and lighting candles for dead relatives. Until his flock attained a personal relationship with the Lord, they would never know the heart of 'the true religion.'

The process by which a man came to terms with original sin was painful for all concerned – but to be called a 'painful' preacher was the highest praise a Puritan minister could hope for. If he could bring some pain into their souls, his congregation would see that their idleness, drunkenness and lechery were not harmless amusements, but way stations on the road to hell.

A painful preacher could not wish for a more receptive audience than the one that gathered in a typical Essex village church, for the county was considered the most Protestant in all England. Long before the Reformation, the people of Essex had demanded an English language Bible that they could read for themselves, and preachers who would help them to understand what God wanted of them. Following publication of the Authorised Version in 1611, the Word of God became daily reading for many, who were soon intoxicated by the poetry of the Bible and the hope for a Heaven on Earth.

In the eyes of the Puritans, the Church of England was still riddled with vestiges of Catholicism, which they regarded as a creed designed by man, not God. According to the Puritan divine Richard Sibbes, the Church of Rome 'knew that children must have baubles, and fools trifles, and empty men must have empty things. They saw what pleased them and the cunning clergy thought, "We will have a religion fit for you."'[10] Catholicism perverted Scripture to pander to man's love of worldly pleasures and smother the pangs of his guilty conscience. If England were to become materially rich, it would first have to become spiritually pure, and that meant driving its people onto the path of righteousness.

To anyone familiar with the stereotypical Puritan, with his prurient attitudes to sex and drink, the liberal good humour of the Earl of Warwick
and his 'loving friends' at the Providence Island Company will come
as some surprise. Robert Rich's daughter-in-law called him 'one of the
best-natured and cheerfullest persons I have in my time met with.' Even
the Royalist Earl of Clarendon, the first historian of the English Civil
War, who hated the earl, admitted that he was 'a man of pleasant and
companionable wit and conversation [and] a universal jollity.'[11]

Nor were the Puritan grandees particularly prudish, as shown by a
letter Sir Thomas Barrington wrote to his wife: 'My dearest, in obedience, in love, in all virtue, there is no mean to be held, nor can there be
excess.'[12] His wife was no wallflower either: Lady Judith's letters show her
to have taken a distinctly unladylike interest in the art of war, being full
of the gory details of the battles being waged by persecuted Protestants
in Europe.

Sir Thomas and his wife certainly would not have approved of illicit
sex, but only because sex between an unmarried young couple invariably
led to bastard offspring, and since neither parent would find work in the
house of a good Christian, the child would likely be raised in the workhouse, which was funded by poor rates levied on property owners like
the Barringtons. Once he was out of sight of his social inferiors, however, Sir Thomas drank, danced and went to the theatre just as often as his
neighbours. His account books show him to have paid fiddlers, harpists,
and morris dancers to entertain him at home. He even bought a case of
Irish whiskey and employed the services of a Welsh conjuror.

What gets overlooked in the rush to mock the Puritan psyche is
their determination to impose a culture of discipline on themselves, and
especially on the poor. It was a message that went down well with 'the
middling sort' – the merchants, lawyers and local government officials
who felt hemmed in between the corrupt rich and the idle poor – which
may explain why Puritanism in Essex was strongest in the cloth towns
where many of them lived.

Understandably, the culture of discipline that the Puritans wanted to
impose did not sit well with most of their countrymen and women. A
typical Church of England minister felt quite at home in the alehouse,
for religious devotion and merrymaking were tightly woven into the fab-

ric of daily life. In *London and the Country Carbonadoed*, Donald Lupton describes a typical alehouse of 1632:

> You shall see the history of Judith, Susanna, Daniel in the lion's den, or Dives (?) and Lazarus painted upon the wall… It may be reckoned a wonder to see or find the house empty, for either the parson, church-warden or clerk, or all are doing some church or court business usually in this place.

No wonder the typical landlady 'prays the parson may not be a puritan.'[13] To a good Puritan, this conflation of the sacred and the profane was sacrilegious and a hypocritical cover for debauchery. Drinking ale after church was all very well in times of plenty, but times of dearth called for austerity. Good Christians had a duty to help the poor, but those who refused to seek the light had to be punished. According to Arthur Hildersam, a Puritan preacher and friend of the Barringtons, 'The poor in all places are for the most part the most devoid of grace.'[14] The poor were weak in the face of temptation, and no amount of mollycoddling would fortify them. As Matthew 10:34 taught them, 'Think not that I am come to send peace on earth: I came not to send peace, but a sword.'

One didn't have to be a Puritan to see the appeal of this punitive reading of Scripture. The poor rates levied on Braintree's property owners had soared in the previous two years, and the parish council laid the blame on the multitude of alehouses in the town. These were frequented by 'journeymen and maids living out of service, [and] idle, loitering people who break hedges and steal wood, playing unlawful games and neglecting their calling.'[15] Parish councillors joined the justice of the peace in evicting squatters from the common lands that circled the town, but they also denied alms to paupers who would not go to church.

Unfortunately for the Puritans, the 'unlawful games' mentioned above were at the heart of village life. Until the Puritans began preaching against their pernicious effects, days dedicated to sports and games occupied a great deal of the working year. The English were especially fond of 'making merry,' and the Christian calendar gave them plenty of 'ho-ly-days' to celebrate. Puritans opposed them, firstly because they fostered sinful behaviour, and secondly because most holidays were vestiges from the days when England was a Catholic country. However, after they had been barred from playing sports or games, most villagers did not spend their Sunday afternoons reading the Bible. Instead, the Puritans' ban on Sunday sports 'set up filthy tippling and drunkenness, and bred a number of idle and discontented speeches in their ale-houses.'[16]

However, even in the most Protestant county in England, plenty of churchgoers felt antagonised by the hectoring of 'painful' Puritan preachers. As George Gifford, the minister of Maldon, complained, 'If the preacher do pass his hour but a little, your buttocks begin to ache and you wish in your heart that the pulpit would fall.'[17] Resistance to the culture of discipline was strongest in 'the dark parishes' of Essex, where the county's drifters, drunkards, and ballad singers held court.[18] They were said to love a Puritan 'as a dog loves a pitchfork.' 'Good sir, spare your pains,' a member of the congregation told the Puritan minister Thomas Hooker after hearing him preach one Sunday. 'We are sinners, and if we be damned, then every tub must stand upon its own bottom. We will bear it as well as we can.'[19]

To be a good Christian had always been a simple affair, bound up with good neighbourliness and the observance of archaic rituals. But the country had changed, and with it, the church. Battered by a recession the likes of which few could remember, many felt nostalgic for better days. But 'now is every man for himself, and all are ready to pull one another by the throat.'[20] According to Gifford, 'The simple sort, which cannot skill of doctrine, speak of the merry world when there was less preaching, and when things were so cheap that they might have twenty eggs for a penny.'[21]

Was the Puritans' culture of discipline the solution to the country's problems, or its cause? As a fog of anxiety and doubt rolled into England's towns and villages, there was a real risk that the Puritans' austere, reproachful outlook would drive many Christians back to the Catholic fold, especially in places like Lancashire, where Protestantism had yet to sink roots. King Charles was concerned that 'the simple sort' might look to a Spanish invasion to take England back to the days when all Christians were ruled from Rome. He only needed to listen to his ambassadors' accounts of the Dutch revolt against their Spanish rulers and the persecution of the Huguenots in France to be reminded of the dangers inherent in religious schisms. The Puritans were a threat to the religious uniformity on which the stability of his kingdom depended.

Through their connections with local church ministers, the Earl of Warwick, Sir Nathaniel Rich and Sir Thomas Barrington found several devout yeomen with the money and inclination to rent a plot of land on a faraway island. They told them that they would have to spend seven years working the fields of Essex to make what they could earn in a year on Providence. But they understood that free land, not free religion, was what enticed most migrants to sign up for passage to the Americas. Land was hard to come by in Essex, especially for younger sons, and fathers were quick to seize any opportunity for the one who did little but play on the tabor and drum. It was the opportunity of a lifetime; all the shareholders asked in return was that the young farmer hand over his harvest to the company, which would retain half of the profits made on its sale in London.

The first English newspaper had only been published in 1620, but colonial adventurers had been luring would-be settlers to the Americas through advertisements posted around towns and villages since the turn of the century. A bill posted in 1609 gave notice:

> to all artificers, smiths and carpenters, coopers, shipwrights, turners, planters, fishermen, metalmen of all sorts, brickmakers, ploughers, weavers, shoemakers, sawyers, spinsters and labouring men and women who are willing to go to the said plantation of Virginia and inhabit there.[22]

The island's farmers and craftsmen were going to need apprentices to work for them. The obvious place for an apprentice to find work was the annual hiring fair, where he could size up a range of employers, before signing up with whoever offered the most palatable terms. The law required that any young person whose parents earned less than £40 per year sign a contract with an employer for at least 12 months. As a result, two thirds of children left home at the age of 15 to become apprentices, and their employers became surrogate parents.

The Braintree fair of 1630 was crowded with young men driven to leave home by land hunger, the collapse of the wool trade, and their exasperated fathers. Some had already travelled to fairs in neighbouring towns in search of work. They had more than hunger to contend with, for a masterless wanderer was akin to an outlaw. If the minister of his local church could vouch for his good character, he might qualify for some relief out of the poor rates, but most vagrants ended up in the workhouse, and persistent offenders were often forced aboard ships bound for the colonies.

A Spaniard who was shipwrecked on the Somers Isles in 1625 was shocked to see that the servants working in the fields were nearly all 'boys, who are either orphans or have been abandoned.'[23] John Dutton, the Earl of Warwick's agent on the Somers Isles, complained that the last three ships to arrive from England had disgorged 'ill chosen men, who, it may be feared, will prove unprofitable servants. As for the benefit accruing to me by them, it is rather a burden, for no man will hire them, for they know not how to work.'[24]

These were just the kind of migrant Sir Thomas could do without. But by wheeling and dealing with his friends among the local yeomanry, he was able to offer indentures to only the most suitable candidates. The indenture was a long-established practice, by which an apprentice contracted himself to a farmer or craftsman for three years. During this time, he received no salary, but his master was obliged to provide him with room, board and the training he needed to learn his trade. Sir Thomas assured his young recruits that they would have 'meat, drink and apparel during their term of service.' After three years, they would each be free from their obligations to their masters, and would be able to buy land of their own.

Naturally, before becoming a free man, an apprentice would have to repay the six pounds – £530 in today's money – that it cost his master to secure his passage to Providence. But Sir Thomas told him that when the time came for him to fend for himself, he would 'receive all convenient assistance and encouragement from the company.'[25] The prospect of becoming a 'freed man' was one that no poor, young Englishman could resist, for it was practically unheard of outside the colonies. Captain John Smith, a Puritan whose writings about New England had already made him one of its best-known planters, asserted that such were the opportunities for freed men in the New World that the day was at hand when 'the very name of servitude will become odious to God and man.'[26] Puritans believed that America was God's gift to the English, in recognition of their enterprise and devotion. The minister William Crashaw gave a sermon to settlers bound for Virginia in 1610 in which he assured them that the voyage to the new colony 'is in that true temper so fair, so safe, so secure, so easy, as though God Himself had built a bridge for men to pass from England to Virginia.'[27]

By February 1631, the shareholders had 100 men and boys ready to start new lives in the New World. Most of them were apprentices aged between 14 and 20, who had borrowed the cost of their fare from their patron, and boarded the *Seaflower* with little more than the clothes on their backs. The sister ship of the *Mayflower*, the *Seaflower* had made the Atlantic crossing before: in 1621, it had carried settlers to the James River in Virginia. Feeding 100 passengers, plus the crew, for the two and a half months it would take the *Seaflower* to reach Providence required careful planning. The shareholders entrusted the job of victualing (supplying food and provisions to) the ship to the company husband, John Dyke. Dyke was the only non-Puritan member of the Providence Island Company, and an experienced colonist who also owned shares in the Somers Isles and Virginia companies. He had bought barrels of salt beef and salt pork, which lasted for up to five years, and casks of butter and hard Suffolk cheese, which would keep for the next six months. He also laid in supplies of biscuit, dried peas, currants, rice, oatmeal and plenty of chewing tobacco.[28]

Most of the settlers' food travelled live – as many tethered cattle, sheep, pigs, goats and caged hens and geese as could be squeezed below deck. A healthy diet was considered a largely meat diet, and no provision was made for citrus fruit or green vegetables. Next, the hold was loaded with demijohns of rum, and hogsheads of claret and brandy for the officers and gentlemen among the passengers. The common sailor and servant had to make do with beer, which was brewed extra strong in the belief that it kept better. Dyke factored on providing each man with a gallon a day. The *Seaflower*'s passengers would spend the next two and a half months living between decks, in the dank, airless space that separated the hold from the upper deck. They built a series of thin-walled cabins to give themselves some privacy, creating a dense warren of chests, trunks, furniture and livestock. By the time they were all aboard, the 75-feet long and less than five-feet high space was severely overcrowded. That was only to be expected, for the likelihood of dying en route was high. Midway across the Atlantic, they would pass 'beyond the line'; if they were captured thereafter they would either be killed or thrown into a Spanish dungeon. Since Captain John Tanner was also carrying letters of marque, they would also need additional men to overcome the crew of any Spanish vessel they might storm on their way to Providence.

The *Seaflower* was embarking on a voyage into the unknown. By using the astrolabe, cross-staff and backstaff, its navigator could determine how far north or south of his home port he had come, but those who navigated by latitude alone were confined to a few well-ploughed sea lanes, where it was easy to fall prey to the enemy. Longitude remained a mystery, and not without reason did the ship's crew refer to the navigator as a 'sea artist.'

But not all the hazards of sea travel were inescapable: only after leaving Deptford did Captain Tanner realise that the bread was mouldy and the beer sour. John Dyke had victualled the ship with the shoddiest goods he could find, and then billed the company at an inflated rate. Once at sea, Captain Tanner proved as unscrupulous as Dyke: he cut his passengers' rations by a third, hoping to sell whatever he could hoard when he got to Providence.

3

THE SEAFLOWER

The first English colony in the Americas was founded in Virginia in 1607. In the hundred years that followed, 375,000 Britons and Irish sailed for the New World.[1] Given that the population of England in 1630 was about 4.3 million, and that it currently stands at 53 million, that's the equivalent of 46,000 people leaving modern England for the Americas every year for the next hundred years.

Migration was not a sign of strength, but weakness. England was a small, relatively weak country on the fringes of Europe. Its population was a fifth that of France, which stood at 20 million, and a fraction of India's, which was over 100 million.[2] When Sir Thomas Roe travelled to Mughal India in 1614 as an emissary of King James I, the East India Company was just a start-up, run from the home of its governor by a permanent staff of six.[3] The towns and cities of Jahangir's empire accounted for around a quarter of global manufacturing, while England's domestic economy accounted for less than two per cent. Its empire was confined to the Somers Isles and Jamestown, Virginia, which was still struggling to recover from the 'starving time,' six fateful months in which 440 of its 500 settlers died of disease.[4]

London, on the other hand, was already one of the world's great cities. In 1630, its population was around 350,000 – half that of Jahangir's capital at Agra, but still larger than that of any other European city.[5] Though a large city, it was not, according to Frederick, Duke of Wurtemberg, who visited the capital in 1600, a worldly one. 'The inhabitants are magnificently apparelled and are extremely proud and overbearing,' he wrote in a letter home. 'And because the greater part, especially the trades people, seldom go into other countries... they care little for foreigners, but scoff and laugh at them.'[6]

Yet England was opening up to the world. By 1642, the year James Howell wrote *Instructions for Forreine Travell*, English travellers with 'a custom to be always relating strange things and wonders' from abroad were common enough to have become figures of fun. 'Such a traveller was he, that reported the Indian fly to be as big as a fox, China birds to be as big as some horses, and their mice to be as big as monkeys,' Howell wrote.[7]

Passing through foreign lands was all very well, but living in them was fraught with danger. Living in a hot climate was likely to throw an Englishman's humours out of kilter.[8] At the very least, it would make him quick-tempered and lazy; at worst, it would kill him. Climate was of immense importance to the English, for it was commonly believed that English culture – its 'mechanical and politic arts' – was the product of the country's temperate climate. Thomas Morton was a Devon man who became a champion of those 'whose economic straits filled new tent-cities, furnished prisons and gallows, and pushed Devon men to the Bristol sea-trades.' After spending a summer in New England, Morton wrote home warning would-be migrants of the risks they ran in journeying to the 'burning zones,' where the Sun was 'unto our complexions intemperate and contagious... Nature has framed the Spaniards, who prosper in dry and burning habitations, apt to such places,' he wrote, 'but in us she abhors such... this torrid zone is good for grasshoppers, and the temperate zone for the ant and bee.'[9]

The yeomen and husbandmen crowded below the *Seaflower*'s deck doubtless saw them themselves as the world's ants and bees: practical, hardworking and co-operative. But for how long would they remain so? Foreign cultures were no less risk-laden than foreign climes, for they were capable of undermining the very foundations of an Englishman's character. England's first colony was Ireland, where William Camden observed the changes that overcame Englishmen once the strictures of the domestic hierarchy were loosened. 'One would not believe in how short a time some English among them degenerate and grow out of kind,' he wrote in *Brittania*, a survey of Great Britain and Ireland published in 1577.[10] Many Englishmen new to Ireland had abandoned the civility of living in towns and villages, and chosen instead to live as semi-nomads. Some, it was said, had even lost their language and 'turned native.'

Ten weeks after their last sight of England, the *Seaflower's* 100 passengers waded through warm, crystal-clear water onto the white sand of Providence's harbour. The new arrivals came bearing gifts for the governor and his council: a staff inscribed with the company seal, and a silver plate bearing the island's ensign of government. The plate was inscribed with a quotation from Job 22:30. *Innocens liberabit insulam* – 'the innocent shall deliver the island,' it read. A second quotation, from Isaiah 42:4, read *legem ejus insulæ expectabunt* – 'the islands shall wait for his law.'[11]

The passengers were also carrying a letter for Philip Bell, in which the shareholders instructed the island's governor to 'distribute all the inhabitants into several families whereof one shall be chief.'[12] The seven tenant farmers among them, most of whom had come with their wives and children, became the 'fathers' of the island's servants, who had come alone. Bell apportioned each 'father' a plot of land, situated at a distance from his neighbour sufficient to avoid disputes, but close enough to hear the sound of the conch shell that signalled a Spanish attack. The settlers moved their belongings into their new quarters, and herded their cattle, sheep, pigs, goats, hens and geese from the hold of the ship into their pens.

If they were to avoid repeating the mistakes made by the Somers Isles' colonists, they would have to become self-sufficient in food. The advance party had made a good start, but there remained a great deal of land to clear before the company would consider sending out more settlers. Each 'father' put his 'children' to work, using the axes, shovels, ploughs and hoes he received from Thomas Fitch, the ensign responsible for the distribution of goods from the company magazine.

In addition to the crops they would need to sustain themselves, the shareholders expected the new arrivals to plant the cash crops that would pay for the materials and manpower they were going to need in the years to come. As the explorer Richard Hakluyt pointed out, the Spanish and Portuguese had taken grapevines to Madeira, sugar cane to Brazil, and ginger to Hispaniola, and now had a thriving trade in all three commodities. With care and attention, the English could grow the tropical crops they needed on Providence, and thereby break their dependence on 'vile Portingal' and the 'perfidious Spaniard.'

Wine and silk were luxuries that the English particularly resented importing. The Virginian colonists had found native vines and mulberry bushes growing wild. Surely, these native variants demonstrated that North America was capable of producing wine and silk? The company issued reams of instructions for the careful cultivation of imported varieties of grape vines and mulberry bushes. The settlers succeeded in producing several barrels of insipid wine, but their vines were dead by the end of the year, killed off by the severe cold of a Virginian winter. The colony's silk farmers fared little better: only after importing French silkworms to eat the profusion of native mulberry bushes did they realise that the American variant was too tough for French worms. In exasperation, the Crown dissolved the Virginia Company in 1624. Left without the patronage of king or company, the settlers turned to tobacco, which proved so well suited to the climate that it was soon growing wild on the streets of Jamestown.

If England's New World colonies were to succeed at anything more than 'a more regulated kind of killing of men,' as a Virginia Company report of 1621 put it, English merchant adventurers would have to secure accurate information about the American climate. Traditional thinking about climate was based on a ragbag of half-baked ideas inherited from classical sources. According to Aristotle, the world's weather was divided into zones, with the most moderate temperatures to be found midway between the equator and the North Pole. Aristotle's a priori reasoning suggested that Virginia would have a climate similar to southern Spain. But as the colonists were to discover, Virginia might be on the same latitude as southern Spain, but oranges and lemons don't thrive in Richmond as they do in Seville.[13]

One of the first Englishmen to challenge Aristotle's deductions was the cleric Samuel Purchas. Though he never traveled '200 miles from Thaxted in Essex, where I was born,' Purchas listened with rapt attention to the stories told by sailors returning to England from foreign voyages. What he heard led him to think that Aristotle and his tradition were impeding rather than advancing his understanding of the world. In 1625, he published *Purchas, his Pilgrimage*, a collection of travel stories and scientific speculations that became required reading for England's first colonial adventurers.[i] Purchas advised anyone wanting to cultivate exotic crops to draw lessons from their own experiences, and not pay too much attention to Aristotle's thoughts on the subject.

---

[i] *Hakluytus Posthumus, or Purchas his Pilgrimes* can be seen as a continuation of Richard Hakluyt's *Principal Navigations*. It is partly based on manuscripts left by Hakluyt, who had died in 1616.

Captain Samuel Axe took all four volumes of Purchas' book to Providence as part of his library of books on farming, botany and general science. The island seemed to offer boundless possibilities for the cultivation of exotic plants. The company prepared a long list of elaborate instructions for the settlers, and told Captain Tanner to remain on the island until the *Seaflower's* hold was full of produce to sell to the apothecaries of London. Mulberry bushes, canary vines, 'Guinea pepper' and pomegranate seedlings were to be procured from the colonists on Barbados, and silk production was 'to be made trial of.'[14] The company was particularly excited about the prospect of growing castor oil plants, which could be used to produce the soap needed by England's woollen manufacturers (English soap was made of fish oil, which left clothes with an ineradicable pong).

The company was also hoping to find a cure for syphilis among the exotic plants growing on the island. Syphilis had been unknown to Europeans when Christopher Columbus first set foot in the Americas, but by 1539, when the Sevillian doctor Ruy Díaz de Isla wrote *The Serpentine Malady*, over a million Europeans had been infected with the disease.[15] Casting around for a scapegoat, the Italians called it 'the French disease,' while the French called it 'the Italian disease.' Syphilis was in fact an American disease, most likely brought to Europe by sailors returning from Columbus' first voyage. Many of them had joined the army of King Charles VIII when the French invaded Italy in 1495. Meeting the low immunity of the natives of Europe, the syphilis bacteria mutated into its deadliest form. Large pustules appeared on the victims' bodies, the flesh fell from their faces, and within a few months of contracting the disease, a third of them were dead.

Syphilis was revenge of sorts for the various infectious diseases that Columbus and his men introduced to the people of the Americas, but it was far from being Europe's biggest killer. Columbus was heir to a long tradition of importing incurable diseases. In medieval times, Genovese merchants had been at the head of the caravans that journeyed to China to buy silk. For the return leg, they were joined by plague-infected rats, which boarded their ships at their trading station in the Crimea, and disembarked at Genoa. During the course of a promenade concocted in the winter of 1627, Cardinal Richelieu sent 8,000 soldiers from Mont-ferrat in the foothills of the Alps to La Rochelle on the Atlantic coast, where they were to assist in laying siege to the Huguenots. The plague pandemic they propagated as they made their way across France caused the death of a million people, none of whom suspected that their grisly end was the inadvertent price to be paid for reducing their country's Protestants to obedience.[16]

Aside from the difficulties inherent in raising exotic plants, the colony on Providence was beset by quarrels from the day the advance party arrived. Many of the servants still found the idea of selling their labour to the highest bidder, irrespective of person or place, quite a novelty. Husbandmen and cottagers were accustomed to working from sunrise to sundown when the farmer's crops needed planting or harvesting, but in the interim, they led lives of relative ease. There were no consumer goods for them to buy, so while their wages only covered the bare necessities, there was little point in earning more. In return for their loyalty, the lord of the manor offered them a degree of security and comfort that the 'free' labourer could only dream of. 'A follower of a great lord was wont to say that he had in effect, as much as his lord, though he were owner of little or nothing,' wrote John Robinson, who was pastor to many of the Pilgrims who sailed aboard the *Mayflower* in 1620.[17]

The prospect of becoming a free man didn't make it any easier to face three years of unpaid labour, working all hours under the tropical sun. The young servants were keen to make a good living, but they were also individualistic, resentful of distant authority, and a long way from the familiar restraints imposed by church, lord and master. Now they were being commanded to follow the orders of men they didn't know from Adam, who in turn took their orders from the governor, who was in turn only doing what the company in London told him to do. As the company council in London put it, 'England has not yet solved the problem of stimulating the poorer sort to work hard in their callings.'[18]

The family heads soon found cause for complaint too. When they took receipt of the tools and seeds they needed from the company magazine, they realised that the company favoured some over others, and that a tenant farmer was only as powerful as his patron on the company council. For as long as there were trees to fell, undergrowth to clear and paths to cut, there was little time to dwell on such trifles, but as time went on, other grumbles came to the fore. The prices of goods sold from the company magazine, and the company's monopoly on the supply of those goods both rankled. Shortly after their arrival, a Dutch ship had dropped anchor in the harbour. Its captain offered them supplies at better prices, but the farmers had to turn him down, as they were only permitted to buy from the company store. It struck them as ironic that, after so much righteous indignation at the Spaniards' refusal to trade with foreigners, an English company should deny the benefits of free trade to its own tenants.

The commander of the settlers, Captain William Rudyerd, had experience of colony building and knew that unity and good order were to be preserved at all costs. But he was not perturbed by the settlers' bickering. He reminded them of their good fortune in having come to such a healthy island, where the 'bloody flux' (probably dysentery) and 'the burning fever' (probably typhoid) that had killed so many settlers in Virginia were unknown.

Rudyerd also reminded them that 'we are environed with enemies,' and that their efforts would be in vain unless the island was capable of resisting a Spanish attack.[19] So in addition to their duties in the fields, the farmers, craftsmen and servants were expected to pitch in with the construction of the island's fortifications. Under the direction of Captain Samuel Axe, they were put to work at Fort Warwick, which was being built on the site of William Blauveldt's little redoubt on a low cliff on the smaller island, where it overlooked the harbour. Since the settlers also had to be able to use firearms, they would receive militia training from the garrison's officers twice a week.

The company hoped that any teething pains the settlers might feel on arrival would be eased by the island's Puritan minister, Reverend Lewis Morgan. Despite being only 22, the company judged Morgan to be 'a very sufficient scholar for his time, and a studious and sober man.' He moved into the governor's house, where he was expected to tend to the spiritual needs of Philip Bell and his family. Morgan liked Bell, calling him 'a man whose countenance proclaims him grave, his words eloquent, his deeds religious – he is all a Christian.' Morgan was delighted by Providence too: in a letter home, he compared it 'to the Eden of God,' and revelled in having found 'all things according to our heart's desire.' He was confident that the settlers would soon have crops sufficient to fill the hold of the *Seaflower*. 'Oranges, lemons, vines, pomegranates, rhubarb we have planted and they prosper. Indigo, cochineal, cloves, pepper, mace, nutmeg, raisins, currants and I doubt not but the land will bear as well as any land under heaven.'[20]

To fulfil his responsibility for the 'well ordering' of the settlers, Reverend Morgan was expected to lead them in prayer at sunrise, before they headed into the fields for the day, and again at sunset, 'so that [God's] blessing may be upon themselves and the whole island.'[21] At the end of evening prayers, Morgan liked to lead the congregation in the singing of psalms. Psalms were the godly alternative to ballads and folk songs, 'which tend only to the nourishing of vice, and the corrupting of youth.'[22]

Captain Rudyerd appreciated the need to inculcate Christian piety in his charges, but he had nothing but contempt for psalm singing, which was never part of traditional church services. Morgan was quick to upbraid the captain for his sacrilegious remarks, and Rudyerd took umbrage. As the younger brother of Sir Benjamin Rudyerd, and a cousin of the Earl of Warwick himself, Captain Rudyerd had left a grand lifestyle and solid connections in England. He demanded the respect of his peers, and the submission of his inferiors, of which a mere priest was undoubtedly one.

But Lewis Morgan stood his ground, and in so doing, became the conduit for the settlers' grievances. He penned a letter to the company in which he complained that Captain Rudyerd's drunkenness and high-handed treatment of the settlers had kept the colony in an uproar for as long as he had been there. He also took aim at the company: far from laying the foundations for a community of devout believers, the shareholders appeared to be 'solely and covetously desirous of profit.' He charged the shareholders with 'putting on a hypocritical show of godliness for the encompassing of ungodly ends.'

While the shareholders awaited the return of the *Seaflower*, they set about 'scouring the world for the richest commodities' to furnish their island.[23] Thanks to their friends at the East India Company and other trading ventures, the company dock at Deptford was soon crowded with barrels of exotic seedlings, shoots and plants waiting to be shipped out to Providence on the next ship. There were rhubarb roots, pots of scorzonera (black salsify, a root vegetable thought to cure snakebite and the plague) and fustic saplings, which yielded a yellow dye coveted by England's cloth manufacturers.

As they waited, their expenses mounted. Hire of the *Seaflower*, which they had already had for more than a year, was costing them £130 a month. Company treasurer John Pym urged patience; only with God's blessing would their efforts be rewarded. The company was not alone in investing large sums in a new colony with little or no return: between 1630 and 1643, England's merchants and adventurers spent £200,000 (almost £18 million in today's money) on hiring and fitting out 200 ships for the voyage to the New World. None would see a return on his investment until the 1650s.

When the *Seaflower* finally made it back to London in March 1632, Captain John Tanner explained that his return voyage had been delayed by an attack by the Spanish coastguard in the Straits of Florida at the end of December. He had lost an eye, many of his crew had been killed, and only after fighting their way clear of the Spanish ships had they been able to head out into the Atlantic. When the company opened the bundle of letters that Tanner was carrying, and read about his mistreatment of the *Seaflower*'s passengers on the outbound voyage, they were tempted to sack him, but in light of his stalwart defence of company property, they chose not to. Company husband John Dyke was not so fortunate; for his sleight of hand in depriving the settlers of their victuals, he was ousted from the board.

When the contents of the *Seaflower*'s hold were brought onto the company dock, the shareholders were disappointed to find that the settlers had only sent home a few sacks of poor quality tobacco. Lewis Morgan's letter explained why: the colony was in a state little short of mutiny. Many of the settlers' complaints – of the company's monopoly on the sale of their produce, and the prices in the company magazine – were to be expected. Others – of the oppressive heat of late summer and the storms that uprooted their young plants in autumn – were inevitable. But Morgan's letter, which was 'stuffed with bitter expressions and savouring a spirit inclined to sedition and mutiny,' cast aspersions on the company's very motives.[24]

Such insubordination was insufferable. In tending to the settlers' spiritual welfare, Reverend Morgan was to be absolutely free from meddling, whether by the island council or the company itself. In return, he was to be consulted on all matters of importance. But he had not been invited to sit on the island council, for the running of the colony was not his business. As far as the Puritan grandees were concerned, Lewis Morgan could never be more than a highly trained and valuable servant. In response to their complaints, the shareholders 'bitterly reproved the people' for their 'infamous libels.' They were akin to the Israelites, 'who were not satisfied with the promise of that good land which God had provided for them.' To punish the Israelites, God had 'let their carcasses fall in the wilderness as men most unworthy to enjoy so great a blessing.' The settlers should take care not to invite the same punishment, the company warned.

The shareholders felt particularly aggrieved by 'the imputation of so dishonourable an end as covetousness.' They had each invested £600 in the colony on Providence. Any City of London merchant would have baulked at being asked to invest so much with so little prospect of a quick return.

> Some of you know that in the other plantations, £25 or £50 a man was a whole adventure [share], and if any man were out £100 before return of profit, he was accounted a great patriot, but scarce a wise adventurer.

Lewis Morgan was clearly too young and inexperienced to bear the weighty responsibility the shareholders had entrusted to him. In a second letter, addressed to Philip Bell, they instructed him to ship the querulous cleric back to London 'in strict confinement.'[25]

The fomenter of the mutiny was gone, but its causes remained. The company received more letters from Providence the following year. 'We do not find here the largeness that was reported,' one settler wrote. Drought had struck for the second year in a row, turning the river running through New Westminster into a trickle, and killing his crops. Governor Bell had managed to procure pomegranate plants and Guinea pepper from Barbados, but they had failed to take root. The fustic saplings were still alive, but it would be many years before they yielded their precious dye. As for the rhubarb roots and scorzonera, nothing had come of them, and the island council was convinced that Providence wasn't suited to sugar.

Although the settlers had had a good tobacco harvest, which they had been counting on to rescue them from penury, they discovered that woodworm had eaten through the rafters of the drying sheds, sprinkling the leaves with a bitter tasting dust that left most of the crop unusable. With no tobacco to trade and the last of their supplies exhausted, they were left feeling 'like forsaken Indians.' Some of them even asked permission to come home.[26]

Had they still been in their home villages, they could have turned to the local alehouse for comfort. But there was no tavern on their Lordships' Isle. 'Take care that idleness, as the nurse of all vice, be carefully eschewed,' the company had warned the island's governor. Members of the island council were allowed to drink – several of them, like Captain Rudyerd, did little else – but the company feared its effects on the lower orders, and instructed Philip Bell to punish any servant found drinking. Swearing, taking the Lord's name in vain, and making atheistic remarks were also punishable offences. If their little island community was to secure God's blessing, it would have to be a godly one.

In the absence of a minister to confide in, those that could write confined their worries to their letters home. Anxious to nip trouble in the bud, the company intercepted them on arrival in London. In one, a settler asked a relative to send 'cards and dice and tables' on the next ship. Company secretary William Jessop told Bell to have them burned on arrival.[27]

Nor did the settlers have female company, for the shareholders judged the island too dangerous for women or children. Valued members of the island council, like Philip Bell, and the wealthier heads of families had been allowed to take their wives and children to Providence, but the other settlers would not be permitted such comforts until the colony was capable of resisting a Spanish attack. Until then, the cooking and washing would have to be done by the island's youngest servants.

This only exacerbated the shortage of manpower in the fields. William Jessop assured the seven family heads that more servants would be sent out on the next ship. In the meantime, the 'fathers' would just have to work their 'children' harder. Servants were commodities to be bought and sold, and wherever possible, the company paid the members of the island council in servants rather than pounds sterling, for cash could be spent in England and might encourage them to come home. Knowing that their servants would be free men in two years' time, they were keen to get as much unpaid labour out of them as they could.

42

Since Captain William Rudyerd had more servants than anyone, he decided to lead by example, taking his whip to a young servant called Floud, who he accused of laziness. Instead of returning to work, Floud complained to the governor. But Philip Bell couldn't overawe an arrogant troublemaker like Rudyerd as he might have at home; experienced military men had to be courted with care, for Bell depended on them to train the militia. So the governor sent Floud back to his master, who tied him to a tree and whipped him again, this time with rods. Three months later, young Floud died, presumably of his wounds. On his return to London in 1634, Captain Rudyerd was brought before the company court and asked to explain his 'cruel usage' of his servant. He told the bench that he had used 'all fair means to prevent the scurvy which through laziness was seizing upon him.' Only when 'fair means' failed did he give Floud 'a blow that might set himself to his business.'

Savage as his treatment of Floud might sound, it was well known that the first signs of scurvy were 'a general laziness and evil disposition of all the faculties and parts of the body.' Poor Floud wasn't able to testify, but one of his friends confirmed that 'through laziness he had got the scurvy,' and that he had been refusing to work for some time before Rudyerd whipped him. Floud's friend also mentioned that 'some in the island had suffered many degrees beyond him,' which suggests that Rudyerd was not the only member of the island council to take a whip to one of his servants.[28]

Scurvy plagued all the colonies, and claimed the lives of more sailors than any contagious illness. The sufferer would complain of 'itching or aching of the limbs' and 'shortness and difficulty of breathing, especially when they move themselves.' His friends might notice his eyes turn 'a leady colour, or like dark violets,' and a 'great swelling of the gums... with the issuings of much filthy blood and other stinking corruption thence,' which caused 'a terrible stinking of the breath.'[29]

The causes of scurvy were 'infinite and unsearchable.' Was it caused by ship's biscuits, salted pork, or a disease of the spleen? Was it contracted from dirty clothes, the damp sea air, or the heat of the day? Without a diagnosis there could be no prognosis. Ships' surgeons had seen sailors recover from scurvy after eating fresh fruit and greens – but they would just as readily prescribe a mug of beer mixed with an egg yolk, bran with almonds and rosewater, or 'a good bath in the blood of beasts.'[30]

The court pronounced itself satisfied with Captain Rudyerd's account. It found his 'drunkenness, swearing, ill carriage towards the governor and other misdemeanours' less than satisfactory, but was unwilling to punish the commander of the settlers, and the trial was abandoned. Before leaving the court, Captain Rudyerd told the company that the only crop ever likely to flourish on Providence was potatoes, and that 'the island in respect of itself is not worth keeping.'[31]

Cruelty to servants was common in the colonies, and it often sparked revolt. Father White witnessed a servant uprising on Barbados in 1634.

> The very day we arrived we found the island all in arms to the number of about 800 men. The servants of the island had conspired to kill their masters and make themselves free, and then handsomely to take the first ship that came, and so go to sea.[32]

Runaway servants often joined forces with runaway sailors, who also faced routine abuse from the authorities. Between them, they made up the best part of the community of buccaneers that had sprung up on Cuba's isolated south coast.

At the company's foundation, the shareholders had raised £3,800 in working capital. By 1633, each 'adventure' had increased in value to the astronomical sum of £1,025, which meant that they had to stump up yet more cash. Although they were all impatient for profits, some shareholders were slow in advancing the company the money it needed to hire and fit the next outbound ship, so company treasurer John Pym came to rely on the largesse of the Lords among them to see the colony through its infancy. They were united by their faith in God, who had led them to Providence. If the settlers' crops failed, it only showed His hatred of sloth. He also disapproved of tobacco farming, which was why tobacco prices in London had slumped; it was just as well that the settlers had sent so little back on the *Seaflower*.

John Pym urged them to concentrate on growing cotton 'till better things may be obtained and brought to perfection, which will in time be greater profit.'[33] He was already victualling the *Long Robert*, and was about to load a mill, which the settlers could use to extract oil from their castor oil plants, and an engine, which would help them process the cotton crop.

John Pym had also contracted several 'special agents' to conduct agronomical experiments on the island. One was Gray Finch, a surgeon whose knowledge of exotic gums, oils, and resins was highly esteemed. Another was Richard Lane, a godly man and acquaintance of Lord Brooke, who would supervise the planting of the madder bulbs Pym had procured. Madder yielded a valuable dye, which cloth makers used to achieve a range of colours, from true red through purple, yellow, orange and light blue. English cloth makers had to import madder from Europe; better that it be grown on Providence.

Richard Lane would also be working with the island's apothecary, Joseph Lidsey, to find the mechoacan potatoes thought to grow on the neighbouring island of San Andrés. Mechoacan was the source of a purgative called 'jalap', much coveted by those prone to constipation. Believing jalap to be a drug of great value, John Pym ordered the despatch to England of a ton of mechoacan potatoes. The realisation of 'the glory of that noble design' was only a matter of time. In anticipation of bumper crops and riches to come, John Pym instructed Philip Bell to clear a further 20 lots of 25 acres each, one for each of the company's shareholders.

4

CAKE, ALE AND PAINFUL PREACHING: A BANBURY TALE

In light of the uproar Captain William Rudyerd had caused, there was a clear need to dilute the influence of the military officers on the island council. Several of the heads of families were invited to sit at the top table, and John Pym drafted instructions to Philip Bell on 'how to proceed against any fractious person.' Since Rudyerd's tirades had clearly been sustained by alcohol, 'strong waters' were prohibited for all but those few 'well-qualified in temperance.'[1]

In March 1632, the company chartered a second ship, the *Charity*, to sail to Providence, and set about recruiting the responsible, God-fearing civilians worthy of settling a Puritan colony. From now on, recruits could expect to keep two-thirds of what they produced, instead of the customary half-share. Shaken by Lewis Morgan's bitter invective, the company also hoped to recruit a good Puritan minister, to reassure the settlers that they were committed to their spiritual, as well as their economic, wellbeing.

They were also going to need more servants. But Sir Thomas Barrington met with a lukewarm response at the annual hiring fairs, for word of the settlers' hardships had got back to the would-be migrants of Essex. Reports of mistreatment at the hands of overweening gentry folk did not go down well with young apprentices, and many of them opted to board ships bound for Virginia or Massachusetts instead. Those who signed up to sail on the *Charity* only did so on condition that their wives and children were allowed to join them. The company relented: not only did they allow women and children to sail for Providence, they assured the existing settlers that they would send out more women and a midwife.

William Fiennes, Lord Saye and Sele, went recruiting around Banbury in Oxfordshire. Lord Saye was among the grandest of the company's Puritan grandees. Like his father before him, he dominated the town and the surrounding villages. His manorial courts, which he presided over personally, were models of efficiency. He was also a Justice of the Peace, with a well-earned reputation for offering sound justice. Lord Saye was well respected by the merchants and yeomen of Banbury, partly because he was more dynamic than the county's other nobles, but more importantly, because he was a Puritan. The town's godliness was well known across England. Banbury's leading families were strict Puritans, and had no time for the hotchpotch of unquestioned beliefs and archaic rituals that passed for religion in England. They wanted to see the Church of England divested of trinkets and baubles, and reduced to its essence: a meeting place for the devout to interpret the word of God. This led them into conflict with traditionalists for whom religion, saints' days and festivals were inextricable parts of daily life.

The town's elaborately carved medieval crosses, made famous by the ballad *Ride a Cockhorse to Banbury Cross*, had not survived the Reformation. Regarded as symbols of popish idolatry, they had been demolished in a fit of iconoclastic fury. Even the morris dancers who led the townspeople in making merry at weekends had been branded pagans and driven away.

In the years that followed, the town had become a recruiting ground for radical sects, like the Separatists and the Independents, 'tradesmen or mechanical fellows who will take upon them to know who shall be saved or condemned.'[2] Traditionalists regarded their sermons as suspect at best, downright seditious at worst, and many of the town's preachers were brought before the church's High Commission to recant their 'mistakes' in interpreting Scripture. The town recorder, Edward Bagshaw, was called to account for a sermon in which he condemned the wealth and earthly power of the bishops who policed the Church of England. At a time when the average merchant was making £45 per year, how could a bishop justify his annual salary of £1,300? Bagshaw wanted to know.[3]

Venal, corrupt, meddlesome bishops were bugbears for Puritans and parliamentary constitutionalists alike – and Lord Saye was both. His nickname of 'Old Subtlety' was given to him by Charles I, as a mark of respect for his formidable skill as a parliamentary strategist. The royalist Earl of Clarendon called Lord Saye 'a man of close and reserved nature,' and 'a notorious enemy of the Church,' who had 'great authority with all the discontented party throughout the kingdom, and a good reputation with many who were not.'[4]

The presence in Banbury of such a shrewd and principled man made it easier for those of the same persuasion to hold their beliefs without fear. Banbury was famous for its cakes, ale and love of a painful preacher, but it was also known for its fierce loyalty to Parliament. King James, who had been a great exponent of the divine right of kings, was well accustomed to dismissing Parliament when it wouldn't let him raise taxes. Lord Saye became his most hard-headed opponent in the House of Lords, and even served time in the Fleet Prison after opposing one of his illegal money-raising ventures.

Thanks to its Puritan families and the Puritan lord who protected them, Banbury was perhaps the foremost town in England in its opposition to the 'forced loan' that King Charles imposed on the country's taxpayers in 1626. Charles was unmoved by their protests and imprisoned four members of the town corporation for their resistance to his tax collectors. The forced loan was not the only royal tax that Parliament refused to authorise. Until King James came to the throne, the Royal Navy was a largely mercenary force that commissioned merchant ships to do its fighting in wartime. King James was, however, blessed in having a talented ship builder in Phineas Pett, whose fleet of 500-ton ships were a match for anything the king's European rivals could put to sea. When Charles came to the throne in 1625, he inherited a navy of 37 warships, but he deemed them insufficient to realize his ambitions, and proposed levying a tax to fund the construction of more.

'Ship money' had been raised before, but only in counties bordering the sea, and only in times of war. By 1634, however, Moorish pirates were regularly taking captives from English coastal towns and selling them into slavery in North Africa. The government's failure to see them off brought disgrace on a seafaring nation, so Charles decided to levy ship money on inland counties like Oxfordshire too. The county's landed gentry resented the new tax, and nowhere more so than in Banbury, where successive writs of ship money met with stout resistance. Such were the men of high principle and unwavering courage that Lord Saye was counting on to become the model settlers of Providence.

Until the late 1620s, Henry Halhead's life had been as respectable and predictable as that of any other Banbury Puritan. He was born in 1577 into the most prominent family of woolen drapers in the town, which was in turn, one of the most notable wool producing towns in England. In 1600, when he was 23 and she was just 17, he married Elizabeth. They had two teenage daughters, Patience and Grace, and an eight-year-old son, Samuel. Unlike his brother Thomas, who was certainly wealthy, Henry was not a taxpayer, yet the brothers rose up through the ranks of the town hierarchy together. Like Thomas, Henry became a constable of the town corporation, a churchwarden, and, in 1630, mayor of the town, just as his brother had two years before. In one of the reports he prepared while mayor, Henry explained how he raised funds for the town's workhouse by levying fines on its 'drunkards, tipsters and swearers,' adding, 'as for rogues and vagabonds, we are little troubled with them, they like their entertainment so ill.' Henry clearly had a sense of humour, albeit a rather heartless one, and was determined to impose the Puritans' 'culture of discipline' on his home town.

Since his father had left his estate to Thomas, Henry was dependent on the wool trade to make his living. Like Essex, Oxfordshire had grown prosperous on the backs of its sheep, and the county was a major supplier of quality wool to clothmakers. Henry made his living selling 'hats, bands, jurkins, dublets, points, breeches, stockings, garters, shoes and all other necessaries' to the yeomen and husbandmen of north Oxfordshire.

But by 1632, the wool trade was in crisis. City of London merchants were buying up land around Banbury, and enclosing it for sheep pastures, just as they were around Braintree in Essex. Henry wrote a pamphlet denouncing the enclosure movement, in which he describes how cottagers turned off the common land were 'constrained to flee into other towns.' Consequently, every town was 'mightily increased with poor people, who press into such towns and erect cottages ... to the great annoyance and charge of the places whither they are driven.' The recession in the cloth trade combined with the influx of landless cottagers to drive up the poor rates paid by the property owners of Banbury, and brought Henry to the point of bankruptcy.

Coincidentally, it was Henry's trenchant opposition to the enclosure movement that first brought him to the attention of Lord Saye, who was the local champion of the landless against the evils of enclosure. Henry found himself on Lord Saye's side again in 1628, when King Charles decided to station a regiment of soldiers in Banbury. Billeting, as it was known, was often used to punish towns that dared resist the king's tax-men. In the pamphlet that Henry wrote denouncing enclosures, he also complains that 'the free quarter of soldiers is so exceeding burthensome,' for the army expected its hosts to pay for its upkeep, and the soldiers often caused trouble in town.

The army was not a popular force. England had no standing army, and the body of men that passed for one was a thoroughly unprofessional organisation. The military commander Edward Cecil described how he went about recruiting men for the anti-Spanish campaign in the Netherlands. 'We disburden the prisons of thieves, we rob the taverns and alehouses of tosspots and ruffians, we scour both towns and country of rogues and vagabonds.'[5] So little-liked was the army that in 1625, when the threat of invasion appeared imminent and Charles ordered his subjects to help the army to fortify the country's defences, his plea went largely unheeded. Indeed, it was the fear that billeting was the beginning of a permanent military presence in the counties of England that convinced many Englishmen and women to leave England for the Americas.

King Charles gave the job of billeting his troops in Banbury to Sir William Knollys, Earl of Banbury. As Lord Lieutenant of Oxfordshire, the ageing earl was responsible for the county's military affairs. He noted that 'the causers of this denial are all neighbours to Lord Saye, who ... has his instruments herein.'[6] One of those instruments was undoubtedly the town's mayor, Henry Halhead. Lord Saye knew Henry well. Apart from their staunch Puritanism and shared opposition to enclosures, the Halheads were old business acquaintances of his Lordship's family. Lord Saye was anxious to recruit someone to act as 'father' to the passengers on the *Charity*, for he didn't want to see a repeat of the casual mistreatment that Captain John Tanner had meted out to his passengers on the *Seaflower*. What could be more natural than his Lordship's suggestion that Henry take up a seat on the island council?

It seems likely that Henry would have heard about the New World from Mary Showell, who was known in Banbury for the Virginian catskin that she wore in the winter months. It was a gift from her son Isaiah, who had sailed for America a few years before. When Isaiah returned to his hometown, word soon spread of the substantial stock of tobacco and property he had built up in Virginia. Lord Saye's promise of a fresh start in a new land caught Henry's imagination. Unlike Virginia, the colony on Providence offered true Christians an opportunity to build a new, more godly society that would, in time, inspire God-fearing Englishmen to challenge the timorous hypocrites running the country's churches.

Whatever Henry's feelings prior to 2 March 1628, matters came to a head that night, when some of the soldiers billeted in Banbury started a fire that burned a third of the buildings in the town to the ground. Nobody was killed, but the loss of property was horrendous, and the town's mayor was among those hardest hit. The town corporation appealed to neighbouring counties for charity, and Henry was one of four townspeople granted £1 by the people of Coventry. The Great Fire of Banbury was a sign from God, he told himself, warning him to go to the beacon the Providence Island Company had lit in the Caribbean.

So it was that Henry and Elizabeth, in late middle age, sold their remaining property – three houses, two shops and a barn – and prepared to join the *Charity*'s voyage 'into the mouth of the Spaniards.' On the last day of December 1631, Henry presented his accounts to the town corporation, and promptly disappeared from the borough records. Had he gone to Massachusetts, his name might today be known to every American schoolchild. Instead, he sailed for a tiny island in the Caribbean, vowing to stay there 'until the isle of Great Britain, being about to be born again into a new and free state, might deservedly be christened the isle of Providence.'[7]

King Charles was determined to prevent 'the promiscuous and disorderly parting out of the realm' of men and women of 'idle and refractory humours, whose only end is to live as much as they can without the reach of authority.' In order to keep Puritans out of the colonies, the Commission for Foreign Plantations issued an order to 'our loving friends, the officers of the Port of London' to interrogate all passengers bound for New England or the Caribbean. Anyone not carrying a letter from his local Justice of the Peace, confirming that he had taken the oath of allegiance to the king and owed no taxes, and a letter from his local clergyman, certifying his good standing in the Church of England, would not be allowed to sail.[8]

But the King's border controls were not difficult to get around. The port authorities paid little attention to poor migrants, so many Puritans boarded ship disguised as servants. Others travelled to the docks with their patrons, who could usually bamboozle their way past the port officers, or were smuggled aboard under cover of night. Consequently, the passenger lists show plenty of ships docking in New England with more passengers than they left with.

Anticipating problems at Deptford, the company arranged for the *Charity* to sail from Plymouth, where no such controls were in place. The Banbury contingent travelled with émigrés from Warwickshire, who had been recruited by Lord Saye's close friend, Lord Brooke. When they reached Plymouth, the company's Devon agent told them to find lodgings in the city while they awaited the arrival of the *Charity* from London. Henry and Elizabeth Halhead took rooms near the docks, and it was in those weeks that they first met Samuel Rishworth, his wife Frances and their young son. They were from Coventry, where Samuel had been prominent in the campaign to raise funds for the victims of the Great Fire of Banbury. Samuel was five years Henry's junior, but his compassion, and his austere, reproving Puritanism bound the two men as brethren. They also had family ties: Samuel's brother was married to Hester Hutchinson of Alford in Lincolnshire; the Hutchinsons were one of the county's leading Puritan families. Many of Frances Rishworth's relatives were also taking leading roles in the Great Migration to New England.[9]

Like Henry, Samuel had been recruited to keep order and good neighbourliness among the settlers. As the son of a Lincolnshire farmer, he too was prime 'middling sort' material, and having served as a churchwarden, member of the Common Council and sheriff of Coventry, he also knew about local government.

Among the other passengers, Henry and Samuel were especially pleased to meet the island's three new ministers. Reverend Hope Sherrard was one of Sir Thomas Barrington's Essex recruits. He would serve as minister at New Westminster's little church, and take the room in the governor's house vacated by Lewis Morgan. Reverend Arthur Rous was John Pym's stepbrother and a cousin of Lt William Rous, the island's deputy commander. He had come to Plymouth with his large family and several servants, and was looking forward to giving lectures at the church. The third minister was Mr Ditloff, a German refugee from the wars of religion raging on the Continent; he had been appointed to tend to the settlers on the east side of the island.

But even before they left England, Henry was given cause to question Arthur Rous' suitability for the post of minister. The Reverend's funds had dwindled away as they waited for the *Charity* to arrive, so he asked Henry to lend him some of the £16 the company's Devon agent had given him to tide him over. Henry went to Rous' lodgings on the outskirts of the city to give him the money, and ended up spending the day with the Reverend and his family. When they joined in prayer for a safe voyage, he was appalled to see that Rous 'was not able to pray extempore,' [i.e. impromptu] and had to read the lines from a prayer book. He was also shocked at the way the Reverend 'would soldier-like beat his men.' Returning to his lodgings, he confided to Mr Ditloff that he considered Rous 'insufficient' to be a minister. The German agreed that their colleague seemed 'fitter for a buff coat than a cassock.'[10]

The *Charity* only arrived from London in March, and the 150 passengers were finally able to board the 200-ton ship for the voyage across the Atlantic. Those with savings paid the £6 fare upfront; the rest agreed to repay it from their first year's earnings. The hold was loaded with supplies for the company magazine and weapons for Fort Warwick. The ship was also carrying letters, some from the settlers' families, most from the company to its governor. Captain Thomas Punt was under instructions to call first at Barbados in order to take on fresh water, cottonseed and pomegranate cuttings. He should then sail to St Martin to buy salt from the Dutch, and then west to Association Island to drop off seven passengers and take on board guinea pepper and tobacco seed. From there it was a week's sailing to Providence.

On their first Sunday at sea, Henry was given more reason to doubt Arthur Rous. As the passengers were kneeling on the deck, rapt in prayer, he heard the Reverend singing 'catches' with Mr Ditloff. What did they mean by singing profane songs on the Sabbath day, he asked them? Protesting his innocence, the German claimed not to have understood the words. Henry was not impressed; he only hoped that the two blasphemers would mend their ways before they reached their Lordships' Isle.

It would have been a hazardous and uncomfortable journey at the best of times, but as feared, it was made worse by the ship's captain. The company had told Thomas Punt to treat his passengers with due consideration, but he was even more callous than Captain John Tanner. Like him, Punt appropriated a third of their biscuit and half their beer, hoping to make a profit on their resale when he reached Barbados. When Henry protested, Punt threatened to clap him in the bilboes, the strong iron bar with two sliding shackles usually reserved for mutineers.

Captain Punt's 'uncivil usage of Mr Halhead' shocked the other passengers, but it didn't raise an eyebrow among the crew. If any of them had complained about the captain's behaviour, they could expect to be flogged.[11] Luke Fox, a seaman from Hull, described the sailor's life in 1635.

> It is not enough to be a seaman, but it is necessary to be a painful seaman. For I do not allow any to be a good seamen that has not undergone the most offices about a ship, and that has not in his youth been both taught and inured to all labours. To keep a warm cabin and lie in sheets is the most ignoble part of a seaman, but to endure and suffer a hard cabin, cold and salt meat, broken sleeps, mouldy bread, dead beer, wet clothes, want of fire – all these are within board.[12]

The difference in outlook between the *Charity*'s passengers and its crew was akin to a chasm. Sailors like Luke Fox took their spiritual bearings from the sea, which was as mysterious as it was powerful. One moment, it was so gentle it could rock a baby to sleep; the next, so furious it threatened to send all hands to the bed where the sleep was endless. The providence of a benevolent God offered no lodestar by which a sailor might navigate a course, for the sailor's creed had no room for a divine plan. To the mind of a typical sailor, the universe was governed by capricious, unbiddable fate, whose weft and warp no man could fathom.

Doubtless Henry would have allowed his understanding of God to temper his reaction to Captain Punt's outburst. The captain's errant behaviour was only to be expected, for as the Bible made plain, most men were little more than worms in the dung heap of human affairs. The typical mariner – greedy for gold, awed by luxury, and committed only to his fellows – was just another lost soul.

Yet Luke Fox's ode to 'the painful seaman' bears a striking resemblance to the Puritans' paeans to the pain of rebirth suffered by repentant sinners. The difference lay in the sense of purpose that Henry's beliefs gave him, and his refusal to bow down in the face of his 'fate.' A series of failed harvests, the growing poverty of the people and the resurgence of the plague in the 1620s were not just bad luck; they were signs of God's displeasure with England. It was the Puritans' conviction that God's wrath was about to descend on England for its wickedness that led so many followers of 'the true religion' to leave for the Americas. Providence promised a new beginning in a new land, free from the restraints imposed by feudal England. Once on their Lordships' Isle, they would live free from meddling priests, churches riddled with corruption and a society benighted by sinfulness.

That arch-Puritan, Oliver Cromwell, called fate 'a paganish' concept. Good Christians lived under divine protection: this was the meaning of providence. It was the light Henry Halhead sought in his prayers, and it was guiding him to the New World. Cromwell's chaplain, John Owen, called providence 'a straight line,' which 'runs through all the darkness, confusion and disorder of the world.' The very idea of chance, and the fatalism it induced, was anathema to the orderly Puritan mindset.

In the face of God's all-sufficiency, mere mortals might be tempted to give thanks and be done with it. Yet, limitless as God's sovereignty was, and powerless as men were to alter His purpose, the Lord's servants were not to 'tempt' providence by just sitting back and doing nothing. The Creator had a plan for mankind, as well as for the world. To trust wholly in the divine plan, while not trusting wholly to it, required the finely attuned sense of balance of a tightrope walker. As Oliver Cromwell put it, the believer had to avoid 'carnal confidence' on the one hand, and 'diffidence' on the other. This entreaty – to be bold and yet submissive – was what marked the Puritans out from the sailors heading to Providence.

To a contemporary observer, this belief in providence might look like literary decoration, or the empty rhetoric of a conventional mind. But it was anything but a cynical cover for self-interest. It was only because Henry had faith in God that he entrusted his life to a crook in a floating wooden box. Henry knew that God intervened continually in the world He had made. His hand could be seen in one man's sickness and another man's recovery; in every disaster at sea, as well as in every safe return. The Bible made plain God's will; once understood, only a fool could regard the fulfillment of His will as anything but necessary.

5

The First Voyage to the Miskito Coast

Captain Daniel Elfrith had no time for the squabbles of priests, farmers and unruly apprentices. In the two years that had passed since the advance party arrived on Providence, the colony's admiral had had no choice but to school them in the rudiments of Caribbean life. But he wasn't suited to the role: it was Providence's position on *la carrera de Indias* that had first excited his interest in the island, and the temptation to return to sea in search of prizes was strong. Providence was an ideal base from which to launch raids on Portobello, Cartagena and the small coastal settlements that lay between them.

In response to the growing numbers of foreign pirates, Spain's colonial authorities had heavily fortified its ports, but once the king's treasure fleet was at sea, his men-of-war were all that stood between the rovers and untold riches. Even in the months before the fleet sailed, there were merchant ships carrying valuable cargos of hides, indigo, wine and gold coins to be had. But a privateer could only sail with letters of marque. They required royal assent, and King Charles had made his peace with Spain. Not that Captain Elfrith expected the peace to last; for as long as he could remember, 'the don' had been Protestant England's principal foe. Spain had tried to get England to rejoin the Catholic fold when it sent its armada to invade England in 1588; given the chance, it was sure to try again.

In April 1632, temptation got the better of Captain Elfrith. Without saying a word to Philip Bell, he gathered a crew, rigged a pinnace and sailed for the coast of Central America. A week later, he returned to the island harbour with a Spanish frigate in tow. It was carrying nothing of great worth, but he hoped his act of piracy would provoke reprisals from the Spanish, which would in turn provoke Charles to authorise a return to privateering.

This was just the kind of rash act that Philip Bell wanted to avoid. Striking at Spanish shipping while Captain Axe was still building the island's forts was an act of stupidity that jeopardised the entire colony. Bell confined Elfrith to land, and told him to write a letter to the shareholders in London to explain himself; only they could pass judgement on such recklessness.

In his letter, Elfrith begged their Lordships' forgiveness; he had sailed for the Main intending to look for sugar cane and fruit trees to plant on the island, he explained, but when he crossed paths with a Spanish merchant ship, the opportunity to grill its crew for intelligence was too good to miss. To curry favour with his patrons, he sent them his rutter, or sailing guide, based on the many voyages he had made around the western Caribbean over the previous 20 years. He kept it for his own private use, but felt moved to 'present these, my labours, unto your Lordships' view,' because the 'ancient seamen' were now all dead, and 'all the drafts and plots which are made in England are very false.'[1]

Their Lordships did not find Elfrith's *mea culpa* very convincing, but his rutter was most impressive. It was far and away the best guide to the Caribbean then available. In careful, accurate prose Elfrith described the sea currents, the shoals to avoid, and the approach to every Spanish port from 'Crackers' (Caracas) to Cartagena; Portobello to Veracruz. It included the hundreds of soundings of the depths he had made, and line drawings of long stretches of the coast of the Spanish Main, including the tiny inlets where a ship's captain might hide from his pursuers.

The drawings were followed by Elfrith's account of his career in the Caribbean, which goes some way to explaining the frustration he must have felt at having to live among inexperienced colonists. It also offers some insight into the problems the company faced in trying to reconcile the divergent interests of the island's Puritans and privateers. 'I have written as several voyages have given me occasion, and so begin with my first entrance, which was in the year of our Lord, 1607,' he wrote.[2] Elfrith had first gone to sea as a member of Sir Walter Raleigh's expedition to found an English settlement in Guyana. From his base on the north coast of South America, Raleigh planned to go in search of the mythical land of El Dorado – the Golden One. Rumours of a chief so rich in gold that he covered himself with gold dust every evening before diving into a sacred lake captivated the imagination of every European who heard them. But Raleigh did not find the source of the rumours, for Lake Guatavita lies high in the Colombian Andes, 1,800 miles from Guyana. His settlement lasted just four years before its inhabitants disappeared without trace.

Daniel Elfrith was luckier: he managed to slip away shortly before disaster struck and in 1613, he turned up in the Somers Isles. Over the next two years, the fledgling colony was overrun by the rats that had boarded Elfrith's ship before he left South America. They swam across the narrow channels separating one island from the next, devouring everything they found. Governor Nathaniel Butler likened their arrival to 'one of the Pharoah's plagues.'[3] He had cats trained to kill them, and then dogs to hunt them, and even had the colonists set fire to their fields, but to no avail, and the Somers Isles endured several years of terrible hardship.

Daniel Elfrith didn't stick around long enough to witness the damage he had caused. By 1614, he was back in England, where he won the patronage of the Earl of Warwick, and turned privateer. In 1618, he took command of the *Treasurer* and launched the first of a series of attacks on Spanish ships that made him one of the most notorious sea robbers of his day. The *Treasurer* was also the first English ship to carry African slaves to North America (which makes Elfrith instrumental in the beginnings of both the transatlantic slave trade and the environmental degradation of the Americas).

The Earl of Warwick was the Somers Isles Company's biggest shareholder, so it was only natural that when Elfrith's options dried up, he returned to his patron's colony. Between 1621 and 1628, he was governor of its castle and a member of its assembly. His experience of high office gave him some understanding of the difficulties inherent in establishing a colony on a small, isolated island, but only confirmed his reputation for being argumentative, and bold to the point of rashness.

The Providence Island Company's shareholders did not hold Elfrith's temperament against him. His rutter was invaluable. Poring over his drawings, they were struck by the only significant stretch of coastline the Spanish had left untouched in their conquest of the lands around the Caribbean basin: the Miskito coast of Central America. The name might have been familiar: in 1623, an article had appeared in one of the first newspapers ever published in England. Entitled *Newes from Spayne*, it reported then-Prince Charles and the Duke of Buckingham's journey to Madrid, and their failed attempt to woo *La Infanta de Castilla*. Unfortunately, the Spanish king had shown no interest in their proposal to unite the Stuart and Habsburg crowns through marriage. The idea hadn't played well at home either, and was soon abandoned.

But the article had gone on to say that while in Madrid, the Duke of Buckingham met a Spanish official who told him about the Miskito Indians. According to 'Don Fennyn,' the Miskitos were more resistant to Spanish encroachment than any other native tribe of Central America. Yet they were 'besotted by a prediction that there shall come a nation unto them, with flaxen hair, white complexion and grey eyes, that shall govern them.'[4] If Don Fennyn was to be believed, the Miskitos looked upon the English as their liberators.

Just as young Spaniards grew up listening to stories of the villainous English pirate *Don Francisco Draco*, so the shareholders had grown up listening to 'the Black Legend' of Spanish cruelty towards the Indians of South America. Several of them were likely to have read the Spanish priest Bartolomé de las Casas' *A Short Account of the Destruction of the Indies*. Published in 1583, it offered a first-hand account of how the Spanish had betrayed their Christian duty to convert the heathens, and had instead enslaved them. Elfrith's rutter showed the Miskito coast to be just 70 miles west of Providence. Was this not a sign from God, reminding the shareholders of their duty to carry the Gospel to the benighted natives of the New World? Company secretary William Jessop hurriedly composed a letter to Philip Bell, instructing him to mount an expedition to the coast.

Christopher Columbus had visited the coast of Central America on his third expedition to the Americas, but it was only on his fourth and final voyage that he actually landed on the isthmus. Shortly afterwards, his ship was engulfed by a storm, and would have been wrecked had he not found shelter in a lagoon close to a headland. '¡*Gracias a Dios que hemos salido de estas honduras!* he declared ('Thank God we've escaped these depths!') As a result, the cape became known as *Cabo Gracias a Dios*, and the gulf that ran west from it, *Honduras*. In the years that followed, the Spanish built prosperous towns at Panama, Granada and Guatemala, but they showed little interest in the Caribbean coast. Between Portobello and the tip of the Yucatan peninsula of Mexico, a distance of over

1,200 miles, they established only two settlements. Their control over the rest of the coast was nominal, and the Miskito coast was still practically unknown.

As the island's admiral, Daniel Elfrith was the natural choice to lead the expedition. But the company was unwilling to give too much leeway to the sailors on the island council, most of whom were veterans of countless skirmishes with the Spanish, and had little understanding of their patrons' evangelism. Elfrith and the other old hands were told to focus their attention on building the island's fortifications, and leadership of the expedition was instead entrusted to Richard Lane, a devout man of God and eminent botanist with a keen interest in the flora and fauna of the New World. Company secretary William Jessop told him 'to ingratiate yourself and your company with the Indians,' find out 'what things are most in esteem' among them, and 'by a civil carriage, modest behaviour, and affable condition, labour to possess them with the natural goodness of the English nation.'[5]

But Richard Lane couldn't be expected to mount an expedition to the Spanish Main alone. Captain Sussex Camock and Captain Samuel Axe, both veterans of the Thirty Years' War, were no diplomats, but at least they knew how to sail. They were authorised to take as many men as they needed. They took fifty, among them William Blauveldt's brother, Albertus, who knew the coast as well as Daniel Elfrith. They sailed on the *Golden Falcon* in 1633.

Each man aboard had his own reasons for befriending the Miskitos. The more trepidatious among them hoped that the coast would serve as a refuge in the event that the Spanish drove them from Providence. The tenant farmers hoped to find precious dyewoods and exotic crops that could be transplanted to the colony. The artificers and servants only hoped to meet some Miskito women, who might alleviate the dearth of female company in the colony.

The Miskito coast stretches for 270 miles from the mouth of the River San Juan, on the border between contemporary Costa Rica and Nicaragua, north to Cape Gracias a Dios, and then west to the mouth of the Black River in Honduras. There are few landmarks in the lagoons and mangrove swamps – so few that Miskitos travelling down the coast in search of turtles navigated by misshapen trees and stands of cabbage palms. Sussex Camock had the crew of the *Golden Falcon* row ashore in longboats, and Richard Lane led a small party to explore the inland savannah. They found it to be boggy, suitable for pasture but not cultivation. Beyond the sandy hills, which were crowded with pines and cedars, were mountains covered with dense jungle.

The party came to the mouth of a large river and headed upstream. The river teemed with turtles and alligators, freshwater sharks and stingrays, and its banks supported great stands of mahogany. Venturing into the jungle beyond, they spotted anteaters, armadillos and wild pigs foraging in the undergrowth. That evening, when they gathered around the campfire to smoke their pipes, they watched monkeys clambering through the branches overhead, and listened to the distant roar of jungle cats.[i] In the days that followed, Lane's party travelled 40 leagues – about 120 miles – upriver, carrying knives, axes, machetes, and glass beads, which they hoped to barter with the inhabitants of the riverside villages they came to. The natives knew nothing of metalworking, and welcomed these strange tools, but had little to offer in return.

Meanwhile, Captain Sussex Camock was cruising the shallow coastal waters. He found that the most desolate stretch ran from Cape Gracias a Dios to what became known as Brancman's Bluff, 60 miles to the south. It was largely barren land and the sand flies were far from hospitable, but it was there that the Miskitos lived. There were no more than 2,000 of them, living in longhouses that accommodated up to 25 people. The Miskitos were happy to act as conduits for Captain Camock's trading venture. In return for the Englishman's knives, axes, machetes and glass beads, they sourced a variety of exotic plants from the tribes that lived further inland. Captain Camock built huts and storage sheds, and a busy trading post soon sprang up at the Cape.

Among the goods the Miskitos brought back from their forays inland was lignum vitae; this was a promising discovery, for resin from 'the wood of life' was believed to be an effective treatment for syphilis. Being the island's only botanist, Richard Lane was also keen to secure supplies of pine gum, agave, and sarsaparilla. These days sarsaparilla is used as a flavouring for drinks, but in seventeenth-century England it was used to treat a variety of maladies, among them syphilis, elephantiasis and

---

[i] But they were most excited by the flocks of parrots they saw. The company had offered ten shillings to any man who sent a live parrot back to London. William Jessop's only stipulation was that they be caged 'in such a way that the boats are not made dirty unnecessarily.' In the years to come, Jessop would send several letters to Providence in which he regretfully acknowledged the arrival of dead parrots.

scrofula. The Miskitos also supplied him with the red annatto berries that they smeared on their skin to ward off the sandflies. Lane thought it would make a good dye for their Lordships' woollens.

Among the other items on Richard Lane's shopping list were several oddities gleaned from stories told by early English travellers to Asia. The Miskitos tried and failed to procure the bezoar stone said to grow in the stomachs of certain small animals, which the English believed to be an antidote to various ailments. Nor could they find 'the stone in the alligator's head' that their strange new friends asked for, though they doubtless cracked a few heads open along the way. Instead, they introduced Camock to the manatee, which 'has a stone in the bladder, very helpful to women in travail.'[6]

Members of the expedition had plenty of time to wonder after the Miskitos during their stay at Cape Gracias a Dios. They were sturdy, squat people who went naked but for a loincloth, which they made by pounding the inner bark of a tree related to the rubber tree into a coarse sheet. They wore ornaments in their noses, lips and ears, and carefully oiled and combed their straight black hair. Theirs looked to be an easy life: in the morning, the men went hunting or fishing. During the rainy season, when rising floodwaters forced the fauna onto isolated knolls, there were plenty of deer and wild pigs to be found; when the floodwaters receded, they revealed alligator, tortoise and lizards' eggs in the riverbanks. The brackish lagoons were home to a variety of fish, including a species of large mullet that they harpooned at night by torchlight. They also ate manatees, which Camock likened to veal, and green turtles, which they harpooned with heavy palm wood spears tipped with flint, attached to twenty feet of silk-grass line.

When Captain Camock first saw the Miskito men whiling away their afternoons in their hammocks, he thought them lazy. But he was astonished by the distances they covered in their canoes, with no sign of fatigue. They seemed to have an almost spiritual affinity with their canoes, which they called 'dories'. When a Miskito boy came of age, his father felled a tree, burned away the core with hot coals, and hollowed it out to make his son a dory. When the old man died, his son would bury his paddle and harpoon alongside his body, and split his dory in two.

On festive occasions, such as followed a successful hunting trip, the men invited neighbours from miles around to come to their village to partake of a fermented brew they called *mishla*. After a few cups of *mishla*, they would start to tell stories, which often ended in drunken brawling. Unsurprisingly, the women hid their weapons as soon as they started drinking *mishla*. The life of a Miskito woman looked similarly relaxed. Apart from gathering fruits, berries and coconuts, there was little to do. They needed maize to make mishla, but they preferred to steal it from neighbouring tribes than grow it themselves.

Aside from their bouts of extreme drunkenness and the casual violence they meted out to neighbouring tribes, Captain Camock was appalled to see that the Miskitos left deformed children on the shore to be eaten by seabirds. But he also noted that they were capable of great tenderness, were quick to forgive and showed no signs of vengefulness. Nor were they divided by rank or property. There was a headman, who was selected for his hunting prowess and called himself a king, but he seemed to have little real authority. His longhouse was set apart from the others, but that was all that marked him out from the rest of the tribe.[7]

Following the expedition's return to Providence, Philip Bell prepared several trunks, packages, earthenware jars, and rolls of hides for dispatch to England. Among the cornucopia of exotic goods to find their way to market in London was sugar cane, the local variant of which Captain Camock judged to be 'as fair as any in the world.'[8] However, the two most promising commodities traded at the Cape were both new to the merchants of the City of London. The first was a tough sea grass that Camock had found growing in abundance on the sandy soil of the Miskito coast. Following trials made by 'Mr White of Dorchester,' who testified that 'Camock's flax' made 'a very fine thread, and spins much better than ordinary flax,' the company judged it to be 'a solid commodity fit for the general manufacture,' worth at least four shillings a pound.[9] The shareholders ordered 200 tons of the stuff, and set about hiring a bigger ship. The Miskitos had also introduced their new friends to an American variant of the vanilla plant, which they called 'dette.' 'Men of understanding' told William Jessop that dette would also prove valuable, so he instructed Camock to source cuttings to grow on Providence.[10]

Jessop's letter acknowledged that Providence's climate had proven too hot for castor oil plants, and drew Philip Bell's attention to his latest procurement of seedlings. These included indigo, which yielded the rich blue dye that had long been the preserve of the Spanish nobility. The company also instructed the governor to plant more food crops, for a second party of colonists would soon be arriving on the *Charity*. As soon as the islanders were producing enough food to feed them, more would follow.

Sussex Camock's expedition to trade with the Miskitos was the first of many. In August 1634, the company instructed him to build a small redoubt at the Cape, in recognition of the trade's importance. On his next trip to the coast, Captain Camock took four cannon, some smaller arms and a supply of ammunition, under strict instructions not to let them fall into the Miskitos' hands. But the Miskitos were fascinated by the guns, and soon became expert in their use, to the delight of the English, and the lasting regret of their neighbours.

As time went on, the English and the Miskitos grew to depend on one another. 'These Indians are extremely skilled in spearing turtles, manatees and fish,' the privateer and surgeon Alexander Exquemelin was to write in the 1670s.[11] 'An Indian is capable of keeping a whole ship's company of 100 men supplied with food.' Turtles were an especially important discovery, for they could be kept alive below decks for months on end, supplying fresh meat to sailors on the longest voyage.

Impressed by their skills as fishermen, Captain Camock invited several Miskito men to return to Providence with him. Each side was amazed at the other's strange customs: the Miskitos were dumbstruck by the wooden world of the *Golden Falcon*, and the thick woollen clothes their new friends wore even at midday. The English couldn't understand how the Miskitos could live without names. In 1684, the privateer William Dampier described how the Miskitos 'take it as a great favour to be named by any of us, saying of themselves that they are poor men and have no name.'[12]

A knowledgeable and willing Indian guide was priceless to anyone unaccustomed to Caribbean life. The Miskitos taught them to use aloe vera to treat their sunburn, and to prepare tea with the young leaves of the annatto plant to treat their diarrhoea. They had brought a supply of iguanas with them from the coast, which they kept as fresh food whenever they went into the hills to cut wood with the carpenters. They also took the English to the cays of Roncador and Quitasueño, where the turtles came ashore to lay their eggs.

When the shareholders learned that there were Miskito men living with the settlers on Providence, they stipulated that if they could not be restrained from practising their idolatrous worship, they were to be removed from the island, 'so there may be no mixture of paganism with the pure religion of Almighty God.' They were reassured to discover that the Miskitos performed no religious ceremonies, had no idols and made no sacrifices. They had many superstitious beliefs – they feared rainbows and believed that certain trees were haunted – but even the most vituperative Puritan could not fail to be struck by their readiness to hear the Word of God.

Converting the natives of Central America to the true religion had always been a priority for the company. As Reverend Hope Sherrard put it in a letter written to his patron, Sir Thomas Barrington, shortly after his arrival, 'The Lord in mercy crowns their honours' noble undertakings in these parts with a glorious purpose, yet the gospel may be planted on the Main. What glory thereby would accrue to God!'[13] The company suggested that Miskito children be invited to live on Providence as well, 'if they may be had with their parents' good liking.' With three new ministers due to arrive on the *Charity*, the heathen children could be given a Christian education whose benefits they could share with the rest of their tribe when they returned to the coast.

Within a year of Sussex Camock's first voyage to the coast, Miskito children had joined the all-male households of New Westminster. The company told their English 'fathers' they were to treat them 'as tenderly careful as if they were your own.' They raised them as they might their servants' children, expecting them to perform simple tasks around the home from the age of ten, and to attend church in the evenings.

While the company found a ready place for Miskito men and their children, Miskito women were more problematic. The company was well aware of the settlers' hunger for female company, but didn't want to antagonise their only allies in the region, and ruled that no Miskito women were to be brought to the island, 'for fear of some inconveniences depending thereon.'[14] Only with time did they realise that most Miskito men would happily barter their wives and daughters with their new friends in exchange for a good knife. In the years to come, several of the islanders took native wives. Even Philip Bell, who had come to Providence with his English wife, had his Indian woman.

Such was the warmth between native and newcomer that the Miskito headman-cum-king even agreed to send his young son to England as a guest of the Earl of Warwick. Perhaps he was fulfilling the prophecy recounted to the Duke of Buckingham by 'Don Fennyn' – that a grey-eyed race of men would come and live among them, and deliver them from the cruelty of the Spaniards? His trust in the English was not blind, however: before he would allow his son to sail for England, he asked that the company send a young Englishman, Lewis Morris, to the coast to act as security for his safe return.

The Miskito prince, whom the English called 'Oldman,' left with an assortment of gifts, among them silk grass, textiles, potions and remedies. He lived in London for three years, was assigned a tutor and soon 'acquired a working knowledge of English, a taste for the accoutrements of European life and a desire to please his new friends.' Young Oldman became a great favourite at the court of King Charles, 'from whom he met with the most gracious reception, and who had him often with him on his private parties of pleasure.' Charles admired 'his activity, strength and many accomplishments.'[15] Oldman would likely have stayed in London longer, but his sojourn was cut short by news of his father's death.

Before he left England, Charles gave him a laced hat to serve as a ceremonial headdress, and a document requesting that he lend assistance to any Englishman who happened upon the Miskito coast in future. Oldman returned home armed with a newfound sense of his own importance, bestowed on him by his powerful benefactors. At his coronation ceremony, he led the Miskito elders in swearing allegiance to his new friend Charles, King of England.

The Providence Island Company now had political, as well as economic and religious motives to build a settlement on the Miskito coast. If they could build plantations there, the potential for expansion was unlimited. Perhaps God had always meant for Providence to serve as the foundation for a mighty English empire in Central America? If the shareholders interpreted His will correctly, the island was destined to flourish as an offshore fort, where crops grown on the mainland could be stored before shipment to England. In time, their new colony would dwarf their outposts in Virginia, Maine and New England, and the settlers of North America would join their more enterprising brethren on the Miskito coast.

6
THE PRIDE OF THE RIGHTEOUS

With the arrival of the *Charity*'s 150 passengers, the population of Providence rose to around 300. All the principal characters in the drama that was to unfold on Providence were now on stage. The Puritan element was represented by Henry Halhead, Samuel Rishworth, Hope Sherrard and Richard Lane; the privateers by Captain Daniel Elfrith, Captain Samuel Axe and Lt William Rous. Adjudicating was the island's austere governor, Philip Bell.

Bell apportioned new plots, and New Westminster gradually expanded across the flat ground at the foot of Cedar Valley. Henry Halhead and Samuel Rishworth were given land and buildings on the east side of the island, which had until recently been occupied by John Essex. He had been co-leader, with Lewis Morgan, of the incipient mutiny against the company, and had returned to London on the *Seaflower* in a bid to draw public attention to the settlers' grievances. Fortunately, for the company at least, he was killed when the ship was attacked by pirates in the Straits of Florida.

With Essex dead and Morgan dismissed, the shareholders hoped that their new tenants would supply the responsible leadership that the islanders needed. Henry and Samuel were assigned a few servants each and apportioned tools and seeds from the company magazine. To reach the windward side of the island, they had to follow the river upstream into Cedar Valley, over the watershed and down onto the ribbon of flat ground that overlooked the reef. It was an idyllic spot: the shallow waters around the reef ran through multiple shades of azure, and a gentle, near-constant breeze sent ripples through the lush grass that rolled down to the shore. The two friends spent their days in their fields, while Elizabeth and Frances looked after the children at home, tended to their livestock, and did the washing and cooking. Close by was a small hut that served as a chapel, where Mr Ditloff would tend to the spiritual needs of the handful of artificial 'families' that lived on the east side of the island. The company assured Ditloff that in time, he too would have land and servants of his own. For the time being, however, he was in the care of Halhead and Rishworth.

Hope Sherrard moved into Lewis Morgan's rooms in the governor's house, and set about making his presence felt as the island's new minister. After preaching his first sermon in New Westminster's little church, he introduced the congregation to his new adjunct, Reverend Arthur Rous. They expected to see the entire community for morning and evening prayers every day, as well as attend the two services they would give on Sundays. They also gave the settlers the option of attending a Saturday evening service at the governor's house, catechism on Sunday afternoons, and another sermon on Wednesday evenings.

There is no record of Sherrard's sermons but if church services in Virginia are anything to go by, he is likely to have ended them with a prayer: 'Lord, bless England, our sweet native country. Save it from Popery, this land from heathenism, and both from atheism.'[1] God would protect them from the enemy, Sherrard assured the congregation, but they would do well not to tempt His wrath. Playing games on Sundays was prohibited, those who slandered His ministers would be whipped and blasphemers could expect to be hanged.

Henry and Samuel were pleased to find themselves in such a godly community, administered by such enlightened rulers. Following the evening service, they often visited the homes of the island's other tenant farmers, who agreed that the presence of such diligent ministers, after so many months living without spiritual guidance, was a great comfort.

Watching their so-called children tend the kitchen fire in the yard, and cook their so-called fathers' dinners, Henry was struck by these curious facsimiles of English domestic life. The company's tenants clearly drew some comfort from their artificial families, and were bound to them all the more tightly by the hardships they had endured.

For almost three years, they had been planting and tending mechoacan potatoes, sarsaparilla and pomegranate, plants that even the company's 'special agents' seemed to know little about. Watching them wither in the dry season, only to be washed away by the autumn rains, they often wondered what sin they had committed to warrant such misfortune. The only crop that brought them any profit was tobacco, and they were obliged to give a third of whatever it raised at market to the company.

When they weren't tending their Lordships' latest whimsy, they were cutting and dressing stone for the walls of Warwick Fort. Lt Rous's demands on their precious time kept them from their fields. Why hadn't their Lordships sent more servants to work on the fortifications, they wanted to know? Like them, Henry also grew to resent the military service they were obliged to perform, for he found Captain Axe's manner all too reminiscent of the overweening army officers that had been billeted in Banbury. He appreciated that in a new colony, everything had to be done 'as in the beginning of the world,' in the words of John Winthrop, the governor of Massachusetts.[2] But that meant clearing land, building houses and planting crops, not marching up and down the little square in front of the governor's house.

Captain Axe and the other soldiers on the island council found the settlers' resistance infuriating. Didn't they see that they had thrown themselves into the the very mouth of the Spanish Empire? If Lucifer was the first rebel, the Puritan yeoman was clearly the second. Philip Bell was equally dismayed, for the arrival of the second contingent of settlers had only exacerbated the acrimony that prevailed in meetings of the island council. He had hoped to spin a comfortable web of mutual obligations that led all concerned to lead productive and virtuous lives. The island's new ministers were supposed to be the oil in the machinery of island government, easing friction and aiding the smooth running of the colony, but they seemed no better suited to colonial life than Lewis Morgan. Bell was shocked by the brutality with which Reverend Arthur Rous treated his servants; such a man would never have been allowed to join a New England congregation. Fortunately for Rous' servants, he died of fever within a year of his arrival.

Mr Ditloff was also quick to create problems. One Sunday, he refused to perform the sacrament – the ritual whereby consecrated bread and wine are offered to the faithful – for Henry Halhead, on the grounds that he was a hypocrite. On the outbound voyage, Henry had told him that the ship's mate, John Wells, was 'a carnal man, who would sometimes swear.' Yet only the previous week, Ditloff had heard him call Wells, 'a good and honest Christian' in front of his friends.

When Hope Sherrard intervened in the dispute, Ditloff told him to mind his own business, and demanded 'parochial independence' for his little congregation. Notwithstanding the fact that his 'church' was no more than a hut on the beach, it was only what the company had promised him, he told Sherrard. The company disagreed: when word got back to London of his declaration of independence, they called him to account for 'the pride and insolency of his carriage.'[3] Mr Ditloff sailed for London on the next ship, never to return.

Since that left Hope Sherrard as the island's only minister, the company was keen not to lose him as well. But Sherrard was a graduate of that bastion of Puritan nonconformity, Emmanuel College, Cambridge, and was just as demanding as his predecessor. Not only did he expect the entire community to attend his sermons, he demanded that each man, woman and child give him an account of their faith, and like Mr Ditloff, was prepared to deny the sacrament to anyone he considered less than godly.

The army officers of Fort Warwick had no interest in plumbing the depths of their consciences for signs of moral laxity and soon tired of their sanctimonious minister. Captain Benjamin Hooke accused Hope Sherrard of 'negligence in his function' and 'debility of memory, whereby he was made unfit for the ministry.' In response, Sherrard told Captain Hooke that he was no longer welcome in his church. It was a rash act, but as he explained in a letter to Sir Thomas Barrington, he had discovered that the captain was 'fomenting a faction against me in the church.'

Not content with alienating the military wing of the island council, Hope Sherrard also criticized the governor. Philip Bell, he alleged,

> maintains this rotten principle that whatsoever he commands, be it either lawful or unlawful, yet we must yield an absolute and active obedience to the same without any questioning power... If this principle may stand good, what are we in this island, but his absolute slaves and vassals?[4]

When he tired of arguing with Captain Hooke and Philip Bell, Sherrard followed Mr Ditloff's example and created a separate congregation, an act symbolic of withdrawal from the Church of England. Like all Puritans, he believed that he was on the cusp of a new understanding of the universe and his place in it. As Lord Brooke put it, 'The light still will, must, cannot but increase.' Religion was no longer a matter of mere adherence to outward forms; indeed, the outward signs of devotion were all too often used as a cloak for sin.

The ability to make compromises for the sake of unity had been a capital virtue of the Pilgrim Fathers who sailed to New England in 1621.

But their minister had tended a small flock, which defined itself by its opposition to the Church of England. By contrast, Hope Sherrard was minister to saints, sinners and the damned alike, and when he wasn't pontificating about the nature of God he was meddling in other people's interpretations of Him. Power was an unfamiliar and intoxicating brew, and Sherrard was not the only Puritan minister to let it go to his head once set loose in the colonies.

Sherrard's self-righteousness might have exasperated the other members of the island council, but it appealed to the powerless, and like Lewis Morgan, he quickly became the pole around which all manner of discontented settlers gathered. Most came to him with prosaic grievances: they resented the company's monopoly on the sale of their crops, and considered the distribution of tools and seeds to those with powerful sponsors unfair. But several of them, including Henry Halhead and Samuel Rishworth, wanted more fundamental changes, starting with the devolution of power from the military officers to the 'visible saints' in Sherrard's congregation.

Ranged against the 'small body of zealots' on the island council was a larger group of army officers, merchant sailors and experienced colonists from the Somers Isles, who were more inclined to look windward than skyward for guidance. They expected Philip Bell, as the former governor of the Somers Isles, to take their side in island council meetings. But Bell was a man of strong religious conviction, who shared the company's patrician high-mindedness. The Somers Islanders didn't thank the governor for his magnanimity.

The governor had other headstrong individuals to contend with too. Barred from setting out to sea for fear he would attack Spanish shipping, Daniel Elfrith had become 'a nuisance to everybody.' The island's admiral interfered with Samuel Axe's authority at Fort Warwick, and the two men quarrelled again when the tobacco harvest was brought in, this time over the portions they had been allotted. In exasperation, Bell expelled his father-in-law from the island council. He took the same tough line with Hope Sherrard, and eventually imprisoned him for 'persistently fronting the authority of the governor and council.' In response, Sherrard's friends on the Puritan wing of the council denounced the governor for his 'impiety and despotism.' Caught between his employers' high hopes and the colonists' low regard for his authority, Bell wrote to the company in despair at the 'disunion of hearts and ends on the island.'[5]

Puritanism was proving no less divisive at home than it was on Providence. The Arminian wing of the Church of England argued for a strong-arm approach to the dissenters. Arminians were determined to unify England's countless nonconformist sects in a single Church of England. They did not believe that heaven was reserved for the Puritan 'elect,' and were convinced that God's grace was available to all who took part in the sacrament. Their greatest champion was William Laud, the Bishop of London. Laud seemed almost embarrassed by the Reformation, which had created a cult of the Bible, without granting the church any authority to insist that its interpretation of the Word of God was better than anyone else's. If Protestant orthodoxy were to be preserved, the Puritans would have to be brought to book.

The Puritan preacher Thomas Shepherd recalled being summoned to appear before Bishop Laud in 1630.

> He asked who maintained me, charging me to deal plainly with him, adding withal that he had been more cheated and equivocated by some of my malignant faction than ever man was by Jesuit, at the speaking of which words, he looked as though blood would have gushed out of his face, and did shake as if he had been haunted of an ague fit.

Laud forbade Shepherd to 'preach, read, marry, bury or exercise any ministerial function' in London, and sent him away.[6]

Bishop Laud and his supporters set about capturing the king's mind, and succeeded in convincing him that all nonconformists were Puritan zealots at heart, and as such, politically subversive. In 1633, Charles appointed Laud Archbishop of Canterbury. Once in office, he embarked on a campaign of religious persecution more severe than anything seen since Elizabeth was on the throne. 'Painful' preachers who disagreed with the new ceremonies, the position of the altar, or the King's *Book of Sports* were charged with heresy and hounded out of church.[i]

The appointment of Archbishop Laud sent shock waves through Puritan ranks. The MP and Providence Island Company shareholder Oliver St John saw Arminianism as another step on the road back to rule from Rome, and called it 'the little thief put into the window of the church to unlock the door.'⁷ Laud's attempts to increase the wealth of the church, and his love of the mystical garb donned by church ministers, convinced many Puritans that he wanted to turn the clock back further, to a time when Englishmen were still in thrall to magic.

Far from listening to the Puritans' concerns, King Charles conspicuously chose Catholics as his friends and advisers, and even befriended George Con, the first papal representative to come to England for over 100 years. To make matters worse, Archbishop Laud became a prominent figure in both the Privy Council and Star Chamber, where he gave his wholehearted support to Charles' drive to raise taxes without the authorisation of Parliament.

Laud was pushing the nonconformist element of the Church of England into an unprecedented radicalism. The Puritans had always seen Catholicism and arbitrary government as two sides of the same coin, but they were powerless to stop the fusion of Church and State that the king seemed intent upon. The world seemed on the verge of the millennium, the thousand-year rule of the Saints prophesised in the Book of Revelation. With both the Church of England and the Palace of Whitehall in the hands of despots, growing numbers of Puritans felt driven to build a new church and a new state in the Americas. One of the most aggressive promoters of migration to New England was Edward Johnson, who remembered 1634 as the year in which 'the yoke of Episcopal persecution in England became so heavy on the necks of the most godly [that] many thousands of them did flee away to join themselves to these American churches.' By then, all of England's colonies had become refuges for nonconformists: not just those established by Puritans, like Providence and Massachusetts, but also commercial ventures like Virginia, Maryland and Connecticut. Had they not left for America, there is every chance that the Earl of Warwick, as Lord Lieutenant of Essex, would have been called upon to put down an insurrection.

Over the course of the 1630s, 60,000 English, Welsh, Scottish and Irish men and women made the crossing to the New World. Two thirds

---

i   The Arminians were essentially traditionalists; they wanted to see the more ceremonial aspects of church services restored, and the altar kept apart from the congregation. The *Book of Sports* was designed to protect the traditional games and physical activities that people played after church on Sundays from the Puritans, who wanted to ban them.

of them headed not for North America, but for the Somers Isles, St Kitts and Barbados.[8] This should have been good news for the Providence Island Company, but most Puritans chose the colony at Massachusetts Bay over Providence, for it offered a degree of freedom unknown on their Lordships' Isle. The founders of Massachusetts had taken the company charter with them, effectively cutting themselves off from rule from England. On arrival, virtually all heads of families were offered the chance to become freeholders of the land they tilled, and company meetings in Boston became the basis of the first representative government in the Americas.

As Archbishop Laud turned the screws on his opponents, Puritan emigration increasingly took the form of vociferous, unbending ministers leading their congregations into exile. Among them was Reverend Henry Roote; so keen were the shareholders to recruit the Reverend and his congregation that they even covered the cost of shipping him and his family to Providence to make a preliminary survey of the island's spiritual life.

Reverend Roote spent a few weeks on Providence, at the end of which time, Philip Bell proclaimed him a man of 'ability, gravity and deserts.' Unfortunately, Roote was unable to return the compliment. Bell and the military men around him had strayed a long way from the Puritan ideal, he told them, for Providence was utterly lacking the machinery for popular participation in government. He returned to London in May 1634, armed with a list of proposals for the shareholders. He was prepared to return to Providence with 100 devout settlers, but they 'would not undertake the voyage, but upon a promise to have the government in their own hand.' If the company agreed to dismiss the soldiers and sailors from the island council, the community could enjoy the leadership of its 'saints,' and thereby ensure the protection of God. No amount of forts could protect their colony from a wrathful God, he reminded them.

Reverend Roote's proposal had the backing of the civilian members of the island council. In a letter to Sir Thomas Barrington, Samuel Rishworth called Roote 'my ancient acquaintance and worthy friend,' and asserted, 'for that short time he has been here, he has begun a Reformation of many things which were amiss.' He urged Sir Thomas to do all he could to accommodate Roote's proposals, 'otherwise I fear we shall be much discouraged, for our hearts are set upon him.'[9]

For a time, the company thought Roote's scheme feasible. Now that the military faction was expending its energies in the trade with the Miskitos, perhaps the Puritan wing could be allowed to hold sway over the island council? Perhaps the company could accommodate both parties, with the pragmatists focusing on the construction of a new colony on the Miskito coast, and the idealists on the construction of a model community on Providence?

But the Puritan grandees could never commit to such a radical redesign of their colony and considered Massachusetts a poor example to follow. By the mid-1630s, the other Puritan colony had passed a law whereby only members of the congregation could hold public office. Since church membership was only offered to 'visible saints' – those in whom the congregation clearly saw 'the work of God's grace' – this amounted to rule by a spiritual elite. Lord Saye, who was the Providence Island Company's principal political thinker, was appalled by the democratic implications of this law, saying, 'No wise man should be so foolish as to live where every man is a master, and masters must not correct their servants; where wise men propound and fools determine, as it was said of the cities of Greece.' The godly settlers of Massachusetts might accuse his Lordship of running scared of the popular will, but Lord Saye insisted that in placing the decision-making power of the congregation above that of its natural, aristocratic rulers, they had overturned the basis of good order and true liberty.

The Providence Island Company's shareholders had always intended to run their colony from London, and were determined to restrict both property rights and political participation. But it was theocracy, not democracy, that Lord Saye most objected to. Church and state should always be kept separate. Ministers should be absolutely free of governmental interference, for no one had the right to chastise them for what they did as religious leaders. But they should play no part in government or law making. Lord Saye respected Hope Sherrard, and was happy to be chastised by him for his personal failings. But his spiritual function 'separated [Sherrard] unto a special work,' which would only be corrupted if he were granted a say in government.

Wasn't Archbishop Laud living proof that the clergy 'always had an itching humour for a coercive power?' Witness too the 'fury approaching outright sadism' that the nonconformists of Boston had provoked, how they had been driven from their churches, and deprived of both civil rights and property. Given the chance, a firebrand like Hope Sherrard would doubtless mete out the same treatment to Captain Axe, Captain Elfrith, and Lt Rous.

Lord Saye was horrified by events in Massachusetts Bay not because they were democratic but because they were tyrannical. Congregational control of political life offered no guarantee of security of property, protection under the law or the other ancient rights of free Englishmen. These could only be guaranteed by good government, checked by the people's representatives in Parliament. Any power not so checked, regardless of the saintliness of the hands that held it, was always liable to become despotic.

Besides, who was to say that Puritans made better farmers than privateers? For as long as the shareholders needed to turn a profit, they were at the mercy of the very men being upbraided for their ungodly conduct. If that meant putting the Puritan ideal on hold, and giving the likes of Samuel Axe, Daniel Elfrith and William Rous control of the island council, so be it. Henry Roote had his answer; he never returned to Providence.

In July 1634, the shareholders held a series of meetings at Brooke House to discuss how best to respond to the economic crisis facing their colony. Their excitement at the prospects for silk grass had proved short-lived: English spinners found that separating the silky fibre from the stiffer part of the grass was fiddly and time-consuming. Since it had 'not yet come to sale or price,' the company had to accept that their hopes for Camock's flax had 'disappeared and come to nothing.'[10]

William Jessop also informed the shareholders that the mechoacan potatoes the settlers had planted were 'not of any value,' and that they had allowed their cattle to eat the dette saplings they had planted. Aside from tobacco, the only crop likely to flourish on Providence was cotton; the shareholders urged their tenants to put the cottonseeds they had procured for them to good use.

The shareholders had no time for the settlers' complaints. There would be no further changes to the profit-sharing scheme, nor would any further investment be made until they started producing marketable commodities. Instead, they castigated them for their indolence. 'The sluggard that will not labour, let him not eat and be clothed in rags,'

THE PRIDE OF THE RIGHTEOUS

they told Philip Bell.[11] Those who refused to contribute to the building of Fort Warwick were clearly under the sway of 'a love to ease and liberty, against which humanity and care of their own reputation should have prevailed.'[12] Such troublemakers would receive no more servants at the company's expense, and those who continued to sow discord in the island council would be expelled.

Philip Bell was told to prepare for the arrival of more settlers on the *Long Robert*. Once they had cleared enough land to build themselves some huts and plant their crops, they were to pitch in with the construction of the new fort that Captain Axe planned to build in the south of the island. As for the news that the servants labouring in the fields wore only linen, the shareholders admitted their 'wonder at the scantiness of clothing,' and ordered Bell to put a stop to such a scandalous practice.[13] Their prudishness speaks volumes about the distance between rulers and ruled. The shareholders were not short on skittish enthusiasm, but they had none of the patience needed to work out which crops would prosper and which would not. They might have been ready to question Aristotle, but they were slow to learn from their tenants' experience of farming in the tropics, and did nothing to tap the Miskitos' knowledge of the environment.

In their first years on the island, the settlers had averred to what they assumed to be their patrons' better judgement, carefully planting and raising the seedlings they received from London. But it was becoming clear that the company knew nothing about the island or its climate. Beset by crop failures, and commanded by men oblivious to their suffering, the settlers' despair turned to defiance. When experienced colonists like Daniel Elfrith urged them to plant more tobacco, they followed their advice, and by late 1634, their fields were full of ripening tobacco plants. Early the following year, they bartered 7,000 pounds of the 'noxious weed' – their entire crop – with a passing Dutch ship.[14] The company's ship was in the harbour at the time, waiting to be loaded with the tobacco crop, but the farmers opted to trade it for the Dutchmen's cargo of wine.

The shareholders were outraged by their audacity. By 1635, they had accumulated debts of £4,599. Unless drastic measures were taken, their colony was heading towards collapse. The causes of the crisis weren't hard to find: the settlers' failure to hit on a valuable crop; the extreme touchiness of the Puritans among them; and the rigid hierarchy through which their grievances were filtered. But at root, the problem came down to a shortage of labour. The more the settlers asserted themselves, the less inclined the company felt to send out more servants. Even when they tried to recruit more servants, they found that most apprentices preferred to try their luck in New England, where there was some prospect of buying land at the end of their indentures, and popular participation in local government was well established.

England's growing population had fed the colonies a steady supply of young men, which kept the price of labour low. But the company was now in competition with employers in New England, Virginia, and the other Caribbean islands. The wealthy merchants and nobles that ran Barbados and the Somers Isles could offer migrants few of the incentives that lured them to New England, and often resorted to violence to raise a work force. So common did the practise of kidnapping servants for the colonies become that a new term – to be 'barbadosed' – was coined to describe the practise.[15]

What was to be done? Enslaving the Indians of Central America was out of the question. The Miskitos' hatred of the Spanish, and their knowledge of the local flora and fauna, made them valuable allies. The company also had ideological reasons for respecting their freedom. The Miskitos were the *tabula rasa* on which the Christian gospel would be written in chalk, as if in a classroom. With the English colonist cast as teacher, and the native as willing pupil, there was no room for a relationship as base as that between master and slave.

Bartolomé de las Casas, the Spanish priest who was first to draw attention to his country's cruel enslavement of the native peoples of the Americas, thought that the only alternative was to import African slaves. Unlike the Indians, the Africans had nothing to offer apart from their labour, for nobody proposed taking the gospel to Africa. Besides, slavery was known to be well-established in Africa, and there was no need to negotiate a contract with an African slave, as there was with a freeborn Englishman, who only agreed to submit to servitude for a limited period of time. As the company put it, 'Negroes, being procured at cheap rates, [can be] more easily kept, and [are] perpetually servants.'[16]

Following a recommendation from Philip Bell, the company instructed Captain Sussex Camock to buy 40 Africans and then sell them to its tenants. But buying slaves was easier said than done. Slavery had yet to become common practice in the other English colonies of the

Caribbean. There were enslaved Africans labouring in the plantations of Virginia, but the Chesapeake Bay was a long way from Providence. The Spanish had literally millions of slaves working in their colonial mines and plantations, but their slaving networks were strictly off-limits. Captain Camock would have to find another way.

7

THE AFRICANS, 'DURING THEIR STRANGENESS FROM CHRISTIANITY'

One day in April 1635, Francisco Fernández Fragoso was walking near the settlement at San Juan del Norte on the Caribbean coast of Nicaragua when he came across a white man stumbling along the shoreline. When the stranger saw the Spaniard, he fell to his knees and put his hands behind his head. 'Negro, negro!' he kept saying, gesturing towards the mouth of the River San Juan two miles down the coast. 'He looks hungry,' Fragoso said to himself, and took him to have something to eat. Over lunch, the stranger babbled away between mouthfuls of fish soup, but the only words he could understand were 'negro' and 'Catalina.' Presumably, the stranger was an Englishman.

The following morning, Fragoso set out in a *chalupa* [canoe] to the mouth of the river. With him went the stranger, two of Fragoso's friends, both armed with arquebuses, and five local Indians, who carried long bows. When they reached the mouth of the San Juan they found another young Englishman, who had a noticeably pockmarked face, and four exhausted Africans. When they saw Fragoso, the Africans jumped to their feet and put their hands up. '*¡Señor, venimos en paz!*– we come in peace' one of them exclaimed. 'We are slaves owned by Doña Mariana de Armas Clavijo, widow of the late Capitan Amador Pérez, a citizen of Cartagena!'

Fragoso took the four Africans and two Englishmen to the hospital of San Sebastián in Portobello, which lay several days sailing down the coast. When they arrived, Fragoso had them eat and bathe while he sent for the *alcalde mayor* (the Spanish equivalent of a Justice of the Peace). Capitán Juan de Ribas arrived promptly, accompanied by the public scribe. He began by asking Francisco Biafara to confirm his name, nation and owner. Then he questioned him about the island from which he claimed to have escaped.

He was 28, Francisco Biafara told the *alcalde mayor*. He came from the Bight of Biafara in contemporary Nigeria, and was one of 11 slaves who worked on Doña Mariana's cargo boat, ferrying goods between Cartagena and Santa Marta. One day, eight or nine months before, they had been carrying a cargo of wine towards the mouth of the River Magdalena when they were attacked by Dutch pirates, who forced their way aboard and took them captive. The pirates towed Doña Mariana's boat back to Santa Marta, where they dumped its captain on the shore, and headed out to sea with the 11 slaves. There were about 14 pirates on board the Dutch ship, led by a short man who Francisco called 'Juan Flamenco' [John Fleming], who he guessed to be about 50. After seven days at sea, they reached a small, mountainous island that the pirates called Catalina. There, Juan Flamenco sold the 11 Africans to an Englishman called Capitán Félix Beles, who gave the pirate a pig and 26 pounds of tobacco for each of them.

Francisco and his companions found themselves in the company of about 300 men, 20 women and a few boys. Some of them were Dutch, like Juan Flamenco, but most of them were English. Although none of the Africans spoke the strangers' language, Félix Beles was clearly their leader. There were two regiments of soldiers on the island, one commanded by a smaller, older man called Capitán Alfero, the other by a tough young man called Capitán Rus.[i] On one occasion, Francisco heard Félix Beles reprimand Capitán Alfero for inviting Diego el Mulatto, the famous Havana-born pirate who sailed under the Dutch flag, to join him on the island.

This was all very interesting, said Juan de Ribas. Were the foreigners well armed? The soldiers carried neither swords nor daggers, but arquebuses, Francisco told him. They also had muskets, pikes, cannon and war drums, all very poorly maintained, which they kept in a large building next to the governor's house.

And was the island well defended? Yes, there were nine small forts, several overlooking the harbour, and one outside the governor's house. Each had between two and five cast iron cannons, either mounted on carriages or laid on wooden frames on the ground.

---

[i] Félix Beles was Philip Bell, Capitán Alfero was Captain Daniel Elfrith, and Capitán Rus was Lt William Rous.

And what of the harbour? Juan de Ribas wanted to know – did it offer good anchorage? Yes, said Francisco, although there were some rocky outcrops. The English had built small forts on either side of the entrance to the harbour, one of which was on a point and had a watchtower. There were no guards in the settlement, but the soldiers kept watch from the forts, and whenever a ship's sails appeared on the horizon, they would fire a cannon. When the men working in the fields heard it, they would throw down their tools and rush to the nearest fort or gun emplacement to take up arms.

How did they sustain themselves? Juan de Ribas inquired. The island had many freshwater streams, which were good to drink from. There were no wild pigs in the woods, but the foreigners kept chickens, pigs, a bull and three cows for breeding. Although most of their fields were given over to tobacco, they also grew some maize and plantains. But their main food crop seemed to be potatoes, which they usually ate raw.

The *alcalde mayor* grimaced and stroked his beard thoughtfully. Had Francisco ever heard the Englishmen talk about a fleet of ships coming to the island from England or Holland? No, Francisco said, although on their way to Catalina, he had heard Juan Flamenco say that he would be back the following year with two big, new ships to take revenge on Don Antonio de Oquendo, a Spanish sea captain who had captured a small Dutch boat and its crew off Havana. Juan Flamenco said that he would kill him and load his ships with tobacco for the journey back to Holland. Did the islanders have a ship of their own? No, only a few *chalupas*, although Francisco overheard Capitán Alfero say that he had ordered a flat-bottomed boat built, so that he could go privateering along the coast.

None of the Africans had enjoyed the experience of working under people of another language and religion, Francisco added. The Englishmen had a little house where they gathered every day after work to hear sermons from a young priest, and he had seen men, women and children go to the house, each with a book in his hand. They forced the Africans to listen to his sermons, but they couldn't understand what he said. Nor did they want to, for the foreigners were clearly heretics – on the day of their arrival, they had watched aghast as the priest snatched their rosaries and crosses from their hands and stamped them into pieces on the ground.

Realising the dire predicament they were in, Francisco and five of his friends – Juan Biafara, Pedro Folupo, Gerónimo Angola, and Damián

Carabali – waited for the next starless night and stole away to the beach. Once at the shoreline, they ran into a group of English servants who were about to make their escape in the governor's *chalupa*. 'This is no way to live,' said one of them. 'If you want to go back to your land, we're going.' Francisco and his friends joined the servants in the governor's *chalupa*, and together, they rowed into the night.

After two days sailing, they caught sight of the Miskito coast. By then, their *chalupa* had been battered by the heavy seas and they were worried that it would sink before they made dry land. They clung to the shore until they came to the Spanish fort at the mouth of the River San Juan, and struggled ashore. One of the Englishmen went to look for help, and came back not long afterwards with Snr. Fernández Fragoso, who took them to Portobello in his boat.

Francisco testified that that was all he knew. The scribe handed him the transcript of his account, so that he could confirm that everything had been recorded correctly. But Francisco could neither read nor sign his name, so the scribe signed the transcript on his behalf. Aided by an interpreter, Juan de Ribas also questioned the two English runaways. One of them was a 40-year-old soldier from London called 'Herbatons'. The other turned out to be a 23-year-old Dutchman called Juan Yons. Both claimed to be Catholics. They told the *alcalde mayor* that they had deserted Catalina because they were tired of eating potatoes.

There are few first-hand accounts of the experience of slavery, and fewer still from the early years of European involvement in the slave trade. The first known account is that of Olaudah Equiano, a leading member of the Sons of Africa, a group that campaigned for an end to the slave trade in London in the 1780s. Although Equiano wrote his *Interesting Narrative* [ii] more than 150 years after Francisco Biafara was sold into slavery on Providence, much of what he remembered of his life in Africa would

---

[ii] *The Interesting Narrative of the Life of Olaudah Equiano, or Gustavus Vassa, the African* was published in 1789. Ironically, Equiano was recruited for a project on the Miskito coast in 1775, by which time he had been a free man for seven years. He used his African background and Igbo language to help select slaves and manage them as labourers on sugar cane plantations.

have been familiar to Biafara, and his description of village life is worth considering in more detail.

Oluadah Equiano writes that he was born 'in the year 1745, in a charming, fruitful vale named Essaka.'[2] The location of Essaka is not clear, but it seems likely that Equiano was referring to the village of Isseke in the Niger Delta, which divides the Bight of Biafara from the Bight of Benin. Equiano came from the Igbo tribe. According to his *Interesting Narrative*, the soils around Essaka were rich and farming was productive. Manners were simple and luxuries few, but the villagers had more than enough to eat, and there were 'no beggars.' The village blacksmith forged iron tools – hoes, axes, shovels and picks – that they used to cultivate crops like yam, which they boiled and pounded to make fufu, their staple food. They also produced cocoyams, plantain, peppers, beans, squashes, Indian corn, black-eyed peas and watermelon. They cultivated tobacco and cotton, which the women spun and wove to make cloth, and raised cattle, goats and poultry. The blacksmith also forged weapons, while other metalworkers manufactured delicate ornaments and jewellery.

Equiano writes that money was 'of little use' in Essaka, since they bartered with neighbouring communities for whatever else they needed. While the land was communally owned and farmed, there was a clear division of labour and status. The villagers prided themselves on their fierce localism and resistance to central authority, and Equiano mentions that, 'our subjection to the king of Benin was little more than nominal.' Equiano owed allegiance to his father, the male head of the household, who was in turn governed by the council of elders. At the other end of the social scale were Essaka's slaves, who were usually prisoners of war, or villagers who had been found guilty of serious crimes, like kidnapping or adultery.

By the time Equiano reached the age of eleven, slave raiding was flourishing around the Igbo's lands. When the adults went out to work in the fields, they took arms with them in case they were attacked by marauding bands in search of people to enslave. The Oye-Eboe were to be treated with particular caution. These 'stout, mahogany-coloured men' were from the southern Aro tribe. They often came through the Igbo's territory to trade the guns, powder and beads that they bought from the Europeans on the coast for the village's slaves. But the Aro also encouraged raids of 'one little state or district on the other,' and

Equiano remembers how any local chief who coveted the Europeans' goods would 'fall on his neighbour, and a desperate battle ensue.'

One day, Equiano was taken prisoner by an Aro slave merchant and shipped downriver to the Bight of Biafara, the vast curve in the coastline where three great rivers – the Niger, Imo and Cross – meet the sea. Slave traders took their captives down these rivers to one of three ports: Old Calabar, Bonny or New Calabar, where they sold them to the Europeans.

Most of the Africans who were sold into slavery had never seen a white man before. An English slave trader by the name of John Matthews recounted his meeting with a man 'of bold constitution' while looking for slaves off the coast of Sierra Leone in the 1780s. The African 'looked at the white man with amazement, but without fear.' He carefully examined the man's skin and hair, compared them with his own, and then 'burst into laughter at the contrast and, to him no doubt, the uncouth appearance of the white man.'

Most slaves boarded John Matthews' ship 'in a state of torpid insensibility.' When he asked them why they were so listless, one of them told him that they believed that 'the white man buys him either to offer him as a sacrifice to his God, or to devour him as food.'[3] This belief in European cannibalism was not universally held – people from the interior, like the Igbo, were more likely to hold it than people from the coast, like the Akan – but Olaudah Equiano certainly came to the slave ship fully expecting to be eaten by his captors.

It took the captain of the *Ogden* eight months to gather enough men, women and children to fill the slaves' quarters. While he waited, Equiano was kept below-decks for days at a time. Many of those on board died, most likely of 'the bloody flux ... thus falling victims to the improvident avarice, as I may call it, of their purchasers.' The ship filled with the troubled spirits of the dead, who the living could neither bury nor placate with offerings. Equiano grew sick and waited to die. In this morbid state, his thoughts settled on the dead who had been thrown to the sharks that circled the *Ogden*. 'I envied them the freedom they enjoyed, and as often wished I could change my condition for theirs.'

By 1756, the year Olaudah Equiano was sold into slavery, British slave traders were frequent visitors to the coast of West Africa. But in 1634, the year Sussex Camock first tried to procure African slaves for the Providence Island Company, slavery was still a complete novelty, for the English at least. The Spanish, however, had long depended on slave labour, and Francisco Biafara was more than likely carried to the Americas aboard a Portuguese slave ship. Between 1600 and 1640, Portuguese merchants shipped over 250,000 Africans to Spanish America. Portuguese slavers, merchants and missionaries had been probing the coast of Guinea Bissau since 1450, and the Spanish relied on them to sell them their wares, human or otherwise.

More than half of the slaves sold by Portuguese merchants came ashore at Cartagena, which was the main port of entry for slaves bound for the silver mines and sugar plantations of the Spanish Empire.[4] Aside from its importance as a port, the city was also of great commercial, political, and military value to the Spanish, and word of its great wealth had been quick to spread across Europe. In 1586, Sir Francis Drake captured the city, and put 200 houses to the torch before the authorities agreed to his ransom demand. Thanks to the depredations of English privateers like Drake, the city's defences were vast, second in size only to those of Havana.

Like everything else in Cartagena, the construction of its walls was only made possible by the seemingly inexhaustible supply of enslaved Africans, and Africans and their creole offspring made up the majority of the city's population. Any white person of standing, whether clergyman, stonemason or cobbler, owned slaves. Most had one or two to look after their household, and those who owned more often rented them out as labourers. Cartagena's slaves worked as cooks, laundresses, nurses, maids, porters, oarsmen and town criers. They made buttons and guarded warehouses; salvaged shipwrecks and cleaned floors; delivered babies and buried the dead. On the farms and ranches around Cartagena, they raised livestock and planted maize, yucca and plantain, and on the boats that carried goods up the River Magdalena towards Bogotá, they worked as navigators, cooks, and deckhands.

The typical *cartagenero* slave might have had few rights, no voice in government, and little protection under (or from) the law, but he was considerably worldlier than the typical English servant on Providence. By 1635, Cartagena was a hundred years old. Slaves like Francisco Biafara were familiar with the comings and goings of the slave ships, and the floating population of sailors, government officials and merchants that passed through the city. Francisco knew the Spaniards' language, religion and way of life, and as a deckhand on Doña Mariana's boat, he was probably more familiar with Santa Marta, Portobello and Havana than his mistress.

86

Although the colony on Providence occupied most of their time and energy, the Providence Island Company had not one, but three colonies. The second was San Andrés, which they largely ignored, and the third was the small island of Association. Located off the coast of Hispaniola, it attracted little of the shareholders' attention, but its governor, Christopher Wormeley, had been permitted to buy African slaves from its inception. In trying to procure slaves for Providence, Sussex Camock turned first to Wormeley.

Nothing had been heard from Association, so in 1635, when a fourth party of settlers sailed for Providence on the *Expectation*, the company told Captain Cornelius Billinge to put in at the island on the way, and find out if it was still under English control. It was not: just a few months before Billinge's arrival, a Spanish fleet carrying 250 soldiers had landed on the island and captured its only settlement. Wormeley was able to make his escape, but the rest of the colonists were not so lucky. One hundred and ninety five of them were hanged, while the remainder were thrown into the hold of a Spanish ship and taken to Caracas, where they were left to waste away in the city's dungeon. It was an object lesson in what interlopers who dared to 'cross the line' could expect from the Spanish authorities.

The loss of Association put paid to any hope of sourcing slaves from the company's other holdings in the Caribbean. Sussex Camock could rely on roving Dutch traders to supply him with a few Africans when they dropped anchor in Providence's harbour. But the Dutch, like the English, were relative newcomers to the Caribbean and could only acquire slaves by robbing the Iberians' ships as they sailed between West Africa and Cartagena, Portobello and Havana. For as long as Spain and England were at peace, such opportunities would be few and far between.

The only dependable supply of slaves came via Captain Camock's Miskito friends, who brought small numbers of Africans to the trading post he had built at Cape Gracias a Dios. The more enterprising of the native tribes had made a business of hunting down and capturing slaves who had escaped from domestic service in Spanish towns like Granada and Trujillo. The life of a runaway slave was a precarious one, and unless he could make his way to the safety of a *palenque* – a fortified stockade of fellow runaways – he was likely to be captured by local Indians. He would then be taken downriver, passing from the hands of one tribesman into those of another until he reached the coast, where the Miskitos would barter him with the 'grey-eyed men' for the iron tools and weapons that they had come to prize. Once on Providence, he would be sold to one of the captains at Fort Warwick, or to one of the island's farmers.

The company was never entirely comfortable with the Africans' presence, and was quick to specify that each household was to have no more than one African for every two English servants. The Miskito children living with them were to be raised as Christians, but no such stipulation was made for the Africans. Watching the rest of his 'family' leave for church every morning and evening, the new arrival must have wondered at his new 'father,' who seemed so dedicated to the monastic way of life, and the God who reigned over this practically all-male society. It was a hard life, but it was not without its pleasures. Most of the island was still virgin forest, and some nights, when his fellow 'children' stole away into the woods, he was invited to join them. Far from their 'fathers,' they were free to drink rum with other young men, listen to the sound of the fiddle and the mandolin and even dance with one of the handful of women living on Providence.

The company's decision to import slaves was a blessing to the tenant farmer. A slave could be had for 150 pounds of tobacco, which was considerably less than the 300 pounds of tobacco he had to pay for an English servant.[5] And because enslaved Africans could be procured locally, they freed the farmer from his dependence on the goodwill of the company, giving him a measure of freedom he had never known before. So it was that the Englishman's freedom came to depend on the African's captivity.

In the second half of the eighteenth century, abolitionists would turn to the Bible to justify their opposition to the commerce in people, but in the early years of English involvement in the slave trade, few Christian consciences were troubled by slavery. Were the Africans not the descendants of Ham, the errant son cursed by Noah and possibly blackened for his sins? For many Christians, it followed that this benighted race of

---

iii According to Martin Luther King Jr, the idea that the curse of Ham justified the enslavement of black people was 'a blasphemy,' and 'against everything that the Christian religion stands for'.

people would only benefit from working as the unpaid apprentices of God's chosen people.[iii]

In seeking to turn a profit in a colony still struggling for breath, the Providence Island Company's shareholders had every reason to forget their avowed intent to take the true religion to the heathen peoples of the world. In a sly re-interpretation of their sacred mission, they argued that the trade in Africans was lawful 'during their strangeness from Christianity.'[6] The ungodly people of the world were mere instruments of God's will, sent by Him to test the faith of His saints on earth. What most provoked God's wrath was not the settlers' cruel treatment of servants, sailors and non-Christians, but their pride, gluttony and sloth. Few things roused the Puritan William Prynne to fury more than the sight of a fringe on a man. 'Lovelocks' were 'an effeminate, unnatural, amorous practice, an incitation of lust [and] an occasion of sodomy.'[7] The oppression of one's social inferiors was a minor infraction by comparison.

The only opponent of slavery on the island council was Samuel Rishworth. Samuel believed that Christianity prohibited the holding of slaves, and he was appalled by the company's easy recourse to forced labour. His was probably the first English voice to raise itself against slavery in the Americas. But the shareholders had no sympathy for his protests. They condemned his 'groundless opinion that Christians may not lawfully keep such persons in a state of servitude,' adding that 'we do utterly dislike Mr Rishworth's behaviour, it being both undiscreet… and also injurious to ourselves.'[8]

When Samuel refused to back down, he was accused of 'defiance of the governor and malfeasance at the council table,' and dismissed from the island council, although he was restored to his seat before the year was out. The shareholders were still trying to entice 'colonists of the solid Puritan sort' to Providence, and could not afford to antagonise a man with close ties to one of the most prominent Puritan families in New England. So Rishworth stayed at the council table, where his defiance earned him the grudging respect of his fellow farmers. Unbeknownst to them, he often crept to the slaves' quarters under cover of night, where he assured them that God was with them, and promised to help them regain their liberty.

8

'A NEST OF THIEVES AND PIRATES'

After hearing Francisco Biafara's account of the time he spent on Santa Catalina, Capitán Juan de Ribas sent a messenger over the mountains from Portobello to Panama with his report. The city's governor consulted with his opposite number in Cartagena over how best to respond to the news that the English had established a colony on the island. But the Spanish state was a bureaucratic monolith that left no room for the initiatives of its colonial officials, so they decided to ask Madrid for advice.

Ordinarily, such petitions met with prevarication from the royal authorities. The *Consejo de Indias* – Council of the Indies - had received similar reports from the Spanish ambassador to London in March 1634 but had not reacted, and even after receiving confirmation from Panama, it did nothing. King Philip IV had more pressing concerns: his armies were bogged down in northern Italy, where his generals found themselves pitted against the combined forces of France, the Papal States and Venice. The situation in Germany and Flanders, where his forces were locked in struggle against the armies of the Protestant nations, was no more encouraging.

Then came a lull in the fighting against France, and in the short interval before battle was resumed, the king and his ministers turned their attention to the problems facing their New World Empire. The English colony on Santa Catalina was the latest in a string of audacious swoops made by the king's uninvited guests. Over the past five years, the English had secured footholds in Antigua, Tobago and St Lucia; the French in Martinique and Guadeloupe; and the Dutch in Curaçao. Yet the gravest threat undoubtedly came from the colony on Santa Catalina: the island was ideally suited for an attack on *la carrera de Indias*, the most important sea lane in the Caribbean. Once a year, a fleet of the king's ships ploughed *la carrera* laden with gold, silver and precious stones sufficient to cover the entire annual expenditure of the most powerful state in Europe. If the English pirates were to capture the king's galleons, his treasury would run dry in a matter of months. In May 1635, a fleet left Cartagena with instructions from the city's governor to destroy New Westminster and restore Spanish dominion over the island.

When rumours of a Spanish attack reached Providence, there were anxious discussions over how best to respond, and several of the company's tenants asked Philip Bell's permission to return to England. The island's governor dismissed their request out of hand, and reminded them that the governor of Cartagena was the infamous *marquis de las murallas*, master builder of the walled city. Among his enslaved workforce were settlers from the English colony on St Kitts. Unless they wanted to join them, they would do well to fall in behind Captain Samuel Axe, who was engaged in a frenetic campaign to put the island's forts in good order.

One day in early July, Captain Axe was at Fort Warwick, scanning the horizon through his spyglass, when he spotted three Spanish ships sounding their way along the reef. Capitán Gregorio de Castellar tried to land his 250 troops on the shore several times, but was driven back at each attempt by heavy musket fire. Amid the tense standoff that followed, he sent a scout ashore under a flag of truce with a letter demanding the island's surrender on pain of the penalties attached to piracy. In his reply, Philip Bell informed the Spanish captain that he would have to put the matter to his superiors in London. With their approval, he could have the settlement dismantled and its inhabitants evacuated within a year. Until he received such approval however, he was obliged to defend the company's property against all trespassers.

Seeing no way of evading the cannon fire from Fort Warwick, Castellar decided to attack the eastern side of the neck of land that connects Providence to the smaller island to its north. Captain Axe had left it unfortified, reasoning that no assault party would choose to sail against the prevailing current. Realising his enemy's intentions, he had the islanders drag cannon from the fort to the windward shore. Battle was renewed, more fiercely this time, and after a week riding at anchor, being 'torn and battered' by shot from the islanders' muskets, the three Spanish ships 'went away in haste and disorder.'[1]

The governor of Cartagena was furious to hear of Captain Castellar's failure to take Santa Catalina. Three months after his ignominious retreat, he sent him back to sea in 'a vessel of no account,' with orders to drive out the English usurpers once and for all.[2] But Castellar had no desire to confront his well-entrenched enemy again. He spent a month cruising off the coast, before heading back to Cartagena, where he assured the city's governor that the pirates had returned to England.

Such was the relief the shareholders felt on reading of the islanders' stoic defence of their property that they wrote off all their outstanding fines for drinking and cursing. They even gave Samuel Rishworth and Henry Halhead a hundredweight of tobacco each, as a token of their gratitude for the parts they had played in rallying the servants and slaves to the island's defence.

While they made a great play of their righteous indignation at the Spanish attack, they knew that it was a blessing in disguise. Five years into their experiment in godly living, and the colonists were barely able to feed themselves, much less turn a profit. Their efforts at growing commercial crops had come to nothing bar regular harvests of mediocre tobacco, and none of the jungle products they had procured on the coast had proven lucrative. For as long as England and Spain were at peace, they had had to turn their backs on the noble tradition of privateering – the Spanish attack gave them the cause for offence they had been waiting for.

In December 1635, they petitioned King Charles for redress. They reminded him that, though diminutive in size, Providence was of 'extraordinary importance' to England, for in time it would 'give his Majesty a great power in the West Indian seas, and a profitable interest in the trade of the richest part of America.' They asked permission to 'right ourselves of this aggression, and former injuries done by the Spaniards,' among them the murderous assault on the *Seaflower* as it made its way back to England in 1632.[3]

King Charles considered the company's request with care. He had been at peace with the King of Spain since 1630, but his allegiances were shifting. He had hoped that the peace would lead to an alliance between their two countries to fight either France or Holland. But King Philip had rebuffed his proposal, so he turned his attention to a suggestion first made by Queen Henrietta and the Earl of Holland: that he forge an alliance with the French against the Spanish. With this in mind, he referred the company's petition to his Secretary of State, Sir John Coke, who was a prominent member of the anti-Spanish party at court.

Providence was indeed of national importance, Sir John reported. The island had 4,000 acres of 'good low ground', another 4,000 acres of hilly land better suited to corn or cattle, and supplied 'all kind of provisions for sustenance… In sum, it will yield provision sufficient for 1000 men besides women and children.' While Providence was of little commercial value, it would make a worthy base for a colony on the Miskito coast, which was a region 'as rich and fertile as any other part of the Indies.'[4] As for the island's strategic importance, it was inestimable, wrote Sir John, for it lay

> in the highway of the Spanish fleets that come from Cartagena and Portobello… All ships that come from these places must pass on the one or other side of the island within 20 leagues, and may be easily discovered from thence.[5]

In 1618, James I had had Sir Walter Raleigh executed to placate Catholic Spain. Now his son would do something to placate Protestant England. Charles could see that Providence was no longer the private concern of a company of gentlemen adventurers, and had become a matter of national importance. In his reply to their Lordships' request, he acknowledged the 'considerableness' of their island, and granted them 'liberty to right themselves,' adding that 'whatever they should take in the West Indies by way of reprisal should be adjudged lawful.'

Throughout February 1636, the shareholders held several meetings to discuss the implications of the king's warrant. In making the island a base for privateering, they ran the risk of jeopardising their entire venture, for a second Spanish attack would only be a matter of time. If the colony were to survive, they would have to spend more money on defence. A decision was taken to send 500 soldiers to reinforce the island's garrison. To finance their deployment, and pay off the company's debts, the wealthier shareholders agreed to stump up a further £10,000. Thanks to the king's warrant, they could reassure one another that they were keeping Providence for 'the honour and public good of the English nation.'[6]

For a pirate to become a privateer, he had to have a license from the Crown, but the Spanish made no distinction between England's pirates and its privateers – and nor did most Englishmen. As Sir Walter Raleigh once said, no one was called pirate when he robbed millions, only when he robbed trifles. Too many English merchants had made money from privateering for a campaign against piracy to win popular support. As the Venetian ambassador noted in a letter home penned in 1620, 'With regard to the mass of the populace, which has acquired such wealth by privateering, and among the common people in particular, [the privateers] are not in ill repute.'[7]

The English liked pirates, and so did its first colonial settlers. Supplies arrived from England so infrequently that no questions were asked when a pirate came through selling plunder. Nathaniel Butler, who was the governor of the Somers Isles between 1618 and 1621, was well aware that most 'pirates' were just free traders fighting for their right to supply protected markets.

> The people here… begin to talk that these strict courses against [the privateers'] admittance are only set on foot for fear lest the poor inhabitants here, by getting some refreshment and clothing from them, should not be tied to the cut-throat prices of the magazine ship.[8]

Naturally, the turn to privateering was not welcomed by Providence's godly faction. The 'Old Councillors', as they had become known, interpreted the change in policy as an admission on the part of the shareholders that they had failed to build a devout, prosperous and peace-loving community. The company assured them that in driving back the Spanish, God had sent them a clear sign of his favour, but their piety would now be rewarded in plunder. Spanish prizes would give the Old Councillors the breathing room they needed to build a just commonwealth, which would in turn inspire other Englishmen to cast themselves into the mouth of the Spanish Empire. Privateering would also act as a spur to the island's farmers, for the 500 soldiers due to join the garrison would need provisions. John Pym instructed the company's tenants to plant more crops, tend their cattle well, and keep their weapons close to hand.

Following the Spanish attack, Philip Bell asked to be 'disburdened' of his post as governor. After casting around for a suitable successor, the shareholders settled on Captain Robert Hunt, 'a religious and able person' well known in Puritan circles as a dependent of Lord Brooke.[9] Like Bell, he would receive no salary; instead, he and his family would be given free travel to and from the island, the services of 20 servants, a 100-acre farm and a new house, to be built at the company's expense. Hunt would sail from London on the *Blessing*, whose captain was William Rous, the deputy commander of the settlers, who had been promoted for his bravery in repelling the Spanish attack.

Sailing with the *Blessing* was the *Expectation* under Captain Cornelius Billinge. Among his passengers were 27 women, each of whom had a husband on Providence; some of the men had paid 300lbs of tobacco – the equivalent of three years' wages – to cover their fares. The ship's captains were under instructions to take their passengers to Providence, and then cruise the waters between the island and the Miskito coast in search of Spanish prizes, which would 'supply the defects of the island, which we conceive will not alone yield profit answerable to our disbursements.'[10]

Their departure from London was delayed by 'a heavy judgement of pestilence,' and only in March 1636 were the two ships able to put to sea. Sailing into the Atlantic, the *Expectation* suffered the horrors of a plague epidemic, and when Captain Billinge fell ill and died, command of the ship passed to his unscrupulous first mate, Giles Merch. By the time the *Expectation* passed into the Caribbean Sea, the passengers were desperate to put in at Providence, but Merch was hungry for prizes. When he came across a Dutch merchant vessel, he exchanged the supplies in the hold for its cargo of slaves, before pushing on towards the Spanish Main in search of a buyer and prizes.

If Robert Hunt hoped to find a like mind in the captain of the *Blessing*, he was to be disappointed. William Rous had long since lost sight of the *Expectation*, but by chance, he caught sight of Merch's ship just a few leagues from Providence, and the two captains decided to attack Santa Marta. They were only persuaded to put in at Providence after Hunt protested in the strongest terms, and no sooner had their passengers disembarked than they were heading southeast. When Merch failed to make their agreed rendezvous off the Main, Rous decided to storm the city alone. It was a reckless act of bravado, for he did not have the firepower needed to outgun the cannons protecting the harbour. The captain of the *Blessing* and his crew were captured and dispatched to jail in Seville. Rous would likely have spent the rest of his life as a galley slave in the Mediterranean, had company treasurer John Pym not sent him the money he needed to bribe his gaolers and make his escape in 1639.

Until the declaration of peace with Spain in 1630, Daniel Elfrith, Sussex Camock and Samuel Axe had been voracious privateers, so they received the news that King Charles had granted the shareholders 'liberty to right themselves' with relief and excitement. They knew that the richest prizes were to be found on *la carrera de Indias*, the sea lane that ran between the principal cities of Spain's American colonies. The annual voyage of the treasure fleet began with the departure of King Philip's galleons from Cádiz. They crossed the Atlantic Ocean and made their way to the Mexican port of Veracruz, where they took on board the silver and gold that had been hewn from the royal mines of Mexico over the previous twelve months. They also took on the contents of the Manila galleons: the spices, silk, and gold that Spanish merchants had accumulated in the Philippines in the course of a year of trading American silver with their Chinese counterparts.

The galleons were just one part of the operation. A second fleet of ships left Cádiz at the same time, this one bound for the north coast of Nueva Granada (modern day Colombia). *La flota* carried men and supplies for Cartagena, and then sailed three days west to Portobello to take delivery of the gold and silver hewn from the king's mines in Peru and Bolivia (the bullion was brought down the Andes to the sea in panniers attached to trains of packhorses, before being shipped up the Pacific coast to Panama, where they were transferred to a mule train that carried them over the mountains to Portobello).

For eleven months of the year, Portobello was a mosquito-infested hothouse where up to four inches of rain could fall in a single day. But the town sprang to life when the mule trains arrived from Panama. So prodigious was the output of the South American mines that it was said that when the slaves unloaded the panniers at Portobello's dock, they left the ingots 'lying around like stones.'[11] The town's annual fair opened at the first sight of *la flota* coming from Cartagena. The fort's cannons fired a salute, which the king's fleet returned as it came into the harbour. While the slaves loaded the ingots into the holds of the ships, the merchants of Panama crowded into the town square to buy the goods they needed to supply the Pacific coast for the next 12 months. When the fair closed, *la flota* sailed to Havana to rendezvous with the galleons, before embarking on the long journey back to Cádiz, and Portobello returned to its slumber.

For the time being, Providence's privateers were too weak to trouble the galleons or *la flota*, but they were still capable of devastating the merchant trade between the ports of Mexico, Honduras and Nueva Granada. In August 1636, Captain Thomas Newman of the *Happy Return* left London having sunk £400 of his own money (and £1,200 of the company's) into the purchase, fitting and victualling of the *Providence*. The company instructed him to take both vessels to the Caribbean, where he was 'to disable Spaniards by every means in his power.'

In the majority of cases, privateers sailed from Providence in ships belonging to either the company, or one of the Earl of Warwick's friends in the City of London. But as word spread of the opportunities awaiting ambitious ship owners, more ships sailed from London to Providence in the hope of sharing in the spoils of privateering. Anxious to see some return on their investments, the company let it be known that they would issue letters of marque to all comers, in return for a fifth of any plunder taken. Among those to receive commissions was William Rudyerd, the overweening gentleman who had whipped his scurvy-suffering servant to death three years before. He returned to Providence in the *Mary Hope* in late 1636, and spent the next four years supplying New Westminster with slaves plundered from Spanish ships.

The privateers' depredations severely hampered seaborne trade along the Spanish Main. The English friar Thomas Gage, who travelled by ship from the Panamanian town of Suere to Portobello in 1637, recounted how:

> the greatest fear that possessed the Spaniards in this voyage was about the island of Providence, whence they feared lest some English ships should come against them with great strength. They cursed the English in it, and called the island 'a den of thieves and pirates,' wishing the King of Spain would take some course with it.[12]

The *Consejo de Indias* called Providence 'the most infamous pirates' lair in the West Indies,' and encouraged the colonial governors to launch another assault on the island.[13] But Madrid committed none of the resources needed, for the budget for colonial defences in the Americas was already accounted for. Spain and Portugal were preparing a joint mission to recapture Brazil from the Dutch, and this left the king with nothing to pay for shipbuilding. The *consejo* instructed the governors to make do with what they had – but being entirely unaccustomed to acting of their own accord, they chose to sit on their hands, and the privateers of Providence were left to roam the western Caribbean largely unopposed.

If the islanders had only known more about the parlous condition of the Spanish king's finances, they might have rested easier in their beds. Instead, they lived in constant fear of a repeat of the previous year's attack. Reverend Hope Sherrard echoed the islanders' preoccupation with security in a letter to Sir Thomas Barrington. His main concern, he told his sponsor, was not the idleness, blasphemy or drunkenness of his congregation, but the woeful lack of ammunition at their disposal – if the Spanish were to make a second attempt on the island, its defenders didn't have enough shot to last a day.

The turn to privateering did nothing for most of the settlers. They saw nothing of the spoils, and everything of the danger that went with sea robbery. Expecting Spanish retaliation, the company ordered that the settlers be 'very regimentily exercised... till they be brought to a perfect knowledge of the use of arms.'[14] Even the governor had his misgivings: Robert Hunt was an experienced soldier, but he was also a deeply religious man, and did not appreciate the military culture in which the island was now steeped. He soon found his natural allies on the island council to be Hope Sherrard, Henry Halhead, Samuel Rishworth and Richard Lane.

The shareholders had not forgotten Lewis Morgan's accusation that they were 'putting on a hypocritical show of godliness for the encompassing of ungodly ends,' and were anxious to reassure the Old Councillors of their ongoing support. They made it clear that they 'utterly disliked' Philip Bell's punishment of Hope Sherrard 'for matters ecclesiastical.' The island's minister was undoubtedly of a contentious nature, but imprisoning him was 'unwarrantable by divine or human law.' Hoping to nip further rancour in the bud, the company's secretary William Jessop advised Sherrard to consult Robert Hunt, who was 'a discreet and godly man,' the next time he felt tempted to excommunicate a member of his congregation.[15]

With Robert Hunt in charge, the 'libertines' on the island council had all the more reason to go roving for Spanish prizes. This left the Old Councillors holding sway in meetings, but they did more to stoke than to calm the islanders' fears, and were no more able to address the problems they faced than the military faction. A coarse grass had invaded their fields – according to Captain Axe, it grew a finger's length every night. Their crops withered in the oppressive heat, and their cattle only gave milk in the rainy season. The only creatures thriving on the island were the rats. Towards the end of 1636, the settlers sent the company another petition, in which they threatened to abandon the island for the Miskito coast unless their grievances were addressed.

Robert Hunt also had to deal with the lingering disputes the military faction had left in its wake. Following Philip Bell's resignation, the company invited him to remain on the island council, and instructed Hunt to show him 'all the respect to his own person that may be convenient,' in the hope that the former governor would not be 'transported with any jealousy.'[16] Hunt did his best to keep relations with his predecessor cordial, but soon realised that Bell had fallen out with his father-in-law, Daniel Elfrith, and several other veterans from the Somers Isles during his time as governor. Despite the company's instructions to mediate between them, Hunt did nothing to protect Bell when the veterans decided to seize his property, servants and slaves. This was the last straw for the former governor: he sold his remaining possessions and sailed for England on the next ship.[i]

No longer able to count on his son-in-law's protection, Daniel Elfrith was exposed to the incriminating zeal of the Old Councillors, who insisted that such 'a carnal and ungodly man' could play no part in the running of a Puritan colony. Captain Samuel Axe also weighed into the fray, complaining that several of the island's forts would have to be rebuilt because of Elfrith's 'mistakes and ignorance.' Like Bell, Elfrith was forced to stand down from the island council; after a period in the wilderness, he was made commander of the fort at Black Rock.[17]

---

[i] Only with the arrival of a letter from the company in March 1637 were all judgements against Bell declared to be null and void, and his property restored to him. The principal actors in Bell's downfall – Lt William Rous and Samuel Rishworth – were ordered home, although the company had no intention of punishing either of them.

Philip Bell returned to England in June 1637, and travelled to Brooke House to present his final report to the company. He offered the shareholders a gloomy assessment of Providence's potential for commercial farming. The good news was that whatever the island lacked in the way of commodities could be found on the Miskito coast, whose soils were 'capable of the richest drugs and merchandise which come from America.'[18] Once the fortifications were complete, Providence would be practically impregnable to attack; perhaps the island was destined to serve as a fortress, garden and storehouse for a new colony in Central America?

Building a new colony would be expensive. The shareholders had already spent the equivalent of £30 for every man sent to Providence, and it was costing them £8,000 per year just to keep the colony going. Yet company treasurer John Pym was confident of attracting a further £100,000 to finance the venture, most of it from the king. Pym's confidence in the king's support would prove misplaced: Charles was already considering a rapprochement with Spain, and his relations with members of the long-dormant Parliament were worse than ever. In November 1637, John Hampden, a prominent MP and Providence Island Company shareholder, was prosecuted for refusing to pay ship money. As well as being one of the king's most forceful critics, Hampden was one of the richest landowners in Buckinghamshire, and his trial became a showdown between the king and the gentryfolk who ran local government in the shires. Hampden was defended in court by another company shareholder, Oliver St John. They lost the case, but their defiance of the royal writ earned them the admiration of many MPs, and Charles received just a fifth of the ship money he had hoped to raise.

Prior to the trial, the Earl of Warwick had appeared before the king to explain his opposition to taxation without representation. His Essex tenants 'were all old, and accustomed to the mild rule of Queen Elizabeth and King James,' he told him. They were unwilling to die 'under the stigma of having, at the end of their lives, signed away the liberties of the realm,' and Warwick would not have them do otherwise. If Charles would only recall Parliament, and make a forceful and effective intervention in the Wars of Religion raging on the Continent, he was confident that the House would grant him whatever he asked. He was himself ready 'to sacrifice his blood as well as his goods for his Majesty.'[19]

Charles listened to the earl's speech with a frosty smile, thanked him for his expression of loyalty, and promptly ignored his advice. Not only had Puritan opposition to his money-making ventures brought his government to the verge of bankruptcy, he had heard rumours that the Providence Island Company had become the pole around which all manner of dissidents were clustering. Company meetings had always been held at Brooke House in London, but its shareholders had taken to gathering at Lord Saye's home at Broughton Castle. The company had always kept thorough minutes of their meetings; suddenly, they became scant. It was whispered in Whitehall that company meetings were being used as cover for the first organised political party in opposition to an English government.

Their Lordships could see that they wouldn't be able to count on Charles' support for much longer. They couldn't even count on the support of their fellow shareholders, most of whom were tired of throwing good money after bad. The Earl of Warwick, Lord Saye and Lord Brooke vowed to go on, partly because they had the deepest pockets, but mainly because of the opportunity they had been given to harass Spain.

In March 1638, their Lordships declared that they would go to Providence and 'settle the affairs of the company' in person. They were growing anxious at the state of England, and privateering looked to be an ideal sphere of action for men of their rank. Only the presence of great men could rescue the islanders from their petty infighting and purposeless drifting. But when they sought Charles' permission to emigrate to Providence, he did not respond to their petition, preferring to keep such 'notorious malcontents' in plain sight.[20] Their Lordships never did get to see Providence for themselves.

Between them, the shareholders managed to raise a further £6,000. This made the building of a new colony unfeasible, and left them with no choice but to consolidate the progress they had made to date, and await the return of more favourable conditions at court. The Earl of Warwick upped his stake in the Caribbean by buying the Earl of Pembroke's holdings in Trinidad, Tobago, St Bernard, and Barbados. He also received a commission from the king, who was keen to see him kept occupied far from home, that empowered him to seize ships and even towns where Englishmen were denied free navigation. This gave the earl practically unlimited power: not only could he set forth as many armed vessels as he liked from any of the king's ports and harbours in the

Americas, he could also storm, occupy or destroy any town or territory belonging to any nation that denied an Englishman his right to trade. In October, he sent the *Warwick* and the *Robert* to Providence, and was soon making serious money from the proceeds of privateering.

Nothing had been heard of Thomas Newman, one of the company's favourite rovers, since his departure from London two years before. But, in August 1638, the *Happy Return* lived up to its name, docking with a cargo of tobacco, tallow and hides worth £4,000. Captain Newman was not aboard, for he had chosen to stay on the Miskito coast with the *Providence*, which he eventually took to Massachusetts with a cargo of sarsaparilla that he sold for £900. Unfortunately his return to England was not a happy one: as the *Providence* approached Dungeness on Christmas Day 1638, it was attacked by pirates from Dunkirk. Most of the crew were killed and Newman was forced to surrender his ship and its valuable cargo. The Frenchmen made off with ambergris, indigo, sarsaparilla and pearls worth £30,000 – ten times the annual income of a member of the House of Lords.[21] Privateering might be a suitable sphere of action for a gentleman, but their Lordships were learning the hard way that there is no honour among thieves.

9

'RAW POTATOES AND TURTLE MEAT'

With the turn to privateering, the company's priority had to be the further fortification of Providence, and a stiffening of the islanders' military preparedness. Robert Hunt had already antagonised the military men on the island council, most of whom were by now roving for prizes at sea. In their absence, he had neglected the forts, several of which were practically in ruins, and had even left the barrels of gunpowder out in the rain. This was 'a great inconsiderateness, and such as might have brought the whole colony into a strange confusion and hazard, if God's wise and gracious providence had not watched over you,' the shareholders told him.[1] The company was by now making most of its money from the capture of Spanish prizes and the trade in slaves. This made it all the more important that the forts were well maintained, and the islanders willing and able to handle firearms. Hunt clearly wasn't cognizant of the more aggressive role the shareholders envisaged for Providence – he would have to go.

In casting around for his replacement, they sought above all 'a man of ability in regard to the danger from the Spaniard.' Early in 1638, they had received reports of 'great preparations in Spain for the West Indies,' and spent the rest of the year in nervous anticipation of a second attempt to destroy their colony. The Earl of Warwick knew just the man for the job: Nathaniel Butler had been governor of the Somers Isles between 1619 and 1622, but was also an experienced captain who had commanded ships in King Charles' ill-fated attempt to lift the siege of French Huguenots at La Rochelle. If Robert Hunt had joined the Old Councillors in looking skyward for signs of divine guidance, Nathaniel Butler was the counter to their righteous wailing. Whatever God's intentions for the island, only a man of action could fulfil them.

Butler was 61 when he arrived on Providence. He was carrying instructions to make the island's fortifications and the military training of its settlers his 'principal care,' and consolidate Providence's role as an eyrie from which to swoop down onto Spanish ships. As the value of prizes seized increased, the island would become the base of operations for the company's new colony in Central America. Daniel Elfrith was ordered home, and Robert Hunt took his place as commander of the fort at Black Rock.

Butler was a sophisticated, urbane man who spoke French and Italian fluently. While his house at New Westminster was considerably less lavish than the little Venetian palace he had occupied on the Somers Isles, he did his best to maintain the style of a Renaissance prince. He always dined in company, and often entertained as many as 100 guests, including the captains of the three or four privateering vessels that came into the harbour every month. He had long been associated with the Earl of Warwick's privateering ventures, and took great pleasure in overseeing the supply of weaponry to outbound ships, and inspecting the prizes they brought back to the island.

Before taking up his new post, Butler had made it clear to the company that endless instructions from London could be no substitute for hard-won experience. He spent his mornings adjudicating in the settlers' disputes over land, slaves and the distribution of supplies from the company store. These were never-ending, and distracted him from more pressing concerns, but he seems to have been a fair judge. After a generous luncheon, he liked to spend his afternoons circumnavigating the island in a small boat, as Captain Axe pointed out the progress of the fortifications being built in the south of the island.

Meetings of the island council were as fractious as ever. The company had advised him not to take sides in the long-running dispute between the godly faction and the island's privateers. He was familiar with such quarrels from the time he had spent on the Somers Isles, and recognised the same belligerent intransigence in the Old Councillors, who stood with the bulk of the settlers in their opposition to privateering and the military preparedness that accompanied it. The islanders had also come to depend on the godly faction to speak up against the mistreatment of servants, and to argue for the recreation of the productive, self-sustaining farming communities they remembered from home.

In response to the deadlock reached whenever the Old Councillors locked horns with the military faction, John Pym had made plans for a general overhaul of the island's government. Among those to arrive on Providence with the new governor were new clerks and council members, and an additional 131 servants to assist in the strengthening of the island's fortifications. The shareholders also created a council of war, to be headed by Butler, in order to circumvent the island council.

Butler allowed the Old Councillors to keep their seats on the island council, but they were now radical protestors, rather than participants in the government of the island. The new governor did his best to assuage the godly faction's concerns: he appreciated that they resented taking orders from army officers, and that life spent on a war footing only heightened their anxiety over the future of the island. But their children would only grow up to become freemen if they were willing and able to defend the island from attack.

Yet the Old Councillors still held court in the island's two little churches, and whatever was discussed in council during the week was sure to figure in Hope Sherrard's Sunday sermon. As well as being a devoted churchgoer, Nathaniel Butler was also a keen diarist, and his journal bears testament to the 'angry,' 'vile,' and 'wild' note that Sherrard was wont to strike in his sermons.[2] As he confessed in a letter to Lord Saye, 'I never lived among men of more spleen, nor of less wit to conceal it.'[3]

Butler had no time for the culture of discipline that the Old Councillors wanted to inculcate in the islanders. Before leaving London, the company had instructed him to investigate allegations that some of the 'families' were spending their evenings in 'riotous feasting.' Butler ignored the order; he was by nature pleasure loving, had no interest in what the islanders did in their free time, and happily sided with the epicureans.

Nor did he share their rabid anti-Catholicism. Shortly after his arrival, he ordered a prison built, for he was already making plans to hold captured Spaniards to ransom. Yet he had no qualms about spending Easter Day 1639 with the two Spanish friars being held in the prison, and even invited them to join him for dinner at his residence, where they prepared a feast to celebrate *la buena Pascua*. Whatever discomfort he might have felt was clearly outweighed by the pleasure he took in antagonising Hope Sherrard, whose next sermon was sure to feature a bitter denunciation of his impious entertainment of the two agents of Rome.

After seven years of the company's experiment in godly living, the colony faced multiple threats. Aside from the failure to find a viable commercial crop, the recurring conflicts that kept the island council feeble and convulsive, and the inevitability of a second Spanish attack, the company's relations with King Charles were getting worse by the day.

Amid so many threats from so many powerful forces, it was easy to overlook those who appeared most powerless: the Africans. In the feverish atmosphere that pervaded the island in the days leading up to the Spanish attack, Philip Bell had promised them that if they helped him to win the coming battle, he would make them free men. They had willingly agreed, but their excitement turned to disappointment after Captain de Castellar returned to Cartagena. Philip Bell not only reneged on his promise, he tightened the yolk around their necks, in the hope that his cruelty would put an end to their talk of freedom.

Many of the slaves were runaways, who had escaped their Spanish masters before being captured by the Indians and sold to the English on Providence. The governor's broken promise caused lasting bitterness, and made them more combustible than ever. Few islanders felt moved to defend them apart from Samuel Rishworth, who had remained true to his convictions and helped several of them escape to the high hills around Palmetto Grove, in the middle of the island. There they created their own community, much like the *palenques* built by runaway slaves from Cartagena to Jamaica. Others followed the example set by Francisco Biafara, and slipped away from the island on stolen boats under cover of the night. Although most of the island's servants were keen to preserve the small but crucial distinction that separated them from the slaves, they too had good reason to flee their masters, and runaways were often mixed groups of Africans and English. Mindful of the surliness of its unpaid workforce, the company issued strict instructions to keep the Africans in small groups, so they would have no chance to plot rebellion en masse.

What turned flight into fight was the example set by the Africans on Association Island. The Spanish had either hanged or imprisoned most of its inhabitants in 1635, but they did not leave a garrison on Association, and it was soon re-occupied by buccaneers, renegades and skin-of-their-teeth planters. Later that year, the company sent a Dartmouth merchant, Nicholas Riskinner, to the island to become its new governor. The following year, they received a report describing conditions on the island. Governor Riskinner had died shortly after arriving, leaving 80 English and 150 Africans to eke out a living by themselves. Although 'the number of negroes in the island was much short of what they first received information,' the settlers were having great difficulty controlling them. 'They are not in subjection, and it may cost some lives, much time and difficulty to bring them in,' one of them warned. No details of the revolt of 1637 have survived; all we know is that within a year of receiving the report, the company had abandoned Association because of 'the great number of negroes' on the island.[4]

The slave revolt on Association was the first to take place in any English colony, and it unnerved shareholders, officers and tenants alike. When news of the revolt reached London, the company issued fresh instructions to Nathaniel Butler: the import of unskilled Africans was to be prohibited, and any slaves captured from Spanish ships sold. In the weeks that followed, William Pierce was one of several shipmasters to load slaves into the hull of his ship, along with the island's tobacco and cotton crops, in the hope of finding a buyer on the docks of Virginia or New England. With luck, he would be able to exchange them for American goods like whisky, molasses and cloth, which were sure to fetch good prices back on Providence.[i]

The ban on the import of more slaves did not go down well with the island's farmers or its fort builders. The Africans had supplied them with the manpower they lacked, and they had acquired a taste for the relative ease and plenty that came with unpaid labour. With so many officers, farmers and servants out privateering, and those that stayed behind reluctant to give their time and energy to Captain Axe's fort-building programme, they were soon short of hands again. With great reluctance, the company agreed to admit more slaves, but insisted on 'a strict watch being kept to prevent plots or any danger to the island.'[5]

---

[i] William Pierce and John Rolfe, the man who married Pocahontas, were among those that met Daniel Elfrith when the *Treasurer* docked in Virginia in 1619. His ship was carrying the first Africans to land in North America. Ironically, the Virginia House of Burgesses, the first representative assembly in the New World, was established the same year. Hillary Rodham Clinton is Pierce's tenth great-granddaughter. See www.findagrave.com/cgi-bin/fg.cgi?page=gr&GRid=103843198.

Yet no amount of planning could calm the fear of a repeat of what had happened on Association. The settlers came to regard the Africans as the enemy within, and complained that such men would readily abet the Spanish when they next attacked the island. By March 1637, the company was again complaining that the island councillors were admitting too many Africans, despite 'knowing how dangerous they may be if you should be assaulted with an enemy, or in case they would grow mutinous.'[6] But the settlers' fear of the Spanish proved stronger than their fear of their slaves. The solution they settled on was to import more Africans, and then work them so hard that they wouldn't have the energy to rise up in revolt.

It was this fear of the slaves that finally pushed the shareholders to make some concession to the English migrant's desire for land of his own, and a voice in how the colony was governed, in the hope that the arrival of more white hands would mitigate the need for black ones. They announced that any family prepared to journey to Providence with six or more servants would immediately be granted the right to buy the land they farmed, and given a say in deciding who sat on the island council.

But these concessions remained vague and unfulfilled, and did nothing to address the lifelong servitude the islanders had imposed on the Africans. On 1 May 1638, they rose up in open revolt. Since Francisco Biafara's testimony is the only record of an African voice on Providence, there is no way of knowing what precipitated the uprising, but they had probably heard about the revolt on Association, and knew that their masters would be distracted by their May Day celebrations.

Nathaniel Butler's diary provides no details of the revolt itself, but the entries he made in the following days show that he was determined to reassert control, and set an example to any African tempted to challenge his bondage in future. The island's governor sent mounted search parties to comb the hills, and a number of runaways were recaptured and brought back to New Westminster. They were executed on the parade ground in front of his house, and another 50 Africans were put to death for conspiracy. Yet a number of slaves found refuge with the runaway community in Palmetto Grove, where they managed to eke out a living as maroons. By day, they raised small plots of corn and potatoes, and tended a few goats. By night, they crept down to the fields where they had once laboured to steal plantains, beans and cassava.

Samuel Rishworth was not on Providence when the slave revolt broke out, having made the ten-week journey to London in order to put the settlers' second petition of complaint before the shareholders. The Old Councillors felt that they had been deliberately sidelined by the new council of war, he told them. The foundations of their godly settlement were being cynically undermined by the traffic in slaves and the privateers who brought them to the island. Unless the shareholders responded with meaningful reforms, he and his fellow Old Councillors would leave Providence for New England.

Rishworth's appeal elicited much handwringing from William Jessop, but by the time he returned to the island in late summer, it was clear that the company had neither the mind nor the means to effect the changes he wanted to see. Samuel, along with his 'great family and many children,' emigrated to Barbados, where slavery had yet to take root.[7] He died there the following spring. His wife and most of his children left no trace on Barbados either, for they soon succumbed to the diseases that ravaged the colony in its early years. However, Samuel Jr survived, and eventually made it back to Coventry, where he died in 1666.

Following the slave revolt of 1638, Providence became the first English colony in which Africans made up the majority of the population and the English became the privileged minority in a racial hierarchy of their own making. Slavery made sound financial sense, but the risk the English ran in giving the Africans a numerical advantage owed just as much to the pact they had made with God. Perhaps they flattered themselves that a Christian minority would only be able to rule over a heathen majority by dint of the special relationship they enjoyed with their maker. Or perhaps the shareholders were simply clutching at straws: their endless prevarication certainly suggests decisions made on the hoof. In 1638, the company gave the go-ahead for the purchase of 100 more slaves to replace the white hands that had been repairing the forts. Yet a few months later, they wrote of their intention to send another 200 English servants to Providence, 'in exchange for negroes.' This proposal, like so many the company made before and after, came to nothing; instead, Nathaniel Butler was authorised to bring another 100 slaves to the island.

The Africans were divided on how best to respond to their bondage. The boldest of them realised that the only lasting solution was to defeat their masters in battle. But their numerical superiority counted for nothing as long as the English held the arquebuses, cutlasses and pikes in the arsenal at Fort Warwick. While some opted for regular meals and shelter over the hunger and endless watchfulness of a runaway, most were determined to join the maroon community in Palmetto Grove at the earliest opportunity. Despite being no more than three miles from New Westminster, the governor's raids had only managed to burn a single cabin, for as Butler noted in his diary, the maroons 'were so nimble as we could scarce get a sight of them.'

With Palmetto Grove and ultimately the Miskito Coast as their beacons, growing numbers of slaves and servants opted to make the break. Butler's diary tells of the sport to be had in hunting runaway slaves, and how his 'tame negroes' could be trusted to bring the rebels back. One Sunday morning, he noted that 'two of our wild negroes being discovered upon a hill near unto my house, my negroes made out after them, and caught one of them, and brought him away with them.'[8] On another occasion, he granted twelve acres in Palmetto Grove to four settlers 'because it was the sanctuary of our rebel negros; yet so by clearing of it I might force them from their freehold.' Yet the organized repression needed to avoid a repeat of the previous year's slave revolt was never made. Perhaps Butler saw the runaways as the Earl of Warwick saw the poachers in his Essex game reserves: as benighted souls whose disobedience was only to be expected.

With militarisation and repression increasing, the mood among the settlers became still more anxious. Weren't the signs of God's displeasure to be seen all around them – in the rats scurrying from kitchen to storehouse, the fields abandoned to the weeds by planters greedy for Spanish gold, and the sullen glances of the heathens plotting to cut their throats? What use were more fortifications if God had withdrawn His blessing? Then, on 15 February 1639, they were blessed with a clear sign of His favour. The captain of a Dutch merchant ship had been passing Roncador, the hook-shaped atoll 90 miles east of Providence, when he spotted a young man lying on the sand. He was close to death, but the crew nursed him back to health, and took him to Providence. The islanders were amazed to see him again, for they had seen neither hide nor hair of him since the night two and half years before, when he and four of his friends had stolen a shallop and sailed for the Miskito coast.

The young man explained that they had been hoping to seize the small Spanish frigate that was known to patrol the coast near Cape Gracias a Dios. But their vessel was enveloped by a storm on the way to the coast and wrecked on Roncador. Only when the tempest abated did the castaways come face to face with their dire predicament. There is no source of fresh water on Roncador, and no shelter from the midday sun. The only way they could stay alive was by drinking the blood of turtles, which they supplemented with the little rainwater they were able to collect in a tattered strip of sailcloth. Aside from raw turtle meat, they ate the eggs of seabirds. After eighteen months of this baneful existence, only one of them was still alive. He spent the next ten months alone, before he was spotted by the Dutch vessel and brought home.

Hope Sherrard proclaimed a day of thanksgiving for the recovery of the shipwrecked mariner. In the sermon he preached that evening, he had him 'offer up public thanksgiving for his deliverance, make confession of his vicious life and register a vow of future atonement.'[9] For the islanders, the return to life of a man given up for dead was a miracle akin to that performed by Jesus to bring Lazarus back to life. Their isolation put them at the mercy of the elements and the Spanish, but God had not forsaken them. Amid the darkness that lay all around, He had lit a beacon to guide them.

Obedience to a wrathful God didn't come easily. In 1650, Ralph Josselin, the Puritan minister of the Essex village of Earls Colne, watched two of his children and his best friend die in the space of a week. In his diary, Josselin wondered why God had seen fit to punish him so; all he could think was that He was angry with him for his 'unseasonable playing at chess.' The Puritans' belief in divine providence might strike the modern reader as the egotism of men with narrow horizons, whose minds had been sealed by the perpetual swirling of a reasoning process devoid of common sense. When things went well, Puritans praised God; when they went badly, they muttered about the impenetrable mystery of His omnipotence. Divine Providence could be used to justify anything, yet it explained nothing. It looks little different from superstition, the irrational belief in the power of inanimate objects that the Puritans were so set on transcending.

But for men like Ralph Josselin, mere mortals were in no position to understand God's intentions – and yet they were obliged to try. For those determined to find consolation in the midst of uncertainty, even a calamity could be taken as a sign of God's mercy. On hearing that a parishioner's newborn daughter had died a few days after falling ill, Josselin wrote that God had done 'wonderful good' by drawing out the infant's agony, for it had prepared her parents for her death.[10]

Listening to Hope Sherrard's interpretation of what God might have meant by saving the young man's life on Roncador, Nathaniel Butler was struck by the minister's selective memory.

> It now brought to every man's mind and observation that, whereas the apparent evidence of God's mercy in as high or a higher nature had been manifested toward Captain Axe and his company in their escape from the enemy; [and] to those five persons that came safe unto us in an extreme leaking boat from St Christopher's [St Kitts]; and towards the forty-nine persons that arrived safely with us from the Barbadoes, and all this done within the space of four months… none of this had been remembered by Mr Sherrard in the same kind, as if the safe being of this one man had either been of more remarkableness in itself, or be of more acceptableness with him than all the rest put together.

By the spring of 1639, the captain of every passing merchant ship was clamouring for letters of marque from Providence's governor. After seven months spent adjudicating in the petty squabbles of grasping planters and pettifogging preachers, Nathaniel Butler was keen to do some privateering of his own. He called a meeting of the island council to inform them of his decision. 'The most by far of the people seemed very well satisfied,' he noted in his diary, although 'some of the Old Councillors would needs be of another mind.'[11]

Ten days later, Butler left Providence for the Miskito coast, accompanied by 80 of the island's most experienced soldiers, among them Captain Parker in the *Spy*, Captain Morgan in the *Gift of God*, and Captain Mathias in the *Hopewell*. In the five years since Captain Camock built the trading post at Cape Gracias a Dios, the coast had become a well-known place of refuge, and Butler found 600 Englishmen living there, along with 200 Miskito Indians.[12] 'The Indians of the Cape came presently unto us and are a very loving people, but the poorest Indians that ever I saw,' he wrote. 'There went with us from the Mosquitoe [Cays] two Indians, and from the Cape five more that were so earnest to go that they would take no denial.'

From the Cape, the three ships sailed west into the Bay of Honduras. They captured the Spanish settlement at Trujillo, but found it 'most miserably poor and utterly empty of inhabitants, having all of them run away one way and conveyed their goods out another way.' Stymied, they made for the little island of Ruatan, 40 miles off the coast from Trujillo. The year before, the Providence Island Company had granted William Claiborne a patent to build a colony on Ruatan, but he was unable to extend much in the way of hospitality to his visitors. Stymied again, they tramped into the bush in search of victuals. 'Some of our men... met with some cassadoe [cassava] roots, which they greedily eating half-raw half-roasted without squeezing out the juice, it made them all very sick, and killed one outright,' Butler recorded.

Captains Parker, Morgan and Mathias decided to make for the Isle of Pines, just south of Cuba, where they hoped to find victuals and fresh water. A week later, they dropped anchor off a small, deserted island. Butler wrote:

> About this island there was a difference of opinion amongst some of our best mariners (such mariners were our best) whether it were the Isle of Pines or some of the small islands called the Keis. We sent off our boat, partly to take a fuller view and partly to look for water here, which returned unto us an hour within night without resolution any way.

Officers and crew were by now close to starvation. Two days later, they met a Dutch ship whose officers gave the three captains a basic lesson in navigation, 'being by them led as the blind man by his dog,' according to Butler. But they were still all at sea three weeks later.

> For all that, our blind guides went on in their mad course, steering away lustily to the leeward for one whole watch. Not being able to cloak any longer their arrogant ignorance, they brought the ship to a tack and lay north-north-east, as if they intended to find where they were at Cuba, since they could not at sea.

By the following Sunday, the three ships had been at sea for nigh on two months. With nothing to eat, and still no sight of a Spanish ship, much less dry land, they were close to despair. 'The alhistical [hysterical] master was in such a diabolical fury, it being the Lord's day, that he… burst out publicly into these words, that surely there were some witches in the ship, and that for his part he cared not though she sunk down right in the sea,' Butler wrote. 'And thus once again am I fallen among the dumb beasts.'

On 9 August, he made the mistake of asking the *Spy*'s officers where they were going.

> But their opinion was not thought fit to be divulged, lest the discovery of so palpable an ignorance in our guides of the round-house might throw them into desperate if not devilish courses, they being well known to be men prostituted to all vileness and rather bent to do anything than to acknowledge their errors.

On 5 September, the three captains told the governor that the Isle of Pines seemed to have disappeared. 'And so once again for Providence,' wrote Butler, 'being a voyage of about six score leagues, and having a small mark to hit and especially by our marksmen, with not full fourteen days victuals of any kind at all save water.' They made it back to Providence on 12 September, 'and thus by the gracious conduct of our most blessed, most merciful and most omnipotent Lord God we finished our tedious and dangerous voyage with rest and comfort.'

Many of the settlers rejoiced when the governor returned from his cruise empty-handed. 'When they heard that we had taken the town of Trujillo and found it empty, some of them showed as much joy as they had been Spaniards,' Butler wrote in his diary.[13] There was more bad news for him when the *Swallow* came into the harbour the following morning. 'By her we had certain intelligence that the Earl of Warwick's pinnace the *Robert*, where Captain Barzie commanded, was taken by the Spanish near the Bay of Tolu and the captain and most of the chief men carried prisoner into Spain by the galleons.' Not only had some of Providence's most successful privateers been captured, the governor of Cartagena was 'very importunate [demanding] with the general of the galleons to make an attempt upon Providence.'

The islanders' news was no less discouraging, for conditions had worsened considerably in Butler's absence. There had been a time when the island was practically self-sufficient in food, but since being given license to raid Spanish shipping, several of the company's tenants had abandoned their fields to the weeds. The supplies of dry food in the islanders' sheds, which had been meagre since the Spanish attack of 1635, were practically exhausted. The same was confirmed by a Spanish prisoner, who described the island as 'a den of pirates living like savages on raw potatoes and turtle meat.'[14] A week after his return, Butler handed William Blauveldt a privateering commission and sent him to sea 'to look abroad for victuals.'

For the next six months, the governor was back in the familiar business of listening to the complaints of the island's most querulous farmers. It was a thankless task, and he committed his growing exasperation to his diary. 'I stayed at home, but had continual business and spent almost the whole day in hearing, examining, preparing and deciding of diverse differences and of sundry natures between party and parties,' reads a typical entry.

At times, he was almost sympathetic to their complaints. When the 'masters of the families' presented him with a petition outlining their grievances, he found 'no cause to mislike their demands.' But on other occasions, their complaints riled him: on 20 November, he was 'all this day much troubled with multiplicity of businesses, and found good cause to wish for the day of my deliverance!'

Picking apart the tangled threads of their grievances, the same names recur time and again: Hope Sherrard, Henry Halhead and Richard Lane. 'There is nothing among the Old Councillors more common than to make themselves parties and judges,' Butler complained to the shareholders. 'There is not an act that has passed in your council of war since it was erected but one way or other some or all of them have secretly attempted to bring it to contempt.'[15] In another letter, he even accused the Old Councillors of plotting to overthrow him while he was away privateering.

As time wore on, Hope Sherrard became the bane of Butler's life. 'I went not to church upon this Lord's Day neither in the morning nor afternoon,' he wrote in early October, 'and the reason was that Mr Sherrard had published that upon this day he would administer the Sacrament of the Supper, but admit only such as would enter into covenant with him.' Two weeks later, he found the island's minister 'strangely possessed with a strain of uncharitable and dangerous suggestions out of the pulpit,' and stopped going to church altogether. 'I found I might far better spend the afternoon at home and so did, and Captain Axe with me,' he wrote. Yet even when he was ensconced in the governor's residence, he was not safe from Sherrard's invective. Two months later, he 'went not at all to church upon this Lord's Day, [yet still] found cause to grieve in hearing what I should have heard if I had been there.'

There was some respite when William Blauveldt returned to the island with several tons of corn, 'which we got at one of our new discovered islands from the cannibal Indians there by force.' These were the Corn Islands, two tiny outcrops 60 miles off the Miskito coast, so-called 'from the abundance of maize or Indian wheat there usually planted by the barbarous natives.'[16] But even the good news was tainted by bad: Blauveldt's frigate was towing an empty Spanish vessel, whose crew 'brought us news of two galleys newly come out of Spain to Cartagena, for the keeping of those coasts.'

In his next letter, Butler informed the shareholders that not only were the settlers growing ever more restless, and the Spanish threatening to attack any day, but their slaves and servants were fleeing to the coast in growing numbers. By New Year 1640, the governor was becoming increasingly cutting.

> I went not to church upon this Lord's Day at all, finding Mr Sherrard's invective sermons to be rather mis-spending of the day than otherwise, and so became wearied with them. By the report of them that heard him, he fell very foul upon one of his own flock, giving out furious and very un-beseeming words in respect of the time and place – though perhaps not in respect of the person.

As the colony entered its tenth year, its governor was increasingly inclined to spend weekdays, as well as Sundays, at home. 'I kept at home all this day and with far less distractions by the country's occasions than ordinary,' he wrote. But the lull proved short; by mid-January, there was 'a return of business, occasioned rather by the general disturbers than the general people.' With the coming of another year, the settlers reiterated that unless the company addressed their grievances, they would join the ramshackle community that had sprung up at Cape Gracias a Dios.

Perusing their petition, Butler found it to contain an interesting proposition. 'They would me to take the pains for them (as despairing of all other help) to make a voyage into England and to solicit a redress.' The islanders' need for a spokesman to present their case at Brooke House gave him the perfect excuse to leave the troubled colony with his honour intact. He spent his last Sunday on Providence at home, 'having nothing but discouragements from Mr Sherrard's preaching.' That evening, 'many of the people dined with me, coming purposely to take their farewells.' The following day he sailed for London.

10

THE LAST DAYS OF
THEIR LORDSHIPS' ISLE

Butler left the government of Providence in the hands of Captain Andrew Carter, who had arrived with him three years before. The company had been sufficiently impressed by Carter's conduct as muster master general of Fort Warwick that it had appointed him to the island council and the council of war the following year. Carter's henchman was the fearsome Elisha Gladman, the keeper of the armaments at Fort Warwick, who was another of the army veterans to have arrived with Butler. Neither man had any sympathy for the Old Councillors, and with Butler out of the picture, Carter was free to rule the island as an autocrat. He spent his days touring the island's forts and driving its servants and slaves to ever greater exertions, and his nights drinking and carousing with visiting privateers in the comfort of the governor's house. The Old Councillors accused the interim governor, and self-styled 'general, admiral, councillor of war and councillor of the land,' of 'executing the office of government without oath, banishing some, imprisoning others without alleging any cause, and winking at horrible crying sins.'[1] Their Lordships' Isle had never seemed so far from God.

Yet its privateers were flourishing. Early in 1640, sailors from Providence captured a Spanish merchant ship off Portobello, which was found to be carrying 80,000 pesos (the equivalent of over £3.3 million today). In the spring, they seized a ship carrying dyewood worth 600,000 ducats (£14.4 million) off the Miskito coast. The English were 'annihilating' Spanish commerce in the Indies, said Don Melchor de Aguilera, the Captain General of Cartagena, who had tried and failed to take the island five years before. On several occasions, the city had been threatened with starvation, and rumours abounded that the English, supported by brigades of 'vile negroes' from the Miskito coast, were planning to invade.[2] Don Melchor renewed his plea to his superiors in Madrid, urging them to take action against the English pirates.

118

For five long years, those pleas had met with obfuscation, as the Spanish government and their Portuguese allies poured their efforts into the struggle to retake Brazil from the Dutch. But with Brazil restored to Portuguese control, the Spanish were finally free to tackle the pirates of Providence. This time, the colonial governors would be granted the men and ships they needed to snuff out the foreigners' colony once and for all. The generals of the king's fleet agreed to take on the challenge (although they turned down Don Melchor's request that his twelve-year-old son be appointed commander of the invasion fleet; the campaign would instead be led by Antonio Maldonado y Texeda, the sergeant major of Cartagena).[3] Two 800-ton galleons, three frigates, two tenders, one caravel and four launches were made ready for the attack. Between them they carried 600 Portuguese troops, 200 Spaniards, and 200 black creoles.

The Spanish attack of May 1640 is described in a letter to the company written by Hope Sherrard.[4] When the islanders first sighted the Spanish fleet approaching from the south, they seemed less than perturbed. 'Some of the inhabitants scoffingly made answer that surely they were [not ships] but so many boobies [i],' wrote Sherrard, and did nothing to be 'any whit more watchful, or to bestir themselves in preparation.'[5] The Spanish did the same, waiting a league off shore,

> partly, as we conjectured, hoping to get some intelligence of the state of our island by renegades, as they might well do, seeing many English and negroes had formerly so desperately adventured to flee from us to them in several boats and canoes.

By the following morning, the alarm had been raised and beacons lit at each of the island's thirteen forts. According to the Spanish account of the attack, Maldonado y Texeda was expecting to find Santa Catalina defended by 200 farm labourers, so the sight of an island 'naturally fortified, and more so by art,' bristling with ranks of armed men, and commanded by experienced officers came as an unwelcome surprise. But as Sherrard's letter makes clear, the English force looked more impressive than it was: most of the militia were at sea and most of the 'officers' were little more than 'ciphers and lookers on.' The men who hurried down

---

[i]   A booby is a seabird common in much of the Caribbean

from their shacks in the hills to Black Rock Fort were 'bareheaded and barefooted, with scarce enough clothes to cover their nakedness.' In their haste to take up their positions, they neglected to take either food or water into the fort, an oversight for which they would later suffer terribly. Although plenty of slaves and servants had fled at the first sight of the sails of the Spaniards' ships, the majority was determined to defend the forts they had laboriously built over the past decade. The 'weaker sex', who were numerous by this time, and included some who were 'big with child', rushed to Warwick Fort with their infants and toddlers, where they and Hope Sherrard 'did by the powerful engine of prayer lay siege to heaven.'[6]

The Spanish ships sailed north, past Southwest Bay and New Westminster, until they reached Fort Warwick. But their guns 'did little hurt at all, unless it were to our trees,' and when the fort returned fire, the invaders were forced to withdraw. An hour before sunset, the bulk of the 1000-strong Spanish force scrambled into launches and made an attempt to land at the mouth of the river that flowed through New Westminster. Robert Hunt was able to keep them at bay with volleys of cannon fire from Black Rock Fort, but due to an oversight on Andrew Carter's part, he only had five cannonballs at his disposal. When his guns fell quiet, the first of the Spanish contingent, among them 'the choicest and stoutest soldiers in the whole fleet,' made for the beach between the fort and the river's mouth.

The English force that Andrew Carter led to the beach consisted of just 17 officers and 100 of the settlers. As the Spanish launches drew closer, the words of a chant, repeated with 'a dreadful and formal tone,' rose above the sound of the breaking surf. '*Perro, diablo, cornudo* [dog, devil, coward], *sa sa sa...*' According to Hope Sherrard, Carter took fright and was seen 'ducking at every shot' from their muskets. He and his clique 'had taken upon them to be our chief commanders,' but in the heat of battle they 'showed no small weakness and pusillanimity, being so far from directing or encouraging others that they needed it most of all themselves.' When the invaders rushed ashore, crying '*Victoria! Victoria!*' they turned tail and made a dash for the safety of Black Rock Fort. In the midst of the ensuing battle, Carter was found hiding in the kitchen, frantically eating his soldiers' supplies. Believing all to be lost, he ordered Captain Hunt to spike the guns and have his men beat a retreat to Warwick Fort, 'so that they might all die together.'

Reinforcements arrived just as the governor was preparing to abandon the fort, and it was only their 'vehement outcries' that forced the garrison to stand its ground. The settlers rained down musket shot on the Spanish soldiers, who were making their way over the rocks at the foot of the small cliff on which the fort stood. When their supplies of gunpowder were exhausted, they were reduced to throwing stones at the enemy. Even in the heat of battle, they did not dare to arm their slaves, but 'our negroes, thinking themselves to be as sufficient as others, did good execution by this means.'[7] The combination of musket shot and stones killed several of the Spanish officers. Suddenly leaderless, the soldiers panicked and ran back to the beach.

> The enemies were now vanquished, yet through the darkness of the night our men knew not of it, being so busied in fight that they could not mind the enemies crying for quarter, so that for half an hour's space, they never ceased pouring in shot among them, till they had scarce an enemy left to shoot at.

Searching the hundreds of sodden corpses strewn across the beach, the islanders found dozens of tiny portraits of the saints, 'besides bread and cheese in the snapsacks, with pumpion [pumpkin] seeds and peas to plant.' The invaders had clearly planned to settle the island for themselves. At daybreak, search parties set out to track down the Spanish soldiers who had fled into the hills. The settlers' prisoners were still in shock when they arrived at Fort Warwick; Don Melchor had assured them that the English 'would fly away like so many sheep at the very sight of an enemy approaching.'

Despite Andrew Carter's promise of quarter to those who surrendered, he had all his prisoners put to death. Capitán Joan de Ibarra, the would-be governor who 'had vowed that he would either take the island or leave his carcass there,' suffered an especially cruel end: Carter cut his arm off so that he could watch him bleed to death. When the captain asked why he had singled him out for such barbarous treatment, Carter told him that he had seen him kill one of his slaves with a rock during the battle.

The 11th June was proclaimed a day of thanksgiving. The islanders, 'both English and heathen', gathered on what they now called 'Bloody Beach' to give thanks to God for their deliverance. Just two of them had

121

been killed in the attack, Sherrard wrote, and they were no great loss, since one had been a 'runaway' and the other a 'miscreant.' Sherrard also recorded, with gratitude and wonder, 'the loyalty in adversity of the negroes who had often rebelled in times of prosperity.' He made a great bonfire of the crosses and icons the Spanish had brought ashore, and explained to the Africans 'that the Gods whom our enemies trusted in and called upon could neither save their worshippers from slaughter, nor themselves from the fire.'

The Old Councillors had witnessed many signs of divine providence when the fighting was at its fiercest, and they emboldened them to confront their cowardly governor. Hope Sherrard led them to the governor's house, where they tried to oust Carter, 'pleading a right by charter to choose their own government,' and demanding that Richard Lane be appointed governor. Enraged, Carter 'privately armed some of the ruder sort,' who seized Lane, Sherrard and Halhead and threw them into the prison that Nathaniel Butler had built to house his Spanish captives. Their only company was the two Spanish friars Butler had celebrated Easter with a year before.

A few months later, they were shipped back to England on the *Hopewell*, which docked at Bristol in January 1641. Carter addressed the letter that went with them not to the shareholders, but to Archbishop William Laud. All four men, he wrote, 'were disaffected to the liturgy and ceremonies of England.' Laud read Carter's letter with interest; it gave him further cause to tighten the screw on the Puritans' influence in the colonies.

The shareholders received the news of the repulsion of the Spanish attack with joy. It gave them 'further arguments of hope' that God had reserved their venture for 'some special services to his own Glory and the honour of this nation.' They found the Old Councillors innocent of all charges, and ordered that they be released from the improvised cell in the hold of the *Hopewell* immediately. Nathaniel Butler had left the island without their permission, and had had no right to appoint Andrew Carter as his successor. As for Carter's execution of his Spanish prisoners, it was a crime 'so heinous, so contrary to religion and to the law of nature and of nations that it ought not to escape without punishment.'[8] He was ordered to return to England immediately.

Although Richard Lane was persuaded to return to Providence, Hope Sherrard and Henry Halhead had had enough. Sherrard left the company's service, and became the vicar of Sandwich in Kent. His parishioners found him 'pious, peaceable in conversation and a great blessing to the town,' but the town's mayor thought otherwise. He was already concerned by the number of non-conformists in the town, and could not countenance the appointment of another painful preacher. He petitioned the House of Lords to have Sherrard removed from his post, and 'incensed rude seamen and others against him.' Driven from Sandwich by his persecutors, Sherrard moved to Dorset, where he disappeared from the records.[9]

When he left Banbury in 1632, Henry Halhead had vowed to stay on the island 'until the Isle of Great Britain might deservedly be christened the Isle of Providence.' But England seemed as far from God as ever, and his hopes for a godlier community in the Indies had been shattered. Henry died shortly after returning to his hometown. However, the pamphlet he had written before leaving for Providence, with its impassioned denunciation of the enclosure movement, found vindication when Parliament came out against large-scale enclosures in 1641. The previous year, enclosures had sparked riots all over England, and MPs agreed that since their introduction, the country's fields had supported less livestock and produced less food. But their opposition proved short-lived: by 1643, the House of Commons was dominated by Puritan landowners, many of whom had been made rich by enclosures. The drive to enclose what had once been common land picked up momentum again, and more husbandmen and cottagers found themselves tramping the country's roads. Some of them walked as far as the docks of London, Bristol and Plymouth, and eventually to new lives in the New World.

While Henry Halhead's hope that England would be 'born again into a new and free state' had yet to be realised, the country was certainly feeling the pains of childbirth. According to the Earl of Clarendon, the English Civil War began with 'a small, scarce discernible cloud in the north, which was shortly after attended with such a storm that never gave over raging till it had shaken, and even rooted up, the greatest and tallest cedar of the three nations.'[10]

In 1637, King Charles had extended his campaign for religious uniformity to Scotland. With typical insensitivity, he tried to impose Archbishop Laud's new prayer book on the Scottish Church. The Scots had their own brand of Presbyterianism; like the Puritans, they believed in a simple liturgy and an active role for preachers, and had no time for the bishops that governed the Church of England. Laud's new prayer book sparked riots across Scotland. In February 1638, the king's opponents came together at Greyfriars Kirk in Edinburgh to sign a covenant urging him to reconsider his insistence on religious orthodoxy. More than a plea to respect the Presbyterian tradition, it signalled the Scottish nobility's determination to resist royal despotism.

By the following February, Charles was writing to his Lords-Lieutenant in England to raise troops to fight the Scottish Covenanters. But Charles' reluctance to defend his fellow Protestants on the Continent, who were still being persecuted in the Netherlands, La Rochelle, and throughout the states of Germany, ensured that his call was not well received. He managed to raise an army of 18,000, which marched to the Scottish Lowlands to meet a far superior Covenanter force. Realising that he was outnumbered, he had little choice but to sign a peace treaty, which bound him to attend a meeting of the General Assembly of the Kirk and the Scottish Parliament, where it was hoped their differences could be ironed out.

The so-called 'Bishops' War' seemed to be at an end. But rather than sit with those who had dared to defy him, Charles reneged on the deal and returned to London in a fury. 'Thereupon,' wrote MP Edmund Ludlow, 'hoping that a Parliament would espouse his quarrel, and furnish him with money for the carrying on of his design, he summoned one to meet at Westminster on the 3rd of April 1640.'[11] Against his own wishes, and in the face of impending bankruptcy, Charles had brought the eleven years of Personal Rule to an end.

As soon as the new session opened, Parliament was flooded with petitions from frustrated MPs anxious to address the many grievances that had been bubbling up through local government over the course of the 1630s. Bills were proposed to put an end to Archbishop Laud's religious innovations and the king's various illegal tax-raising ventures, and to ensure that he would never again try to govern his kingdom without consulting Parliament. The man who emerged as leader of the Commons was the Providence Island Company's treasurer, John Pym. According to an MP who was present at his first, two hour-long speech to the House, Pym 'left not anything untouched – ship money, forests, knighthoods, recusants, monopolies, the present inclination of our church to popery, and more than my memory can suggest to me.'[12]

Ship money was not a legal tax, but a form of usurpation, Pym thundered. The king's insistence on depriving his people of the fruits of their labour had brought them to 'the condition of slaves.' Those taxed without representation 'will easily grow into a slavish disposition, who having nothing to lose, do commonly show more boldness in disturbing than in defending a kingdom.'[13] Although the irony would probably have been lost on him, the same words could have come from the mouth of any of the settlers on Providence.

Under duress, and keen to move on to more pressing business, Charles agreed to stop collecting ship money. It was an unprecedented climb down, and a major victory for the country's property owners, but Pym was not satisfied yet, and urged the king to address the members' other grievances. Charles found such insolence unforgiveable; just three weeks into the session, he dissolved the assembly, bringing the curtain down on what became known as the 'Short Parliament'.

'There could not a greater damp have seized upon the spirits of the whole nation than this dissolution caused,' lamented the Earl of Clarendon.

> But I was observed, that in the countenances of those who had most opposed all that was desired by His Majesty, there was a marvellous serenity... for they knew enough of what was to come to conclude that the King would shortly be compelled to call another parliament, and they were as sure that so many grave and unbiased men would never be elected again.[14]

Looking out over the River Thames from the Palace of Whitehall, Charles must have rued the day he granted a patent to the Providence Island Company. After his dismissal of Parliament in 1629, the company had provided an outlet for the energies of ambitious men no longer able to influence national affairs from Westminster. But in the years of his Personal Rule, it had clearly become a disguise for a rather more dangerous creation: England's first political party, and the first organised resistance to its government. Among the company's shareholders were 22 members of Parliament, most of whom had played prominent roles in stymieing his plans in the Short Parliament. John Pym was leader of the Commons, Lord Saye was leader of the Lords, and every other opponent of his government seemed to own shares in their company. Charles had even heard it said that they were actively colluding with the Scottish Covenanters to undermine his closest allies and advisors. He had the offices of John Pym, John Hampden, the Earl of Warwick and Lord Saye searched for incriminating evidence. Nothing was found, but still his doubts lingered.

Had he openly charged the company's shareholders with treason, they would have denied it, for in spite of their opposition to the king's government, they considered themselves his most loyal subjects. In 1628, which was the last time they had had a chance to meet Charles in Parliament, they had been at the forefront of the campaign to put his finances on a firmer footing. But their programme had been voted down by traditionalist MPs from the shires, who had a vested interest in keeping central government underfunded and ineffectual. Their opposition to Charles' government had only become implacable in the last two or three years – but implacable it had indeed become, and it was gathering popular support. When John Pym had his speech to the Short Parliament published, his belligerence found favour with all manner of disaffected people, and tension began to mount on the streets of London. Anti-Catholic mobs attacked bishops in the street, and even tried to drag Archbishop Laud from Lambeth Palace.

Rather than ease the strife between the king and his people, the end of Personal Rule had only brought it into the open. In June 1640, Charles raised his standard, and once again commanded England's nobles to join him in putting down the threat posed by the Scottish Covenanters. The First Bishops' War had been the most unpopular military campaign in 400 years, and the Second was an even greater fiasco. English nobles who might ordinarily have come to Charles' aid were horrified by his plan to recruit an army of Irish Catholics to invade Scotland. It was a supremely ill-judged move, as it united the discontented rich and the discontented poor of England in a flurry of religiously inspired jingoism. Hostility to Catholicism had been commonplace for years; in seeking to defeat his opponents in Scotland, Charles was seen to be taking the wrong side in his kingdom's long-running sectarian dispute with Rome. Nobleman and husbandman had other interests in common – their resentment of arbitrary taxation, for example. But their alliance was not a natural one, and it took all of Charles' incompetence to hold it together until the outbreak of war the following year.

Military conscription brought poor men from all over England together, and their numbers taught them their strength. Those who didn't desert became increasingly insubordinate, demanding better pay and insulting their commanding officers with abandon. Yet when the Earl of Warwick went to talk to a regiment of the king's soldiers, they told him that they had only insulted the officers after they had declined to take communion with them. Perhaps it was at that point that the earl realised the power that radical Protestantism had given to the poor of England. When one soldier toasted him as 'the king of Essex', he had him arrested, but as he made clear to Charles when they next met, if the order had come from a royalist officer, the entire company would have risen in arms against him. In seeking to unite the country around the royal banner the king had raised an army of gravediggers.

Charles' army met the Scottish Covenanters in battle at Newburn and was roundly defeated. By the end of August, the Scots had taken Newcastle, and he was forced to call an emergency meeting of his leading nobles at York. He agreed to make peace with the Covenanters, return to London, and recall Parliament again. This would be the Long Parliament, and King Charles would not live to see the end of it.

Not that regicide was on anyone's mind in 1640. The Providence Island Company's members certainly planned something like an aristocratic coup d'état, and saw Parliament as the vehicle through which to achieve it. With the help of wise, well-placed friends like Sir Gilbert Gerard and Sir Benjamin Rudyerd, John Pym had come up with a radical, thoroughgoing programme for raising new taxes for the king's government. Pym would become Chancellor of the Exchequer, and their ally, the Duke of Bedford, would become Treasurer. In return for their support in Parliament, they hoped that Charles would strike a more aggressive stance in the Caribbean, and provide state funding for empire building on a large scale.

But the Puritan imperialists were just one of two groups opposing the king in the Long Parliament. Both were determined to resist the tyranny of arbitrary power, but while one was imperialist and visionary, the other was localist and entirely negative. The dominant spirit in the Commons came not from the ambitious but responsible opposition of John Pym, but the small-minded, irresponsible opposition of MPs like Sir Robert Phelips and Sir Francis Seymour. Phelips' outlook, like that of most country MPs, was rooted in distrust of central government. He resented royal interference in local affairs, and wanted to keep things the way they were, whatever the state of Charles' finances, and despite the rising costs of government and war.

When the MPs first took their seats, the king wasted no time in denouncing the Scottish Covenanters for their treachery, and demanding that the House give him the funds needed to quash their rebellion. But MPs saw no good reason to grant Charles the authority to raise new taxes, if he planned to use the money to fund a war on the very people who had secured their assembly. And the Puritan nobles had reasons of their own to oppose the king's call to arms: because they had no army to call upon, they had struck an agreement with their Scottish counterparts, whereby a Scottish army would be stationed in England until the coup they planned had been realised.

'We must enquire from what fountain these waters of bitterness flowed,' John Pym said, with no little guile. 'What persons they were who had so far insinuated themselves into his royal affections, as to be able to pervert his excellent judgement.'[15] Pym already knew the answer to his question: Thomas Wentworth, Earl of Stafford, Lord Lieutenant of Ireland and Lord President of the council established in York. For their Lordships' scheme to stand any chance of success, the king's most effective operator would have to go. When the House was told that the Earl of Stafford had solicited Spanish help in putting down the Scottish revolt, he was impeached on a charge of high treason and imprisoned in the Tower of London. Bills were drafted to ensure that, in future, any royal advisor would have to meet with the approval of both Houses, and all taxation without the consent of Parliament was declared illegal. Charles had expected trouble from the Long Parliament, but such hostile and organised opposition to his rule was unprecedented.

The same spirit of revolt could be felt in the streets outside Parliament. Puritan ministers at the head of a huge crowd presented the king's government with the 'root and branch petition,' which demanded the repeal of the reforms Archbishop Laud had foisted upon the Church of England, and quickly attracted 15,000 signatories. The following week, Laud too was charged with high treason and taken to the Tower. With the king's most powerful ministers behind bars, the political and religious authoritarianism that Charles had brandished like a talisman was losing its power to awe. The Puritan elite, and England's God-fearing, hungry and impatient masses were each becoming aware of the other's power.

With England locked in a political and constitutional crisis, the share-holders felt hard pressed to attend to the crisis on Providence, for the MPs among them had urgent business to attend to in the House. The Earl of Warwick was also kept busy, either by discussions with the Scottish Covenanters, or his ventures in the Somers Isles, Tobago and Massachusetts. So it was left to John Pym, Lord Saye and Lord Brooke to pen a letter to the island council. Although 'the many public occasions now lying upon us in respect of the sitting of Parliament' had diverted their attention from Providence, they had no intention of giving up on their colony, they assured the councillors.[16]

This was not strictly true. In 1637, the Dutch West India Company had offered the shareholders £70,000 (about £6 million in today's money) for the island, as part of its plans to steal a march on the Spanish in the Caribbean. The Earl of Warwick had been keen to sell, and even raised the matter with King Charles. But with anti-Spanish feeling running high at court, the king had persuaded him to keep the island. He acknowledged that Providence had become 'a place of charge rather than of benefit' to the nation, and suggested that the company reconsider their plans. Shortly afterwards, John Pym began drawing up his scheme for the colonisation of the Miskito coast. At the end of 1639, the Dutch West India Company renewed its offer, and even upped it to 600,000 pieces of eight. By then, Charles could see what a nest of vipers the Providence Island Company had become, and was more than amenable to the sale. The Earl of Warwick asked his agent in Amsterdam to probe the offer further, but he was unable 'to bring the proposition to a reasonable issue.'[17]

In all likelihood, no offer would have persuaded the remaining share-holders to part with their island. Things clearly could not continue as they were, but whether as a refuge for godly migrants, base for the evangelization of the Miskito Indians, or fortress to protect a future English colony in Central America, Providence remained of vital importance to England's imperial mission.

As ever, much would depend on the fate of the other Puritan colony. Ties between Providence and Massachusetts had grown close over the course of the 1630s. Much of the cotton and tobacco and many of the slaves shipped from Providence were sold in Boston, and the town had become an entrepôt for the dispatch of hides, tallow and sarsaparilla to England. Following the company's move into privateering in 1636, merchants on both sides of the Atlantic had been making good money from the trade in stolen Spanish ships, cargos and slaves.

After 1637 however, trade had slowed to a trickle, as the New England economy first slowed, and then lurched into a full-blown recession. Migration to Massachusetts fell dramatically, and many of its settlers sold up and went looking for a more promising location for their divinely inspired efforts. Thomas Gorges, the young Puritan governor of Maine, visited Boston in 1641 and found the place 'in a distracted condition, men unresolved in their minds what to do, some for the West Indies, some for Long Island, and some for old England.'

Lord Saye interpreted the downturn in the colony's fortunes as a sign that God had withdrawn His favour. He exchanged a series of angry letters with John Winthrop, the governor of Massachusetts, in which each claimed his colony to be the divinely sanctioned refuge for followers of the true religion. According to Lord Saye, the recession in New England was proof that 'God appointed Massachusetts only for a temporary abiding place, and did not mean His people to settle there forever.' Winthrop retorted that his Lordship was only trying to 'enthrall' the New Englanders 'to advance other men's posterity.' It was an argument neither side was prepared to lose, with both men accusing the other of wilfully misinterpreting the Bible to justify their claims. In his last letter to Winthrop, Lord Saye signed off by expressing his hope that the New Englanders would 'carry themselves moderately, be content with their own freedom and leave others to theirs.'[18]

In March 1641, the Providence Island Company named John Humphrey as the island's new governor. Captain Humphrey was an excellent choice; he had been one of the original organisers of the Massachusetts Bay Company and had risen to become sergeant major general, the most senior military post in the colony. He was well liked and highly influential, and the company hoped that their appointment of so prominent a Puritan would encourage colonists 'of the middling sort' to journey south from New England. Once sufficient numbers of them were settled on Providence, they too could move to the mighty English colony that the company planned to build in Central America. In his letter notifying Captain Humphrey of his appointment, Lord Saye flattered him that governorship of Providence was 'below his merit,' and encouraged him to pursue any designs he might make on the Miskito coast.[19] Humphrey returned the compliment, saying that his Lordship clearly had 'the deep dye of Christ's blood' on him.

John Humphrey had always had his doubts about the long-term viability of the colony in Massachusetts, and already had 200 good Christians willing and able to accompany him to Providence, with the prospect of many more to follow. His recruitment drive provoked bitter arguments; while many New Englanders were ready to believe that the soil and climate of Central America were better than those of Massachusetts, moving to their Lordships' island would mean a return to tenant farming and government from London. News of how the soldiers and sailors on the island council had combined to stymie the Old Councillors' efforts had been quick to spread. They also knew about the bad-tempered letters that Lord Saye had exchanged with the Governor of Massachusetts, John Winthrop, and many of them had only harsh words for those who decided to journey south with John Humphrey. 'They wanted a warmer country, and every northwest wind that blew, they crept into some odd chimney-corner or other to discourse of the diversity of climates in the southern parts,' said one weather-beaten New Englander.[20]

The shareholders were incredulous that anyone would choose to own a piece of cold, rocky New England when they could rent land on balmy, fertile Providence. But Humphrey advised them not to put 'clogs or burdens' on the New Englanders 'any more than they have here been acquainted with, either in civil or ecclesiastical matters.'[21] The newcomers were not to be fobbed off with idle promises; they wanted land of their own, as well as a voice in how the colony was run. Desperate to find new blood among the impoverished but godly farmers of Massachusetts, the company relented. Over the past ten years, the shareholders had made several modifications to the island's constitution: their tenants no longer had to hand over half of their produce in rent, and by 1638, they could lease land for just 20 pounds of tobacco a year. Now the shareholders went a step further, offering migrants the chance to become freehold landowners, with a say in drafting laws. They even agreed to disband the council of war, and give more power to the Old Councillors.

John Winthrop watched anxiously as growing numbers of New Englanders opted to follow John Humphrey to Providence. The first contingent of 30 men, five women and eight children left Boston harbour in two sloops under the command of the merchant William Pierce in

May 1641. The Spanish attack had threatened to undo all the company's good work, but God had intervened to fend the enemy off, the new governor told them. With the promise of hundreds of experienced colonists journeying south to a new English colony in Central America, prospects looked bright for the Puritans of Providence.

General Francisco Díaz Pimienta was commander of *la flota*, the fleet of ships that carried supplies to Cartagena every year, and a veteran of the struggle to expel the Dutch from Brazil. The general took the failure to prise the pirates' grasp from Santa Catalina as a slight on his country's honour, and was determined to exact his revenge. After journeying to Madrid to remonstrate with King Philip IV in person, permission was duly granted for a third attempt to dislodge the heretics. The king put three galleons at the general's disposal, his only condition being that the expedition should be complete before his treasure fleet sailed in January.

This time, the Spanish invasion was planned with extreme care and precision. General Díaz Pimienta waited until the hurricane season was well passed, calculating that the pirates who had sought shelter in the island's harbour would be roving once more by then. He interrogated four Englishmen in the dungeon at Portobello to find out more about the island's defences, took on a Moorish pirate who had spent time on the island as his pilot, and personally oversaw the outfitting of eleven warships in the docks of Cartagena. His second-in-command, Admiral Rodrigo Lobo, would sail as commander of the 1,400 infantrymen, while Antonio Maldonado y Texeda, a veteran of the previous year's attack, would command the 600 seamen.

Two weeks later, as Humphrey was still at sea the general's flagship dropped anchor off the reef. The following day, he sent out a launch to reconnoitre the island, bravely drawing the enemy's fire to test the range of their weapons. He would invade from the east, he decided. But on the night he assembled his forces, a storm moved in from the west and his fleet narrowly escaped being swept onto the reef. He tried again the following night, but there was 'so much rain that they were almost drowned,' and they had to retreat to their ships for a second time.

The islanders had by now spotted the Spaniards' landing craft and lit beacons to warn of an imminent attack. Watching hundreds of militia-men spread out along the coast, the Spanish officers were so disheart-ened that they urged their general to abandon the enterprise. But Díaz Pimienta was determined to make one more attempt at a landing. Since the winds were still blowing from the west, they would sail around the northern tip of the smaller island and gamble on being driven into the harbour. If they were fast enough, they would escape the worst of the cannon fire from Warwick Fort. It was an audacious proposal, and as the report prepared for the king when it was all over made clear, Díaz Pimienta had 'more trouble overcoming the opposition of his friends than his enemies.'

As the sun rose on the morning of 24 May, the general waved his handkerchief from the bow of his flagship, the attack standard was run up, a signal shot fired, sails raised, and a brisk breeze blew the Spanish longboats into the harbour below Warwick Fort. Although cannon balls rained down on them from the fort, 'carrying away masts, sails and some men, the speed of the launches spoiled the enemy's aim.' Eighty of the islanders, accompanied by many Africans, ran to the beach to confront the invaders, and in fierce hand-to-hand fighting, 'defended themselves with great valour.' But they were outnumbered by the hundreds of Span-ish soldiers that rushed ashore; 20 of them were killed, and the survivors were forced to retreat to Fort Warwick.

General Díaz Pimienta marched into New Westminster at the head of the invading force, took possession of the governor's house and raised the Spanish standard over its roof. He told Antonio Maldonado y Texeda to have his men track the survivors into the bush, flush out any pockets of resistance, and station a garrison in each of the other 12 forts.

The scout sent to investigate Fort Warwick estimated there to be 500 well-armed Englishmen within its stone walls. Díaz Pimienta had nei-ther the time nor the resources to lay siege to the fort; what he did have however, was the unwitting collusion of the island's cowardly interim governor. The general was still considering his options when a launch flying a white flag came aside the pier in New Westminster. On board were the two Spanish friars from the island's prison. They came bearing a message: in return for safe passage to Cádiz, and the same rations af-forded the passengers of a Spanish ship, Andrew Carter was prepared to surrender the island.

Shortly afterwards, General Díaz Pimienta took possession of Fort Warwick 'in the name of the king, with the solemnity belonging to such acts.' After disarming the island's militiamen and their commanding officers, he requisitioned 60 cannon of between four and twelve pounds apiece, 32 smaller cannon and four large catapults. In an adjoining storehouse, he found large quantities of muskets, arquebuses and munitions, which Carter had been preparing for the new colony on the Miskito coast. The 398 Englishmen, women and children the general took prisoner were spared the sword, the *Junta de Guerra de las Indias* having decided it advisable to 'grant the privileges of surrender with mercy, although it was not usually granted in those parts.'

Díaz Pimienta had expected to find 1,500 slaves living on Providence, so he was surprised to find just 380 Africans on the inventory. What he didn't know was that for fear of another insurrection, Captain Carter had just sold 1,000 slaves to the colonists of St Kitts and the Somers Isles. The general divided the Africans into two groups: 305 of them were sent to Cartagena and sold at auction; another 53 were destined for the marketplace in Portobello; and he gave the remaining 22 slaves to his officers by way of reward. That evening, the Spaniards sang a festal Te Deum on the parade ground in front of the governor's house, before going to Hope Sherrard's little church to celebrate Mass. When the service was over, General Díaz Pimienta let it be known that from now on, the island would be known as 'Santa Catalina de la Providencia'.

Spanish reports had always painted the English colony as a near-destitute den of unrepentant pirates and heretical seers, so Díaz Pimienta was surprised to find the Englishmen's fields full of ripening corn and beans, and their pens stocked with thousands of well-fed pigs. Despite its diminutive size and utter isolation, the island was blessed with rich soils and a gentle climate, and if the vial of quicksilver he found in the governor's house was any indication, it also had deposits of precious metals.

Even if the king chose not to settle the island, the general could see that it was always likely to attract unwelcome attention from Spain's European rivals. So instead of dismantling the fortifications, as he had been instructed by the *Consejo de Indias*, he decided to improve on them. He appointed his most trusted lieutenant, Gerónimo de Ojeda, governor of the island and put at his disposal a garrison of 150 Spanish and 50 Portuguese soldiers. Before embarking for Cartagena, the general made sure that they had enough corn and beans to last them until the next harvest, and wished them well. His parting instruction was that they 'live model Christian lives, go to mass regularly and demonstrate other exercises of virtue, so as to be a good example to foreigners, and to God.'

The sale of the indigo, gold and cochineal that Díaz Pimienta recovered from the foreigners' storehouse raised 500,000 ducats (the contemporary equivalent of £12 million) at auction in Cartagena, which more than paid for the expedition (tellingly, Andrew Carter had declared none of these prizes to the company's shareholders). News of the fall of the pirates' lair prompted joyous relief on the city's streets, and grand festivities were held to celebrate the king's victory. In the following two months, more merchant ships entered the Cartagena's harbour than in the previous two years. Similar celebrations erupted in Portobello, Santa Marta, Tolú and every other port on the Spanish Main that had suffered at the hands of Providence's privateers. In gratitude for his leadership of the campaign that expelled them, General Díaz Pimienta was summoned to Madrid, where he was feted as a hero, and awarded the Military Order of the Knights of Santiago by Philip IV himself.[22]

The English prisoners spent the summer of 1641 in Cartagena, waiting for the arrival of the armada that would take them to Cádiz. Since none of them spoke Spanish, they could only guess at what their captors were saying about them, but after years of listening to the Black Legend of Spanish cruelty, they were shocked by how well they were treated. The men were lodged in quarters supplied by the *Compañía de Jesús*, and given a generous allowance for food and drink, while their wives and children stayed with private citizens, who 'had asked for them with pleasure.'

But not all of the islanders had been captured. Around 150 of them escaped into the hills, and watched with the maroons of Palmetto Grove as their friends were rowed out to the galleons waiting in the harbour. When the Spanish ships had sailed out of sight, they made their way down to the wooded bluff overlooking New Westminster and watched a crowd of strangers toast their good fortune around the fire pit that had been their meeting place for the last ten years. They were homeless; at nightfall, they dragged their dories from the mangroves and began rowing for the Miskito Coast.

Nor had all the slaves fallen into the Spaniards' clutches. In the latter stages of the battle, a group had commandeered one of the privateers' ships riding at anchor in the harbour and made their escape. The English had been careful not to teach slaves skills as valuable as navigation, but somehow they too made it to the Miskito coast, where their ship was wrecked just south of Cape Gracias a Dios. The previous year, a slave ship called the *Newton* had been wrecked further south at Karata. Its human cargo had become the first Africans to land on the Miskito coast as free men, and it seems likely that the escapees joined them.

In the years that followed, the fall of Providence spurred the creation of other English-speaking outposts. Refugees from their Lordships' Isle were instrumental in founding isolated coastal settlements from Panama to Campeche on the Yucatan peninsula. Some found shelter in the ramshackle pirate communities that had sprung up on the Miskito coast, particularly at Bluefields, which had been named after the Dutch buccaneers William and Abraham Blauveldt. Others found their way to William Claiborne's outpost on the island of Ruatan, where Samuel Axe had recently built an armed stockade. The following year, they were driven out by a Spanish expedition, so Captain Axe led them first to St Kitts, and then to the Earl of Warwick's short-lived colony on Tobago, an exodus that would in turn lead to the creation of an equally short-lived settlement on Trinidad in 1649. Other refugees from Providence sailed under a Scotsman by the name of Captain Wallace, and founded the village that eventually became Belize City.[ii]

As for John Humphrey and the contingent of settlers from New England, they were on St Kitts taking on fresh water when they first heard that a fleet of Spanish ships had been sighted off Providence. Their captain, William Pierce, recommended that they return to Massachusetts, but his passengers insisted on pressing on. 'Then I am a dead man!' he said. He dropped anchor in Providence harbour just a few days after the departure of the Spanish fleet for Cartagena. There were no other ships to be seen; nor did there seem to be anyone working in the fields. Pierce was approaching the shore, hailing for the harbour master as he went, when his ship came under a barrage of cannon fire. Most of it did little more than rip holes in his sails, but one hit him in the chest. The first mate pulled the sloop out of range of the Spaniards' guns, but within an hour Captain Pierce was dead.

[ii] The name 'Belize' is thought to be a corruption of 'Wallace.'

It would appear that God did not mean for the New Englanders to make Providence their home after all. They spent an anxious night at anchor a league off shore, arguing over their next move. John Humphrey convinced the first mate to make for Cape Gracias a Dios, but the discussion over what God wanted them to do next only became more heated when they arrived on the Miskito coast. Having turned their backs on Massachusetts, most of them were reluctant to return – but living with buccaneers, runaway slaves and heathen Indians was none too appetising a prospect either. Humphrey chose to stay at the Cape, but most of his followers opted to return. They reached Boston in September, just as the first of the colony's birds were flying south for the winter. By November, Humphrey too was ready to give up on the Caribbean. He sailed for England, and docked at Deptford shortly after Andrew Carter and the rest of the islanders who had been imprisoned in Cartagena arrived from Cádiz.

The last ship to leave the company dock for New Westminster had sailed six months before. Among the latest contingent looking to start over on Providence were Richard Lane and the island's new minister, Nicholas Leverton, who were still flush with hopes for the rejuvenation of the island's divine mission. As the familiar electric blue of the reef came into view, it didn't take them long to realise that the island had been taken for the Antichrist. Reverend Leverton suggested that they 'venture a brush' with the Spanish, 'wherein they killed a great many of their men, and forced their armed longboats ashore.' But they too were eventually driven away.

They spent the next two years careering around the Caribbean, during which time they 'had many preservations (almost miraculous) from famine, the Spaniards, and violent storms.' Richard Lane's luck eventually ran out: he was drowned off the coast of Eleuthera in the Bahamas. Nicholas Leverton fared better: he spent a year preaching in the Somers Isles before returning to England, where 'he was received with great honour and respect by the Lords proprietors of the island of Providence.'

The loss of their island was a terrible blow, but their Lordships didn't give up their claim to Providence. As King Charles had himself acknowledged five years before, the island had become the business of all Protestant England, and would remain so for as long as Spain denied England the right to trade in the Americas. In a letter to John Humphrey written

137

in August 1641, the shareholders assured him of their continued support, and invited him to consider some 'public undertakings, which may shortly come to a resolution here touching the West Indies.' They felt sure that such ventures could only 'further improve and advance your beginnings.'[23] It was to be the Providence Island Company's last letter.

PART TWO

11

'LITTLE MORE THAN
THE SUMMIT OF A HILL'

In June 1641, the Long Parliament passed an act declaring ship money illegal. Charles gave the act his assent in August, but if his concession was supposed to mollify his opponents in Parliament, it was forgotten in the crisis created by his stand off with the Scots. Then, in October, news reached London of a second, still more dangerous rebellion, this time against English settlers in Ireland. Tensions between natives and newcomers had been rising for years, but the uprising was sparked by fears that Charles was about to give in to the Puritans' call to curb Catholicism in Ireland. The prospect of a religious crackdown, combined with popular frustration at the passivity of the Dublin Parliament, drove people to take matters into their own hands. Across Ulster, native Irish vented their anger at their Protestant neighbours, who had taken their best lands and persecuted their religious leaders. By the time the bloodletting came to an end, over 15,000 Protestants and Catholics were dead.

In the minds of jingoistic English, the Irish rebellion of 1641 showed their obsessive dread of a Catholic conspiracy to be well founded. Graphic woodcuts depicting bloodthirsty mobs of rampaging Irishmen were prepared, and bills posted across the country. The number of dead was said to have passed 200,000, and rumours spread that the rebels were on their way to England. In Puritan circles, the rising was assumed to have had the king's blessing, for allegations of Charles' latent Catholicism had never gone away. But the king was no less appalled by the rebellion than the Puritans, and immediately asked Parliament for the resources needed to mount a full-scale offensive against the rebels. For the time being, most English were still prepared to rally around their monarch. But John Pym was not; he responded to the Irish Rebellion with the Grand Remonstrance, which reiterated Parliament's grievances and proposed a dramatic increase in its powers to keep the king in check.

Charles was furious: he accused Pym and his colleagues of treason for their collusion with the Scottish Covenanters, and even stormed into the Commons to arrest the culprits himself. 'All the birds are flown,' he said, on finding his tormenters absent from the chamber. Turning on his heel, he stormed out, as cries of "Privilege! Privilege!" rang out from the benches. The same cry went up from angry crowds outside Parliament. Charles' bad-tempered attempt to interdict his opponents was interpreted as a failed coup by a despot who certainly could not be trusted with command of the army. Suspected Catholics and courtiers were attacked in the street, and some were even killed. London was rapidly turning against the king.

In February 1642, Charles put Queen Henrietta Maria and their three children on a boat to Holland with the crown jewels. She was sure to find sympathy from monarchs on the Continent, he told her; she should pawn the jewels and use the money to raise an invasion force. But with the navy now at the command of the Earl of Warwick, there was little hope that any troops the Queen mustered would make it across the Channel. Although King and Parliament continued to affect friendship and express hopes for an amicable end to their disagreements, each side was now racing to gain control of the armed forces. In March, Parliament issued the Militia Ordinance, which provided for the raising of forces 'for the safety of his Majesty's person' against 'the bloody councils of papists and other ill-affected persons.'[1] Naturally, Charles refused to sign the bill, so Parliament reissued it as a legally enforceable Ordinance without Royal Assent.

Charles retaliated by issuing the Commission of Array, commanding the country's Lords Lieutenant to raise troops, and forbidding his subjects from taking any part in Parliament's 'mischievous designs and intentions against the peace of this, our kingdom.'[2] As far as the Royalists were concerned, the source of those 'mischievous designs' was the Puritans in Parliament. As the tension mounted, staunch opposition turned to outright abuse, and 'Puritan' became a catch-all term for anyone who dared to question the king's authority. Colonel Hutchinson came from a distinguished Puritan family that fought for Parliament during the Civil War. 'If any, out of mere morality and civil honesty, discountenanced the abominations of those days, he was a Puritan, however he conformed to their superstitious worship,' he wrote in his *Memoirs*,

If any showed favour to any godly honest person, kept them company, relieved them in want, or protected them against violent, unjust oppression, he was a puritan. If any gentleman in the country maintained the good laws of the land, or stood up for any public interest, for good order or government, he was a puritan.[3]

With King and Parliament making competing demands on the people's loyalty, neutrality was no longer an option. Families, villages and entire towns were divided, pulled in one direction by their commitment to 'the true religion', another by their loyalty to the king, and still another by their ties to local nobles and landowners. But the fault lines were far from clear, and they shifted over the course of the war to come.

On 22 August 1642, Charles declared war on Parliament. The first engagement between the two sides – and the first battle between Englishmen since the War of the Roses – came on the road between Banbury and Kineton, at a dramatic escarpment known as Edgehill. Among the regiments that rallied to the cause of Parliament was Lord Saye's; all four of his sons enlisted, and the Banbury men who served under them wore uniforms dyed blue with woad grown on his his estate. A lifelong opponent of arbitrary government, Lord Saye was destined to play a leading role in the Civil War. According to the Earl of Clarendon, he was 'the pilot that steered all those vessels that were freighted with sedition to destroy the government.'[4] His Lordship had mixed motives for going to war: aside from his commitment to Parliament's right to hold the monarch to account, he had spent as much as £25,000 on his colony, most of which he lost with the Spanish invasion. As a Parliamentary Commissioner of the Treasury during the war, large sums of money passed through his hands, and since he kept only primitive accounts, he may well have profited substantially.

The other shareholders also played leading parts in the war with King Charles. Lord Brooke commanded the armies of Warwickshire and Staffordshire (and paid for his soldiers' upkeep out of his own pocket). Sir Thomas Barrington served under Lord Mandeville, now Earl of Manchester, another prominent shareholder, who headed the armies of the Eastern Association. Company secretary William Jessop became secretary to the Admiralty commissioners, and the MP Gilbert Gerard was paymaster to the Parliamentary armies.

The English Civil War raged for most of the 1640s. Although the fighting was interrupted by ceasefires and negotiations, neither side entered into them confident of securing the concessions they demanded, and they soon returned to the fray. Armies tens of thousands strong fought pitched battles from Lostwithiel in Cornwall to Inverlochy in the Highlands. When Charles' English reserves flagged, Scottish and Irish soldiers were drafted in to bolster them. As the fighting rolled through one year and into another, the death toll rose, and the pillaging of towns and destruction of houses and farms dragged the country into ever-deeper poverty. Yet the cries of the avengers rang louder than the groans of the war-weary. The days of gentle persuasion were long gone: now terror was deployed from street to street, as each side tried to frighten away local support for the other.

The man who emerged from the ranks of the Parliamentary armies to drag its leaders to victory was Oliver Cromwell. At the start of the war, Cromwell had served under Lord Mandeville, Earl of Manchester, as leader of the cavalry regiment known as the Ironsides. He proved himself an obedient, loyal and determined officer, and was rapidly promoted. When it came his turn to select the men who would fight at his side, he showed himself a believer in meritocracy, as well as a devout Puritan. Prior to the outbreak of war, the Puritans had pushed aside their less resolute allies in Parliament. Now they did the same on the battlefield.

The turning point came in 1644, as the high command of the Parliamentary armies was mulling the consequences of the inconclusive Battle of Newbury. The King's forces had been driven back towards Bath, but the battle was not the emphatic victory that it should have been. MP Sir Arthur Haselrig urged Lord Mandeville to give chase to the enemy, but the Earl was content to watch them retreat. His Lordship had grown war-weary, and turned on Sir Arthur, saying, 'You are a bloody fellow! God send us peace, for God does never prosper us in our victories to make them clear victories.'[5]

Cromwell saw that the war would never be won as long as the armies for Parliament were led by ambivalent commanders desperate to find a compromise peace, and anxious not to promote poor men to positions of authority. In an unsparing internal enquiry, he accused Lord Mandeville of laziness, incompetence, and most damning of all, a fear of victory. Cromwell orchestrated his Lordship's demotion, and became leader of the Eastern Association in his stead. This was the first step in a thorough reorganisation of the army that saw aristocratic commanders like the Earls of Manchester, Essex and Bedford replaced by men with proven leadership ability.

For Cromwell, that meant his most God-fearing soldiers. 'Truly, I think that those who pray best will fight best,' he once said. Plenty of the men who rose through the ranks under Cromwell's leadership were 'poor and of mean parentage, such as have filled dung carts, both before they were captains and since.'[6] But even the aristocrats had to admit that Cromwell's New Model Army was possessed of a remarkable self-confidence. Lord Mandeville observed the serenity that came with their certainty of victory, and the evangelism that bound them to their leader. 'If you look upon his own regiment of horse, see what a swarm there is of those that call themselves the godly. Some of them profess that they have seen visions and had revelations.'[7]

The visionary power of the convinced Puritan stemmed from his belief in divine providence. In the years leading up to the outbreak of war, Puritan congregations had been told that God was intervening in the affairs of England on a scale not seen 'since the first day of the creation of the world.'[8] God had delivered his followers from Laudian persecution; now He blessed them with a series of spectacular, even miraculous, victories on the battlefield.

Cromwell had a devout faith in God, but he was not a clairvoyant, and when it came time to consider the political reforms the country needed, he was an arch-pragmatist. In his *Memoirs*, the Parliamentary commander Edmund Ludlow recalled that in 1648, Cromwell's high command 'would not declare themselves either for a monarchical, aristocratical or democratical government, maintaining that any of them might be good in themselves, or for us, as providence should direct us.' It was a peculiar combination of activity and passivity, but one typical of the Puritan frame of mind. After sweeping across the country in 1647, the New Model Army marched on London to put a wholly new set of demands to the king. The Heads of Proposals demanded extensive reforms, including the widening of the franchise, decentralisation of power to the regions, full accountability of government ministers to Parliament, and complete religious toleration for the country's nonconformists.

The story of the democratic forces stirred by the Diggers and the Levellers, mobilised by the New Model Army, debated at Putney and put down as part of the post-war settlement is a fascinating one, but this is not the place to tell it. Suffice to say, Cromwell's role changed following the Parliamentary armies' victory over the king's forces. In raising an army capable of defeating the king, Parliament had conjured a genie: the devout religiosity of the majority of English people. For many radical Protestants, the beauty of the true religion lay in its indifference to property, rank and social status, and this had profound implications for the government of England. Concurrent with the recession, the rise of the Puritans' culture of discipline and the drift to war, growing numbers of poor people had been politicised. Radical preachers and pamphleteers were disseminating novel ideas about power and politics, and unprecedented numbers of people were stirred by their message. But the widening of the franchise was a demand that few property owners could consent to, Cromwell included. He assured the Parliamentary leaders that he considered his victory to be God's, not the people's, and set about returning the genie to its bottle. In so doing, he earned a measure of gratitude from England's property owners, but betrayed 'the poor and mean of this kingdom, who had been the means of its preservation.'[9]

But before the soldiers of the Parliamentary armies would consent to return to civilian life, they demanded their pound of flesh. Among the proposals to emerge from the Putney Debates was the Army Remonstrance of 1648, which called for the trial of King Charles on a charge of high treason. In January 1649, elections were held to return a new Parliament, and the Puritans emerged as far and away the most powerful element. Parliament decreed itself the supreme authority in the country, and appointed a lowly provincial judge, John Bradshaw, to become President of the High Court of Justice that was hastily assembled to try the king. 'I tell you we will cut off his head with the crown on it,'[10] Cromwell said to a Royalist who questioned the court's legitimacy. Fittingly, the man chosen to bear the sword of state of the High Court was John Humphrey, the last governor of Providence. Days later, John Bradshaw condemned Charles to become the first king of England to be sentenced to death by execution.

On the morning of 30 January 1649, Charles was led to the scaffold that had been mounted in front of Whitehall gate. Philip Henry, an undergraduate at Christ Church, Oxford, was in the crowd that had gathered to watch the King's last moments. 'I stood and saw what was done, but was not so near as to hear anything,' he later wrote. '[But] the blow I saw given, and can truly say, with a sad heart... there was such a groan by the thousands then present as I never heard before and desire I may never hear again.'[11]

Had he been governor of any other colonial settlement in the Americas, Gerónimo de Ojeda would have had a team of stonemasons, carpenters and labourers ready to build a town in the Spanish style, with streets laid out on a grid around a modest church. But the governor of Santa Catalina de Providencia had neither the skilled craftsmen nor the materials needed, so his soldiers had to be content with squatting in the abandoned buildings of New Westminster. So began the only period of occupation by Spanish speakers in the island's history. Not that their dominion was complete, for they had heard about the community of runaway slaves living at Palmetto Grove from their English prisoners. Rather than flush them out, Ojeda warned his men not to wander the high hills alone.

Life on the island soon began to grate. The Spanish soldiers bickered with their Portuguese counterparts, who wanted to go home, and both sides complained of being abandoned by their superiors in Cartagena. During the winter of 1643, the island's Portuguese surgeon emerged as leader of a plot to kill Gerónimo de Ojeda and join the foreign pirates living on the Miskito coast. The governor got wind of the conspiracy just in time to avert a mutiny, and had the surgeon and seven other ringleaders shot. A further eleven Portuguese were condemned to six years in the galleys at Cádiz, but they escaped punishment when the ship transporting them to Spain was hit by a storm that sent all hands to the bottom of the Atlantic.

The English migrants to Providence might have baulked at building forts and roads, but their Spanish counterparts, whether noble *hidalgo* or common *peón*, regarded all forms of manual labour as beneath them and left the business of sowing, cultivating and harvesting to the 15 Africans that General Díaz Pimienta had left behind. But 15 slaves were incapable of supplying food sufficient to feed an entire garrison, so Ojeda told his men that they would have to work the land or starve. The slaves showed the younger conscripts how to tend corn, beans and yucca, and where to find the deer and wild pigeons that lived in the woods, while the older soldiers learned the rudiments of animal husbandry.

For the Africans, the Spanish regime was less onerous than the English, and in time, they even reached some accommodation with their new masters. In the evenings, they gathered around the fire pit to smoke a little tobacco together. The absence of women afflicted them with loneliness no less than it had the English, but few ships visited, for the soldiers had nothing to sell, and no money to buy the new clothes and strong liquor they dreamed of, let alone prostitutes.

Once a year, Governor Ojeda sent a letter to his superiors in Madrid. He began his dispatch with a reminder that he had been a loyal officer of the *Armada Real* for over 25 years, had fought in many battles and sustained several injuries. Then he described conditions on the island and listed the supplies his men needed, most important of which were women, 'to avoid the great damage that can otherwise result.' His letter travelled with the supply ship that, in theory at least, visited Santa Catalina once a year. If he were lucky, he would receive a reply two years later.

One year, he received a letter from the governor of Cartagena, who informed him that he was mooting the idea of dispatching some 'unattached or licentious ladies… so that the soldiers will carry out their duties with greater pleasure.'[12] But nothing came of the governor's proposal. As for Ojeda's request that new recruits be sent out to relieve the garrison, he admitted that nobody in the city could be persuaded to live on the island, 'except by force.'[13] Ojeda rarely received the provisions he had asked for, and all he got in the way of reinforcements was the occasional stowaway from the galleons, rebellious slave or criminal, who was invariably 'condemned to serve on the island without hope of leaving, even after completing his term.'[14]

The little garrison on Santa Catalina was practically forgotten in Madrid. The *Consejo de Indias* only kept it going to defend the island from the English – although, as one official admitted, the only reason the pirates had not taken it back was that they had not tried. Although none of them dared say as much, officials in Cartagena believed the king would be better off dismantling the forts and sending the garrison somewhere it could be put to better use. Yet in spite of his superiors' indifference, Ojeda continued to send them regular requests for new recruits, fresh supplies and female company. After receiving his letter of 1646, an official at the *Consejo de Indias* noted in the margin that it was 'word for word the same as his letter of '44.'

Gradually, the soldiers grew resigned to their isolation. Some of them even came to see the advantages of island life, for while Madrid and Lisbon laboured under the continual threat of plague, and the denizens of Cartagena suffered regular outbreaks of smallpox and dysentery, no epidemic ever reached Santa Catalina. Resignation soon turned to apathy. When the chief of the *guardacostas* visited the island from Cartagena in 1648, he was shocked by the neglect into which Fort Warwick had been allowed to sink. The garrison had built their principal redoubt, *El Castillo Santa Teresa*, next to the English fort, but the chief of the *guardacostas* was not impressed. 'The fortifications on the island are of such little importance that they can be considered non-existent,' he reported. The so-called castle was 'little more than the summit of a hill,' and its weapons and munitions were deficient in both quantity and quality.[15]

By 1660, many of the veterans of 1641 had died of old age, leaving just 100 men still able to bear arms. In a letter to the king, Governor Ojeda lamented that such was their misery that many of them were deserting the island, 'risking their lives to cross 60 leagues of water on little more than a log.' Even those that reached the Miskito coast 'ended up more dead than alive,' he wrote, and most were 'lucky enough not to be eaten by Indians.'[16]

Being at war with their king, the chief financiers of England's fledgling empire were in no position to mount an expedition to wrest back control of Providence. But in July 1641, just two months after Andrew Carter and the other settlers were taken to Cartagena, the Earl of Warwick had given Captain William Jackson command of the 350-ton *Charles* and a fleet of five smaller vessels, and told him to avenge the Spanish invasion. Jackson, a man 'stern almost to the point of cruelty and not overburdened with scruples,' had been a frequent visitor to Providence before its capture. He set sail on what would become a groundbreaking, three-year voyage.

His first prize was a Spanish slave ship, which he took off Trujillo and successfully ransomed for 8,000 lbs of indigo, two enormous gold chains, and 2,000 pieces of eight (£96,000 in modern money). He returned to England, where he sold his prizes to the earl's friends in the City of London, before heading back to the Caribbean to round up the remaining privateers of Providence. In July 1642, he rendezvoused with Samuel Axe and William Rous, the former commanders of Fort Warwick, on the island of St Kitts. He made Axe his vice admiral, and captain of the 240-ton *Valentine*, and appointed Rous commander of his land forces. Next, he hired the *Dolphin* to serve as his supply ship. Its master was Lewis Morris, another Providence veteran, who as a teenager had spent three years living with the Miskitos as security for Prince Oldman's safe return from England.

Providence's former privateers were akin to a lodestone, attracting loose particles wherever they went. On Barbados, they found no end of men willing to sign up on the usual principle of 'no purchase, no pay.' Jackson took on 500 men, and turned away twice that number, with 'every one that was denied entertainment reputing himself unfortunate,' according to the voyage's anonymous journal keeper.[17] The six vessels in Jackson's fleet sailed north, aiming for the island of Hispaniola. The Spaniards' first and largest Caribbean colony had miles of unguarded coastline on its southern shore, where runaway servants and slaves eked out a living from hunting the huge herds of cattle that the island's first Spanish settlers had abandoned to roam wild. They lived on beef, which they grilled on 'boucans' (hence the name 'buccaneer') traded cowhides for gunpowder and rum, and made a name for themselves as soldiers for hire.

William Jackson was a formidable soldier, but like so many of the first English adventurers to venture into Caribbean waters, he was a terrible mariner. He sailed without a rutter, and soon got lost en route to Hispaniola. When the crew began suffering for want of victuals, William Rous 'did greatly encourage and suscitate the dropping spirits of his men, and by showing himself a forward pattern of plausible patience, taught them the readiest way to support languishing nature by eating of boiled hides.'

By the time they reached Hispaniola in December, Jackson was having second thoughts about attacking such a well-fortified colony, and announced that they would instead mount an assault of the smaller island of Jamaica. He found more willing volunteers among the buccaneers, and sailed west with 890 men and 16 ships under his command. The Spanish authorities had not afforded Jamaica much importance, and Jackson's men were able to rout its 2,000 defenders without a fight. So taken were they by the island that they wanted to settle it right away. 'The temperature of the clement, and salubrity of the air may be well discerned in the good complexion and long life of the inhabitants, who here attain to greater age than those in many of the neighbouring islands,' wrote the journal keeper. The fertility of the island soils, the wealth of fruit growing in its trees, and the prosperity of the Spaniards' plantations inspired him to flights of rhapsody not heard since the discovery of Providence. 'Whatsoever is fabled by the poets, or maintained by historians concerning the Arcadian plains or the Thessalian Tempe, may here be verified and truly affirmed,' he raved.

Long before the first party of Englishmen had ventured ashore at Cape Gracias a Dios, the Miskitos had prophesised that a grey-eyed race of men would come and save them from Spanish tyranny. William Jackson found the same divine validation for their voyage to Jamaica after speaking to the Spaniards' African slaves, who told him of 'the inward desire they had to change their old masters.' He assured them that the English would soon be back to drive the Spaniards out for good. On hearing this, the Africans 'seemed greatly to rejoice,' for it corresponded with 'a confident opinion long rooted in them, that they shall one day come under the subjection of the English.'

Jackson ransomed Jamaica for '200 beaves [cattle] and 10,000 pound weight of cassavy bread for the victualing of our ships... and 17,000 pieces of eight (£816,000 in today's money).' After returning the island to its governor, his men spent the next two weeks slaughtering and salting their cattle. It was at this point that a letter arrived from England, informing William Rous that he had been elected MP for Dartmouth. He sailed for England, and took his seat in the Long Parliament in time to celebrate Oliver Cromwell's promotion to the head of the largest of the Parliamentary armies.

Jackson and the rest of the privateers sailed on to Trujillo, 'where each man expected to make himself a second Croesus.'[i] But the port had been plundered by Dutch and French privateers since the captain's last visit, and they found it 'in a very poor and ruinous condition.' Upon diligent search, we found diverse chests of sugar, tobacco, sarsaparilla and some

---

i   Croesus (595 BC – c. 546 BC) was the King of Lydia. He was renowned for his fabulous wealth, and is credited with being the first monarch to issue true gold coins with a standardised purity for general circulation.

THE ISLAND THAT DISAPPEARED

small quantity of plate, but nothing of any considerable value.' Before leaving the town, they were approached by a group of 120 Miskitos who had been evacuated from the island of Ruatan after the capture of William Claiborne's tiny colony. They humbly requested that their grey-eyed friends take them home, so Jackson made for Cape Gracias a Dios, where:

> the Indians in their canoes came aboard our Vice Admiral to visit their old acquaintances, Captain Axe and Lewis Morris, the master who had formerly lived among them. These Cape Indians are our friends and diverse of them speak and understand our language, by reason of the great correspondence they held with the islanders of Providence before it was taken up by the Spaniards.

From the Miskito coast, the privateers headed south, in the hope of finding gold in the colonial villages of Central America. Their initial forays inland came to nothing, 'yet it is certain that the Spaniards enjoy and possess incredible mass of wealth in those parts... for Castilia de Oro, or Golden Castle, has not his name for nothing.' Not to be discouraged, they made for Bogo del Drago (today's Bocas del Toro, on the border between Panama and Costa Rica), where 'Captain Wolner with some of his men, going unadvisedly on shore, were suddenly seized by a company of cannibals and man eaters, and never after seen.' It was a timely reminder that not all the native peoples of the Americas regarded the English as their liberators.

Undeterred, Jackson made for Tolú, 'the garden of Cartagena, from whence that magnificent metropolis is furnished with all manner of dainty provisions.' Finding 'good pillage' in the town, they stayed for four days, but the inhabitants refused to negotiate a ransom. Incensed by their stubbornness, Jackson burned their town to the ground, 'leaving them to cuddle their crosses in dust and ashes.' His contempt for the Spaniards' religion only grew more bitter when he reached the indigenous village of Chaupotón, where the Indians' 'heathenish temples are now become the monasteries of Franciscan friars.' Not only were the Spanish 'mixing paganism with the pure religion of Almighty God,' they kept:

> these poor Indians under a miserable servitude and subjection, and they themselves living in all manner of luxury and excess, of which we had

sufficient proof by taking two of these epicures in the night time, whilst they were drinking and revelling with their whores.

Captain Jackson had seen enough; after almost four years of roving, raiding and pillaging, he was feeling both sated and inspired, and decided to sail for England. For want of firepower, he had failed to intercept the Spanish treasure fleet, but he returned to Deptford with a welcome taste of things to come: a huge cargo of indigo worth 150,000 pesos (£7 million in today's money). But he was also carrying something of even greater value: knowledge, both of the Caribbean and Spain's weakening hold on it.

The strength of the Spaniards in these occidental regions is far inferior to what they have themselves so much boasted of ... These American Spaniards are an idle, cowardly and effeminate people, not exercised nor brought up in war-like discipline, but much degenerating from the spirits of their ancestors, who first conquered those parts.

William Jackson's account tallied with the reports of the English ambassador in Madrid. Dependency on American gold and silver had sapped the strength from Spain's domestic economy. The king's treasury was empty and the foreign bankers he had come to depend on were unwilling to extend him more credit. Not only were foreign privateers disrupting legal commerce between Spain's Caribbean ports, the country's merchants were being undercut by their foreign rivals. Spain still held the three big islands of the Greater Antilles – Cuba, Hispaniola and Puerto Rico. English, French and Dutch colonists were still confined to islands so small they barely warranted inclusion on Spanish maps – the English had Barbados, Antigua, St Kitts, Nevis and Montserrat. But the Spanish had neither the ships nor the men needed to evict them, and the interlopers were intent on extending their reach in the Caribbean basin.

Even in the midst of the Civil War, England's imperialists had kept a careful eye on their colonies. During the Long Parliament, which continued to sit for the duration of the war, the Earl of Warwick was appointed both Lord Admiral of the Navy and Governor-in-Chief of the Colonies. In September 1641, just two months after he had given Jackson his letters of marque, a parliamentary committee renewed the call he had first made in the 1620s, for the incorporation of an English company to rival the Dutch West India Company. Such a company would combine the functions of a private company with those of a national army, building colonies in the Caribbean, attacking Spanish ports and storming the ships that sailed between them. But its broader purpose was to split Spain's American empire in two, and pave the way for the creation of a Protestant empire in Central America.

In 1643, Parliament established a Committee for the Colonies, whose members included the Earl of Warwick, John Pym and Oliver Cromwell, to supplant the King's Commission for Foreign Plantations. A pamphlet published the same year, *Certain Inducements to Well Minded People*, reiterated the imperial ideal espoused by the Providence Island Company, by calling for the creation of an English colony on the Miskito coast. It was addressed to the many thousands who had suffered 'by the plundering and utter ruin of their estates, by the cruelty of the Cavaliers, or through the decay of trading.'

By moving to the Miskito coast, Englishmen would become 'more free to each other, in acts of hospitality, courtesy, relief and commerce,' as well as 'more liberal to God in public and domestic duties.'[18] Migrants were offered 60 acres, on lifelong freehold leases. They would have houses and gardens in the colony's capital, and their servants would be granted the same when they completed their indentures. The proposed colony would be built on a familiar conflation of private gain and public duty: an ambitious Englishman could become rich in Central America, and by taking the light of the true religion to the benighted Indians, save his soul in the process. Many of the Providence Island Company's former shareholders backed the scheme, and set about raising the £300,000 they judged necessary to put it on a firm footing.

12
THE WESTERN DESIGN

Following the execution of King Charles, England was declared a republican Commonwealth, to be governed by Parliament, aided by a General Council, and presided over by Oliver Cromwell. The mightiest organs of state, including the House of Lords, were abolished and power was devolved from London to the regions. Encouraged by the Puritan scythe that had cut the Royalists down to size, as much as by the end of royal censorship, the country was swept up on a wave of preaching, proselytising and pamphleteering that would not be seen again until the mass mobilisations of the Victorian era.

Parliament had abolished episcopacy in 1646; with no bishops to police the religious life of the country, sects multiplied. According to a Royalist church minister from London,

> every day begets a new opinion, it faring with them, as with the ancient heretics, who having once forsaken the truth wandered from one error to another, that they agreed only in this one thing: to do mischief to the Church of God.[1]

The execution of the king had put an end to the war in England, but it continued to rage in Ireland and Scotland. In August 1649, Oliver Cromwell sailed to Ireland to put down the insurrection that had begun with the rebellion of 1641. At Drogheda and Wexford, his troops engaged in mass slaughter, supposedly to avenge the deaths of Protestant settlers. If the Irish campaign stopped up the gap through which foreign powers might have come to the relief of their fellow Catholics, it also paved the way for the large-scale appropriation of lands that Cromwell had earmarked for his friends in the City of London who had financed the campaign. He treated the rebels much as the first settlers of New England had treated rebellious Indians: he had them shipped to Barbados in chains. In July

1650, his army crossed the River Tweed and routed the Scottish forces at Dunbar and the following year, he crushed the combined Royalist and Scottish armies at Worcester.

After nine years of intermittent conflict, the civil wars were at an end, and Cromwell was free to roll out his Commonwealth across the three kingdoms. Preoccupation with domestic affairs gave way to an energetic interest in foreign pursuits.[2] With a newfound confidence in the ability of the army and navy, the Caribbean still looked to many Englishmen a suitable arena for the national effort in empire building. Providence might have fallen to the Spanish, but over the next 40 years, it would continue to inspire England's most bellicose soldiers, sailors, ministers and settlers. The island had become their talisman, and the prospect of retaking it fired their imaginations, just as William Jackson's voyage around Spain's decadent empire had in the war years.

The lessons of the fall of Providence were far from clear. Some of the company's shareholders blamed the lack of government support for the venture; others, the company's failure to find a profitable crop. The contradiction at the heart of Puritan imperialism seems to have passed them by: the company had failed to attract the industrious 'middling sort' that had made a success of New England in sufficient numbers. In the absence of right-minded settlers, the godly had been outnumbered by the earthly, and by the time the shareholders offered their tenants the opportunity to buy the land they farmed, and a say in who governed them, it was too late.

Back in 1628, John Pym had opposed extra-parliamentary taxation in Parliament, asking 'who will contend, who will endanger himself for that which is not his own?'[3] The same words might have been etched on the epitaph for the colony on Providence. By 1640, there were six representative assemblies in the colonies: Barbados, Massachusetts, Maryland, Connecticut, Plymouth and New Haven. As in England, the franchise was limited to property owners, but the colonists' demand for more autonomy still caused alarm at home, for there were no nobles in the colonies to steer the voters' judgement, and commoners were considered incapable of wielding authority responsibly.

The Somers Isles Company had more success than the Providence Island Company, both in building a devout community of believers, and in replicating the life of an English village. By 1638, the company had built nine churches, a chapel, and five houses for the island's ministers.

Unlike Providence's Old Councillors, the Somers Isles' godlier settlers were brought low, not by privateers, but by the Privy Council in London, which interfered in the religious life of the colony to a degree never attempted on Providence. Prior to his imprisonment, Archbishop Laud had condemned unlicensed ministers who went to the Somers Isles to 'preserve their factious and schismatical humours,' and ordered them back to England.[4]

Oliver Cromwell had no intention of persecuting his fellow believers for their interpretation of Scripture – at least, not unless they were Catholics. 'In things of the mind, we look for no compulsion but that of light and reason,' he once said.[5] His abiding purpose was to make the reformed religion secure, which meant protecting England from its enemies within, as well as preparing for a potential invasion by the Spanish. Neither danger would go away until the link between Spain and the source of its riches had been severed.

Yet Cromwell was unsure of how best to proceed. Seeking the counsel of men more learned than himself, in 1651 he initiated a correspondence with John Cotton, New England's foremost interpreter of Biblical prophecy. 'What is the Lord doing? What prophesies are now fulfilling?' he asked him. The minister told him that 'to take from the Spaniards in America would be to dry up the Euphrates,' and reminded him of the prophesy made in Revelation 16:12. Mankind's last days on earth would begin when 'the sixth angel poured out his vial upon the great river Euphrates; and the water thereof was dried up, that the way of the kings of the east might be prepared.' Cotton's suggestion that Cromwell might be one of 'the kings of the east,' and that the Euphrates could be interpreted to mean the Caribbean was all the justification England's leader needed.

In 1653, Cromwell took the title of Lord Protector. The *Manifesto of the Lord Protector* was the work of a committee that included among its members Lord Saye's son, Nathaniel Fiennes, and Cromwell's Latin (or Foreign) Secretary, the poet and arch-Puritan John Milton. The *Manifesto* asserted that Spain's claim to exclusivity over America, whether by papal gift, discovery or even settlement, was baseless. England had both natural and treaty rights to trade in the Caribbean, and Spain's depredations against its merchants and colonies, to say nothing of their 'outrageous' treatment of the Miskitos, were justification enough for English aggression. 'We must have war, where the Spaniards will not let us have peace,' the *Manifesto* concluded.[6]

After months of planning and consulting, Cromwell and his colleagues came up with an audacious plan to hit back at the archenemy of Protestantism. The Western Design was inspired by the Spanish invasion of Providence. Cromwell had four cousins among the Providence Island Company's shareholders, and when the time came to put together a coherent programme for imperial expansion, he consulted them closely. Several of the shareholders had died in the war years – John Pym and Lord Brooke in 1643, and Sir Thomas Barrington the following year. But the Earl of Warwick was Lord Admiral of the Navy and Governor-in-Chief of the Colonies, and William Jessop was effectively Secretary to the Admiralty, and they were instrumental in shaping the Design.

Among the plan's other designers was another man determined to avenge the Spaniards' capture of Providence: Thomas Gage, whose book *The English American, or A New Survey of the West Indies*, had been published to great acclaim in 1648. A lively account of the author's travels in Central America and the Caribbean, it was the first such book to be written in English. No Englishman had immersed himself in Spanish colonial life as Gage had. He came from a family of Catholic priests, and as a child had been sent to French Flanders to attend a Jesuit college sponsored by the King of Spain. But he turned his back on his Jesuit upbringing, and embraced the Dominican Order, an act of defiance that earned him the contempt of his father, who disinherited him and forbade him from returning to England.

In 1625, Gage travelled to Spain, where he joined a group of fellow Dominicans who were bound for the Indies. Despite the King of Spain's ban on foreigners in the New World, he managed to hide himself in a barrel of ship's biscuit, and spent the next twelve years ministering to the natives of Guatemala. It was while there that he began to question the Catholic faith, and asked to be allowed to return to England. But his request was denied, so he began amassing the money he would need to make his escape. This he managed to do in 1637, making his way from Guatemala to Nicaragua and eventually boarding a ship bound for Cádiz. By chance, the ship was also carrying William Rous and the crew of the *Blessing*, who had been languishing in the city's dungeon since their disastrous attempt on Santa Marta the year before.

He made it back to London in time for Christmas 1637; he had been out of the country for 24 years. He was welcomed by his family, his father being long dead, and in 1642, he converted to Protestantism.

Thomas Gage went on to become an especially zealous Puritan, whose exposure of recusant Catholics went some way towards assuaging the doubts of his fellow ministers. He was granted a living near Deal, and settled down to write an account of his extraordinary adventures. *The English American* confirmed everything the English had heard of the 'Black Legend' of Spanish cruelty. He described the oppressive *encomienda* under which the native peoples of the Americas were forced to work, and echoed William Jackson's condemnation of the decadent state the Catholic Church had fallen into. But he also drew his readers' attention to the fabulous mineral wealth of the Spanish Empire, and the wonderful opportunity to ransack it that had been lost with the fall of Providence. 'Though but little, [Providence] might have been of a great, nay greater advantage to our kingdom than any other of our plantations in America,' he wrote.[7] It was a wrong that many of his readers were determined to put right.

Another key contributor to the Western Design was the Barbados planter Thomas Modyford. Barbados had been settled just two years before Providence, but it was burdened with none of the scruples attending the Puritan colony. The island's planters were a notoriously hardnosed bunch; the shipping agent Peter Hay complained that they were 'so unfaithful that I can have no payment of them but by violence.' They attracted indentured servants from England with promises of the new El Dorado, and then drove them into the bush to clear ground for tobacco fields. But the island's soil did not yield a good crop; after trying some Barbadian tobacco, John Winthrop called it 'foul, full of stalks and evil coloured.' Barbadian tobacco was worth so little that merchant ships didn't even bother calling at the island, and by 1639, its settlers were 'wearied out with the small profits they reaped in their toilsome labours,' and desperate to leave the island for a more promising location.[8]

Later the same year, the Earl of Warwick offered to buy the island for £12,000 (just over £1 million in today's money), thinking it might be a good place to try his hand at growing sugar cane. The deal fell through, but the turn to sugar was made the following decade under Philip Bell, the former governor of Providence, who ran Barbados for the best part of the Civil War years. Bell invited Dutch experts to the island to impart what they had learned about growing sugar in Brazil, and by a process of trial and error, the island's farmers learned how to produce high quality, refined white sugar.[9]

Until then, they had struggled to replicate the workings of a typical English village, with white servants labouring in the fields, but the Dutch told them that better results could be had by using African slaves. The first sugar crop was shipped in 1643, and with the money made from sales in England, they were able to invest in the plantations, slaves and mills they needed to produce sugar on a large scale. Nowhere in England could investors count on such a disciplined, unpaid workforce – or such gargantuan profits. Sugar cultivation was so lucrative that Barbados was soon producing nothing else. Such was its dominance that it became an alternative currency on the island: a pair of shoes could be had for 30 lbs of sugar and a good horse for 3,000 lbs.

In putting together his Western Design, Oliver Cromwell also sought the advice of his merchant friends in the City of London. During the Civil War years, England's merchants and financiers had looked on with jealous impotence as their Dutch rivals reaped huge profits from their trade with the Caribbean. With the victory of Parliament and the return of more stable trading conditions, they put pressure on Cromwell to take measures against the Dutch. The result was the Navigation Act of 1651, whose chief architect was the Providence Island Company's former agent in the City, Maurice Thompson.

The Navigation Act marked a turn towards mercantilism, the economic theory that would guide England's colonial policy for the next 150 years. Mercantilists believed that for any colony to thrive, it needed at least one of three things: a precious metal, a cheap supply of labour, and a staple crop or commodity to sell at home. They insisted that England's colonies existed for the benefit of the mother country, and as such, should not be allowed to trade with her commercial rivals. It was hardly free trade, and it was bitterly resented in the colonies, but mercantilism gave English manufacturers a firm footing on which to build an export trade.

The Western Design was the first, fantastically ambitious attempt by an English government to devise a strategy for world domination. While it signalled another attempt by bombastic Puritans to return to the glory days of Queen Elizabeth, it was much more than an exercise in nostalgia. The Design was the first step in the transformation of the colonial model, away from the self-sufficient English farm idealised by Puritans like Lord Saye, and towards the slave-driven rural factories favoured by planters like Thomas Modyford. Yet Cromwell's motives were ultimately religious: if the Spanish could be dislodged, and the mercantilist model rolled out across the Caribbean, the true religion would be safe from its enemies forever.

The expedition charged with realising the Western Design was headed by General Robert Venables, a veteran of the Parliamentary army who had spent the past five years fighting in Ireland, and Vice Admiral William Penn.[i] Although Penn was able to recruit well-trained sailors and his ships were in good shape, the recruitment of the expedition's land forces was a cack-handed affair. All the regiments of England were instructed to send volunteers, and this gave the officers of the New Model Army an opportunity to rid themselves of their worst soldiers. When numbers rose no higher than 2,500, press gangs marched through the streets of English towns 'by beat of drum,' collaring 'common cheats, thieves, cutpurses and suchlike lewd persons.'[10]

It was not an auspicious beginning, but on Christmas Day 1654, 18 warships, 20 transport vessels and 3,000 soldiers and sailors left Portsmouth for the Caribbean. Following their arrival in Barbados, the drum went out again on the streets of Bridgetown, offering freedom to any indentured servant who volunteered for the campaign to break the Spanish hold on the New World. Among those to sign up were many of the 150 men who had fled Providence after the Spanish invasion of 1641, including Samuel Axe and Andrew Carter, who was back in the Caribbean after his spell in a dungeon in Cádiz.

Lewis Morris, the Providence veteran who had rampaged around the Caribbean with William Jackson in 1642, was made colonel of 'the Barbado Regiment.' He managed to recruit 3,500 men, but General Venables was not impressed by them, calling them 'the most profane, debauched persons that we ever saw, and so cowardly as not to be made to fight.' Finding able-bodied recruits on Barbados was far from easy; the island might have been England's wealthiest colony, but it was also its most drunken. One of the products of sugar refining is rum, and on an island chronically short of fresh water, the 'hot, hellish and terrible liquor' was cheap and plentiful.[11] The combination of ambitious plant-

---

[i] His son was the Quaker who went on to found Pennsylvania.

ers freed from the strictures of home, servants impatient to improve their lot and Irish prisoners of war was a heady mix. Drunkenness was so rife on Barbados that men were often seen lying comatose at the side of the road, where they were bitten and sometimes even eaten by land crabs.

Prior to the fleet's departure, Cromwell had told Venables and Penn that he would not 'tie you up to a method of any particular instructions.'[12] He had complete faith in his Western Design, if only because 'providence seemed to lead us hither.' Free to strike where they liked, Thomas Gage, who was returning to the Caribbean as the soldiers' chaplain, advocated a wholesale attack on Central America. With its long coastlines and weak defences, the Spanish dominions were there for the taking, and he was confident that the entire region could be secured within two years.

But Venables and Penn ignored Gage's advice, and opted instead to attack Santo Domingo, the capital of Hispaniola, which was conveniently situated to leeward of Barbados. The commander of the expedition's land forces was Major-General Robert Sedgwick, a New Englander who had sailed in the *Mayflower*. He decided to copy the tactics used by Sir Francis Drake when he had attacked the city almost seventy years before. But the assault was a fiasco. From their camp on the outskirts of the city, Venables had his men march as far as the city walls, but contrary to Gage's confident prediction, the local Indians chose to fight alongside their Spanish masters, and their stout resistance prompted a wholesale retreat.

Back at camp, the English soldiers found that the supply ships had yet to arrive; with no tents to protect them from the torrential downpours, their leather breeches rotted on their bodies, and their gunpowder turned to a sodden cake. Knowing little of basic hygiene, they soon came down with typhoid, malaria and yellow fever. The ships' surgeons blamed the vapours of the night air and bled them but this only drained what little strength they had left. Those who didn't die from disease succumbed to heatstroke brought on by wearing too many clothes, or dysentery from eating rotten rations and putrid meat. By the time the 8,000-strong English force left Hispaniola, 2,000 of them were dead. Among the victims was Thomas Gage, who contracted malaria on Hispaniola and died the following year.

In the aftermath of the botched attack on Santo Domingo, Venables and Penn fell upon one another in a bout of mutual recrimination. If they were to avoid disgrace in London, they would have to secure an easy but suitably spectacular success elsewhere. Lewis Morris reminded them of Captain Jackson's rout of Spanish Town in 1642, and the decision was hastily made to attack Jamaica. The Blue Mountains came into view early on 8 May 1655, and by the end of the following day, the island was in English hands.

The Western Design had struck a victory of sorts. It was one that no one had foreseen, and it would have profound implications for the future of England's nascent empire. Two weeks later, William Penn and two thirds of the fleet sailed for home, leaving Robert Venables on Jamaica to recover from a bout of dysentery. As soon as he was able, he followed Penn back to England, supposedly at the request of his men, who asked that he inform the Lord Protector of the atrocious conditions they were living in.

On their return, Cromwell charged both men with deserting their posts, relieved them of their commands, and imprisoned them, if only briefly, in the Tower of London. The capture of Jamaica was small recompense for the failure to take Santo Domingo. News of their failure to break the Spaniards' hold on the Caribbean was quick to spread through Puritan circles. God had laid England 'low in the dust' – but why? Cromwell repeatedly called for days of fasting and humiliation in the hope of an answer, but none came. The army that he had assembled to take Hispaniola had not been a godly one, he told himself. Opportunistic servants eager to escape their indentures made poor substitutes for the devout yeomen who had supplied the backbone of the New Model Army.

'God is angry,' said Robert Sedgwick, the commander of the expedition's land forces. 'What God will do with this Design I know not. I was willing some time to believe God was in it, but He yet seems to disown us.' Unlike its authors, Sedgwick saw a fundamental flaw in the Western Design. 'It is not honourable that Your Highness's fleet should follow this old trade of West India cruisers and privateers, to ruin and plunder poor towns and so leave them,' he told Cromwell.[13] Providence's Old Councillors had long railed against the reckless folly that brought the curtain down on their colony, but this was the first time a senior Puritan had acknowledged that pillage and plunder were no way to finance the building of a godly community. With the failure of the Western Design, the bridge between the Elizabethan ideal of a foreign policy directed

165

by devout Protestants and the more pragmatic, commercially-minded policy espoused by merchants in the City of London was broken. Oliver Cromwell was left to wonder at the wreck of his venture, and appealed to his advisors to tell him 'what they thought the mind of God was.'[14]

As the first reports came back from Jamaica, he began to get an inkling of His intentions. The island had all the blessings of Providence in abundance. It was perfectly situated to harry the sea traffic passing along the Yucatan Channel and the Windward Passage, two of the Caribbean's principal sea lanes, which the Spanish galleons used as they made their way from Cartagena to Havana. It also had a magnificent natural harbour, almost entirely enclosed from the sea, and of a size sufficient to shelter the entire English fleet. Buoyed by a conquest he had neither ordered nor foreseen, the Lord Protector sent Robert Sedgwick back to Jamaica with 800 soldiers from the New Model Army.

Their delight in the island's potential was irrepressible. Jamaica was extraordinarily fertile, and being 25 times the size of Barbados, it offered endless opportunities for Englishmen with the ambition, capital and slaves needed to clear the bush for sugar plantations.[15] Sedgwick found just 1,500 Spaniards living on the island, and an equal number of slaves. They had cleared little of the bush, and when he headed inland, the only signs of their presence were the pigs and cattle they had abandoned to roam wild in the hills. To a convinced Puritan like Sedgwick, such neglect of God's bounty was testament to the decadence and sloth that had overcome the Spanish imperialists since their conquest of the New World.

The infant colony on Jamaica became 'the Lord Protector's darling.' For the first time, an English colony would be settled not by lone entrepreneurs or private companies, but by the government. But the capture of Jamaica could only ever be partial recompense for the loss of Providence. 'It is much designed amongst us to strive with the Spaniards for the mastery of all those seas, and therefore we could heartily wish that the island of Providence were in our hands again,' Cromwell wrote in a letter to Jamaica's first governor. 'It lies so advantageously in reference to the Main, and especially for the hindrance of the Peru trade and Cartagena, that you might not only have great advantage thereby of intelligence and surprise, but even block up the same.'[16] The Western Design had struck its first victory, but the Lord Protector would not sleep easy until Providence was in English hands again.

166

Jamaica's Spanish settlers were taken to Cartagena, where they spread the news of Cromwell's capture of the island, and his plan to retake Providence. The city's colonial officials might have considered such an outcome a blessing; keeping a garrison on Santa Catalina was costing them 20,000 pesos (£960,000) a year, but without significant investment in its fortifications, it was practically indefensible. Yet Madrid was determined to hold on to it, and the loss of Jamaica only brought into stark relief the need to repair its fortifications. Muskets, powder and arquebuses were dispatched on the next ship. In a letter to King Philip IV, Gerónimo de Ojeda admitted that he and his men awaited the heretics' arrival 'with infinite concern.'[17] Over the course of 1657, they saw English vessels reconnoitring the island on three occasions, but the enemy stayed several leagues offshore, and by the following year, they had returned to their melancholy slumber.

Two years later, Fernando de la Riva Agüero, Captain-General of the Spanish Main in Panama, wrote to His Majesty to remind him of the neglected garrison on Santa Catalina, and 'the travail that soldiers in that solitude have so long suffered.' Were it not for Governor Ojeda, their plight would have been considerably worse. 'I have heard for many years that only his good nature, care and tenderness have conserved the garrison in peace and happiness,' Riva Agüero wrote. Perhaps some new recruits might be sent to relieve the soldiers? He also suggested dispatching 400 slaves to clear land for plantations capable of yielding crops on a large scale, and 50 'women who have been leading scandalous lives in Cartagena and Panama.'[18]

Any surprise Gerónimo de Ojeda might have felt at Riva Agüero's sudden interest in his island was tempered by his advancing age. The island's governor was by then in his fiftieth year of service to his king. The soldiers in the garrison had been with him since driving the English out in 1641, and they had grown old together. Despite their country's independence from Spain and the repeated requests to be repatriated that they had made as young men, even the Portuguese soldiers had become resigned to island life. The garrison was past caring what the colonial authorities had planned for them.

Notwithstanding Riva Agüero's late show of concern, no new recruits, slaves or licentious women were ever sent to Santa Catalina. Ojeda's repeated request for a promotion did eventually meet with a positive response, however: he was appointed governor of the Andean city of Popayán, one of the wealthiest cities in Nueva Granada, and a fitting setting in which to see out the closing years of his long career. But the governor didn't get to read the letter informing him of his new posting; he died – the records don't say how or why – shortly before the ship carrying that year's post reached the island.

In capturing Jamaica the Western Design had struck its first victory, but the Puritan revolution that inspired it had run its course. In April 1653, Oliver Cromwell moved against the Commonwealth he presided over, denounced the MPs sitting in Parliament as drunkards and whoremasters, and dissolved the assembly. In its place, he and the Army's Council of Officers ordained the Nominated, or Barebone's Parliament, named after one of its most devoutly Puritan members, Praise-god Barebone. Like the assembly in Massachusetts, nominations to the new parliament were confined to the godly. 'God hath called you to this work by, I think, as wonderful providences as ever passed upon the sons of men in so short a time,' the Lord Protector told the assembled MPs.[19]

Barebone's Parliament was supposed to usher in the rule of the Saints, but its members' radicalism, distinct lack of political experience, and the bitter infighting into which they fell earned them widespread ridicule. One pamphleteer branded them 'pettifoggers, innkeepers, millwrights, stockingmongers and such a rabble as never had hopes to be of a Grand Jury.' Another journalist reported Cromwell as saying that he was 'more troubled now with the fool than before now with the knave.'[20] When it became clear that the new parliament was only hampering his campaign to unify their divided country, the Lord Protector decided to govern without Parliament altogether, advised only by his Council of State.

The same frustration was evident in his treatment of the army that had brought him victory. Puritanism's innate hostility to authority was all very well when the highest authority was the king; now that England's champion of radical nonconformity was in power, his brethren's argumentativeness became insufferable to him. The Lord Protector had the New Model Army's godliest officers removed, to the dismay of the many ordinary people who had pinned their hopes on him as a champion of what had come to be known as 'the Good Old Cause.' The Puritan Lucy Hutchinson lamented that in the wake of the purge, 'many of the religious soldiers went off, and in their room abundance of the king's dissolute soldiers were entertained.'[21]

It would be unfair to accuse Oliver Cromwell of becoming as tyrannical as the king he had deposed; Puritan MPs guided only by providence were in no position to put the radical changes they demanded into effect, let alone bring peace to a country weary of war, and their incompetence compelled him to take matters into his own hands. But Cromwell was undoubtedly better suited to the soldier's life than he was to the statesman's. Bereft of new ideas and apparently deserted by providence, the Lord Protector cut an increasingly forlorn figure. He made a heartfelt attempt to reconcile royalists and parliamentarians, and was feted by the City of London for his efforts. But on the day he rode in state through its streets, the crowds watched him pass in silence.

Cromwell died on 3 September 1658, the anniversary of his victories at Dunbar and Worcester, probably of malaria contracted in the fens of East Anglia. His son, Richard Cromwell, made an attempt at maintaining the Protectorate, but even his father's most steadfast allies had little faith in him, and he resigned his post nine months after coming to power. It fell to the leader of the New Model Army, George Monck, Duke of Albemarle, to open negotiations with the late king's son, who was living in exile in France. Cromwell had often discussed the idea of restoring the monarchy, believing it to be the only guarantor of property and the social order. But he had dismissed out of hand a proposal to crown Charles Stuart, saying, 'He is so damnably debauched, he would undo us all. Give him a shoulder of mutton and a whore, that's all he cares for.'[22]

That the heir to the throne was a libertine, a cynic in political matters, and insincere in his defence of the true religion mattered little to a population that had grown tired of Puritan austerity. Following his triumphant return to London, Charles Stuart was crowned Charles II. The diarist John Evelyn was in the Strand on 29 May 1660 to watch the royal procession make its way to Whitehall, and joined the crowds in rejoicing at 'the ways strewn with flowers, the bells ringing, the streets hung with tapestry [and] fountains running with wine... and all this without one drop of blood and by that very army which rebelled against him.'[23]

'Old, silent George Monck' went on to become the young king's most trusted advisor. The Duke of Albemarle was a thoroughly unprincipled operator; he had switched his allegiance from king to Parliament as soon as it became clear that the Roundheads were going to win the war, and he changed sides again when he realised that they were going to lose the peace. As he set about organising a peaceful return to royal government, the structure of power in England was reconfigured from the top down. Some were pardoned, others were brought out of the woodwork, and more than a few were sent scrambling for refuge in the colonies.

The Earl of Warwick had also died in 1658, and the surviving members of the Providence Island Company were now old men. Lord Saye had broken with Cromwell over the execution of Charles I, and withdrew from public life thereafter. Had he been able, he might have made good on his promise to move to Providence, but since that was no longer an option, he had to be content with hiding out on the island of Lundy in the Bristol Channel. He regarded the restoration of the monarchy as the not wholly satisfactory fulfillment of 'the Good Old Cause' he had taken up arms to defend in 1642: a balanced constitution of King, Lords and Commons. Following the coronation of Charles II, he returned to London, and like many who had sided with Parliament in the war years, did his best to ingratiate himself with the young king, assuring him of his loyalty and scrabbling to find a place for himself in the new scheme of things. In recognition of his cunning, no less than his experience, Charles II made the man he called 'Old Subtlety' Lord Privy Seal. His Lordship occupied the post for just two years, and died at Broughton Castle in 1662.

With the restoration of king and court, the refinement and exclusivity the aristocracy had enjoyed before the war returned with renewed vigour. The House of Lords renewed its long alliance with the monarch, while the Puritans' austere morality was confined to the Commons, which has been making a virtue of argumentativeness ever since. Puritans had varied attitudes to their new king. The Bible taught that, like Jesus Christ, even the mightiest prince had been 'born on a dung hill.' God's law should always take precedence over laws passed by Parliament, which they had always regarded as an assembly of 'silly worms.' But most Puritans were not political radicals; Charles II might have been a worm, but he was still a royal worm, with a divine right to rule over his subjects.

Such theological debates were no longer heard in Parliament, for

Charles II insisted that all but the most accommodating Puritans be removed from office. But their legacy is hard to overstate. The English owe three centuries of constitutional government to the belligerence of the Puritans in Parliament. Rebellion and intransigence were intrinsic parts of the Puritan creed, and their challenge to the King's late father was a powerful spur to democracy. Their conviction that anyone, even a child, was capable of appreciating and following the word of God was revolutionary. They expected every Englishman and woman to be able to read the Bible, and to enter into a personal pact with God. It was a painful process (the English tendency to self-criticise may well be another aspect of the Puritan legacy), but it raised a man's self-esteem, at least when he compared himself to the blinkered souls around him. Far from teaching passive resignation to the will of God, Puritanism taught courage, and the possibility that mind could win out over matter. In the eyes of God, a man might be no more than a 'clod of dust,' but he was more than the equal of his neighbour, and his social standing became less important the closer he grew to God.

The belief that God would provide for his people was not particular to the Puritans; nor was the idea that when He didn't, it was because He was punishing them for their sinfulness. But there was certainly something inherently masochistic in the Puritan psyche. Their belief that God smites those He loves best betrays a fatal combination of self-regard, self-pity and a strangely perverse pride, that may explain the English love of moaning. There is also something sadistic in the culture of discipline that the Puritans championed; certainly, the distinction they made between the deserving and the undeserving poor can still be heard today in talk of 'strivers' and 'skivers.' Seventeenth-century strivers heard God's call and knew that 'without running, fighting, sweating and wrestling, heaven is not taken.'[24] Skivers, or as the English Puritan theologian William Perkins put it, 'such as live in no calling, but spend their time in eating, drinking and sleeping and sporting,' were rebelling against God.

But the Puritan legacy is broader and subtler than the stereotypical repressed and repressive New Englander suggests. In repudiating the collectivism of Catholic ritual, Puritan ministers made individuals of their followers, and that individualism was the making of many of the entrepreneurs and merchants who would grow rich under Charles II.

The Puritan revolution also had a significant impact on the world of finance. Christians had long believed that a man's investments should not exceed the capital he had at his disposal, and that borrowing and lending money at interest were equally wrong. As a consequence, the Providence Island Company's ambition had been curtailed by the difficulties it faced in borrowing money. Before the development of the mortgage in the 1630s, the only way of securing capital for serious investment was through savings. Lord Saye did not resort to a mortgage until 1638, by which time he was practically broke. His campaign to legalise money lending and the charging of interest saw him branded as 'the White Jew of the Upper House,' but following the Restoration, both were recognised by an Act of Parliament. This was a crucial development, both in the history of money and the imperial project that Lord Saye did so much to advance, and it came at a crucial stage in England's journey to becoming a modern country.

At first sight, the Providence Island Company shareholders' cack-handed attempts at raising pomegranates and olives, ardent study of the Bible's teachings on government, and general indifference to whatever was new about the New World make them unlikely heralds of the modern age. But in casting out the superstition and magic they believed to be latent in the Catholic faith, in favour of a rational approach to understanding God's purpose for man on earth, Puritan thinkers trained the minds of ambitious men to wrestle with thorny questions. 'God sees not as man sees,' said one Puritan minister, 'and yet he that will judge uprightly ought to see as God sees, and not as man.'[25] Although the English gradually stopped looking skywards for guidance after the Restoration, the conviction that God had created an orderly, rational world only grew stronger as England's scientists found favour under the new king.

The English love of science was also shaped by the first colonists' experiences in the Americas. In addition to gold chains, parrots' feathers and smokers' coughs, Providence's Puritans returned to England with a newfound sense of the size and variety of the world. It was a mind-expanding experience, and one that allowed them to shake off the trappings of the medieval world. As a young man, Lord Saye had been one of the first English nobles to visit the ruins of ancient Greece and Rome. By the time he died, the Grand Tour had become a rite of passage; as educated Englishmen reassessed the lessons of antiquity, they learned to think for themselves, both at home and in the colonies.

Puritanism had a lasting impact on how the English regarded their country, and themselves. Until the Puritan revolution, books had been weighty affairs that remained cloistered in wealthy men's libraries. The the welter of bills, broadsides, newspapers and pamphlets hawked in the streets of London in the war years were testament to the rising self-esteem, as well as the rising literacy of the English people. Neither Charles II nor his successors would ever attempt to govern without consulting the people's representatives in Parliament. But just as importantly, England's property owners were forced to respect the millions of English men and women who had yet to be represented by the honourable members.

The Puritan revolution and the Civil War it gave rise to have been largely forgotten. To the contemporary ear, its theological disputes sound arcane, and the advances it secured are taken for granted. But Puritanism remains crucial to any understanding of the United Kingdom's rise to world dominance. The Puritan Revolution was the first modern revolution, in that it was driven by ideological conviction, and this had a profound effect on how the English saw themselves and their place in the world. Until the 1620s, when a man spoke of his 'country,' he usually meant the county in which he had been born. But England's self-appointed role as defender of 'the true religion' gave it a distinct national identity. While Puritanism was fervently anti-Catholic and anti-Spanish, it was never parochial. It might have been born in the pulpits of England's village churches, but as personified in Oliver Cromwell, it had far-reaching consequences for the balance of power in Europe, and the vast empire that Britain would build over the course of the following 200 years.

The Empire was built on a policy of aggressive, state-backed mercantilism and colony building, first promoted as part of Cromwell's Western Design. Although the Western Design was interpreted as a failure at the time, Cromwell's decision to prioritise English sea power resulted in a string of successes closer to home. Admiral Robert Blake in the Mediterranean and Vice-Admiral William Goodson in the Baltic made the seas safe for English merchant shipping, and paved the way for the establishment of English naval bases at Tunis and Gibraltar. The Navy also managed to subdue the pirates of Dunkirk and Algiers, a feat that no other European power had been able to accomplish. By the time Cromwell died, England was Europe's pre-eminent maritime power, and the way was clear for Charles II to capitalise on the capture of Jamaica, a colony that would make Englishmen rich like no other.

The historian Christopher Hill describes how Cromwell marks the transition from the divine right of kings to the divine right of the nation.

He also suggests that the archetypal eighteenth-century Englishman, John Bull, was basically 'Oliver Cromwell minus ideology.'[26] It is not a flattering comparison, but at least Cromwell was happy to be portrayed 'warts and all.' Unfortunately, the same cannot be said for the empire builders who would take John Bull as a role model in the years to come.

13

THE RISE OF PORT ROYAL AND THE RECAPTURE OF PROVIDENCE

The end of England's Puritan Commonwealth also marked the end of the idealistic phase in English empire building. Despite the Lord Protector's best efforts, Jamaica failed to attract Puritan settlers from New England, and the seven nonconformist ministers that he sent to the island soon died of disease. With the Restoration of the monarchy, the colonies swore allegiance to the new king, and the Caribbean lost its religious purpose for the English.

Oliver Cromwell might have been the architect of the Western Design, but the man who turned the blueprint's vaunting ambition into the prosaic reality of slave ships and sugar plantations was one of its less devout exponents, Colonel Thomas Modyford. Born the first of five sons of a former mayor of Exeter, Modyford was a barrister by training, but became commander of a royalist regiment during the Civil War. Smarting from a series of defeats, and finding little to like in the grim austerity of Puritan England, he decided to seek his fortune in Barbados. In 1648, he spent £7,000 on a 500-acre estate; its previous owner had bought it for just £200, but that was in the days before sugar cane was planted on the island. Still, it was a canny investment, for Barbadians were making annual returns of 50 per cent on their plantations, and he soon became rich.

Despite the part Modyford had played in Charles I's army, when the King was executed in 1649 he switched his allegiance to the Parliamentarians, claiming that he had always 'utterly abhorred and abjured the interest of the Stuarts.' By the time of the Restoration, he had risen to become Speaker of the Barbados Assembly. Such an ambitious, unscrupulous operator was always at risk of falling foul of political developments in England, but Modyford was an opportunist of the highest order, and was quick to swear loyalty to Charles II. His switch failed

175

to win over the new king, however, who had him arrested and charged with high treason, and he was only released at the intercession of George Monck, who happened to be his cousin. The Privy Council ordered that Modyford 'be not disturbed or further prosecuted for anything he had formerly acted,' and that he 'be permitted to enjoy the full benefit of His Majesty's Gracious Act of Oblivion.'[1] As the name suggests, the Act was the new king's way of letting bygones be bygones. It offered a general pardon to all those who had committed crimes during the Civil War, with the exception of those found guilty of the regicide of Charles' father, murder, piracy, buggery, rape and witchcraft.

Since George Monck also happened to be chairman of the Committee for Foreign Plantations, when the time came to appoint a new governor of Jamaica, he proposed that the job be given to his young cousin. The island offered unlimited opportunities to the ambitious, and the Speaker of the Barbados Assembly was well placed to act as its recruiting sergeant. Modyford rounded up a gaggle of footloose servants and impoverished freemen, who were soon joined by Irishmen driven into exile by Cromwell's plantations in Ireland. Together, they formed a corps charged with overseeing the African slaves that were being shipped to the island in ever-greater numbers. He sailed for Jamaica in June 1664, taking 800 Barbadians with him. Lady Modyford and the 80 members of his private household followed shortly afterwards.

Thomas Modyford's policies, and the men he hired to realise them would shape Jamaica forever. George Monck was keen to maintain the aggressive intent that had inspired the Western Design, and thanks to his counsel, the new king was no less committed to empire building than Cromwell. Memories of Providence were uppermost in the minds of the Committee for Foreign Plantations' members, and they kept English plans for the colonisation of Central America alive. In March 1666, Modyford remarked that the Miskito coast and the River San Juan remained 'the properest and most probable places to lay a foundation for the conquest of the whole of Central America, if ever the reason of state at home require any attempt.'[2]

For the time being, however, reasons of state kept his attention focused on Jamaica. There were still pockets of resistant Spanish settlers and runaway slaves in the island's mountainous interior, and although Admiral Robert Blake had destroyed the Spanish fleet at Santa Cruz in the Canary Islands in 1657, the Spanish had already made two attempts to retake the island, both of which were repulsed.

Charles II had reasons of his own to adopt a belligerent stance. In 1656, he had sent Lord Arlington to Madrid to seek Philip IV's help in recovering the throne. He had offered to return Jamaica, and even to deny his merchants access to Spain's colonies, but Philip had stood aloof, and his indifference earned him the new king's lasting resentment.

Once the Crown was firmly sitting on his head, Charles demanded 'good correspondence and free commerce with the plantations and territories belonging to the King of Spain or his subjects in the West Indies.'[3] This went down well in Port Royal, which had supplanted Spanish Town as Jamaica's capital, in recognition of the importance of trade. Until land was cleared for sugar plantations, the island's prosperity would depend on its role as an entrepôt for English canvas, rope, cloth and iron, all of which were in strong demand in the towns and villages of the Spanish Main.

But free trade was a concept alien to Philip IV. Despite his country's inability to supply basic goods to its colonies, and the exorbitant prices its merchants charged for what little they did, traders on the Spanish Main were forbidden to trade with foreigners. The Spanish monopoly on trade with its colonies created economic stagnation at home, and made it even more dependent on American silver and gold. It also gave rise to corruption, inefficiency and smuggling on a vast scale in the Caribbean.

The chief beneficiaries of the trade in contraband goods were the myriad small workshops that sprang up in England in the years after the Restoration, and by extension, Charles' tax collectors. In 1662, the Committee for Foreign Plantations had told Modyford's predecessor that, 'If the governors of the King of Spain shall refuse to admit our subjects to trade, you shall in such case endeavour to procure and settle a trade with his subjects in those parts by force.'[4]

Since Philip had no intention of granting the English the right to trade with his colonies, and Jamaica's position 'within his bowels and in the heart of his trade,' was always likely to provoke another attempt to recapture the island, Modyford made defence his top priority.[5] Without it, the planters could have no confidence in the long-term future of the colony, and would not invest in the sugar plantations and mills the island needed to thrive.

The Royal Navy might have been dominant in European waters, but it was not yet able to offer Jamaica permanent protection, so he was dependent on English merchant ships to defend the island from attack. Fear of a surprise Spanish attack would bind Jamaica's governor to its privateers for the next 20 years, and Modyford made no attempt to disguise his ties to these private armies. Instead, he assumed the right to grant privateering commissions to the captain of any merchant ship willing to combine legal trade with 'the subduing of all our enemies by sea or land within and upon the coasts of America.'[6] A letter of marque from the governor of Jamaica was indispensible for any captain hoping to plunder Spanish ships and settlements; without it, he was little better than a pirate. This was no concession to the Spanish; rather, it was a guarantee that Modyford – and King Charles – would get a cut of whatever booty was landed in Port Royal.

The martial spirit was good for England's colonies. Stolen Spanish goods brought New England merchants to Port Royal, and their cargos of fish, corn and hides were welcomed by Jamaicans. Yet when Thomas Modyford arrived to take up the post of governor in 1664, he was carrying orders to cease all attacks on Spanish shipping. For the time being at least, Charles was keen to placate the Spanish. This left Port Royal's sea captains high and dry. Takings from privateering shrank to a pittance, and many sailors were left practically destitute. With no reason to stay in Port Royal, most privateers left for the ramshackle buccaneer settlements on the island of Tortuga, which had been ungoverned since the days when it was known as Association Island. The 'lawless motions' of the privateers were always of great concern to Thomas Modyford, for as he watched them leave, he knew that it would only be a matter of time before they turned pirate and started attacking the English ships that supplied Jamaica. He also knew that without them, the island was virtually defenceless. The governor of Jamaica considered the king's order to rein in the privateers 'the saddest error of all governments in this most active age.'

Fortunately for Modyford and his privateering friends, a war for international commercial supremacy broke out between England and Holland in 1665. To induce the island's only defenders to return to Port Royal, he began issuing letters of marque, authorising them to attack Dutch ships. Sailors from Jamaica were soon waging an aggressive privateering campaign against the Dutch, but Modyford continued to commission attacks on Spanish interests too, reasoning that, 'it must be force alone that can cut in sunder that un-neighbourly maxim [of the Spanish government] to deny all access of strangers.'[7] Later that year, he 'caused a war against the Spaniards to be solemnly proclaimed by beat of drum and proclamation at Port Royal,' and privateers returned in droves, their appetites whetted by the prospect of renewed attacks on Spanish ships and settlements.[8]

In declaring war on Spain's colonies, Modyford was defying the Committee for Foreign Plantations, but both parties recognised the tightrope he was being asked to walk. King Charles didn't want to antagonise the Spanish any more than he had to, but he admitted that, 'It is not easy for us to prescribe rules and directions for you as our service and the benefit of that island may require.'[9] The lack of definitive instructions from London made Modyford's balancing act a little easier. In his reply to the king's letter, he expressed his hope that Charles would grant him:

> that commission which the wise Romans gave their generals, so well did they understand the rule of trusting him that was on the place, who clearly sees what cannot be imagined by much wiser men at so great a distance.[10]

In another letter to the king, this one written in August 1665, Thomas Modyford makes his first mention of Henry Morgan, the man who would do more than any other to shape Jamaica in the early years of English rule. Henry was born in 1635, and had grown up with war and soldiering. Looking back on his life in 1680, he admitted,

> The office of Judge Admiral was not given me for my understanding of the business better than others, nor for the profitableness thereof, for I left school too young to be a great proficient in that or other laws, and have been more used to the pike than the book.[11]

Henry arrived in the Caribbean at the age of 20, as a soldier in the army charged with realising the Western Design, and took part in the failed attack on Santo Domingo. Following the capture of Jamaica, George Monck nominated Henry's uncle, Colonel Edward Morgan, to become Lieutenant Governor of the new colony. The young Welshman was also fortunate in that another uncle, Thomas Morgan, had been Monck's right-hand man in his subjugation of Scotland after the Battle of Dunbar. Between them, his two uncles smoothed Henry's path to the governor's house.

In January 1665, Modyford made Henry an officer in the fleet of small ships that sailed from Port Royal under Jamaica's best-known privateers, Captain Jackman and Captain Morris. Guided by the ever-present William Blauveldt, the Dutch veteran whom Daniel Elfrith had met when he first came ashore on Providence, Jackman and Morris rounded Cape Gracias a Dios and sailed down the Miskito coast. If they were to storm a ship or town of any size, they would have to take on more men, for successful privateering was all about weight of numbers (while the typical crew of a 100-ton merchant ship was around 12, a privateer of the same size would likely carry at least 80 men). Blauveldt was their introduction to the community of 600 foreigners who lived on the coast, many at Bluefields, a community of itinerant buccaneers that had been named after the old Dutchman.[i]

Most of Bluefields' inhabitants were English or African, and many were veterans of the colony on Providence. The contrast between life in New Westminster and life on the Miskito coast could not have been starker. On Providence, they had long wrestled with the competing claims of hectoring preachers and abusive captains, and they had no interest in returning to the life of the indentured servant. Lord Saye had warned against democracy, a world in which 'every man is a master, and masters must not correct their servants.' Yet the buccaneers lived with so little government (indeed, so little subordination to any form of authority) that for a time they were indeed all masters.

The democratic spirit that prevailed on the coast owed much to the culture of their Miskito hosts. When the first settlers of North America called the natives 'faithless, lawless and kingless,' they had meant it as an insult.[12] The buccaneers would have considered it a compliment, for their indomitability was akin to a badge of honour. The humble toil and patient accumulation urged on them by Providence's Puritan ministers

---

[i] Strictly speaking, the community of foreigners living on the Miskito coast were not buccaneers, since they didn't hunt cattle, or roast beef on a 'boucan,' like their better-known brethren on Tortuga. But they were similar in most other respects.

meant nothing to them, and after 24 years of buccaneering, the routine humiliation they had suffered at the hands of their employers was a distant memory. Free to live as they liked, they fashioned dice from the teeth of the manatee, and gambled away what little they had. No longer tied by the strictures of Providence's artificial 'families', or Reverend Hope Sherrard's watchful censoriousness, they were free to drink *mishla* with the Miskito men, take their friends' sisters as wives, and raise families of their own.

Like the Miskitos, their lives were often idle, broken by spells of frenetic, sometimes violent activity. They learned to sleep in hammocks strung between poles, and preferred to hunt fish than till fields. They made what little money they needed by cutting dyewoods, which they sold to passing merchant ships from Jamaica, and running contraband to isolated Spanish settlements further down the coast. Sometimes, guided by their Miskito friends, they ventured inland to raid the Spaniards' cocoa plantations.

Like the Miskitos, they produced no cloth, pottery or basketry. But they appreciated the fruits of other men's labour: they relied on the leather and metal goods they were able to procure from the merchant ships, and whenever they came by a cargo of clothing destined for the wealthy households of Granada or Panama, they lavished attention on their costumes. To parade on the beach in stolen ruffs and silk shirts was a form of drag, as subversive as it was ridiculous (although the suggestion that they wore earrings is a figment of a Victorian writer's imagination).

In place of the indenture, which committed the servant to his master, they committed themselves to one another. They became 'the Brethren of the Coast,' a brotherhood that encompassed all buccaneers. According to James Burney, an early chronicler of piracy in the Caribbean,

> Every buccaneer had his chosen and declared comrade, between whom property was in common, and if one died, the survivor was inheritor of the whole... Bolts, locks, and every species of fastening, were prohibited, it being held that the use of such securities would have impeached the honour of their vocation.[13]

The buccaneers' sense of honour was one of the few fragments of European life they kept, for it bound them to their mother country's imperial mission, and ennobled a journey that had begun when they first joined the army of vagrants tramping the country lanes of England. Judging by James Burney's account, some of the buccaneers also kept up a keen hatred of the Spanish.

> It is related of a Frenchman, a native of Languedoc named Montbars, that on reading a history of the cruelty of the Spaniards to the Americans, he conceived such an implacable hatred against the Spaniards that he determined on going to the West Indies to join the buccaneers; and that he there pursued his vengeance with so much ardour as to acquire the surname of the Exterminator.[14]

When William Blauveldt told the Brethren of the Coast that Jackman and Morris were looking for crew to join them on a privateering cruise down the coast, there was no shortage of takers. From Bluefields, he guided the little fleet down the coast to the mouth of the River San Juan, where they transferred to their canoes and began paddling upriver. The river was wide and still, and its banks were crowded with tall, verdant rushes. On distant sandbanks, crocodiles could be seen sunning themselves to warm their cold blood amid the huge beached logs that rushed downstream in the rainy season. They heard howler monkeys roaring from distant treetops, and watched as troupes of spider monkeys swung from tree to tree on the far bank. After rowing 100 miles upriver, they came to Lake Nicaragua, a magnificent inland sea whose surface is broken by two towering volcanoes. On the far shore stood Granada, a city of wealthy merchants and storehouses stacked to the rafters with barrels of rum, gunpowder and powdered gold. Its garrison was no match for 80 heavily armed buccaneers, and the raiders soon had the run of the place.

The buccaneers' raid of Granada was the most audacious strike the English had made against the Spanish, and set a precedent for a wave of marauding on the Spanish Main. Over the next six years, buccaneers from the Miskito coast, Port Royal, Tortuga and the south coast of Cuba stormed and plundered four Spanish cities, 18 towns and 35 villages. They were led by the privateers of Port Royal – captains of merchant ships and hardened veterans of the English Civil War like Henry Morgan, who played an ever more decisive role in each raid. Thus Jamaica's need for defence bound the governor to the flotsam of England.

The rise of Jamaica as a sugar producing colony, and Port Royal as a privateering base, also revived relations between the English and the

Miskitos. Following the attack on Granada, several Miskito men sailed back to Port Royal with Jackman and Morris, some to help put down the island's first slave revolt, others to work as harpoonists on future privateering expeditions. It proved an enduring relationship, and Spain's colonial authorities would spend the next 150 years trying to eliminate 'the zambo and Miskito whip' hanging over the traders of Granada and León.[ii] Neighbouring tribes also came to dread a visit from the buccaneers for they captured their young men and sold them into slavery, and forced their young women to become their wives. The Indians around Bocas del Toro had once been keen to trade with the Brethren of the Coast, but as they melded into the fabric of Miskito life, they learned to flee at their approach.

The Brethren of the Coast's 'admiral' was Edward Mansveldt, a Dutch sea captain that the English called Mansfield. While they lauded him as a brave and noble privateer, the Spanish cursed him as the most notorious of the pirates roving the western Caribbean. Mansveldt had received his first commission from the governor of Jamaica in 1659, and his exploits earned him the gratitude of the merchants and landowners who sat in the Jamaican Assembly. In 1666, he assembled a fleet of 15 ships under his casual command, and 500 of his Brethren. Most of them were English, Dutch or French, but there were also Africans, Miskitos, Flemings, Genoese, Greeks, Levantines and Portuguese among their number. In recognition of the leading role Henry Morgan had played in the sack of Granada, Mansveldt made the young Welshman his vice admiral.

As ever, once at sea the decision-making process was far removed from the vertical hierarchy that governed life in an English colony. Although the Admiral of the Brethren and the ships' captains determined strategy, every member of the crew had a say in their goals and where they should try to realise them. Thomas Modyford had given Edward Mansveldt a commission to attack the island of Curaçao, but men accustomed to fighting the Spanish were reluctant to rob a Dutch colony and

---

ii 'Zambo' was the name given to the offspring of unions between the Africans and their Indian hosts.

the Brethren argued that there would be 'more profit with less hazard' in raiding a Spanish settlement. The democratic spirit prevailed, and Mansveldt bent to their disobedience.

His fleet sailed for the coast of modern-day Costa Rica, where the buccaneers marched inland to sack the cocoa-producing towns in the Valley of Matina. But it was not a profitable raid, and after limping back to the coast, several of the ships' captains opted to return to Bluefields. The remaining vessels regrouped at Bocas del Toro, a tiny archipelago whose mangroves had long provided shelter to itinerant buccaneers. They spent several days there, and it was while fishing and recuperating that the Admiral of the Brethren resolved to retake Providence. His first loyalty was to his fellow buccaneers, who hoped to make the island a secure and permanent base from which they could raid the Spanish Main without waiting for the governor of Jamaica's authorisation.

On 25 May 1666, five ships dropped anchor on the edge of the reef that runs down Providence's eastern flank. The Brethren lowered long-boats into the water and rowed their way along the reef, until they came to a narrow passage near to the southern tip of the island, 'where they say ship never came.' According to Thomas Modyford, Mansveldt was 'an excellent coaster,' a skill that was 'his chief, if not only, virtue.'[15] Passing through a breach in the coral, one longboat made for the beach at Southwest Bay (which the Spanish called *Playa Grande*), while the other headed for Manchineel Bay (which they called *Playa de los Naranjos*).[iiii]

While the Spanish soldiers slept in their scattered farmsteads, the Brethren used the light of the moon to familiarize themselves with what would soon be theirs. By sunrise they were well placed to stifle any alarm. The official who had been appointed to take Gerónimo de Ojeda's place as governor of Santa Catalina was Esteban de Ocampo. His garrison was 200-strong, but many of its soldiers were elderly, none had had any experience of combat since driving the English off the island 25 years before, and most of them were incapable of handling, much less firing, a musket. He awoke fully expecting to pass another day of resigned contentedness, so the sight of the Brethren of the Coast's ensign, with its leering skull over two crossed cutlasses, was the realization of his worst

---

[iiii] *Playa de los Naranjos* means Orange Tree Beach, which is a fatal misnomer since the trees lining the bay are not orange but manchineel, whose fruit is highly poisonous.

fears. He surrendered without a fight, and by eight o'clock that morning, an English flag was flying over the the ramshackle battery once known as Fort Warwick.

Reviewing the fort's munitions, Henry Morgan was surprised to see Queen Elizabeth's coat of arms on the rusting cannons – relics from the days when the English government was run by stouter hearts than those at the present King's court, they had been pressed into service to defend their Lordships' colony. For the old Providence men among the Brethren, it was something of a homecoming. To the surprise of the Spanish veterans, the invaders treated them well. They were locked in the church, but the French Catholics among the Brethren insisted that no harm should come to them. One of them even asked Ocampo's chaplain to celebrate mass, and invited the governor and his men to join them. Having given thanks – whether to God, Neptune or fate – they spent the next three days looting the island's stores. By the time they had finished, the garrison's veterans were left with nothing but the clothes they were standing in. When they protested, Mansveldt ordered that they be given a change of clothes, by way of thanks for surrendering so willingly. The Admiral of the Brethren left a small garrison on Providence, took his 180 prisoners to his ship, and sailed for Portobello to put them ashore.

Esteban de Ocampo and his Spanish, Portuguese and African veterans must have watched the island recede from view with relief, as well as some foreboding. While Philip IV had done little to fortify the island or relieve their terrible solitude, he was sure to find a scapegoat for its capture, for it allowed the English to plant a foot in the door to his Treasury.

From Portobello, Mansveldt and Morgan sailed back to Port Royal to inform Thomas Modyford that they had recovered Providence for its rightful owners. The governor rebuked 'the old man' for taking the island without a commission, but he knew that if he were to punish him, he risked jeopardizing the Brethren's allegiance to the Crown. Besides, the capture of Providence was undoubtedly a triumph, whether he had ordered it or not. In the face of a *fait accompli*, he told the Admiral that he could not 'without manifest impudence but accept the tender of [the island] on his Majesty's behalf.'[16]

The merchants of Port Royal, who did not have to feign circumspection, welcomed Mansveldt's recapture of Providence. Emboldened by their reception, the Admiral of the Brethren asked the governor's permission to recruit men for the resettlement of the island. But for reasons of his own more than reasons of state, Modyford told him to look elsewhere, so he sailed for Tortuga, where he hoped to find recruits among the French buccaneers living on the island. It was to be his last voyage: Mansveldt was captured en route by a Spanish *guardacosta* and taken to Cuba, where he was executed.

On hearing of the capture of Providence, the Spanish ambassador to the Court of St James protested to Lord Arlington in the strongest possible terms. But the Secretary of State denied all responsibility for the attack, insisting that it had not been ordered by his government or the governor of Jamaica. Having made his excuses, Arlington wrote to Modyford thanking him for his 'gift,' and the governor made hurried arrangements for the resettlement of Providence.

Among the first to heed Modyford's call for volunteers was Sir Thomas Whetstone. A nephew of Oliver Cromwell, Whetstone had won royal patronage after encouraging the officers of the Navy to switch their allegiances to the new king. That done, he financed the fitting and victualing of four vessels, and left London for the Caribbean with a group of adventurer friends, hoping to go privateering in the South Seas (the Pacific Ocean, in modern parlance). Once in Port Royal, he fell in with Edward Mansveldt, who persuaded him to join another expedition to plunder the Spaniards' cocoa plantations. Flush with the spoils of another audacious raid, Whetstone invested in land in Jamaica, and was elected to the Jamaican House of Assembly. He was eventually appointed its Speaker, though 'more by the desire of the general [Modyford] than the election of the gentlemen.'[17]

Cromwell's nephew was determined to play a leading part in resettling his uncle's cherished island. Such was Whetstone's enthusiasm for Providence, he even offered to transport reinforcements for the garrison in his own ship. Touched by his generosity, Modyford appointed him deputy governor of the island, and put at his command Major Samuel Smith, Captain Stanley Steven, and a troop of 32 soldiers. He reserved the governorship for his brother, Sir James Modyford, doubtless at the intercession of their uncle George Monck. Sir James' contribution was an important one: in 1664, King Charles had granted him a five-year license to carry reprieved felons to Jamaica. With a ready, if not willing workforce at their disposal, the Modyford brothers were well placed to realise Edward Mansveldt's plan to make Providence a private fiefdom, from which they could plunder Spanish ships, whatever the state of diplomatic relations between the two countries. Naturally, they could not admit so base a motive to anyone but themselves, and they assured anyone who asked that Providence had been taken in the name of King Charles.

Thrilled by a familiar concoction of patriotic zeal and the prospect of private gain, Modyford ordered a broad seal for the island to be etched onto a silver plate, just as the Providence Island Company had in 1630. His brother would carry it ashore when the island was deemed ready to receive him. Sir Thomas Whetstone, Major Samuel Smith, and the other members of the advance party set sail in June 1666. Whetstone was carrying letters of marque authorising him to attack Dutch or Spanish vessels 'wherever they might be found to the southward of the Tropic of Cancer.' The governor of Jamaica also granted him permission, 'if you find it prudential, to invade any of the lands, colonies or plantations in America.' The first step in the grandiose scheme to build an English empire in Central America looked set to be reprised.

Royal Field Marshal Juan Pérez de Guzmán, governor and captain general of Panama, president of the *audiencia* of *Tierra Firme* and Caballero of the Order of Santiago could barely contain his rage when he was told that Santa Catalina had fallen to the English. Although Edward Mansveldt had spared the lives of the island's 180 inhabitants – a rare act of mercy from such a bloodthirsty pirate – he had not spared them their honour, showing them 'so little esteem' that he had them 'unceremoniously thrown ashore' at Portobello.[18]

Pérez de Guzmán's rage was only heightened by the cowardice of the relevant authorities. Instead of coming to the islanders' aid, the governor of Cuba had parroted the absurd rumour that 50 ships, carrying 3,000 pirates, were about to conquer Central America and thereby divide the Spanish Caribbean in two. Pérez de Guzmán reserved particular ire for Esteban de Ocampo, who had surrendered the island without so much as a show of resistance. The governor of Santa Catalina had 'committed a serious and atrocious crime worthy of repugnance and punishment,' he wrote to his superiors in Madrid. Criminal charges were brought against Ocampo and seven of his officers, who were sent to Seville, and imprisoned in *La Casa de Contración*.

In an impassioned speech to the *junta de guerra* in Panama, Pérez de Guzmán argued, 'it was absolutely necessary to send forces unto Santa Catalina, sufficient to take it from the pirates, the honour and interest of his Majesty of Spain being very narrowly concerned herein.'[19] The retaliatory expedition should be mounted immediately, if the pirates were not to fortify the island as a base for more raids on the King's settlements. Flushed with righteous indignation, the junta voted 'as one would expect from hearts as Catholic as they were Spanish: to destroy the encroaching thieves.' Some of its members even suggested that the expedition be extended to include the retaking of Jamaica. Pérez de Guzmán convinced them that, for the time being at least, they should focus on Santa Catalina.

The Spanish government was no less outraged than the governor of Panama. It assured the *junta de guerra* of its wholehearted support, and promised to send 1,000 men to the Caribbean to join the expedition. Its only condition was that the island be recaptured before January 1667, so as not to delay the annual sailing of the treasure galleons. As ever, the king had creditors to consider, and was entirely dependent on American gold and silver to pay them.

Pérez de Guzmán put 185 troops under the immediate command of Captain José Sánchez Ximénez, the mayor of Portobello. Forty-five soldiers from the original garrison on Santa Catalina signed up for the retaliatory expedition. According to Pérez de Guzmán, the veterans had 'lion hearts,' and were 'zealous to return to reclaim their honour.'[20] What he didn't tell his superiors in Madrid was that half of them were without arms and their rations were woefully inadequate, for he had connived with a local magistrate to defraud the paymaster of the funds the Crown had allocated to the expedition.

Captain Sánchez Ximénez's fleet sailed from Portobello on 1 August 1666. Once at sea, a rumour swirled below-decks that the pirate army on Santa Catalina had swollen, and was now 1,000-strong. As if portending trouble to come, they hit a storm, which battered their ships and made them miserably seasick. It was 10 days before the fleet caught sight of Santa Catalina, and it took the ships another two days to beat their way through the high seas to the island's harbour.

On coming ashore, Captain Sánchez Ximénez could see no sign of the pirates, so he sent an advance party to reconnoiter the abandoned shell of New Westminster. The pirates had retreated to the fort, so he sent a scout with a letter informing the usurpers of his instructions to retake Santa Catalina. Major Samuel Smith replied that 'the island had once belonged unto the government and dominions of the King of England, and that instead of surrendering it, they preferred to lose their lives.'

Sánchez Ximénez retired to his flagship, and was considering the best course of action to take when three Africans approached in a canoe. Contrary to appearances, they told him, Fort Warwick was occupied not by a 1,000-strong pirate army, but a small contingent of ordinary soldiers. The following morning, Sánchez Ximénez laid siege to the fort and settled in for a long wait. Two days later, he was puzzled to hear what sounded like cannon balls ricocheting off the rocks behind their redoubt. Being without ammunition, the English had resorted to cutting down the organ pipes from the abandoned church before their retreat to the fort. They had sawn them into short lengths, and were now using them as missiles, 'discharging in every shot three score pipes at a time.'[21] Sánchez Ximénez sent word that unless Major Smith surrendered immediately and unconditionally he would put them all to the sword. After consulting Sir Thomas Whetstone, Smith accepted the terms of surrender at midnight on 17 August 1666. Providence had been in English hands for just 81 days.

Sánchez Ximénez had his prisoners clapped in irons, and began interrogating them. Among the incriminating documents his men found were blank letters of marque and Thomas Modyford's instructions for the formation of a government. They also recovered his order to send all Spanish prisoners to Port Royal, 'so that they might be treated in the same manner that English captives had been treated by the enemy.' What did this mean? the Spanish captain demanded to know. The governor of Jamaica clearly intended to retain the island whether it was taken in peacetime or not. Sánchez Ximénez also discovered that among his prisoners was Sir Thomas Whetstone, 'whose other name was Cromwell.' Hearing the name of the late Lord Protector, he had his prisoners bound and chained in the hull of one of his ships, and told its captain to take them to Governor Pérez de Guzmán in Panama.

When news of the fall of the pirates' lair reached the streets of Panama, 'the city blazed like midday at nine that night.' The city's bishop sang 'Te Deum' and a procession of Jesuits circled the cathedral repeatedly, giving solemn thanks to God for delivering Santa Catalina from the heretics for a second time. Sánchez Ximénez had agreed to treat his prisoners according to the articles of good quarter, but Pérez de Guzmán had no time for such niceties. The 32 English soldiers were put to work building Portobello's *Castillo de San Geronimo*. Even their guards admitted that each of them was expected to do the work of three slaves, despite being perpetually weak from hunger and lack of sleep. However, the officers among them were not expected to perform manual labour. Instead, Pérez de Guzmán ordered that Sir Thomas Whetstone, Major Samuel Smith and Captain Stanley Steven be chained to the floor of their ten foot by twelve foot dungeon 'forever.' At the end of each day, they were joined by the 32 emaciated soldiers, who fell into a cramped and fitful slumber while Franciscan friars abused them, their king and their religion.

Such was the fate that awaited any Protestant found 'beyond the line.' The only way out was to pay a bribe, or 'turn Papist.' Many Englishmen considered the latter a fate worse than death, but others converted to Catholicism, and in sufficient numbers for foreign converts to become a novelty on the Spanish Main. Most became servants to local worthies, but a few became street attractions. One English privateer, who the Spanish had captured and forcibly baptized in the cathedral of Mexico City, was put on display in one of the city's marketplaces. His keeper kept him covered in oil, and offered a swab of cotton to passersby. A swab taken from the head of a converted heretic was considered a blessing, and fetched a good price from penitential Catholics seeking forgiveness for their sins.[22]

Despite clear evidence of the Modyford brothers' plan to re-settle Santa Catalina, Captain Sánchez Ximénez was no more able to defend the island than his disgraced predecessor. He appealed to the *junta de guerra*, whose secretary assured him that work was underway on the construction of an *armada de barlovento* (Windward Fleet). Until it was complete, the new governor would have to make do with the 450 men under his command. A third of them were Africans or black creoles; some slaves, others free men. Another third were soldiers, among them several veterans from the days of Gerónimo de Ojeda, and the rest were common criminals. According to Alexander Esquemelin, whose *History of the Buccaneers of America* would do so much to romanticise the lives of the privateers in the century to come, the Spanish authorities used Santa Catalina as a penal colony, to which they 'commonly banished all malefactors of the Spanish dominions in the West Indies.'[23]

The island soon returned to the somnambulant state it had fallen into under Gerónimo de Ojeda. Overworked in the fields, soldier, slave and prisoner alike sickened and died in alarming numbers. Eight months after relief supplies were supposed to have arrived from Cartagena, and in protest at his miserable existence, a soldier who had been court-martialled and banished to the island for an unspecified crime slipped through Captain Sánchez Ximénez's window, crept to his bedside and stabbed him to death 'with such disgrace that he didn't even have time to confess.'[24]

14
HENRY MORGAN,
ADMIRAL OF THE BRETHREN

In August 1668, two years after the Spanish recapture of Santa Catalina, a man arrived in Port Royal from Havana, little more than a skeleton in rags, his arms and legs heavily scarred and covered in sores. Major Samuel Smith was taken to the governor's house, where he told Thomas Modyford that after being dragged from the dungeon at Portobello the previous month, he had been shipped to Cuba to await passage back to Spain with the annual *flota*. He had managed to escape his captors, but had done so alone, and had no idea what had become of the other officers. Presumably they had been lost, most likely to disease, somewhere between Portobello and Havana.

By 1668, King Charles was in negotiations with the Spanish and was in no position to issue privateering commissions, at least not openly. But Thomas Modyford could, and he gave one to his friend Henry Morgan, who was keen to avenge the Spanish attack, rescue the other members of the advance party, and recapture Providence. Henry set about recruiting an army. There were more than 2,000 buccaneers living in Port Royal in 1668, and their presence contributed to the port's reputation as 'a gilded Hades where Mammon held sway.' They 'gambled with heavy gold coins whose value no one cared to estimate,' and drank from cups embellished with 'gems torn from half a hundred cathedrals.'[1] At the death of Edward Mansveldt, the Brethren of the Coast had made Henry Morgan their admiral, so when he told them that he had 12 ships ready to sail for Providence, 700 buccaneers signed up for the voyage.

From Port Royal, the buccaneer fleet headed towards Cape Gracias a Dios. En route, Morgan seized a Spanish merchant ship and, after rigorously interrogating its captain, ascertained that Sir Thomas Whetstone, Captain Stanley Steven and the 32 soldiers captured on Providence were still languishing in the dungeon at Portobello. The ship's captain also confirmed that the authorities in Panama and Cuba were indeed raising levies to finance another attempt to retake Jamaica. This suited Morgan well, since the threat of such an attack was what kept the privateering commissions coming.

After spending a few days at the Cape, Henry's fleet made its way down the Miskito coast to Bocas del Toro, where he and 400 of his men transferred to a convoy of small launches and travelled another 40 leagues down the coast to Portobello. After a series of battles in the outlying villages, they were able to breach the town's walls and fight their way to the dungeon beneath the town's castle. Morgan found just 11 of the prisoners alive; one of them told him that while a few of his fellows had been able to escape, most of them had died. Sir Thomas Whetstone was never heard of again. 'If our number is small, our hearts are great,' Morgan declared to his men. 'And the fewer we are, the better shares we shall have in the spoil.'[2] He had the emaciated prisoners removed to his ship, and sent a ransom demand to the governor of Panama for the safe return of Portobello.

When Juan Pérez de Guzmán received word of the famous pirate's arrival, he 'was brought into extreme admiration, considering that 400 men had been able to take such a great city with so many strong castles, especially seeing they had no piece of cannon.' The governor of Panama raised 3,000 troops and set out on the track used by the mule trains that carried the King's bullion over the mountains to Portobello. But their movements were betrayed by the local tribesmen as they made their way down to the Caribbean coast, and this gave Morgan the chance to make the first move. Hoping to catch Pérez de Guzmán unawares, he led 100 of his Brethren to a narrow ravine through which his adversary's army was sure to pass. Alexander Esquemelin, who was a surgeon in the buccaneer force, described their meeting in his *Buccaneers of America*.

> At the first encounter, the hundred buccaneers put to flight a good party of those of Panama… with considerable damage, in so much that the next day [Pérez de Guzmán] proffered 100,000 pieces of eight for the delivery of the towns and castles in as good condition as we found them.

Esquemelin records that the governor of Panama's offer was accompanied by a request that Morgan supply him with 'some small pattern of those arms wherewith he had taken with such violence so great a city.' Morgan treated the governor's messenger with great civility, and gave him a pistol with a few lead bullets. His master could 'keep them for a twelve month,' he told him, 'after which time he would come to Panama and fetch them away.'[3] Morgan insisted that Pérez de Guzmán up his offer, and a few days later, his flotilla left the dock at Portobello with 250,000 pieces of eight (£12 million in today's money).

Crossing the bay where Sir Francis Drake's lead-lined coffin had been dispatched to a watery grave 70 years before, the Brethren could congratulate themselves on pulling off an feat of bravado not seen since the days of the Elizabethan seafaring heroes. Little did they know that in addition to their magnificent plunder, their ships were carrying plague-stricken rats. Once ashore, they would kill off many of the denizens of Port Royal, among them the governor's wife, Lady Elizabeth Modyford, before they had time to enjoy their share of the spoils.

In retaliation for the raid on Portobello, Pérez de Guzmán let it be known that he would issue a privateering commission to any ship's captain willing and able to seize an English merchant ship. By the time Henry Morgan made it back to Port Royal, the Spanish had already taken several English prizes, and the town's merchants were clamouring for redress. Thomas Modyford was again forced to walk a tightrope: he recognised the importance of keeping Jamaica's privateers in business, for the sake of the island's defence as much as to keep them from wanton piracy. But he was also aware that Sir William Godolphin, the king's ambassador to Madrid, was in negotiations towards a comprehensive peace treaty between their two countries. In concert with Henry Morgan, he hurried to cement his own grand design for the Carribean.

In June 1669, Modyford made Henry 'Admiral and Commander-in-chief of His Majesty's fleet belonging to the island of Jamaica,' and gave him orders 'to put to sea for the guard and defence of this island.' The Admiral of the Brethren was now Admiral of Jamaica as well, an act of collusion between organised crime and the English state never seen before or since. The Jamaica Assembly also lent their support to the enterprise, commissioning Morgan to 'attack, seize and destroy all the enemy's vessels that come within his reach,' and granting him 'power to land in the enemy's country as many of his men as he shall judge needful, and with them to march out to such places as he shall be informed the said magazines and forces are.'[4] In a letter to the Secretary of State, Modyford expressed his regret at having to appeal to the buccaneers, but lamented that he had no choice, 'there being no other way to encourage these men.'[5]

Encouraged they certainly were: in return for posting a £1,000 bond, and a cut of any booty seized, the captains of English merchant ships were authorised to seize any Spanish ship and storm any settlement in the name of the Crown. In August 1670, Henry sailed from Port Royal with 11 ships and 600 men, among them several of the prisoners that he had sprung from the dungeon in Portobello. Some of the Brethren were arguing for an attack on Santiago de Cuba, but Morgan rejected the idea – the city was known to be well defended, and the risk of being struck by a hurricane was strong in the months of late summer. Others suggested Cartagena, but that too was ruled out because, according to Morgan's Spanish prisoners, the city was already 'all in arms against the English.'[6]

The third and most daring option was to mount an assault on Panama. The city was 'the greatest mart for silver and gold in the whole world,' said Morgan, 'for it receives the goods into it that come from Old Spain in the King's great fleet, and likewise delivers to the fleet all the silver and gold that comes from the mines of Peru and Potosi.'[7] Panama was the finest gem in Spain's imperial crown, and the gateway to the Pacific coast. Strike a blow there, and all the silver and gold of Peru and Mexico would fall into English hands, a setback from which the King of Spain would never recover. Every buccaneer and privateer in the Caribbean dreamed of attacking Panama. Situated on the Pacific coast, less than 50 miles from Portobello as the crow flies, it had never been attacked with any force, and its inhabitants seemed oblivious to the threat from marauding foreigners. Their city was graced with 2,000 houses 'of curious and magnificent structure', according to Alexander Esquemelin, built by the merchants who had made their fortunes in the bullion trade, and surrounded by beautiful gardens and prosperous plantations.

But Henry's plan suffered an early setback: the day after his fleet sailed from Port Royal, a pinnace drew up alongside his flagship, the *Satisfaction*, carrying a copy of the Secretary of State's latest letter to Thomas Modyford. King Charles was unmoved by the governor's complaint that the Spanish were attacking English shipping. 'The Spanish men-of-war attacking English ships is not to be wondered at after such hostilities as your men have acted upon their territories,' wrote Lord Arlington. 'This way of warring is neither honourable nor profitable to His Majesty.'[8] His letter was accompanied by a copy of the articles of peace that had just been signed by Charles II and Philip IV.

The Treaty of Madrid was a breakthrough in relations between the rival powers. Philip had finally relinquished his country's 200-year-old claim to exclusivity over the lands 'beyond the line,' and acknowledged English sovereignty over its territories in the New World. The treaty was a triumph for the settlers of Jamaica, who Philip had always regarded as little better than jackdaws in a Spanish nest, for it opened the way for peaceful trade between English merchants and their customers in the Spanish colonies.

But for those who made their living from sea robbery, contraband and raids on the Spanish Main, it was a disaster. It also dashed Sir James Modyford's hopes of taking up his post as governor of Providence, for in accepting the status quo, Philip had made it clear that he would tolerate no more assaults on his American territories, of which Santa Catalina was indisputably one.

Ever since the loss of Providence in 1666, Thomas Modyford had urged his brother to be patient while he waited for the opportune moment to take up the governorship of the island. He had appointed him sole judge of customs in Port Royal, an extremely lucrative post, and then commander of the town's castle. When he wasn't counting his money or stalking the sea walls, Sir James was to be found in his plantation house, writing letters to friends in high places in London. 'We may certainly have [Providence] again if His Majesty pleases,' he wrote to one. He confessed that whenever he heard of the arrival of a ship carrying the king's latest instructions to his brother, he would ride down to Port Royal, always 'hoping it may be the retaking of the said island.'[9] But the order for a renewed assault on Providence never came.

Perusing the terms of the Treaty of Madrid aboard the *Satisfaction*, Henry wondered who could have dispatched a copy of a peace treaty that had yet to be made public? It could only have come from someone in high office who knew of his plans, expected to profit by them, and hoped that they would be realised before the treaty came into force. It could well have come from the king himself, or his brother James, Duke of York, both of whom were friends of Thomas Modyford, and could expect a substantial cut of any booty Henry brought back to Port Royal. In fact, it came from the governor himself; in an accompanying letter,

Modyford gave Henry advance warning that while he had 'no orders to call him in, yet thought fit to let him see [the treaty] and to advise him to do nothing that might prevent the accomplishment of His Majesty's peaceable intentions.'

Modyford's letter put the Admiral of the Brethren in a quandary: word that he was about to embark on the most audacious raid of his career had already travelled through the buccaneering communities. Mariners, castaways and renegades from every secluded cove and isolated cay in the Caribbean had flocked to join his fleet, and the *Satisfaction* was now at the head of the largest fleet of privateers ever seen. There were 28 English vessels, with a combined crew of 1,320 men, and eight French vessels, carrying a further 530 men.[10] Far from discouraging them, the Treaty of Madrid only lent urgency to his plan to attack Panama.

Henry gathered the 36 captains under his command, among them renowned privateers like Edward Collier, Lawrence Prince, Joseph Bradley and John Morris. They agreed that before they launched their assault on Panama, they would retake Providence. As their surgeon, Alexander Esquemelin noted, 'No place could be more fit [to take],' the island 'being the King's ancient property.'[11] They also had reasons of their own for retaking the island: if they were to cross the mountains from Portobello to Panama without being detected, they would have to avoid the royal road used by the mule trains. Providence, being 'a place of banishment for all the Spanish felons of the region,' was a likely place to find a knowledgeable man with nothing to lose who might guide them along the local Indians' jungle paths.

Henry's fleet reached Providence in the dead of night. Guided by the English soldiers he had sprung from the dungeon in Portobello, his ships passed through a channel in the northern reef and glided towards the mouth of the island's harbour. To prevent any attempt at escape, two ships dropped anchor within sight of Fort Warwick, while the other 34 vessels drifted with the current as far as Southwest Bay, where 1,000 men clambered into launches and coasted around the island's southern tip to Manchineel Bay. By daybreak, they were marching through the woods towards New Westminster.

The man who replaced the murdered governor of Santa Catalina was José Ramírez de Leiba. According to Esquemelin, Henry and his men reached the governor's residence that afternoon but found it deserted. In what had become a familiar ritual, the Spanish governor and his garri-

THE ISLAND THAT DISAPPEARED

son had taken refuge in *El Castillo Santa Teresa*, formerly known as Fort Warwick.[12] After coming under fire from the fort's guns, Henry and his men withdrew 'to sleep under the stars, according to their old habit, with no surfeit of supper in their stomachs, for they'd eaten nothing all day.' Soon after midnight, a cold, heavy rain began to fall. There was some let-up at dawn, but no sooner had the Brethren dried and primed their weapons than it began to rain heavier than ever, 'as if the skies were melted into the waters.' In the midst of the downpour, the Spanish renewed their bombardment, 'to demonstrate that their powder was not wet.' In such dispiriting conditions, Henry grew fearful of mutiny, and began to turn the screws on his opponent. He sent a message to Ramírez de Leiba, warning him that unless he surrendered immediately, his men 'would most certainly put them all to the sword, without granting quarter to any.'

Shortly afterwards, the island's governor agreed to Henry's terms – but on one condition. To save his reputation, and to avoid being garroted by his superiors on his return to Madrid, he asked that the Admiral of the Brethren join him in a curious compact. If the buccaneers pretended to mount a furious attack, Ramírez de Leiba would have his men make an equally pretentious show of resistance. Much powder would be burned by both sides, and shots would be fired, 'but in the air, or with blanks, so that no one should suffer from it.' The governor would then allow himself to be 'captured' and surrender his fort. This comic twist to the handover of power speaks volumes about the hollowed-out shell that Spain had become since its Golden Age. Behind the imperial edifice were ranks of cowardly soldiers and corrupt priests united only by their dependence on the king, and their evasion of all responsibility for the protection of his empire.

Henry agreed to the governor's scheme with a good-natured laugh – and a stipulation of his own. If any of his men sustained as much as a scratch in the charade, he would have every last Spaniard on the island executed. Ramírez de Leiba had little choice but to agree, and the play was enacted to the satisfaction of both parties. When the compact with the Spanish had been carried out and all was calm, the war against the hens, pigs and sheep began,' wrote Esquemelin. With the handful of creole women on the island held captive in Hope Sherrard's abandoned church, the Spanish soldiers were compelled to head into the fields to gather yucca, plantain and sweet potatoes for the hungry buccaneers.

'The boiling and roasting went on all night.' When all bellies were full, Ramírez de Leiba was permitted to sail for Cartagena with his reputation as a loyal servant of the king intact.

The Brethren finally had their island. As Henry knew from his visit in 1666, Providence offered great advantages to the ambitious buccaneer, and he was pleased to see that it had been well fortified in the interim. The island's nine forts and batteries were well stocked with all kinds of munitions, including 30,000 lbs of gunpowder. The Spanish might have been shadows of their former selves, but they were bound to attempt another assault on Providence at some point, so the 130 Brethren who would hold the island until their Admiral returned from Panama would need strong defences. He had 49 cannon brought ashore and mounted, most of them in Fort Warwick, which had the added advantage of being ringed by a 20 foot-deep dry ditch.

Prior to Ramírez de Leiba's departure, Henry had enlisted three felons willing to guide the buccaneers across the mountains to Panama. In return, he offered them their freedom and 'as much booty as they could gather.' Esquemelin recalled that one of them was:

> happy of an opportunity to revenge the wrong he thought had been done him – as indeed it had, for he did not deserve banishment, but rather to have been broken alive on the wheel for all the murders, rapes and robberies he had committed.

On 10 January 1671, the Admiral and his Brethren returned to their ships and hoisted their sails. Guided by this villain, the *Satisfaction* led the 36 ships of Morgan's fleet to the mouth of the River Chagres, where their most daring raid to date would begin in earnest.

After storming the castle at the mouth of the River Chagres, the buccaneers sailed upriver. As they approached the watershed, its course narrowed and they had to transfer to their dories. When the water became too shallow for dories, they enlisted the aid of the local tribesmen, and 'betook themselves to the wild woods.' Their journey upriver had not gone unnoticed: every village they came to had been stripped of anything of value or succour, and Spanish ambushes prevented them from foraging for food in the woods. Esquemelin noted that by the fifth day 'many were complaining of Captain Morgan and his conduct... and desiring to return home.'[13] But the promise of plunder stoked their resolve; the threat of desertion was averted when they found a few horses that the Spaniards had overlooked, and were finally able to sate their hunger.

Traversing a pass in the chain of mountains that runs down the spine of the isthmus, they caught their first glimpse of the South Sea. Arrayed on the plain before them was Pérez de Guzmán's large but ragged force of 3,600 men, among them 400 cavalry, 300 Darien Indian archers, and 2,000 foot soldiers 'of all castes.' The army that Henry assembled to meet them in battle was less than half the size, but still larger than anything the Spanish could have prepared for. At its vanguard was a battalion of 360 men, led by Lieutenant Colonel Lawrence Prince and Major John Morris. On the left flank, Colonel Edward Collier commanded 300 men, while on the right were another 300 men under the Admiral himself. The rear guard, also of 300 men, was led by his valiant, if obese, cousin Colonel Bledry Morgan. Henry sent a message to Pérez de Guzmán: he had come to retrieve the pistol that he had lent him two years before.

As the buccaneer army closed in on the Spanish force, Pérez de Guzmán ordered his cavalry to charge, 'wherewith the battle was instantly kindled very hot.' His horsemen found themselves galloping across marshland and were soon cut down by volleys of shot from Lawrence Prince's vanguard. In Henry's words, as the survivors veered away to make room for the foot soldiers, 'they were met with such a warm welcome, and were pursued so close, that their retreat came to plain running.'

In desperation, the Spanish 'did work such a stratagem as has seldom been heard of, viz. attempting to drive two droves of 1,500 cattle into our rear.' It was a cunning move, but the Brethren were accustomed to hunting wild cattle, and managed to turn the herd back to charge its keepers. What followed was by all accounts a rout, and after pursuing the fleeing soldiers for three miles, Henry declared the battle won. The Brethren had lost less than a dozen of their number; the Spanish over 600.

Charging down the lanes that separated the city's palatial gardens, they took the first of Panama's forts with ease. The second was better protected, and the struggle to take it raged for several hours. In the midst of the fighting, Henry's men considered retreating from the fray, but their luck turned when a Spanish patrol happened to return to the fort, accompanied by a group of monks and nuns. The buccaneers put them into service as human shields, and the second fort soon fell.

With events spiralling beyond his control, Pérez de Guzmán retreated to a neighbourhood on the edge of the city and ordered that the city's principal fort be detonated. Such was the rush to destroy what could not be saved that 40 of its 200-strong garrison died in the ensuing blaze. Undeterred, the governor ordered his soldiers to burn the entire city to the ground, in the hope that the invaders would lose heart and head back over the mountains. Most of Panama's houses were built of resinous cedar and were ablaze in minutes. As fires raged across the city, attacker and defender alike sought to douse the flames; the former in the hope that they might save their prize, the latter, their property. They struggled in vain, and by midnight, the wealthiest city in the Americas had been reduced to ashes.

The buccaneers were exhausted and hungry, and many of them were showing the first symptoms of the malaria, yellow fever and dysentery they had contracted on their journey over the mountains. But they wanted their prize as greedily as a king wants his taxes, or a bishop his tithes, and they were no less ruthless.[14] They knew that the city's merchants, clerics and officials had spirited away their valuables at the first word of their approach, so the following morning, and every morning that followed for the next month, Henry sent armed groups to search the ruined city and the outlying farmsteads. Three thousand of the city's inhabitants were seized and dragged to the Admiral's makeshift headquarters for questioning. Under duress, those that had hidden their valuables in cellars and attics divulged their hiding places. But many admitted that they had loaded their goods onto ships bound for Peru, before hiding themselves as best they could in the surrounding villages.

According to one citizen, Henry Morgan was the only one of the pirates 'noble enough to the vanquished enemy.' But his Brethren recognised no such bounds, and embarked on a chaotic campaign of killing, robbing and raping the people of Panama. As secrets were spilled, caches uncovered, and loot dragged back to the Admiral's headquarters, their haul increased in size until it reached the ceiling. While Henry waited for the next eminent citizen to be brought before him, he counted and recounted the pieces of eight, doubloons, cruzados and crowns arrayed before him. Only when he was confident that the last coin, gold bar and precious stone in the city were in his possession did he give the order to load the king's 175 pack mules, and make ready for the return journey to Portobello.

The raiders set out on 14 February 1671. The journey back proved more arduous than the one that had brought them to Panama, for many of them were ailing, and once they were in the mountains they soon ran out of food. Such was their hunger, they were reduced to eating jungle rats. When the rats ran out, and with no prospect of the sea to sustain them, they loaded the panniers onto their backs and ate their mules.

The Admiral of the Brethren only divvied up the spoils of the sack of Panama when they made it back to the mouth of the River Chagres. Each of the buccaneers received between £15 and £18 (£1,494 in modern currency), a share that would be the source of bitter complaints in the taverns of Port Royal for years to come.[15] Allegations of Henry's skulduggery were supported by his personal surgeon, Richard Browne, who claimed that he 'cheated the soldiers of a very vast sum, each man having but £10 a share [in money and plate].' Browne also claimed that before sailing for Jamaica, he saw Henry 'cast away' 19 of the 36 ships in his fleet, abandoning their crews at the mouth of the Chagres. Once at sea, several other ships 'were forced to leeward, where hundreds were lost, starved,' and just ten of the Admiral's ships made it back to Port Royal. Having invested heavily in his audacious raid of the wealthiest city in the Americas, many of Jamaica's merchants now faced ruin. Richard Browne called the sack of Panama, 'half the undoing of this island.'[16]

But Browne and Esquemelin – and the many later writers who drew from their accounts of the sack of Panama – may have been mistaken about the supposed treachery of the Admiral of the Brethren. Browne reckoned the total value of the plunder to be £70,000, but Henry's secretary, John Peake, put it at just £30,000 – half the value of what had been captured in his attack on Maracaibo two years before. The Jamaica Assembly certainly didn't feel swindled: its members passed a motion giving the island's Admiral 'many thanks for executing his last commission,' with the Speaker noting that the Assembly 'approves very well of his acting therein.'[17]

It may simply be that Henry's greatest military exploit was his least profitable. Even if he was as duplicitous as Browne alleged, the Assembly's members had no cause for complaint. In the two and a half years since he was appointed the island's Admiral, Henry and his Brethren had brought pieces of eight worth £237,000 into Port Royal. Considering that in 1669, the total value of England's exports to its Caribbean colonies was just £107,000, their contribution to the governor's finances is astonishing.[18] Thanks to them, the colony had rushed through its infancy, and was now well able to stand on its own two feet.

Back in London, the diarist John Evelyn expressed his wonder at the sack of Panama, a feat that 'had not been done since the famous Drake.'[19] The story of how the Brethren of the Coast had burned Spain's greatest American city to the ground became a favourite yarn in London's taverns, just as it was in Port Royal's. According to Sir William Godolphin, the English ambassador to the Spanish court, the news threw the Queen Regent into 'such a distemper and excess of weeping and violent passion, as those about her feared it might shorten her life.' In his investigation of the circumstances leading up to the disaster, the Spanish Crown prosecutor found that the city's defenders, from the governor down to the lowliest Indian archer, had fled the approaching enemy 'like chickens.' In terms reminiscent of Pérez de Guzmán's own condemnation of Esteban de Ocampo in 1666, the *fiscal* opined that Panama's governor 'should receive the greatest and gravest punishment possible.'[20] Pérez de Guzmán was sent back to Seville to stand trial, but he escaped due process by dying shortly after his arrival in Cádiz.

Spanish fury took time to subside, but it soon became apparent that the sack of Panama was not a sign of things to come, but the last spasm of the criminal monster the governor of Jamaica had created. Neither Spain nor England wanted to jeopardise the treaty they had signed the previous year. Article seven of the treaty, which granted England jurisdiction over the territories it held in 1670, would cause friction and occasional conflict for the next hundred years, but the Spanish were largely resigned to the English presence in the Caribbean. In return, the English dropped all talk of building an empire in Central America.

The Spanish did not know it yet, but the sack of Panama was to be Henry's last great raid. Following the proclamation of peace, Jamaica's merchants turned their backs on the Brethren of the Coast and headed inland to invest their ill-gotten gains in land for plantations and sugar mills. The buccaneers' depredations had broken the Spaniards' hold on the Caribbean, and forced them to acknowledge the English presence in the region. They had protected the English at Jamaica from expulsion, imprisonment and death itself, just as they had the Dutch at Curaçao and the French in Saint-Dominigue. But with the King of Spain reconciled to the foreigners' colonies, Jamaica's merchants could live without the sea rovers.

Their change in outlook found favour at court, for King Charles was coming to the realisation that privateering was not worth the grief, notwithstanding the cut he stood to take from the enterprise. Privateering and the peaceful pursuit of trade had never been compatible. Royal patronage of the privateers had been sound policy when the English were newcomers to the Caribbean, but now that England, Holland and France had naval squadrons capable of taking on and defeating Spanish men-of-war in battle, the Brethren of the Coast were surplus to requirements.

As Admiral and now Lieutenant Governor, it fell to Henry to persuade them to abandon the rover's life for more mundane pursuits. Those who had not gambled away their cut of the spoils invested it in land, and in time joined Jamaica's 'plantocracy' – the cabal of wealthy landowners that would make a killing from sugar in the years to come. But those lacking the ambition, capital or commercial nous required to build a plantation had few options open to them. Henry had orders to hang those who refused to move with the times, and would no doubt have strung up more of them had so many not succumbed to malaria, snakebite or starvation in the jungles of Panama.

With the gallows of Port Royal straining under the weight of their brethren's rotting corpses, most buccaneers didn't need telling twice. Some went to the Bay of Campeche on the coast of Mexico, where they turned to the logwood trade to make a living. Others returned to the Miskito coast and the contraband trade, which continued to thrive long after Spain had declared itself open to free trade. Thomas Modyford was quick to encourage such ventures. By keeping 'these soldierly men within peaceful bounds,' he had a reserve army 'always ready to serve His Majesty in any new rupture.'[21]

Those who didn't settle in Campeche or Bluefields passed northeast, through the Straits of Florida to Carolina or the Bahamas, where a new generation of pirates would emerge in the opening years of the eighteenth century. These were the men of all nations who became renowned for their brutality under fearsome villains like Edward 'Blackbeard' Teach and 'Black' Sam Bellamy. No longer welcome in Port Royal, they ensconced themselves at New Providence in the Bahamas, which was named in memory of the island that has since been known as Old Providence.

Their Lordships' Isle also fell victim to the peaceable tide lapping Caribbean shores. In time, the buccaneers that Henry left to man the garrison grew tired of waiting for him to return from Panama and sailed to Port Royal. Still, Sir James Modyford was confident that Providence would be resettled once he found an acting governor to take the place of the emaciated Major Samuel Smith. In the meantime, he commissioned Henry's cousin, Colonel Bledry Morgan, to sail for New Westminster and hold the island on his behalf, while he went about recruiting the 300 soldiers he would need to keep it in English hands for good.

But Bledry Morgan's departure was delayed, and by the time he was ready to sail, Providence's would-be colonisers had been overtaken by events beyond their control. Lord Arlington, the Secretary of State who had done so much to secure the peace with Spain, was a typical Restoration statesman. Henry's biographer writes that while 'outwardly charming,' he was 'thoroughly unscrupulous and self-seeking. Patriotism meant little to him and he was faithless even to a good cause, regarding public office solely as a means of procuring his own pleasure and profit.' Lord Arlington had little faith in Thomas Modyford or Henry Morgan to observe the Treaty of Madrid, so in June 1671, he sent Sir Thomas Lynch to Port Royal to take up the post of Lieutenant Governor, with orders 'not to permit any pirates whatsoever to set forth from Jamaica.'

On his arrival, Lord Arlington's man 'apprehended several of the chiefest actors herein and condemned them to be hanged.' Lynch was also carrying orders to arrest Modyford on a charge of 'making war and committing depredations and acts of hostility upon the subjects and territories of the King of Spain in America, contrary to his Majesty's express order and command.' Jamaica's governor was taken prisoner and sent back to London on the next ship.[22] After 24 years in the Caribbean, seven as governor, Thomas Modyford found himself a prisoner in a damp stone cell in the Tower of London. Charles II was quite prepared to sacrifice England's colonial heroes to appease the King of Spain when he saw fit. Fifty-four years before, his grandfather, King James I, had had Sir Walter Raleigh executed in the Tower's courtyard. Now it was Thomas Modyford's turn to wonder how a loyal patriot could have fallen so foul of his monarch.

A few months later, Henry was also sent home, partly to explain his decision to attack Panama, but mainly to appease the King of Spain, who was still demanding the return of the six million Spanish crowns he was alleged to have stolen. Just two weeks prior to Lynch's arrival, his friend, the governor of Jamaica, had given Henry a formal reception to thank him for his services to the island. Now he too was stripped of his titles and sent back to London in disgrace.

Henry had not been home for seventeen years. He had left in the days when England was a Commonwealth governed by the Lord Protector, but by 1672, Oliver Cromwell was not only dead, his corpse had been dug up by vengeful royalists and hanged at Tyburn. London was still recovering from the Great Fire of 1666, but it was already being shaped by the gaiety, refinement and corruption that came to be associated with the Restoration of the House of Stuart. Struggling to get his bearings in a city so utterly changed, Henry and the money he had brought back from Panama dropped out of sight. 'Oppressed by a lingering consumption, the coldness of this climate and his vexations…[and] under the perpetual malice of a prevailing court faction, he wasted the remaining part of his life,' lamented Sir Thomas Dalby, author of an early history of the Caribbean published shortly after Morgan's return.[23]

With his brother and Jamaica's greatest privateer out of the picture, Sir James Modyford's dream of governing his own private island seemed destined never to be realised. Providence held little appeal for Thomas Lynch, and the merchants who might once have backed his venture were kept busy by their new plantations. In the decade to come Jamaica would become the most valuable, as well as the gaudiest, jewel in England's Crown, but Sir James never mustered the energy needed to partake of its rise to prosperity. He died a bitter man in 1673, in his plantation house in the hills overlooking Port Royal. The Spanish were equally unmoved by the island's potential. Juan Pérez de Guzmán's successor visited Santa Catalina in 1672 and found it deserted. In his report to the authorities in Cartagena, he suggested that the *guardacostas* pass by from time to time to ensure it had not been resettled, but otherwise to forget about it, the island being 'worthless to everyone.'

When the last ship had left the island harbour and the last official report had been filed away in some distant colonial city, the name of Old Providence disappeared. Officially, at least, the island became an un-place. Captain William Dampier, the pirate who would later become governor of New Providence in the Bahamas, passed by Providence in 1680, and judged the island to be 'without interest for the English.'[24]

Yet the freshwater streams and fertile soils that had lured Providence's first settlers ashore did not disappear, and in the century that followed, the island may well have served as an occasional haven for pirates roaming the western Caribbean. Sailors who broke the rules aboard ship were often punished by being marooned on remote islands, and it may have become home to such castaways. Perhaps they found shelter and sustenance with the original maroons? Nathaniel Butler had tried and failed to dislodge the runaway slaves of Palmetto Grove in the years before the collapse of the Puritan colony. Perhaps they survived, to be absorbed into Gerónimo de Ojeda's geriatric garrison and then evacuated to Portobello in 1666? Or perhaps they managed to evade detection by Ojeda, and then by Mansveldt, Whetstone, Sánchez Ximénez, Ramírez de Leiba and Henry Morgan, and on sighting Dampier's ship, dowsed their fires and waited for the tip of the mast to drop over the horizon, before returning to their bucolic un-existence? In the absence of written records, there is simply no way of knowing what became of them – just as there is no way of knowing if there were Miskitos living on Providence before the arrival of Daniel Elfrith, or other Amerindian tribes before them.

PART THREE

15
MARINERS, CASTAWAYS
AND RENEGADES

Before leaving England, I tried to find some trace of Providence. I found the Providence Island Company's journal at the National Archives at Kew, and a few letters from the company's shareholders to its colonists in the British Library. But that was all. I heard that there was a plaque commemorating the company's pioneering role in empire building at the Naval Museum in Dartmouth, but if it ever existed, its librarian wasn't aware of it. Nor was there any mention of Providence in the National Maritime Museum at Greenwich. The only other traces were in the names of Brooke Street and Warwick Court, the Holborn streets where two of the company's most illustrious founders once lived.

At some point in the 345 years that have passed since the *Satisfaction* carried Henry Morgan away from the island for the last time, Providence also drifted over the horizon. Old Providence might prompt a flicker of recognition in the minds of a handful of Britons, but few would be able to put a face to the name. Of the few to know anything about the Providence Island Company, only one has seen it in its modern guise. David Fiennes, Lord Saye's grandson ten times removed, spent a few days on Providence in 1977 on his way back from a business trip to Panama. In an article he wrote for the journal of the Banbury Historical Society, he recalled that the Colombian Embassy in London hadn't been able to tell him how to get to the island, and he had ended up hitching a ride to the island on a cargo ship from Colón. He found it a backwater. "There is no hotel," he wrote.

> 'Good' was the reply to every enquiry of local people as to their life, health, and government... Only one old man had a complaint; having spent his working life in North America as a mechanic, he could find nothing mechanical which needed repair. Being no good at ponies, he was bored.[1]

The journey to Providence was a long one, involving a flight from London to Bogotá, and a connecting flight to San Andrés, from where I could take a catamaran to Providence. The price at least, had not changed since 1629. As David Fiennes observed, "In Henry Halhead's day the fare from England to Providence was £6. If one takes a factor of 50 for currency inflation, the fare is the same today, give or take a few pounds." I decided to break the journey by spending a day and a night on the bigger island. All Colombians know San Andrés: if they haven't been there on holiday, they know that of the 32 departments in their country, *el archepiélago de Providencia, San Andrés y Santa Catalina* is the only one where English is the official language.

My hostel was run by Colombians from the coast, and was decked out with the fishing nets, ships' wheels and hardboard cutlasses you would expect to find in any tourist town that trades on its piratical past. There were brochures in reception intended to lure me to the 'must-see' sights at Morgan's Cave and the Pirate Museum. Outside Morgan's Hotel, the tourists milled around with their kids, or perused the imported booze and digital cameras on offer in the duty-free shops. They wandered the aisles with an air of disdain. Even the 'native crafts' – carved coconut shells painted to depict scenes from old-time Caribbean life – were made in China. I recognised their beer bellies and sunburned arms from home, and imagined them working as taxi drivers or shopkeepers in Medellín, Bucaramanga or Bogotá. They were 'the middling sort,' still hemmed in between the corrupt rich and the idle poor, with a tenuous grip on respectability and not enough money for a trip to Miami.

Until the 1950s, San Andrés had a population of 5,000; these days, it is close to 80,000. The *Avenida 20 de Julio*, named in commemoration of the day Colombia won its independence from Spain, had barely warranted the name in 1950, for it was less an avenue than a sandy track leading from the wharf to the office of the *intendente* (the Colombian appointed to oversee goings-on on the islands). Until the late 1950s, when Colombians began flocking to the island, the avenue had been flanked by large, two-storey wooden houses with corrugated iron roofs and verandas bound by crosshatch woodwork. I spotted a few remaining traditional Caribbean houses, but in most cases, the ground floor had been sold to ambitious shopkeepers from the mainland, who were quick to brick up the veranda and replace the wooden shutters on the windows with iron bars.

212

Slouching in the shadows cast by the shops' awnings were the island's beggars: skinny, old black men with no shoes on their feet, who gazed absently beyond the unseeing eyes of the tourists in their sunglasses. As young men, they had been fishermen or farmers, but they had been made redundant by their island's tourist-friendly transformation, and had gradually melted into the shadows, like ghosts tied to a world in which they no longer had any part to play.

Early the next morning, I went to the wharf to catch the catamaran. Few of the Colombians that visit San Andrés bother to travel the additional 40 miles north to Providencia, and most of the passengers were locals. I found a seat on the open deck at the stern and promptly fell asleep. When I woke up, we were in the middle of the sea, and there was no sign of land in any direction. A little girl had instinctively taken shelter in the arms of the old man sitting opposite me, and was clinging to his neck as if he were a buoy. He was tall, still well-built, and kept his eyes fixed on the horizon. The only thing that distracted his gaze were the man-of-war birds cruising overhead, following the catamaran as they have every vessel to have passed through those waters. He told me that the man-of-war is much admired on Providence, and not only for its impressive wingspan. Like the islanders' piratical forebears, it doesn't fish for itself, preferring to snatch its food from the beaks of other seabirds.

When a speck of land appeared on the horizon, the passengers gravitated towards the bow to watch it grow, and we were soon skirting the low cliffs of Providence's western shore. They receded into steep slopes, dotted with coconut palms and ragged plantains, whose fronds reflected silver the light of late morning. We passed Black Rock, the site of the fort where Captain Andrew Carter had made his last stand against the invading Spanish, and came into the curve of the bay, where the low ground runs a mile inland from the shore. The old man pointed out Old Town, which had once been known as New Westminster, and behind it, the black cliffs at the end of the the ridge that runs into the mountainous heart of the island.

From the catamaran, we piled onto the wharf and into the little square in front of the harbourmaster's office. It was all very quiet in the village that the locals call Town. A few old people were sitting on benches set in a low wall, silently watching the visitors melt away, giving the odd slow nod to those they knew. I sensed the deep familiarity seeping between them, and my own strangeness. For the last four months, I had tried to picture the lie of this land. Now it was real, and suddenly I felt completely foreign.

My email enquiries from England hadn't met with much response, but I'd managed to negotiate rental of a flat on the second floor of a concrete block at Maracaibo, in the northeast corner of the island. The owner had recommended that I pay a visit to Luis Dann Newball when I arrived. Since the only road on the island is a twelve mile-long ring, few islanders own cars, but practically everyone had a scooter. As well as being the island's only builders' merchant, Luis Dann's was the only place to rent scooters. We agreed a price for a four-month rental, and after dropping off my luggage and the box of history books I had brought out from London, I set off to explore.

I headed clockwise. There was no one on the road, the sun was warm on my face, and a light breeze was blowing from the northeast. For the first time in ages, I felt free to do what I liked, when I liked. From Town, the road headed up to the island's only clinic, and then down to its only electricity generating plant. I puttered past the warehouse where the beer deliveries were kept and the island's little airport, and then crossed the tail end of a long spur that ran from the Peak to the Three Brothers cays, where the Man-of-War birds were circling over their offshore eyries.

Philip Bell was right: by anyone's standards, Providence must be accounted utterly beautiful. Thirteen million years ago, a string of volcanoes threw up lava that bridged the straits that divided North from South America. Providence was created by a stray volcano, 70 miles off the coast of what would become Central America. The island is dominated by the Peak, whose spurs run down to the sea, creating steep valleys and the sheltered coves where most of the islanders live. This accounts for the strange combination of round boulders and what must once have been lava: a fine, sandy adhesive that binds them together like mortar. It was as if the island began as a vast cathedral of soaring spires and buttresses, which had gradually been eroded to create its rich soil, leaving only the pinnacles to blacken under the combined onslaught of brilliant sunshine and torrential rain. From the road, some of these rocky outcrops resembled the ruins of the forts that had once defended the island from attack. But as I would discover in tramping its hills and valleys, no trace of the Puritan colony has survived. Once Hope Sherrard's church collapsed, termites would have bored their way into its timbers, and the sun and rain would have turned them near weightless, like corpses in a desert.

214

Five thousand people live on Providence today, clustered in any one of seven villages. Each has its plain church, and each is the domain of a small group of families. The Huffingtons and McLaughlins can be found in Lazy Hill; the Livingstons and Bryans in Southwest Bay; and the Newballs and Archbolds in Town. Before leaving Bogotá, I had visited the Biblioteca Luís Angél Arango, one of Latin America's most important public libraries, in search of books about Providence. One of my finds was *The Genealogical History of Providencia Island* by J. Cordell Robinson. Over page after page of family trees, I had tried to establish which Newball, Livingston or Howard had married which Archbold, Taylor or Robinson over the past nine generations.

It was nigh-on impossible, but it was clear that until the 1950s, the island's white families were obsessively close-knit. The Newballs and the Robinsons in particular were known for marrying their cousins, and as the gene pool shrank, growing numbers of Newballs were born deaf, the result of a mutant gene that the first Newball, an English lawyer called Francis, brought to the island in the 1830s. The last wholly white islander died in the 1950s, and although race remains Providence's prime divider, the majority of islanders fall somewhere between black and white. 'Some is white and some is black, but most is the colour of chewed tabac,' as a visiting anthropologist was told in the early 1970s.

Beyond Rocky Point, the road was shaded by the boughs of great cotton trees, whose beard-like blossom littered the corrugated iron roofs of the old wooden houses. Towards the south of the island, the faces grew darker, and by the time I reached the woods at Bottom House, I was the only white person around. From there, it was a long climb to the army base at the top of Morris Hill, from where the Colombian military scans the seas for the first sign of incursion by the Nicaraguans, who have long maintained that the islands are theirs. Coiling back down to meet the sea at Southwest Bay, the road took me past garden hotels and the porches of simple concrete houses, where families gathered to shelter from the sun and watch the scooters go by. The bay was an archetypal Caribbean idyll of white sand beach fringed by coconut palms, and was completely deserted.

I realised that I had given my last cigarette to the island's only beggar, so I turned off the road at the foot of Morris Hill, past a paddock where three hale old black men were admiring a mare, and down a little road to what looked to be a corner shop. There was no one behind the counter, so I called hello, but no one came. For the first time in my life, I found myself alone in a shop with only the goods for company. My eyes wandered over the shelves of washing powder, tinned vegetables and long life milk. I had half a mind to take a pack of Bostons from the other side of the counter, but found that I didn't have $3,000 pesos in change, so I walked towards the light spilling through the back door, and onto the veranda of the house behind. After hallowing over the sound of a Colombian *telenovela* [soap opera] I heard a woman shout, and a big-boned boy of 16 came out rubbing his doe eyes. He mumbled a greeting and shuffled past me in his flip-flops to the shop, where he sold me my Bostons.

Heading back to Town, I passed the tourists' chalets at Freshwater Bay, and parked up next to a sign that pointed down a steep flight of concrete steps to Almond Bay. Next to the sign was a concrete bus shelter in the shape of a huge octopus balancing on its tentacles – not that the island had any buses. Luis Dann Newball had told me that the bus shelters had been built by the last mayor, but his successor didn't want to pay for the bus service (I was never able to work out whether this was a cause or a consequence of the islanders' dependence on their scooters). I walked down the path, as little bright blue and green lizards scampered into the bush. In the field beyond, an egret was perching on the back of a recumbent cow, which was chewing the cud and appeared to be looking out to sea.

There wasn't much to see at Almond Bay, apart from a rickety wooden hut with a dirt floor, where a *mestizo* man was offering *empanadas* to the handful of tourists on the beach. A skinny old man with knobbly white knees, a flat cap *al estilo inglés* and a delighted look on his face was picking his way across the pebbles in his bare feet. He looked familiar, for I had only been out of London a couple of days, and I wondered if he might be English. "*¿Que maravilla es esta isla, no?*" he asked me with the air of one rejuvenated. I could not have agreed more. He bought a coconut from the man in the hut, who lopped off the top with his machete and stuck a straw in the hole, and headed back up the path.

"*Un cachaco,*" [someone from the mountains around Bogotá] said the man in the hut, who was wearing the *boltiao* hat of woven cream and brown straw popular on the Colombian coast. I bought a coconut, and asked him where he was from. His parents were from La Guajira, the desert peninsula that protrudes into the Caribbean from Colombia's

216

north coast, he said. But he had been born on the island, and had never left it. When I told him where I was from, Delmar looked at me with curiosity, as if meeting a character he had only read about in stories. "The English was here one time," he said, switching from Spanish to English. I gave him what I hoped was a look of complete surprise, for I was keen to find out what the islanders knew of Providence's history. "English come in the fourteenth century. About the time Christopher Come-bust-us discover America." But that was all he had for me; he didn't know who the English visitors were, or why they had come.

But Delmar knew all about Henry Morgan. "In the cave on Ketleena is where he buried his treasure," he told me, pointing across the glittering water of the bay to the smaller, adjoining island of Santa Catalina.[i] Morgan's Cave looked to be just short of Morgan's Head, the rocky outcrop that a Victorian visitor likened to 'the profile of an elderly ruffian.' If Delmar was to be believed, it was there that the Admiral of the Brethren stashed the gold and silver he amassed during the raid of Panama in 1671. My response was as obvious as it was naïve: if they all knew the location of the treasure, why had none of them managed to find it?

This prompted Delmar to talk of riptides, savage barracudas and old William Archbold, who had found Morgan's loot and spent the rest of his life in a wheelchair as a result. No, recovering the treasure was far from straightforward, for it was protected by ghosts. When Morgan returned to Providence from Panama, he ordered his four most loyal slaves to dig him a ditch. After burying his haul, he beheaded each of them in turn and had their headless corpses thrown into the ditch, in the belief that their 'duppies' would guard his treasure against future interlopers.[ii]

In the months to come, I would hear many stories of pirates' treasure, buried either on Santa Catalina or in the hills of Providence. Somewhere

---

i   In colonial times, the English called the island Providence, while the Spanish called it Santa Catalina (or sometimes Santa Catalina de Providencia). Since becoming part of Colombia, the island has become known as Providencia, while the adjoining island has been called Santa Catalina. But the islanders continue to call them Providence and Ketleena.

ii   'Duppy' is a Caribbean corruption of the Adangme word *adope*, meaning ghost. The Ga-Adangme people are prevalent in Ghana and Togo; between the late seventeenth and early nineteenth centuries many of them were enslaved and sold to English slave traders.

under the solid, black bubbles of volcanic rock lie the spoils of war accrued by Morgan and every other pirate to have stopped at Providence on his way back from the Spanish Main, among them Francis Drake, John Hawkins and Edward Mansveldt. I had heard similar stories in the mountain villages around Bogotá, where the indigenous Muisca people are said to have hidden their gold from the invading conquistadores. In Colombia, such sites are known as *guacas*; like all ghost stories, they reflect an ancestral conviction that the dead will one day avenge past misdeeds. Providence might have been conquered by Spanish speakers since the last of the buccaneers' ships faded out of sight, but the true wealth of its English-speaking inhabitants lay hidden, waiting for the day when an islander suitably qualified in the appeasement of angry spirits reclaimed it.

Delmar's hoary musings amounted to little more than I had learned from the tourist brochures on San Andrés, but I couldn't blame him for his ignorance of the island's history. The story of how Providence was resettled went largely unwritten, and the little that was recorded was lost when a hurricane destroyed the *intendente*'s archives in 1940. The islanders certainly felt some kinship with the buccaneers, but the events that bound them to the Brethren survived only in anecdotes passed down from grandparent to grandchild. The further back in time the story went, the hazier the details became, until all they could call upon were a few names and dates, bobbing unmoored on time's tide. Without a clear line of descent, the islanders had grown accustomed to an intangible sense of being on the wrong side of history, ignored by mainlanders, and caricatured as pirates by the few tourists to make it this far north.

The truth, of a sort, could be found in the National Archives in Kew, but the prospect of an islander visiting London was so unlikely that it might as well have been the Ancient Library of Alexandria. Besides, what could the volumes of correspondence between the governor of Jamaica and the Secretary of State in Whitehall really tell them about the Brethren of the Coast? Even when Providence was key to England's nascent empire, the rank and files' opinions went unwritten. To the extent that pirate stories have any basis in the reality of what happened in the Caribbean in the seventeenth century, the facts either come from Alexander Esquemelin's *History of the Buccaneers of America* or Captain Charles Johnson's *A General History of the Robberies and Murders of the most notorious Pyrates.*[iii] But neither author has much to say about the wider meaning of the Brethren, and both dismiss their ambitions as extending no further than fame and fortune.

I might have done likewise had I not come across James Burney's *History of the Buccaneers of America,* which was published in 1816. Burney was an English Rear Admiral who retired from the sea to write about its best-known villains. He, at least, was in no doubt about the buccaneers' radical intent, or how close they came to realising it. 'It was fortunate for the Spaniards, and perhaps for the other maritime nations of Europe, that the buccaneers... took no step towards making themselves independent whilst it was in their power,' he writes.

> [While] only two of them, [Edward] Mansveldt and [Henry] Morgan, appear to have contemplated any scheme of regular settlement independent of the European governments... before Tortuga was taken possession of for the Crown of France, such a project might have been undertaken with great advantage. The English and French buccaneers were then united, England was deeply engaged and fully occupied by a civil war, and the jealousy which the Spaniards entertained... kept at a distance all probability of their coalescing to suppress the buccaneers. If they had chosen at that time to form for themselves any regular mode of government, it appears not very improbable that they might have become a powerful, independent state.[2]

There is no way of knowing how Burney regarded the prospect of an independent pirate republic, but it is hard to resist the temptation to see him as sympathetic. By 1816, the pirates' villainy had been far exceeded by that of the law-abiding men who sentenced them to hang. The scale and savagery of the slave trade made a mockery of Europe's claim to moral superiority over the people of Africa and the Americas.

> In the history of so much robbery and outrage, the rapacity shown in some instances by the European governments in their West India transactions, and by governors of their appointment, appears in a worse light than that of the buccaneers, from whom, they being professed ruffians, nothing better was expected.

---

iii   Charles Johnson was long believed to be a pseudonym for Daniel Defoe. These days, that theory isn't much respected, and the author's true identity remains a mystery.

While 'the superior attainments of Europeans' had 'done much towards their own civilization,' they had done next to nothing for the native inhabitants, 'who have, with few exceptions, been made the instruments of usurpation and extortion.'[3]

Despite James Burney's claim that Morgan wanted to create an independent pirate state, and the stories that he envisaged Providence as its site, his biographers have little to say on the matter. To them, the Admiral of the Brethren was a lifelong rover, and Providence was never more than a stepping stone in a career that bloomed, and then withered in Jamaica. Far from leading his men to freedom on Providence, Morgan ditched them as soon as his employers could find no further use for them. The poacher was happy to turn gamekeeper, for by the time he returned to Port Royal from Panama in 1671, Jamaica's anarchic defenders were akin to the stalks of sugar cane that emerge dry and ragged on the other side of the mill; they were trash, only good as fuel for the fire that turns the juice they have just given up into precious sugar. Yet it is not entirely fanciful that Providence remained Morgan's fondest dream, even after he had deserted his Brethren for Mammon.

Before I left Almond Bay, Delmar told me another story, one that shows that Providence continues to be a haven, whether for religious radicals, castaways, renegades or criminals. Deep in the bush beyond Morgan's Head stand the ruins of a large, modern house, and the island's only swimming pool, now little more than a mildewed fish tank. The property was occupied until the early 1990s, supposedly by Pablo Escobar. It seemed a tall story, but it wasn't beyond the bounds of reason. By the early 1990s, Escobar was one of the wealthiest men on the planet, and certainly its most wanted. Where better for a man in constant fear of betrayal to hole up than the most isolated corner of one of the most remote islands in the Caribbean?

I wondered how he might have felt, looking out to sea from his hilltop hideaway. Did he ever consider the parallels between his life and that of Henry Morgan? Both men became folk heroes in their lifetimes, before being brought to book by authorities whose nefarious hypocrisy they knew only too well. In championing the poor of Medellín, wasn't Escobar, in his own way, claiming the mantle of Admiral of the Brethren? Hadn't both men defied the cant of the moralisers and the might of the most powerful nation on the planet? In Morgan's day, that meant Spain, which closed its ports to foreign traders, and denied its colonists the right to buy the well-made, reasonably priced products of England's workshops. By the time Escobar came to prominence, the roles had been reversed. The villain of the piece was now the United States, which denied its people the right to buy the no less well-made product of Colombia's workshops. Cocaine might be extortionately priced, but that only reflected the the authorities' determination to keep it from the market.

Perhaps the true heirs to the Caribbean's privateering tradition are its cocaine smugglers. They certainly use the same boltholes: Providence, Bluefields, Kingston and the myriad hidden coves and inlets of the Miskito coast. The parallels between pirates and drug traffickers aren't lost on Johnny Depp: before he starred as Jack Sparrow in *Pirates of the Caribbean*, he played another anti-hero in *Blow*: George Jung, who became the biggest importer of Escobar's cocaine into the United States. Ultimately, the meaning of the pirates is sufficiently elastic to hold multiple, sometimes contradictory interpretations, and this goes a long way to explaining their near-universal appeal today. Of course, not all pirate fans would appreciate the comparison between Henry Morgan and Pablo Escobar. If the islanders consider themselves heirs to Morgan's legacy, it isn't because so many of them have been lured into cocaine trafficking, but because they, like the Brethren of the Coast, live in a world skewed to benefit men more powerful than themselves. That means not only murderous drug barons, but also corrupt politicians, rampaging corporations and the behemoths of the international tourist trade. Between them, they have overrun the entire Caribbean, and the islanders regard them as scourges, to be kept from their shores wherever possible.

"Tank's empty," said the attendant at the island's only petrol station, who I found dozing in a hammock strung up between the pumps. It wasn't a problem, he assured me – any cargo ship leaving San Andrés for Providence knew to bring petrol. One would be arriving the following day – probably. I used the little fuel I had left to scooter back to Town for something to eat. I found nothing open bar a white-tiled, fluorescent-lit box opposite the mayor's office, where I bought a hotdog bursting with salty, molten fat and topped with broken crisps. There were a few more options for the handful of Colombian tourists staying in the chalets at Freshwater Bay, but they weren't cheap.

The following morning I headed to what looked to be the most popular of the three little supermarkets in Town for a look around. The wooden shelves were laden with tins of spaghetti and meatballs from Ohio, pork and beans from Medellín, tomatoes from Nebraska and spam from Brazil. In the vegetable aisle were some pitifully shrivelled onions, garlic and red peppers, which had been flown in from Costa Rica, and some Chilean apples. The only things that hadn't been imported were the shelves, which had been coated in thick layers of gloss paint to keep the termites at bay.

On the back wall was a large, brightly coloured map of the world. I found plenty of the world's other tiny islands: Tristan da Cunha, South Georgia, and even Pitcairn, which has a population of just 50. But Providence wasn't marked, and neither was San Andrés. Perhaps it was because their distant relatives have the initials 'UK' in brackets after their names, whereas the inhabitants of *el archepiélago de Providencia, San Andrés y Santa Catalina* lost touch with their progenitor state long ago. Providence is a fragment chipped off an Empire that no longer exists. Even if the chip were restored to the block from which it fell, it would no longer match, for its contours have been worn smooth by the passage of time. But perhaps 'fragment' is a misnomer. Empires are not as clearly delineated as the solid blocks of colour on the old maps suggest. Alive, they are dynamic, porous, and hybrid creations, but even once dead, the colours continue to bleed. The British might have forgotten about Providence, but for the islanders, England remained as real, and as unattainable, as an absent father.

It was strange to think that the hopes of a generation of British empire-builders had once rested on Providence. Those who sailed on the *Seaflower* in 1631 believed that their Puritan colony would in time eclipse the one that had been built by the passengers of the *Mayflower* ten years before. But New Westminster was abandoned just eleven years after the foundation stone of the governor's house was put in place, while New Plymouth went on to become a beacon of righteous autonomy for the generations that succeeded the Pilgrim Fathers. Cold, barren New England had trumped balmy, verdant Providence. Wasn't that what all those tins, packets, and cartons from the United States were trying to tell me?

Outside the supermarket, I bought a soft drink from a short, elderly woman who was sitting in the shade of an almond tree. "My name is Miss Amparo," she said with a smile when I told her why I'd come to Providence. *Amparo* is the Spanish for protection, and she was the picture of kindness. She had a round face, and distinctly Miskito features, which were not common on the island. "I am Archbold, but my father is Archbold Taylor, so I am Taylor from my father's mother's side. She was Taylor, so he becomes Taylor from his mother, and Archbold through his father. And I have Archbold Newball from my mother. Her father was Newball, and my grandmother was Archbold."

I was confused. I asked her where the first Taylors had come from. "My people told me that they were from Central America. You goes to Nicaragua, you find Taylors, because the pirates and those English people get to Central America before they get to Providence." This wasn't qute true, but I wasn't going to hold it against her.

"Do you know when they came here?" I asked. "I really can't tell you," said Miss Amparo apologetically. "My father used to read the history book, but maybe I was foolish them time to intercede more about it, because I don't have that thing."

We were interrupted by a delivery for her little shop, which she was having fitted out with sinks and fridges. Miss Amparo was going to open a fried chicken shop. We watched as the deliveryman struggled with box after box of frozen chicken legs from vast American and Canadian farms with names like Happy Valley and Imperial Foods.

"The food must have changed a lot since you were young," I remarked. "Yes," she said, "in our days, we didn't know what was tomatoes. We didn't know what was cabbage, or carrots. Up 'til now, nobody plant those things. From Monday to Saturday, we used to eat fish. We used to roast the fish. We used to steam the fish. And we used to corn the fish."

Miss Amparo's home had been one of the few that didn't have a fisherman, as her late husband had been the island's mayor – or "major," as she phrased it. "But who didn't have a fisherman in their home, they used to say, 'You give me fish and I will give you yucca.'" With so many vegetables, and so much fruit and fish to eat, it never occurred to them to eat anything else.

The only day they did not eat fish was Sunday, when the woman of the house would kill one of the chickens in her yard. "But now nobody kill a chicken," Miss Amparo said in wonderment. "They buy the chick-

223

en in the store." Until recently, the islanders had been among the healthiest people on the planet, and she seemed bewildered by her memories of how they had lived.

Over the next four months, I would speak to a lot of old islanders, and hear endless nostalgia, not just for the diet they had enjoyed, but for the collective effort required to bring it to the dining table. The island economy had effectively been cashless, for they shared what they had with those that needed it. This bounteous co-operation stemmed from their shared interest in fishing and farming, which they did together.

We were interrupted again, this time by a schoolboy wanting to buy a can of fizzy drink. Our conversation was proving surprisingly difficult; in the short time we had been talking, Miss Amparo had had to attend to customers, delivery men, a census taker and a woman looking for the cemetery. Even when we'd been free to talk, our words were drowned out by the *reggaetón* ringtones of mobile phones, and the incessant buzz of passing scooters. Half a mile in either direction were spots of utmost tranquillity, but the island's main settlement was noisier than Oxford Street.

"In our days everything was coconut," Miss Amparo said in a lull in trade. "If you want to fry the fish, you need coconut oil. If you want to cook the rice, you had to cook it with coconut oil. So every day we had to grate coconut. And practically every home had one or two cows, so they could always get the natural cow milk. But now nobody milk a cow."

I had noticed that her younger customers tended to be on the large side – had people got bigger since she was young? "Yes, because they eat too much tinned goods and fried things. In the past, they was big because they was descended from tall and stout people, not because of fatness. But now," she said, gesturing at the cardboard boxes around her, "the food is very different from those days."

Miss Amparo told me that if I wanted to know more about how, why and by whom the island was resettled, I should talk to Antonio Archbold on the smaller, adjoining island of Ketleena. I found him peeling an apple in a rocking chair on the porch of his clapboard bungalow. The steps that led onto his porch were worn and crowded with old tubs of vegetable oil that he had converted into flowerpots for his bougainvillea and hibiscus. Like most of the older islanders, Tony Archbold looked to be in good health. I had him down as being about 60, though he later told me that he was 76. He put it down to all the fish he ate. "I start learn how to eat the fish before I could even talk, because my parents would always put a piece of the fish meat in my mouth."

Mr Archbold spoke in a measured, unhurried way, and had an slow and easy laugh. He had found an idyllic spot that gave him an excellent vantage point from which to survey the length of the wooden bridge that led back to the main island. "I does not come out of my house to cross that bridge if I don't have to," he told me. "It's just me and my wife is here now and we're trying to enjoy our old age."

Through the unglazed window behind his head, I could see an old map of the island on the back wall. It was the first and last time I would see such an artefact on Providence, and a token of his keen interest in the island's past. In places with so little written history, the title of historian goes to the oldest or wisest member of the community. Tony Archbold had earned his title over the course of a life at sea, for on Providence, there was no profession more worthy of respect than that of ship's captain. "At the age of 18, I worked on a motor sailor that used to go from San Andrés to Cartagena, and then come back to Providence and then Colón. I started at second cook, and when I quit the sea, I was the navigator of a 500-ton ship that used to take all the electro-domestics from the free zone in Panama to San Andrés."

I asked him about the first Archbold to come to Providence. "I really don't know where Francis Archbold came from. According to history, he migrate from Scotland to the Caymans as a net builder, and then he migrate to this island. He taught his son-in-law how to build his nets, he taught my grandfather, my father taught me and I taught my children. But that's all we know. If I were younger, if I had that privilege, I would really go and do some investigation because there are so many things…"

Tony's voice trailed away, and his gaze drifted to the patch of lush sea grass growing in his little front garden. Beyond the grass, the soil was black and smooth, for the tide had only just receded into the mangroves, whose black fingers probed the sunlit water.

"I was very curious as a young man. When this island was destroyed by a hurricane in 1940, I was three years old, so there wasn't any school. What I have learned, I learn it by travelling. At the age of ten, I thought every white man could read and write. But I begin to do some investigation on my travelling. I read every book on the coloured race, and I begin to learn, not only about the negro race, but also about the white race. My great-grandfather was Scottish, and he didn't know how to read and write. My great-grandmother was an African, with a Spanish title, but she knew to read and write."

But that was all Tony Archbold knew about the black members of his family. Even after poring over the few books he'd been able to lay his hands on, he knew next to nothing about their original language, religion, or even which part of Africa they came from. Listening to his voice, I thought I detected a West Country burr. As subtly as I could, I scrutinised his light brown eyes, and through them, pictured Francis Archbold sitting quietly inside his descendant's body. If I'd known more about the Africans in his family tree, I might have made them out too, but *The Genealogical History of Providencia Island* makes no mention of the first Africans that went to Providence.

While Tony had little to tell me about how the island came to be resettled, he was all too aware of how history can be spun for gain, whether personal, political, or commercial. "To sell San Andrés, they begin to sell Henry Morgan. But Morgan was never in San Andrés!" he told me. "They get it from the internet, and from what Alexander Esquemelin wrote, but they don't mention that Morgan took him to court and Esquemelin had to retract what he said about him!"

As the surgeon on several of Morgan's voyages, Alexander Esquemelin was well placed to turn the events he had witnessed into riveting tales. In 1684, Thomas Malthus published an English translation of his *History of the Buccaneers of America*. It was an immediate success, and no book of the seventeenth century in any language was the parent of so many imitations, or the source of so much fabulous fiction. Sir Henry Morgan has exercised a fascination over the reading public unlike any other pirate ever since. He is the embodiment of adventure and cruelty, a servant of the Crown who was licensed to rob; and a pirate who was celebrated, condemned and then celebrated again by both Charles II and the country at large.

After several years of regaling the leading lights of Restoration London with his tales of singeing the Don's beard, Henry realised that respectable society was beginning to lose interest in him. But respectability mattered little to him, for he had something of far greater value to protect. He had a reputation, and in the closing years of his life, he spent his sober hours vociferously defending it. Morgan took issue with Esquemelin's account of his life, which he considered full of slights against his character and career. He was neither a buccaneer nor a pirate, he asserted. At his height, he had been both Admiral and Lieutenant-Governor of Jamaica, and the suggestion that the Crown might appoint a pirate to such eminent posts was no less libellous. Sir Henry sued Thomas Malthus for libel, won the case and was awarded £200 damages. In subsequent editions of the *History of the Buccaneers of America*, Malthus made it clear that Morgan 'never was a servant to anybody in his life, unless unto his Majesty. Neither did he ever sail but by commission from the governor of those parts.'[4]

The story is telling for two reasons: not only does it show how slippery the truth becomes in the hands of men determined to spin a good yarn, it inadvertently lays bare the organised criminality on which England's wealthiest Caribbean colony was built. But no holidaymaker can resist the lure of a good pirate story, however tenuously anchored it may be to the truth. If Morgan were ever to return to the Caribbean, he would make his fortune not by licensed piracy, but by suing all the hotel proprietors, restaurant owners, and owners of shoreline caves who have appropriated his name to advertise places that he never even visited.

Shortly before leaving Providence, I paid another visit to Tony Archbold's clapboard bungalow on Ketleena to give him a photocopy I had made of Henry Morgan's family tree. It showed that, contrary to popular myth, the Admiral of the Brethren was no philanderer. He remained faithful to his wife to the end, and died childless. He left half of his estate to Elizabeth and divided the other half between the children of the two men who had risen through the ranks of the Jamaican plantocracy with him. The first of those men was Charles Byndloss; the second was Henry Archbold.

"This is very, very important," Tony said, and a wonderful smile spread across his face. Morgan's family tree put paid to the long-held assumption that the Archbolds were descendants of Henry Morgan. But for the first time, an islander could corroborate that he indeed shared a connection with the Admiral of the Brethren, not by blood, but by love. A month after leaving Providence, I was travelling through the English-speaking towns on the Caribbean coast of Central America when I heard that Tony Archbold had died. What follows is the story of how

Providence was resettled, gleaned from the books, articles and assorted old papers that the island's historian never got to read.

1789: emerging from a sea that shimmered near silver in the light of mid-morning, the island looked like a black peaked hat. As Captain Francis Archbold drew closer, he saw that it was no more than five miles wide, but its greenery suggested that its soils were rich. When his sloop was just a league from shore, the seabed rose from the depths, turning the cobalt water a brilliant turquoise. Francis dropped anchor on the edge of the reef, rowed ashore in his canoe and stepped onto a short beach of white sand partially shaded by coconut palms. He made for a deep crease in the greenery, where a fast-flowing stream coursed down from the Peak to the sea. It was his first taste of freshwater since leaving Kingston, 410 miles to the north.

Francis decided to settle the flat ground in the south of the island. He had arrived with several of his family's slaves, who he set to work felling trees and clearing rocks. Among the white men to have accompanied him was a carpenter, who went into the woods to fell cedar and ironwood. He made foundation posts and planking, and set about building some rudimentary huts.

No white family could claim to have deep roots on Jamaica, but Francis Archbold had a better claim than most. There had been Archbolds on the island since 1655, the year the English wrested it from the Spanish. Colonel Henry Archbold had served under Henry Morgan when the latter was the island's Lieutenant Governor, and had risen to become a powerful member of the Jamaican Assembly. But the principal heir to the family's holdings had sold up and returned to England in 1770. Francis had been left with nothing, and joined the growing ranks of men with no prospect of owning land for themselves.

By 1789, Jamaica had changed beyond recognition since Henry Morgan's day. There was an insatiable demand for tropical goods like sugar, cocoa, tobacco, coffee and cotton in Britain, and it was met by the plantation owners of its Caribbean colonies. The islands accounted for four fifths of Britain's income from colonial trade, and the sugar business had paid for some of the grandest public buildings of Georgian London, Liverpool and Bristol. Sugar was also a vital spur to British industry. By

1789, half of Britain's exports were destined for its colonies. That year, trade with India was worth £2 million, whereas trade with the Caribbean was worth over £4 million, half of which was with Jamaica.[5]

Although Jamaica had risen to become Britain's wealthiest colony, it was entirely dependent on the mother country. Britain took all it produced, but also ensured that an island capable of supplying practically every tropical crop known to man grew little apart from sugar and cotton. Such was the island's self-neglect that it had to import most of its food from the Thirteen Colonies, and when trade was cut off by the outbreak of the American War of Independence in 1776, 15,000 Jamaican slaves died of starvation.[6] In return for Jamaica's sugar and cotton, Britain exported the lessons it was learning from its Industrial Revolution. The division of labour and the creation of specialist professions, first developed in Britain's textile mills, were transplanted to Jamaica, where the sugar estates became more akin to rural factories than any English farm.

Back in 1658, when Colonel Henry Archbold had bought his first plot on Jamaica, most of the land belonged to men like himself: old soldiers and sailors keen to leave the sea behind and make a living from farming. Plenty of them had been privateers, and they brought ashore the attitudes they had learned over thirty years of colonial rivalry, plunder and war. One observer described the island's first landowners as typically illiterate and 'all trained up from boys in rebellion and murder.'[7] They had relatively little money, but land was cheap, so they spent what they had on buying land and taking on servants. It took them some time to work out how best to raise sugar cane, but demand for sugar was strong in Britain, and they had every reason to be hopeful.

There were just 1,400 slaves on Jamaica in 1658, but following the foundation of the Royal Africa Company in 1672, the supply of slaves became a Crown monopoly. By the time Francis Archbold left Jamaica in 1789, there were 250,000 slaves on the island, and most of its smallholders had been muscled out by those with capital to invest in plantations and sugar mills.[8] Once the plantations were up and running, their owners saw no reason to stay in Jamaica, and returned to London to enjoy their fortunes in style.

In their absence, their servants took over the day-to-day running of the colony. They too had changed since Morgan's day. Over the course of the eighteenth century, Irish and Scots had come to Jamaica in growing numbers, and by 1789, Scots made up the majority of

229

the white population.[9] Charles Leslie, whose *New and Exact History of Jamaica* was published in 1739, did not hold these newcomers in high regard. 'Many of these menial servants, who are retained for the sake of saving a deficiency, are the very dregs of the three kingdoms,' he wrote. By 1789, many of these 'dregs' had joined the resident elite of estate managers, merchants, lawyers and magistrates. Members of the 'plantocracy' enjoyed an idle life. In return for filing an occasional report for his employer in London, an attorney could expect an annual salary equivalent in value to 6 per cent of his estate's output. Most white Jamaicans drank to excess (Governor Nugent's wife Maria noted that, 'the men of this country eat like cormorants and drink like porpoises'). They were also renowned for their choleric tempers and several of them embezzled funds from their employers' accounts.

On leaving Jamaica for a fresh start on another island, Francis Archbold would likely first have considered San Andrés. When Daniel Elfrith stopped by the island in 1629, he thought its low hills and lack of a natural harbour made it indefensible, and had sailed on to Providence. But potential settlers no longer had to make a priority of defence. Following Britain's defeat in the American War of Independence, it was forced to recognise the independence of its 13 North American colonies. But the Treaties of Versailles that Britain signed in 1783 went further than that, for the war had united Britain's European enemies, and they were determined to win back what they had lost over a century of rising British sea power. In their negotiations with Spain, Britain agreed to evacuate all settlers living in proximity to Spanish territories, including those on the Miskito coast, and to resettle them in British Honduras – modern day Belize – further up the coast.

The treaty brought peace to the Caribbean, but it left the status of Providence and San Andrés unclear. Although British ships evacuated 89 English settlers from San Andrés, some of those living on the island defied the order to leave, and asked King Charles III of Spain's permission to remain.[10] They had headed south from Jamaica in search of new beginnings, they explained. Since they were looking to raise sugar or cotton, most of them had opted to settle on San Andrés, which had more flat ground than Providence. They wanted no part in the tug of war between England and Spain, and only wanted to be left in peace.

The Viceroy of Nueva Granada granted the settlers their request, only for a court in Madrid to overrule him, and there followed several years of limbo, as Bogotá and Madrid jostled over who had the authority to consider the islanders' request. Finally, an official was despatched from Cartagena to enforce the expulsion order. Had he spoken English, San Andrés and Providence might be Spanish speaking today. But he did not, and the interpreter who accompanied him from the Spanish Main was evidently no royalist. When the official returned to Cartagena, promising to present the islanders' case to his superiors, Tomás O'Neille chose to stay on San Andrés. O'Neille was a Spanish-speaking creole who had been born in the Canary Islands to Irish parents, and in this bilingual child of the Atlantic world, the islanders found their champion.

They waited three years for a definitive answer to their request. Finally, in May 1792, a letter arrived from Madrid informing them that they would be allowed to stay. Tomás O'Neille was appointed governor of *las islas de Providencia y San Andrés*, which would henceforth fall under the jurisdiction of the Captain-General of Guatemala. The King of Spain clearly thought it better to have a band of English farmers living on one distant island than a garrison of impoverished Spanish soldiers wasting away on another.

After the English were driven off Providence by the Spanish in 1641, a handful of refugees had made their way to the Miskito coast, where they waited for a time when they would be able to return to the island. After 1670, they were joined by some of the pirates and privateers that Henry Morgan had driven out of Jamaica. Among the other refugees to find shelter on the coast over the next 100 years were runaway slaves and servants, and smallholders muscled out of Jamaica by the sugar barons. Their forays on land and sea supplied them with sarsaparilla, mahogany, dyewoods and vanilla, which they bartered with Jamaican merchant ships for arms, ammunition and farming tools. Most of them took Miskito wives, and light-skinned Miskito children were soon growing up with English as their first language. In 1739, the governor of Jamaica reported that there were 537 whites and 1677 slaves living on the coast, 'the majority of whom could live nowhere else.'[11]

By 1789, most of them had left for British Honduras, but some, perhaps the great-great-grandchildren of those who had fled Providence in 1641, opted to return to the island. Among them were John Britton and Thomas Taylor, who were both of Anglo-Miskito heritage. Once on Providence, they joined Francis Archbold in asking for the clemency of the King of Spain. They had come to the island not to engage in piracy or war, they protested, but to cut wood and tend crops. They proclaimed their loyalty to the king, promised not to trade with the English merchants of Jamaica, and agreed to convert to Catholicism as soon as the king sent a priest to the islands.

In theory at least, Tomás O'Neille was responsible for both islands, but his control over what happened on Providence was nominal, and he left Francis Archbold in peace. Francis' house in the south of the island became known as 'Bottom House'. When the work was complete, the men who had helped him to build it gathered around the island's first table and watched as he sketched a rudimentary map of the island. He drew a series of lines running from the Peak to the shore, and apportioned a plot of land to each of them. That done, each man began clearing the bush for cultivation.

After three years, their number had risen to 32, including wives and children.[12] Each family had its own house and garden, where they grew corn, yucca and potatoes. They gathered fruit from the wild trees that grew in the woods, and hunted pigeons and wild pigs. Like those who had settled the island 160 years before, they became skilled fishermen, for the reef was a feeding ground for shoals of snapper, grouper and sea bass, and enjoyed the tender meat of the green turtle.

But if they were to advance beyond basic subsistence, they would need to clear much more ground, and plant crops to sell to the merchant ships. So in 1792, Francis sailed for the Gold Coast of Africa, home of the Coromantis. It was a journey Francis had made many times before, for he had once been a slave trader, and knew the Gold Coast well. Thanks to the role the Coromantis played in fomenting revolt among their fellow slaves, Barbadian planters had passed a law prohibiting their purchase. Yet perversely, Jamaican planters actually preferred them over other ethnicities, and Francis was similarly undeterred.

There is no record of how many enslaved Coromantis boarded his ship, but of the 21 that survived the voyage across the Atlantic, there were likely to have been more women than men. Women were given more spacious accommodation, where they could move about unchained, and they could also trade sex for favours from the sailors. Conditions for men were worse, and any who dared resist Archbold's crew could expect cruel punishment.[13] Francis sold one or two slaves to each of the settlers, keeping most of them for himself. His foreman, an African who he called Loyalty, put them to work clearing the bush around Bottom House, and when that was done, he had them plant cottonseeds.

Although the first years Francis Archbold and the other settlers spent on Providence are largely a matter of guesswork, thanks to a government inspector's visit to San Andrés in 1793, a picture emerges of a thriving community. José del Rio found ten large white families and 293 slaves living on the larger island. There was no central settlement, for each family had its own little plot of land, and these were scattered all over the island. They enjoyed an excellent diet of maize, squash, yam, oranges, avocados, plantain and coconut. They grew tobacco, coffee, sugar cane and indigo – just enough for themselves – and raised pigs, chickens and turkeys. They also grew allspice trees, whose fruit they traded with merchants from Cartagena, and cardamom plants, which they fed to their turtles.

Although they had cut down most of the island's biggest cedar trees to serve as planking for Jamaican merchant ships, they still found enough timber to build houses for themselves, and José del Rio was much impressed by their skills with axe and hammer. The island's slave owners told him that cotton from Saint Andrew's, as they insisted on calling their island, was the best in the world, and fetched much better prices in Liverpool than did cotton from Santo Domingo. What they didn't tell him was that despite the ban on trade with Kingston, they had sold their entire cotton crop to the captain of a Jamaican merchant ship. With the money they made from the sale, they were able to buy goods like rum, butter and Madeira wine.

One day, Governor Tomás O'Neille invited José del Rio to a banquet in the home of the island's biggest slave owner. In addition to the splendid spread, the government inspector was struck by how the islanders' general industriousness allowed them to 'cultivate a certain degree of mutual friendship.' Thanks to their peaceful contentedness, they were 'able to keep order without need of magistrates or an official religion,' which was unheard of in a Spanish colony.[14] Their only complaint was the poor quality of the drinking water; since there were few streams on the island, they had had to build tanks in which to store the rainwater that ran off their roofs.

But José del Rio knew more than he let on. Despite the islanders' subterfuge, he could see that the source of their wealth was not farming, but the trade in contraband goods, which they smuggled from Jamaica to the Miskito coast. This was in clear breach of the terms of the Treaty of Versailles, so on his return to the Main, he recommended that the islanders be removed to Bluefields. In 1795, the Captain-General of Guatemala issued another order for the islands to be evacuated.

Once again, O'Neille appealed to Madrid for protection. The Captain-General was right to complain about the English merchants of Jamaica, for they were interfering in Spain's legitimate trade with its colonies, he wrote. But it would be quite wrong to blame the islanders, who remained loyal subjects of the King of Spain, and would be only too glad to see the back of the smugglers. He suggested that the Captain-General send out one of the *guardacostas'* ships to drive them away. Once again, the order to leave was rescinded.

But the idea that the settlers were loyal to Spain could only ever be pretence: the only Spanish speakers on the island were O'Neille and the 30 soldiers who had been dispatched from Guatemala. The colonial authorities had always been keen to see Spanish taught on the islands, and had even suggested sending Spanish families to San Andrés, in the hope that the islanders would 'get to know our language and customs,' and in time, 'feel themselves Spanish.' But as O'Neille wrote in a report some time afterwards, 'the islanders still speak English and know nothing of Spanish.'

A few years later, another inspector was dispatched to San Andrés to investigate reports that that the islanders were not only buying and selling from the Jamaicans, but had started trading with the Americans, whose merchant ships were roving the Caribbean with growing confidence. Their stores were said to be full of English and American goods waiting to be smuggled up the River San Juan to the townspeople of Granada and León. What everybody knew, and nobody wanted to admit, was that official connivance in the smuggling of English goods into Spanish ports had been going on for years. Moreover, Tomás O'Neille was sharing the spoils of the smuggling business with his commercial agent in León, who happened to be his father-in-law. With everyone bar the King of Spain getting a cut of the action, contraband was a boat that nobody wanted to rock. The inspector's inquiries were met with bemused shrugs, and he returned to the Spanish Main none the wiser, venturing only that it was 'evident that neither the islanders nor the English want to see a change of governor.'[15]

But even this was enough to unnerve Tomás O'Neille. For as long as the islands were under the jurisdiction of the Captain-General of Guatemala, there would always be meddlesome inspectors prowling the rickety jetty that served as the island's dock. If only colonial jurisdiction over the islands could be reverted to Cartagena, 480 miles due south, the island's smugglers might get some peace. O'Neille made his case in a latter to Madrid; he explained that while Cartagena was further away than Guatemala, it was to windward of San Andrés, whereas Central America was to leeward. This meant that the *guardacostas* would always find it easier to reach the island from Cartagena than from Guatemala. In 1803, O'Neille got the response he had been hoping for: the authorities confirmed that all Spanish territories between Cape Gracias a Dios and Veraguas, including San Andrés and Providencia, would henceforth be considered part of the Viceroyalty of Nueva Granada, and administered from Cartagena.

The steep slopes running from the Peak to the sea made Providence less suited to cotton cultivation than San Andrés. This deterred more ambitious settlers, made the large-scale importation of slaves unnecessary, and ensured that while San Andrés prospered, Providence remained a backwater. From time to time, a Jamaican merchant ship would arrive in the harbour to buy dried turtle meat, timber and the little cotton Francis Archbold was able to produce at Bottom House. In return, the islanders were able to buy hammers and nails, pots and pans, shoes and cloth, canvas for their sails, and the clay pipes in which they smoked their tobacco.

However, the frugality and isolation of life on Providence did not put off all comers, and Francis and his friends were soon joined by more English speakers. Following the American War of Independence, many of those who had remained loyal to the British Crown sought refuge in the Caribbean. Finding few opportunities for poor whites around Kingston, some founded new communities in the west of Jamaica. Others heard about the little islands 410 miles south, where the people spoke English and land was cheap.

Among them was Philip Beekman Livingston, a sailor and merchant of Scottish descent who arrived on Providence in 1800. During the war years, Livingston had travelled widely aboard an American man-o'-war. When his ship was captured by the Spanish off the coast of Chile, he made his way into the Andes and then north to Cartagena, where he found passage on a ship bound for the United States. But he had made it no further than Kingston when the ship began to take on water and eventually sank in the harbour. Taking this for an omen, he boarded a merchant ship bound for Providence, where Francis Archbold sold him land and slaves, and he started growing a little cotton.

If Providence's settlers were looking forward to a future of peaceful productivity, they were to be disappointed. 'History' – the awesome rumbling of great nations on the move – was poised to sweep through the islands again. The Americans' triumph over their colonial masters had inspired few emulators in Britain's Caribbean colonies, but its impact on the instigators of the revolt that became the French Revolution cannot be exaggerated. The revolution in turn brought Napoleon Bonaparte to power. Combining the tradition of the absolutist king with the ideals of the revolution, Napoleon led his armies across Europe in an unprecedented campaign against the *anciens régimes*. Among the decrepit structures in his sights was Spain's Habsburg monarchy. In 1808 Napoleon invaded Spain, deposed King Charles IV, and put a Bourbon king on the throne.

The French invasion sounded the death knell for the Spanish Empire. Not only did the crisis distract attention from the colonies, where even the highest-ranking colonial officials seemed indifferent to the fate of their European masters, it forced Spain to find common cause with England in the struggle to expel the invaders. Like France, England turned to its colonies to finance its military campaigns, for it could not keep large armies in the field for years at a time without imposing high taxes on imports of sugar, cotton and rum.

Yet the country most at risk of losing its Caribbean possessions was not Spain, but France. The jewel in France's imperial crown was Saint-Domingue – modern-day Haiti – which had first been settled in 1659, just four years after the English captured Jamaica. In 1794, France's revolutionary government had abolished slavery in all of France's overseas territories. But swayed by the country's merchants, his wife's Caribbean connections, and his own racism, Napoleon set about restoring slavery in France's wealthiest colony.

The leader of the revolution for a Free Haiti was General François-Dominique Toussaint L'Ouverture, who had been born into slavery as the son of Coromanti parents. He rose to prominence espousing the revolutionary ideals of republican France, which ennobled the huge revolt that spread through the plantations in 1801.[iv] Although Napoleon's Grand Army defeated the black general the same year, its victory was short-lived. The French forces might have marched across Europe and defeated its most renowned armies, but they proved no match for yellow fever. Brought low by 'Yellow Jack,' the foreigners were seen off with little difficulty when the Haitians next took to the battlefield, and in 1804, Haiti declared its independence.

Among the forces Napoleon sent to Haiti to restore French rule were the 3rd and 4th Polish demi-brigades, which had been created in 1794, in the wake of attempts by Russia, Prussia and Austria to further partition Poland. In desperation, remnants of the Polish army had retreated west, in the hope of persuading Napoleon to establish a professional Polish army in exile. The French Emperor made them his 'Polish Legions,' and after several years fighting alongside his Grand Army in Italy, France and Austria, he sent them to Haiti, where they set about smothering one people's aspirations for freedom in the hope that Napoleon would revive their own. It was an irony of the age of nationalism that sickened many of the Polish soldiers, and when the time came to board the supply ships for home, many of them chose to stay behind.

Among these renegades was a Polish aristocrat by the name of Teodor Birelski, who clearly saw a brighter future for himself in the Caribbean. The Haitian revolt had prompted the first rumble of the wars the Spanish colonies would fight to secure independence from Spain. Men of all nations rushed to put themselves at the service of the creole patriots, and this led to a revival of the privateering tradition in the Caribbean. They sailed under the flags of the the aspirant republics of Peru and Argentina, and considered all Spanish ships legitimate targets for plunder. In 1805, Teodor Birelski had been fighting in Haiti as one of 60 Polish and French troops assigned to the *Mosquito*, but captain and crew turned

---

[iv] Toussaint L'Ouverture changed the island's name from Saint-Dominigue to Haiti, which was the original, Arawak name.

to privateering and began robbing British ships as they made their way home from Kingston. So successful were these Franco-Polish pirates that the governor of Jamaica sent out a warship to pursue them. The *Renard* chased the *Mosquito* from Cuba into Charleston, and then back down to Veracruz in the Gulf of Mexico, with the ship's French captain managing to escape what seemed certain capture on several occasions.

It was while cruising off the Miskito coast that the *Mosquito* put in at Providence for victuals. None of his descendants know why Birelski chose to stay on the island; it may be that he was deliberately marooned after falling foul of the ship's captain; or maybe, after years of fighting, he was simply taken by the romance of living on an isolated island.

Given that he changed his name to John Robinson shortly after his arrival, the last explanation seems the most likely. Since its first publication in 1719, *The Life and Adventures of Robinson Crusoe* had been translated into most European languages. Teodor Birelski was an educated man, and was likely familiar with Daniel Defoe's novel. If so, his arrival on Providence would have struck him as more than a coincidence, for the island's name chimes with one of the book's recurring themes – the providence of God over even the most benighted members of his flock.[16]

Twenty years after Francis Archbold first came ashore, the population of Providence had risen to 300. The men and women who resettled the island spawned offspring at a rate only found among people on the brink of extinction. Francis Archbold had six more children, by whom we don't know. Philip Beekman Livington married Francis' daughter Mary, thereby uniting the two families that have dominated island life from that day to this. Thomas Taylor, who had come to the island from the Miskito coast, went on to have children by five different women, and his friend John Britton was no less promiscuous.[17]

Stable, monogamous households were few and far between on Providence, for while most island men had wives, they also had mistresses. Polygamy was the norm for both settlers and slaves on Jamaica, and the mores of the bigger island provided the template for family life on Providence. That polygamy should have been so prevalent on Jamaica should come as little surprise, for the lack of churches and schools on the island caused a complete breakdown of the institution of marriage. There were very few white women available to the overseers and men of their ilk, since most were the wives or sisters of their employers, and strictly off-limits. So it became customary to seduce the 'wives' of the slaves.

In a society as cruel and hierarchical as Jamaica, it should come as little surprise to find that poor whites took particular pleasure in seducing the wives of the 'better sort' of slave – those with skills to offer or some authority in the community. The whites were 'heartily despised' for this last, most intimate act of robbery.[18]

16

THE LAST ENGLISHMAN

Tomás O'Neille's diplomatic skills had served him well. He was the Spanish governor of two isolated islands of English speakers, mostly the descendants of wandering pirates and castaways. While he gave the colonial authorities no reason to doubt his loyalty to the King of Spain, he made his living running contraband into their ports, a duplicitous balancing act that was the basis for the bigger island's prosperity. By 1805, San Andrés was a thriving cotton producer, where 800 slaves toiled in the plantations, while 400 settlers worked as overseers, administrators and smallholders. But it was not Jamaica: many of the settlers were of mixed race, and the island's biggest slave owner, Francis Bent, was a black man.

Then Francis Archbold, the leader of the settlers on Providence, rocked the boat. That year, he appealed to the governor of Jamaica, Sir George Nugent, for protection. Notwithstanding his declaration of loyalty to the King of Spain, he had always considered himself a British subject, he told him. Sir George sympathised. In March 1806, Captain John Bligh landed on San Andrés aboard the *Surveillante* with 144 soldiers, and proclaimed the island a territory of the British Crown. Overawed by the cannon bristling at the warship's gunwales, Tomás O'Neille offered no resistance when Bligh arrested him, shipped him and the 30 soldiers at his command to Cartagena, and unceremoniously dumped them on the beach.

The free population of San Andrés welcomed the arrival of the British, for like Francis Archbold, they had always considered themselves Crown subjects. Yet memories of how the British had deserted them in signing the Treaty of Versailles were still fresh in their minds. Hedging their bets, they asked that as and when Captain Bligh left the island, he take them with him. It was all very well being scooped back into the Anglosphere, but if the islands were left undefended, they would rather be evacuated to Jamaica or the Miskito coast than stay and face reprisals from the Spanish.

240

But Bligh proved a blithe spirit: he departed San Andrés just two months after he had arrived, leaving behind a handful of soldiers to fend off the inevitable counter-attack. Sure enough, the *junta de guerra* wasted no time in putting Tomás O'Neille at the head of a contingent of 50 soldiers with orders to retake the island, and in October 1807, the governor retook San Andrés for Spain. When he found that several prominent landowners had been fomenting relations with the governor of Jamaica prior to the invasion, he had them charged with high treason (although Francis Archbold managed to escape punishment).

It was a bad time to be proclaiming loyalty to the Spanish crown. O'Neille's imperial masters were in crisis: with the king driven into exile, and Napoleon's army still occupying the country, the fragility of Spain's empire was plain for all to see. When, in July 1810, the new Viceroy of Nueva Granada wrote to the islands' governor to ratify his term of office, O'Neille hastily stepped down, alleging ill health. His timing was impeccable; on 20th July, Nueva Granada declared its independence. The following year, Venezuela did the same. This prompted a fierce backlash from Madrid, and both colonies were soon embroiled in a war for liberation from European rule.

For many years after the outbreak of hostilities, Providence was unscathed by the wars of independence. Jacob Dunham, an American who made his living trading around the western Caribbean, had no trouble reaching the island from New York in the summer of 1817. 'We arrived at Old Providence in 17 days,' he wrote in his diary, and were greeted by:

> a motley group of English, Spanish and Curaccoa natives of all colors … [who] urgently requested me to give them a ball… I had a trunk full of sheepskin morocco ladies' shoes on board, which cost at auction thirty-one cents per pair. I sold most of them here at two dollars per pair. Many of them were danced out in one night.[1]

Dunham spent the following day enticing the islanders with his cargo of 'one hundred and sixty different articles to be sold at retail,' including 'calicoes, jackonets, muslins, shoes, ribbons, jewelry, cologne water, pomatum, beads and liquors.'

Yet when Dunham returned two years later, he found that the war for independence had finally caught up with the island. 'On our arrival at Old Providence, I found a small fleet of vessels there called patriots (another name for pirates), who had taken possession of the island and hoisted the Columbian flag.' On entering the harbour, Dunham's ship was embargoed, and he was taken ashore for questioning. 'They had hanged one American, and severely flogged another for some crime, giving him one hundred lashes under the gallows,' he wrote. Although the occupiers 'pretended to hold some commission from General Bolivar (sic),' Dunham demanded that they return his vessel, and was able to escape the island with his precious cargo intact.

The leader of these patriot-cum-pirates was 31-year-old Louis-Michel Aury, a French privateer who would spend his short, roving life clamouring for official recognition as a committed fighter for the independence of Latin America. He had first heard about Providence in the summer of 1818, as he was trying to curry favour with the diplomatic representatives of the half a dozen Latin American governments in exile that had found sanctuary in Kingston. The governor of Jamaica was happy to sponsor their plans to throw off the Spanish yoke, and offered no objection when his guests began issuing letters of marque to willing privateers. The combination of public glory and private enrichment enticed Louis-Michel Aury to accept a commission from the Argentine consul, who told him about a small island off the coast of Nicaragua that would make an ideal base from which to run arms to the mainland.

Aury was delighted to be accepted into the patriot fold, and began casting around for recruits in Kingston. By the time his flotilla of 14 ships was ready to sail, he had been joined by 800 soldiers and sailors with a stake in the overthrow of the Spanish. Most were French veterans of the Napoleonic Wars, but there were also Mexican, Chilean and Argentine patriots and 200 battle-hardened Haitians. He also recruited 150 white Jamaicans and a large contingent from the southern United States. Some of them were attracted by the lure of privateering, others by the opportunity to overthrow the Spanish Empire, which remained the principal obstacle to free trade in the Caribbean, in spite of the assurances made in the Treaties of Versailles in 1783.

Aury sailed first to San Andrés, where he deposed the man who had taken Tomás O'Neille's place as governor without firing a shot. The prominent slave owners who sat on the island council breathed a sigh of relief when he told them that their island was of no interest to him, and that he intended to base his force on the neighbouring island. Within days of his arrival on Providence, the island had become a vast barracks, divided into an English camp, a French camp and an American camp. While he awaited the arrival of the reinforcements he needed to launch an assault on the mainland, Aury set about fortifying the island against a Spanish attack, aided by his second-in-command, Agustín Codazzi, a 24-year-old Italian engineer and naval gunner who was no less committed to the patriot cause. In his *Memorias*, Codazzi writes that Providence:

> was certainly the best outpost we could have wished for, and the most suitable for espionage. The island is completely surrounded by reefs that extend for several leagues in all directions, so there is no danger of being surprised by the enemy at night.[2]

To make the smaller, adjoining island of Santa Catalina better able to withstand a siege, Codazzi had his men remove the sand bar that joined it to the main island (thanks to the channel they dredged, the two islands have been separated by 100 metres of water ever since). Meanwhile, he had the island's battery, which had been in ruins since the departure of Henry Morgan, equipped with heavy calibre cannons. For the first time in almost 150 years, Fort Warwick would serve as an anti-Spanish bastion 'in the heart of the Indies and the mouth of the Spaniards.' Pressed into service by a new generation of patriots, it became known as Fort Liberty.

Codazzi was enamoured of Providence. Thanks to the huge variety of crops the islanders cultivated in the hills, he enjoyed a healthy diet of corn, bananas, yucca, sweet potatoes, peppers, mangoes, pineapples, papaya, tamarind, oranges, watermelon and coconuts. Like the islanders, he ate iguanas often and with relish, for 'guana' was delicious meat. At the end of every meal, he smoked home-grown tobacco and drank home-roasted coffee, which he sweetened with home-made cane syrup. Unlike the denizens of the other Caribbean towns he had visited, the inhabitants of the little town the newcomers called Santa Isabel lived in well-built wooden houses with solid doors and windows, each set well apart from its neighbour. Every householder kept a well-stocked drinks cabinet, and most of them seemed to have a black mistress as well as a white wife. Surrounding the main house were the shacks of their slaves, 'of whom there are a great number.'

The arrival of an army of liberation on such a prosperous, self-contained island threw the community into turmoil. Several of the islanders, including Philip Beekman Livingston, found common cause with the newcomers, and dedicated themselves to the struggle for independence. They put their slaves to work alongside the soldiers in fortifying the island against attack, and when Louis-Michel Aury announced plans to raid the Spanish settlements on the coast of Central America, several of them willingly signed up. Aury's first privateering voyage from Providence was a great success: he captured a Spanish ship off Santa Marta, which was found to be carrying 50,000 escudos (£4 million in today's money). He sent half of the prize to General Simón Bolívar, the head of Nueva Granada's government in exile, and distributed the rest among the members of his crew. He even looted Trujillo, which hadn't been sacked since Henry Morgan's day.

Next, Aury sailed north to New Orleans to buy weapons and ammunition for the patriot forces that were fighting near Cartagena. The rendezvous with his creole comrades at a little fishing port near Cartagena went smoothly, but Aury and his men were arrested by the colonial authorities as they headed back out to sea. They were taken in for questioning, but having already delivered their consignment of weapons, the authorities had no evidence to implicate them in any wrongdoing. Philip Beekman Livingston, who had thrown in his lot with the patriots, told them that they were just fishermen from Providence who had been caught up in a storm and swept south. He assured them of their steadfast loyalty to the Spanish crown and the authorities let them go.

Louis-Michel Aury's greatest stumbling block was not colonial Spain, but the difficulty he faced in convincing General Simón Bolívar of his trustworthiness. Agustín Codazzi went to Bogotá on various occasions to petition Bolívar in Aury's favour, but *el Gran Libertador* regarded Aury as little more than a pirate, and he met Codazzi's pleas with indifference bordering on contempt. So the war went on without Aury, and as the prospect of expelling the last royalist soldier from Nueva Granada became ever more realistic, the Frenchman and his pirate army was soon forgotten.

Aury did his best to live down the inevitable disappointment he felt at being spurned by the man he idolised above all others. The fortification of Fort Liberty was complete, and the island was regularly patrolled by a well-drilled artillery corps and a cavalry corps of 100 horses. He had

12 warships in the harbour, all ready to carry his 600 soldiers and 400 sailors to war in Nueva Granada. But until General Bolívar entrusted him with a mission on the mainland, he was a rebel without a cause.

He and his fellow officers found girlfriends in Kingston and Santo Domingo, and brought them back to Providence to enjoy the proceeds of their privateering raids. When funds ran low, they went out in search of more plunder, for in spite of General Bolívar's opprobrium, the Allied Republics of Chile and Argentina were still prepared to issue Aury with letters of marque. But without a war to fight, privateering in the name of colonial freedom soon became robbery for nothing nobler than base greed. Aury and his men began attacking not just Spanish ships, but any vessel that happened to be cruising the western Caribbean. Idle soldiers waiting for the call to arms became wealthy raiders, waiting only for the next outbound ship. There were no end of men with reason to join the pirates on their fortified island. Creole patriots, Haitian insurrectionists, Yankee adventurers, Italian republicans and English sailors made redundant by the end of the Napoleonic Wars arrived from Port-au-Prince, New Orleans and Kingston. The island's harbour became crowded with privateering vessels, and sailors comparing the prizes they had seized in Havana, Portobello and Santa Marta.

Providence's storehouses were soon packed with merchandise, bullion and cash worth sums the islanders could only imagine. In Kingston, it was said that the island's pirates had amassed booty worth $250,000 (over £50 million in today's money). The American captain of a ship that Aury captured in 1819 called him 'the most stubborn bandit facing us today.'[3] But the governor of Jamaica was keen to see the triumph of the patriot cause, in Spanish America at least, and recognised Aury's piracy as legal. It was a return to the buccaneering days, only this time the privateers sailed not under the flag of England, but that of the Allied Republics of Chile and Argentina.

Thanks to Louis-Michel Aury, Providence and San Andrés played a prominent, yet rarely acknowledged part in Latin America's struggle for independence. Most Colombians are unaware that the islands were actually the first territories of Nueva Granada to be liberated from Spanish rule. And yet in spite of the great service Aury made to the patriot cause by running weapons across the Caribbean, and coming to the aid of the besieged patriots of Cartagena, Simón Bolívar was never able to overcome his disdain for the Frenchman. In 1821, Bolívar made his true feelings known in a cutting letter. 'I no longer need the services of pirates that only besmirch the national flag in the eyes of the world,' he wrote.[4]

This was not the first time a pirate from Providence had fallen foul of an erstwhile ally. Spurned by his idol, Aury wrote letters to members of Congress in Bogotá to convince them of his patriot credentials, in the hope that they would give him a position in the new government. He was waiting to hear back from them when he was thrown from his horse and severely injured. 'Arriving in Providence, I discovered that the general had fallen from a horse and was not at all well,' wrote Codazzi. 'After just six days, I watched him pass away in my arms amid the sobbing of his lover, a slave and another woman who had given him lodging.' Aury's second-in-command had never had anything but admiration for Aury's courage and devotion to the cause of colonial freedom. 'The loss of this man was irreparable,' he wrote.

With the Spanish driven from Nueva Granada and their leader dead, the revolutionary era came to a close for Aury's men. 'Suddenly Providence turned chaotic, because everyone wanted to govern, and none to obey,' wrote Codazzi.[5] Peace was only restored when a ship arrived from Cartagena with money to pay off the foreign soldiers and sailors, most of whom soon left the island for pastures new. The same ship brought news from the Andean town of Cúcuta, where a congress of patriot generals and prominent creoles had declared Simón Bolívar president of an independent Republic of Gran Colombia. The scattered territories of Nueva Granada were to be consolidated as a unified, independent state and provisions made for a new constitution.

On 23 July 1822, Providence proclaimed its allegiance to the new republic. The chaplain of Fort Liberty led the soldiers in singing 'Te Deum', and offering thanks to God for their deliverance from colonial oppression. Bells were rung, and rounds of artillery fired as the Colombian tricolour was raised over the fort. Providence was now part of the *Intendencia de Providencia y San Andrés,* which would become the sixth canton of Cartagena.[6]

There is no record of how the islanders felt about the 'independence' that was foisted on them, just as there is no way of knowing how they felt about the four-year occupation of their island. Several prominent islanders, including Francis Archbold and Philip Beekman Livingston, certainly added their signatures to the pledge of allegiance to Gran Colombia. But with the island's government effectively still in the hands of Lt Colonel Jean-Baptiste Faiquere, the Frenchman who Aury had appointed Providence's governor, they are unlikely to have had much say in the matter.

In his speech to the Congress of Cúcuta, Simón Bolívar had said, 'Once this work, born of our wisdom and my zeal, is done, nothing will remain for us to achieve but peace.' It was a vain hope: no sooner had the ink dried on the Declaration of Cúcuta than the government of Gran Colombia came under attack from within, as the regions comprising the new state fought to keep control of their land, slaves and authority. Unable to find a compromise with the government in Bogotá, the constituent states of what are today Venezuela and Ecuador seceded. What was left of Nueva Granada – modern Colombia and Panama – descended into a civil war that pitted secular liberal against Catholic conservative, centralist against federalist, and slave owner against slave. It was the first of what would prove to be a series of internal conflicts that would keep the Colombian government occupied for the next 80 years.

Cartagena's distant sixth canton was to all intents and purposes forgotten in Bogotá. The position of *intendente* of Providence and San Andrés was not a coveted posting. Bogotanos with friends in the Secretariat of the Interior only knew the islands as a good place to send the black sheep of the handful of families that ran the country. Typical of the tragicomic figures charged with overseeing the islands' affairs was Antonio Escalona, who was appointed *intendente* in 1833. During the outbound voyage from Cartagena, his ship was engulfed by a storm. As high waves crashed onto the deck, and the vessel began to list, its passengers became violently seasick, none more so than Escalona. So traumatised was the new *intendente* that when they eventually docked at San Andrés, he swore that he would never board another ship for as long as he lived.

His oath must have amused the islanders, for in addition to Providence and San Andrés, the sixth canton included the Corn Islands – Big Corn and Little Corn – two tiny islands off the Miskito coast that had been settled by men from San Andrés sometime before 1810. Faced with the prospect of a regular, stomach-churning 90-mile round trip to report on conditions in San Luis, the only settlement on Big Corn, the new *intendente* came up with a novel solution. He decided to give the same name to a group of shacks in the south of San Andrés. This would allow him to report back from 'San Luis' without having to go to sea again. Befitting such a duplicitous man, Escalona also had two wives, one in North End, and the other in 'San Luis.' His ruse was only discovered in 1844, after the governor of Cartagena decided to investigate the islanders' complaints about their *intendente*. Fearing the consequences of an official investigation – to say nothing of the voyage back to Cartagena – Escalona shot himself through the head in 1845.

With the wars of independence at an end, most of Aury's men had drifted away. But some chose to stay. One was Simon Howard, a soldier turned pastor from Georgia, who went on have two children with Mary Tayler, and another seven with Ana Pabla de los Ríos, a Colombian from Cimití in the new department of Bolívar, who had come to the island 25 years before to work as Tomás O'Neille's housekeeper. Another was Ralph McBean, a Scottish captain in Aury's army, who bought land around the lagoon on the east side of the island. Another Scot who chose to stay was John Hawkins, the namesake of the legendary privateer who is credited with being the first Englishman to carry African slaves to the New World.

Naturally, Antonio Escalona never visited Providence, and in his absence, the island reverted to the self-government it had enjoyed before Aury's arrival. The only resident Colombians on the island were the magistrate and his two assistants, whose only task was to feed the handful of dissidents from the mainland languishing in the island's jail.[7] The islanders still traded with Kingston, and as late as 1871, the US State Department seemed to think that the UK still had a claim on Providence. But neither island held much interest for the British either. With the wars of independence over, San Andrés and Providence became strategically insignificant, and with the promulgation of the Monroe Doctrine in 1823, the United States sent a clear signal to the old colonial powers that it was embarking on a new, expansionist phase, and would have no truck with European meddling in American affairs. Echoes of Captain Bligh's claim that the British were the islands' rightful rulers were heard long after he returned to Kingston, and many islanders believed that the island would continue to maintain some kind of connection with Britain. But the

British claim to the islands went over the horizon with Bligh's ship, and the islanders have been strangers in their own land ever since.

So utterly insignificant did Providence become that, were it not for the account of a foreign visitor, it might have been entirely forgotten in Britain. In 1835, the Royal Navy commissioned the captain of HMS *Thunder* to prepare a survey of the Caribbean coast of Central America. En route to the coast, the crew spent several weeks on Providence, and one of the officers, C. F. Collett, described life on the remote island in an article that was published in the *Journal of the Royal Geographical Society*. Collett had heard of Providence even before he reached the island, perhaps from childhood stories of Henry Morgan, for he mentions 'the notoriety of its having been the resort of both former buccaneers and more modern privateers.' But there was 'no late authentic description' of the island for him to draw upon, and he had no idea 'from whom, or when, it received its present name of Old Providence.'[8]

Collett was rowed to shore from HMS *Thunder* by the harbour pilot, Mr McKellar, who claimed to be one of the island's oldest inhabitants, and 'boasts of being a Scotchman.' McKellar was another of the patriot soldiers who had arrived under Aury and decided to stay. He had settled down with one of Francis Archbold's daughters, and went on to have several children with her. Collett recalled that he 'was in the habit of amusing us with many interesting anecdotes of the exploits of General Aury and his followers, in which he generally figured as a principal character.'

Jacob Dunham would have found few takers for his moccasins on post-war Providence. With the patriot soldiers gone, just nine houses remained in the once-flourishing town of Santa Isabel. But each family still had its own house, built on ironwood piles hewn from the woods on Ralph McBean's land, and their slaves still lived in the shack in the garden. Half of the 342 people on the island were enslaved – but that is not to say that every white man on the island owned slaves. A slave cost a lot of money – 113 silver pesos on average (ten times the value of a cow, and the modern day equivalent of £21,000).[9] The magistrate, John James Davidson, had five or six slaves; William Newball, an English barrister who had come to Providence with his wife, had three. But Ralph McBean and his wife had just one, and many islanders did not have the money to buy a slave. Instead, they worked the land with their wives and children.

The islanders' plots were scattered across the island, and despite the adjustments made to accommodate the growing number of heirs and new arrivals, the oldest islanders could still recognise the boundaries that Francis Archbold had sketched at his kitchen table 43 years before. Collett spent a good part of his day on horseback, riding the rough path that followed the shoreline, or following the tracks that led up into the hills. The islanders' horses were 'a fine breed, rather small, and purchased at £3 to £4 sterling a head,' he noted.[i] Southwest Bay was still lined with manchineel trees, and in the steeper valleys there were still a few stands of the cedar trees that the Puritan settlers had used to build their huts. Yet much of the interior remained uncultivated, and it was there that 'the animal creation' was afforded 'the greatest profusion.'

When the islanders wanted to travel to other parts of the island, most of them took to their dories.[ii] They had learned to make dugout canoes from the Miskitos, and were as comfortable on the water as they were on land. Collett began his day by paddling his dory offshore and dropping a plumb line into the water to take soundings for the nautical chart that he had been instructed to prepare. From his dory, he could see fields of sugar cane ripening in the sun, and noted that the fertility of the island's volcanic soil was such that it required little cultivation to produce 'a sufficiency for the inhabitants.' In addition to their kitchen gardens, they had planted hundreds of fruit trees, and 'sapodillas, mangoes, oranges, tamarinds, plums, and limes are plentiful... Nature appears here in abundant luxuriance,' he marvelled.

The owners of the best of the flat ground were Francis Archbold's three sons: James, Pierce, and Francis Jr. Most of their fields were given over to cotton, but the resemblance to San Andrés ended there. Collett says that on Providence cotton was 'cultivated more or less by everyone,' whether free or enslaved, and the working day lasted only until noon. On Tuesdays, Thursdays and Friday afternoons, the islanders tended their kitchen gardens. On Mondays, Wednesdays and Saturdays, they went fishing. The cattle that Francis had brought over from Jamaica had flourished on the rich pasture that fringed the island, and Collett judged

---

[i]   £3–£4 in 1830 would be worth £148–£197 today.
[ii] The Miskito term for a dugout canoe was one of the few native words the English speakers adopted.

their descendants to be 'generally in good order.' But they were outnumbered 20 to 1 by the island's pigs, which didn't need pasture and were good receptacles for kitchen waste.

Although the islanders bartered the produce of their plots with their neighbours, they needed cash to trade with passing merchant ships, and Collett was pleasantly surprised to be able to buy fresh meat, vegetables and fruit for the crew of HMS *Thunder* with pounds sterling. Aside from the cotton crop, their main source of cash was the turtles that nested on the cays of Serrana, Roncador and Serranilla, 75 to 100 miles northeast of Providence. 'Tortoiseshell' had been coveted since the days of Cleopatra, who is said to have used it to decorate the walls of her palace. The first Spaniards to reach the coast of Central America had seen the native chiefs use tortoiseshell for ornamentation, and it had returned to vogue thereafter. By the 1830s, it was in such demand in London and New York that a single turtle was worth $50 (almost £12,000 today).

At the start of the turtle-hunting season, Pierce Archbold would run up to the cays in his sloop with a crew of young turtle hunters, who often spent a month there, leaving only when he picked them up again on his return from the Miskito coast. Their principal object was the hawksbill turtle, which has tougher meat than the green turtle, but better quality shells. Because of its value, and the opportunity to interact with outsiders that it provided, only whites were allowed to go turtle hunting.

Few traders stopped at Providence, and this put the islanders at a disadvantage when Peter Shepherd's boat came into the harbour. Every year, traders like Shepherd sailed away from Providence with 30,000 lbs of raw cotton, tropical woods like cedar, ironwood, manzanilla and dyewoods, and smaller quantities of honey and coconuts.[10] In exchange for the islanders' produce, he supplied them with everything they needed for the months ahead, be it rope, hoes, tar, kerosene lamps, fishing hooks, hooped barrels or earthenware jars. Most of their earnings went on cloth, which arrived from Britain via Jamaica. Cloth was exorbitantly expensive, and the irony of a community of cotton producers having to pay over the odds for the finished article was not lost on the islanders, most of whom had permanent black marks against their names in Shepherd's ledger. His near monopoly on trade gave him enormous leverage, which he often exploited to his own advantage, but he could be munificent too. When the price of tortoiseshell slumped in 1830, forcing the islanders to the edge of penury, he extended them the credit they needed to see out another year.

The most eagerly awaited event in the island calendar was the grinding of the sugar cane, when the Archbold brothers invited their neighbours to spend a few days cutting cane and loading it on to carts for the horses to carry to the island's only sugar mill. After a day in the brothers' cane fields, the workers would gather at the mill to bottle the precious raw cane juice, which they used to sweeten their coffee, cakes and preserves. Cane juice was also the source of 'cumfire,' the rough liquor that sustained those who chose to stay at the mill for the night. Illuminated only by the light of the moon and a kerosene lamp, they would tell stories of buried treasure, and the ghosts that stood guard over it. The scene was enlivened by their ballads, which were sung to the accompaniment of a fiddle, a mandolin, and an accordion.

Sailors and fishermen from the Cayman Islands often timed their visits to Providence to coincide with the cane-cutting season. They came south in their catboats, attracted by the tortoiseshell trade, the delicious meat of the green turtle and the good times to be had at the mill.[11] When they left, they took word of the islanders' knowledge of the sea with them, and Providence men were soon in demand as pilots for the merchant ships that traded up and down the Miskito coast. Some settled there, taking the names of Archbold, Howard and Robinson to the English-speaking communities on the coast. Their places were taken by the Cayman islanders who settled on Providence between 1830 and 1880. Most of them were also of Scottish descent, and they added their names – McLaughlin, Rankin and Bush – to the island's family tree.

It was an idyllic life. While they knew little, if anything, about the original Puritan colony, by the time they passed away, the men and women who had resettled Providence with Francis Archbold in 1789 had realised the ideal of the self-sustaining farm so cherished by the Puritans. They grew their own food, built their own houses and boats, sewed their own clothes, and even made their own hats. Archbold's sons laboured in the fields alongside their slaves, and nobody was idle or insubordinate. There was no overweening governor to answer to, and no company lecturing them on how best to raise vanilla plants. Their trade with Peter Shepherd could hardly be called free, but they made up for any deficiencies by bartering with their neighbours. They lived in peace, were remarkably long-lived, and undoubtedly more prosperous than the inhabitants of a typical English village of 1835.

Yet they were impoverished, and their isolation was never splendid, for the piratical element had triumphed. The only law they recognised was the one that condemned black men and women to lives of perpetual slavery. All they knew of the modern world was what they learned from Jamaica, which had all of the material comforts that the modern world could offer, and none of its civilisation. Since Collett only hints at the islanders' moral shortcomings, we can only assume that they were similar to those of the white community 410 miles to the north. White Jamaicans had not been guided to the island by an ideal, and the idea that they might be fulfilling a divinely ordained plan would have struck them as laughable. They had come to take their places in a vast machine owned by their absent employers, and protected by their employers' allies in the House of Commons.

With the plantation owners absent in England, laziness, lack of initiative, callousness and egotism became defining characteristics of the plantocracy. They found nothing on the island to give them cause to improve themselves, and the semi-literate majority viewed the very idea of schools with disdain. According to Charles Leslie, whose *New History of Jamaica* was published in 1739, teachers were 'looked upon as contemptible, and no gentleman keeps company with one of that character.'[12]

Nor did white Jamaicans have a religious life to speak of. To become a clergyman in Jamaica was the office of last resort for an Englishman who had failed in every other profession. Charles Leslie found the island's clergymen to be 'the most finished of our debauchers.' Another historian has called the story of the Church of England's Jamaican outpost 'perhaps the most disgraceful episode in the history of that institution.'[13] The colony's planters and army officers dutifully attended church every Sunday, but the service was an empty ritual, whose main purpose was to convince one another of their shared superiority over their heathen slaves, and give their wives a chance to show off their finest clothes. Describing the situation in a letter to the Bishop of London in around 1720, the Rector of Kingston wrote that most members of the plantocracy 'have no maxims of Church or State, but what are absolutely anarchical.'[14]

'To what, I say, can we attribute this?' wondered Charles Corbett in his *Essay Concerning Slavery*, which was published in 1746. 'To indolence in some, and perhaps stupidity in others; but in far the greatest part 'tis owing to a narrow selfishness, and total unconcern for everything that does not regard their immediate interest.'[15] It is not hard to see why Samuel Johnson referred to Jamaica's planters as 'English barbarians,' and called on his friends to drink a toast to the next slave insurrection.[16]

Did Francis Archbold migrate to Providence to perpetuate this benightedness, or to escape it? Fifty years after his arrival, there was still no church on Providence or San Andrés. In a report he prepared for the Captain-General of Guatemala, Tomás O'Neille admitted that while 'youths of both sex have already travelled to England and the United States … all they know of Christianity is the baptism.'[17] He asked the Captain-General to send him an Irish priest – 'the Irish are well liked here because they speak English' – but nothing had come of his request. As for C.F. Collett, the Royal Navy officer who visited Providence in 1835, he appreciated the islanders' hospitality but noted they had:

> neither form nor observance of religious duties. Marriages are contracted by civil ceremony and bargain, and their only recognition of a supreme power is in the respect they pay to Sunday, which is marked by a total cessation of labour, and attention to external appearance.

In the absence of a minister, newborns were baptised by the chaplain of the Colombian *guardacosta* [coastguard], and since there were no schools on the islands either, they grew up unable to read or write. To one raised in the belief that Christianity was the bedrock on which civilised life rested, as Collett undoubtedly was, the idea of a prosperous and contented community living without religion was baffling. Yet he found the islanders to be perfectly upstanding. 'They have few temptations to drunkenness, restrictions being placed on the introduction of spirituous liquors,' he wrote approvingly, before adding that 'to speak of the moral character of these people would perhaps be hazardous.'

Considering the conflict between Puritanism and piracy that defined the original colony on Providence, what was the 'moral character' of the men and women who succeeded them? Collett makes no mention of the the drunken singsongs of the cane-cutting season, the islanders' promiscuity, or the lives of the enslaved population, and it's hard to avoid the conclusion that he only saw what his hosts wanted him to see. He spent much of his time with the island's magistrate, but John James Davidson didn't have much call to practise his legal skills, and for want of an income, he had turned to farming. On the rare occasions when a crime was committed, he left it to fathers to punish their children, and owners to punish their slaves.

Collett noted that theft was dealt with 'severely,' which probably meant flogging. On an island of British runaways and former mariners, most of whom had learned the rudiments of colonial life in Jamaica, the whip was likely the chief censure. In England, the whip had been used to punish recalcitrant soldiers, sailors and servants for generations, and the same hard line was taken in Jamaica, where it was customary to flog slaves judged to be lazy or argumentative. The punishment for repeat offenders was one that John James Davidson had learned from the Miskitos: a dory would be loaded with fruit and water, and the culprit banished from the island for life.

As well as having no religion, education or law, neither island had a doctor. If someone fell ill, he might be taken to Kingston, but that was 450 miles away, so in all but the most extreme cases, the islanders fell back on the bush medicine practised by the Miskito, black and zambo women, who would comb the hills for the plants they needed to treat everything from labour pains to dysentery.

And then there was slavery. In the years following the arrival of the 21 Coromanti slaves that Francis brought to Providence from the Gold Coast, more slaves were brought to the island from the west coast of Africa, via Kingston. According to the late Oscar Bryan, Providence's wise fool and most knowledgeable historian, the new arrivals included Mongala from the Congo and the kingdom of Benguela (who were usually classed as Angolan), and Ibo and Montete from Nigeria.[18] Jamaica's first historian, Edward Long, says that Gold Coast slaves tended to dominate those from other regions of Africa. Whether they played the same role on Providence is a matter of guesswork, but it seems unlikely. Although the slaves were sent to different parts of the island, they often found themselves working together, and many of them were bound by the strong ties of friendship they had forged in the terrible conditions that prevailed in the Middle Passage. It was customary for slaves who arrived on the same ship to call one another 'shipmate,' and the term became synonymous with brother or sister. So strong were the bonds that sexual intercourse between these 'shipmates' was considered taboo.

Jamaican planters referred to the one to three years that it took an African to adjust to his new life on the plantation as the 'seasoning' period. In Henry Archbold's day, slave owners had a vested interest in keeping their slaves healthy, for they wanted them to reproduce. They bought male and female slaves in equal numbers and tried to recreate some semblance of family life. But that changed once large-scale sugar production got off the ground, and the planters began trafficking slaves from Africa in their thousands. Natural reproduction became unfeasible, because a quarter of their enslaved workers died during seasoning, whether of malnourishment, illnesses contracted during the Middle Passage, or the savage treatment meted out by their overseers. *Practical Rules for the Management of Negro Slaves* urged that 'no encouragement [be] given to bring up families, the general opinion being that it is better to purchase new Negroes than to rear Negro children.'[19]

Although there are few clues to the daily lives of the island's enslaved population, the life of a slave on Providence is unlikely to have been as grim as that of a Jamaican slave, or a slave on San Andrés for that matter. Their owners had every interest in ensuring that they had the strength needed to produce children. Cotton wasn't the mainstay that it was on San Andrés, and aside from the Archbold brothers, most of the islanders were poor smallholders, who could not afford to send for more slaves every time one of them died. Nor did the enslaved population live as a distinct, separate community, as they did on San Andrés. Instead, they lived in artificial families of between three and six men and women, in wattle and daub shacks built at the end of their owners' gardens. Such close proximity couldn't help but create a certain intimacy between master and slave.

But the fundamentals of the relationship remained the same: a puerile game of one-upmanship based on deprivation, humiliation and endless petty rules. The slaves' only days off work were Sundays, and every third Saturday, which they spent tending their own vegetable patches and working in their shacks, for they were expected to feed, clothe and house themselves. Some of the men would take to their dories of a Saturday to catch fish, but they weren't allowed to trade with Peter Shepherd. Turtle hunting at the cays was not allowed, but some masters allowed their slaves to catch the odd hawksbill turtle in McBean's Lagoon. With the proceeds, they were able to buy a little cloth, but never enough to clothe a family, so most of them spent their lives wearing their owners' castoffs. Never far from destitution, they had little choice but steal from their masters' gardens. Even in death they were kept separate and unequal. White islanders were buried in the cemetery in Town, where their graves were marked with a token wooden cross. Black islanders were buried in 'the heathen burial ground' in Southwest Bay, where nothing marked a man's final resting place but a clump of weeds.

17

'A Sort of Lying That Makes a Great Hole in the Heart'

By 1831, few Britons had heard of Providence, and fewer still were aware of its role in the development of the Empire. So little was known about the island that the *Dictionaire Geographique Universal*, published in Paris that year, could state with confidence that it was 'not inhabited.' On the rare occasions that the name came up, it was usually in reference to New Providence in the Bahamas, or Providence, Rhode Island. The planters and merchants of Jamaica and Barbados, who were making a killing from slave labour and the English sweet tooth, had no use for Providence, for it was too small and too mountainous for sugar plantations. The island had played its part, luring the adventurers of the Providence Island Company to New Westminster with the promise of riches and righteousness.

But William Dampier, the pirate who visited the island in 1680, was mistaken in thinking that Providence was 'without interest to the English.' The imperial drama might have shifted to Jamaica, but as timeserving bookkeepers and sadistic overseers took the places once occupied by Puritans and privateers, England's swashbuckling days were revived in literary form. Readers thrilled by the tales of derring-do in Alexander Esquemelin's *History of the Buccaneers of America* were given another treat in 1724, when Captain Charles Johnson published *A General History of the Pirates*. These books became templates for a welter of stories about pirates, castaways, and buried treasure that captured the public imagination just as the events on which they were based receded further into the past. The rise of the adventure story coincided with an era of momentous changes that kept England in a state of fear and uncertainty. As London luxuriated in its new finery, nostalgia became a feature of modern life no less than consumer luxuries. Not that nostalgia was anything new for the English, for among the spurs that drove the colonists of the Providence Island Company to cross the Atlantic in the 1630s was their nostalgia for the glory days of 'Good Queen Bess.'

As noted earlier, Charles Johnson was long thought to be a pseudonym for Daniel Defoe, author of *The Life and Adventures of Robinson Crusoe* (the true author was most likely Nathaniel Mist, a sailor turned publisher). Both writers were quick to realise that stories from the early days of colony building could be turned into money-spinners, once suitably tailored to flatter the prejudices of the book-buying public. Tales of adventure set in distant lands amid a cast of strange peoples highlighted the qualities thought to be common to all Britons: self-sufficiency, daring and enterprise.

As well as being a pioneer of the true crime genre, Daniel Defoe was perhaps the first writer to dramatise a real life story: in his hands, the facts were made to serve his imagination. Yet the author of *Robinson Crusoe* felt strangely deflated by the book's success.

> This supplying a story by invention is certainly a most scandalous crime, and yet very little regarded in that part. It is a sort of lying that makes a great hole in the heart, at which by degrees a habit of lying enters in.[1]

By 1831, the Empire had become more than a source of materials and markets; it was a venture in which the entire country had a stake, and a useful way of cohering a nation that was increasingly prone to internal strife. Yet the Empire had also changed, as the centre of gravity moved away from the Caribbean colonies to India and beyond. Not all of Britain's imperial subjects appreciated the three Cs – Christianity, commerce and civilisation – that the mother country was offering them, and the British found themselves embroiled in several colonial wars. Victorian thinkers worried that the Empire had lost its moral purpose, and as the typical Briton grew more anxious, the ideal Briton, unfazed by wild natives or wild nature, became more appealing.

1831 also saw the publication of *Sir Edward Seaward's Narrative of his Shipwreck and Consequent Discovery of Certain Islands in the Caribbean Sea*, an extraordinary re-imagining of the English colony on Providence. Its author, Jane Porter, is little remembered today, but she was one of the most successful novelists of her day. Much of her success was down to her obsessive interest in Britain's national heroes and *The Scottish Chiefs*, her retelling of the life of William Wallace, was one of the first historical novels ever written. Her rose-tinted perspective owes much to the pride she took in being related to one of the chiefs of the MacGregor clan.

The same vanity inspired *Sir Edward's Narrative*, which holds a mirror to Britannia's bloated glory, and shows the historical imagination at its most deluded.

The virtual disappearance of Providence gave Porter a blank slate on which to re-write the history of the island, and thereby Britain's role in the Caribbean. The story is set in 1731 – exactly 100 years before the book was written, and 100 years after the Providence Island Company dispatched the *Seaflower* to the island. Edward Seaward is the son of a 'poor but honest farmer' from the suitably saccharine-sounding village of Awbury, near Bristol.[2] Like Robinson Crusoe, Edward's story begins with an irrepressible desire to go to sea. His nephew invites him to join him as a merchant in British Honduras (modern day Belize), but he cannot imagine going without his childhood sweetheart, 'the simple-hearted, single-minded daughter of the curate of Awbury.' Like all of Porter's heroines, Eliza is brave, intelligent and determined to do what is right, and as the author points out in the preface, she and Edward exemplify 'sound and truly British principles, religious and moral.' Far from discouraging Edward's flight of fancy, Eliza tells him, 'the providence of God is with you, whether in England or in the solitary desert.' They get married, and when the time comes for the newly-weds to leave for Bristol docks, Edward's father gives him 'his blessing and my mother's Bible.'

They sail first to Kingston, the capital of England's wealthiest colony. But the city was built by its slave traders, plantation owners and sugar merchants, not its church ministers, and the Seawards soon realize that it is no godlier than Port Royal, the swashbuckling city it was built to replace. When Eliza asks a local merchant how many churches Kingston has, he replies, 'One, I believe; but I never have been in it.' 'Never in it!' repeated my Eliza, with an emotion of surprise. 'O no,' resumed he; 'scarcely any one here ever thinks of going to church. We have too much to do…'

Leaving Kingston for British Honduras, the Seawards' ship is engulfed by a terrible storm. Driven onto the jagged reef of an isolated island, the ship is wrecked and the crew drowned, leaving our twin pillars of Christian rectitude as the only survivors. On coming ashore, Eliza is overcome by an ancestral fear of being eaten by the natives, but in the days that follow, she realizes that she and Edward are the island's only inhabitants, and that far from being a desert, they have been cast into a latter-day Garden of Eden. But what saves them from starvation is not the mercy of God, but the wreck of their ship. What they call the 'ark of our deliverance' is packed with all the accoutrements of modern life, and at every challenge to the nous of this quintessentially Victorian couple, Edward roots around in the hold until he finds a solution, be it a bow saw, steam iron, coffee cup or inkpot.

Thanks to 'the workshop of the world,' they are able to replicate a typical middle class Victorian household on the island. Spared the indignity of eating earthworms and binding broken limbs with her last scrap of clothing, Eliza goes about putting her kitchen back in order. Fidele, their King Charles spaniel, has also survived the shipwreck, and when he catches an iguana, Edward uses his spyglass to light a fire. He cooks the strange lizard on the embers; the merchant they met in Kingston was right: it tastes like chicken. They supplement their diet with sea biscuit from the hold of the ship and fruit from the trees, 'never omitting to gather up the seeds of our fruits as we used them.' The following day, Edward plants the pumpkin, orange and watermelon seeds, while Eliza turns her hand to basket weaving. As she admires her handiwork, she is quick to draw lessons from their misfortune. 'I now began to think a good basket-maker no despicable personage in society,' she says to herself.

'Gentlefolk often wonder how servants and other working people can eat so much,' says Edward, as he sits down to dinner. 'If I had ever entertained such a wonder, it was now no longer to me a mystery.' In a passage that must have delighted and appalled Porter's readers in equal measure, he not only washes their clothes, but prepares a pepper pot for dinner, while his wife 'lies down on our friendly settee to repose.' As he helps her to wring out the sheets, he tells her, 'Our situation shows how much is to be effected by mutual assistance... To such a lesson, at least, is the tendency of God's providence in the order of His creation.'

Sitting on the wooden platform between the plank-house and the stone kitchen Edward has built, 'each on a commodious chair, and our dear little dog in front of us,' they reflect on the lives they have left behind. They agree that they are 'experiencing more real enjoyment than the world's society, with all its blandishments, could bestow!' Edward even manages to enjoy himself: one evening, reminiscing about his struggle to catch a fish, he 'laughed heartily again and again,' in 'an excess of mirth neither natural nor habitual to me.'

The Seawards have no idea:

> whose dominions we were in, or even of the probable name of the spot where we were, for our situation did not exactly answer to any island, or islands, laid down in the chart I had found in the captain's chest.

The only clue is the brass belt buckle that Edward comes across while clearing piles of bird manure from the mouth of a cave. 'I rubbed the plate with some sand, and thought I made it out to be Spanish… it must have lain there a long time; perhaps a century.' Using a crowbar – another miraculous find in the hold of the wrecked ship – he breaks through a fissure at the back of the cave, and stumbles across a chamber piled high with canvas bags, each of which contains 500 gold doubloons. In one of them, he spots an English coin dating from 1670. Eliza is wary of the corruption that wealth brings in its train, but Edward soon reasons his way to taking ownership of the treasure. Still, his sleep is troubled by strange dreams that night.

One morning, three months after coming ashore, they are 'struck dumb by the sudden appearance of a large canoe between us and the opposite island.' It is carrying two men, two women, and a girl, all of whom are black.

> The elder of the men stepped out, and stooping before me, embraced my knees. I raised him up, while my wife, with the look of an angel, gave him the melon, and I, to show him I had no misgivings, took a clasp-knife from my pocket, and putting it into his hand unopened, made signs to him to cut the melon and divide it among his party.

This is Diego, his wife Rota, and Xavier and his wife Hyacinthe, Cuban slaves, and the only survivors of a second wreck on the reef. Edward tells them that they are free to return to Cuba or stay on the island – they choose to stay.

'I hope we shall be able in time to teach them to know that God who delivered them from death, and placed them here in security and abundance,' Eliza says to her husband that evening. But before they can make acolytes of their new friends, the Seawards must teach them the natural order of things. 'For their happiness and our own, they must be accustomed to look up to us for everything, and therefore be made to serve us as servants, but not as slaves,' Edward tells Eliza. He puts Diego to work tending their crops, while Eliza instructs Rota in gutting a fish for their dinner. Xavier turns out to be a carpenter, so Edward finds a saw, axe and adze in the hold of the ship, and puts him to work building a plantation house, whose 'elevation was sufficiently commanding, when compared with the huts of Diego and Xavier, to give it an air of superior consequence.'

Elevated to their rightful place, Edward has the pleasure of seeing his wife 'restored to her former gentlewomanly condition by His providence, relieved from toil, and all the menial offices of culinary labour.' The Seawards are now 'able to read a good deal, and enjoy frequent walks, arm in arm, in intellectual converse: happy in ourselves, and happier still in seeing those around us happy.' They spend their days decorating their new home with the shells they find on the beach, and building a shelf for their books, which include 'the noble Shakespeare... the nobler Bible... the *Spectator*, and Bunyan's *Pilgrim's Progress.*'

One Sunday, their servants are amazed when Edward tells them that they are not to work on the Sabbath. But Diego crosses himself when he hears the words 'Jesu Cristo,' and prostrates himself at his master's feet. 'I took a little water, and dipping my finger in it, moved it on the forehead of each one present, saying, "May it please Thee, God, to add this individual to Thy holy Church."' The sight of their crops ripening in the sun, and their commodious accommodation gives Edward great satisfaction, but

> the happy condition of our negro friends was still more gratifying even than all this. Their orderly conduct, their attachment, their progress in speaking English, and the pleasure they seemed to take in learning what God had revealed to man in the Scriptures, gave us a deep feeling of holy joy.

But the idyll cannot go undisturbed by villainy. One morning the castaways are awoken by the sound of cannon fire. Running to the shore, they see a Spanish brig firing on an English schooner. After Edward shoots at them with his musket, the brig wheels away, and the schooner's crew are able to come ashore. Over dinner, their captain expresses his amazement at landing on an island of free blacks – why doesn't Edward sell them in Kingston, he asks him? This is Edward's chance to school an old Caribbean hand in the rudiments of Christian morality. 'These much-valued negroes that surround me are as free as I am,' he tells him.

With these words, Edward realises God's purpose for the island: far from being a lucky escape, 'the providential arrival of the poor castaway negroes, and then of the schooner worked together to give us the means of planting a colony of refuge in that blessed haven.' Convinced of the godly role they have been assigned to play, he sails to Kingston with the schooner's captain, returning with provisions and more settlers, including a group of wandering New Englanders, and the 22-year-old Captain Francis Drake, 'an excellent fellow,' who has 'no pretensions to modish attire.' The Seawards leave the island in Drake's capable hands, and return to London to secure official recognition of their island.

At a meeting in Whitehall, Prime Minister Sir Robert Walpole asks Edward to show him the island's location on a map of the West Indies. But it is not marked, for as Edward explains, 'neither England, nor Spain, nor any other country, has ever thought it worth their while to take possession of those rocks.' The process of granting a patent is far from straightforward, says Sir Robert, and Edward will have to be patient. But as old Caribbean hands know from bitter experience, politicians are a duplicitous breed, and it is only the intervention of good Queen Caroline that saves Edward's request from endless bureaucratic wrangling. The Queen has heard all about their little settlement from Eliza, and tells Sir Robert to grant Edward the patent without delay. He pays five shillings an acre, is appointed governor of Seaward Island, and knighted Sir Edward Seaward.

Before they return to their transatlantic home, Eliza orders 'low-heeled boots and some new articles of furniture, besides an outfit of glass and china and crockery ware, damask linen and cutlery.' While his wife is shopping, Sir Edward goes to inspect the weapons at the Tower of London. England and Spain have fought several wars since Henry Morgan's day, and the *guardacosta* continues to harass British shipping. Yet far from throwing their weight behind the region's privateers, the Commissioners of Trade and Foreign Plantations have 'sat three years on the British claims for redress.' Sir Edward has no more trust in Whitehall's commitment to defending the colonies than Thomas Modyford did, and orders 'ten guns for the battery... to be prepared on the open ground below the mansion.'

The island's new governor also contracts a doctor to join him on Seaward Island. He promises Dr Gordon a salary of £50 a year, with 'the medicines to be found at the public expense, or at mine.' To tend to the islanders' spiritual ailments, he also employs the services of Reverend

Rowley, who has weak lungs that he hopes will benefit from the warm air of the Caribbean. 'I liked his appearance and his manner,' says Edward. 'Being much subdued, either by religion or want of health, [they] stamped on him that air of meekness which seems the distinctive mark of a true Christian.' Sir Edward's last recruit is Rosalie, the teenage daughter of 'a Protestant clergyman, of the remnant of the Huguenots.' She is presented to the Seawards by her mother, a Frenchwoman who 'has sought in your country that protection we could not find in our own.'

Upon their arrival in the island harbour, Diego rows out to meet them 'in the six-oared boat, with his men neatly equipped in white frocks and trousers, and straw hats.' Rev. Rowley is struck by the warmth of the welcome. 'It is delightful to see such love between the negro and his lord,' he tells Sir Edward. 'Why is it not so everywhere?' 'Because,' I replied, 'I am not their lord. I teach them, as you will teach them, that God is their Lord; and I only his servant, though their benefactor.' That evening, governor, first lady, doctor and minister sit down to enjoy 'the greatest rarity in the tropical world: good English wedder mutton!' which they round off with coffee and cigars, 'giving three cheers to King George and the Governor.'

The following Sunday, Rev. Rowley gathers his flock at the island's cotton tree, where boards have been placed on bricks to make rudimentary pews. The minister leads them in prayer, 'and if there was not a general devotion in his congregation, there was every appearance of it.' In the weeks that follow, he baptizes them, and marries several couples who had hitherto 'lived together merely by consent, as is the custom with all negroes and people of colour in Jamaica.'

The islanders' new-found faith sanctifies their prosperity. After two years, their tobacco is 'unrivalled' and they are producing 'the best cigars in the world.' Thanks to their friendship with the Miskitos on the coast, they have hit on another valuable export: arrowroot, a source of starch, which is much in demand among London's clerks and scribes. Francis Drake has twice visited the Spanish Main, 'near to Cape Gracias a Dios and succeeded in procuring a family who understood in perfection the making of plait and fine hats from the leaves of the palm tree.' The island's principal merchant, a Dutchman called Van Kempen, 'approved entirely of my project to establish a manufactory for straw hats from the palmetto.' Van Kempen sets up a workshop, where the island's women 'are kept at work with their wheels and distaffs, spinning cotton.'

265

Thanks to their general industriousness, the islanders are soon producing valuable exports, 'especially hats, Indian arrow-root, cigars, and stockings.' With their earnings from the export trade, they build 20 large and comfortable houses at Black Rock, which form the island's first street. Among the shopkeepers on George St. is William Gortz, a German butcher who makes 'capital sausages of the turtle.' Further up the street are the premises of 'Hart the mason, Herbert the tailor, Gerard Onder the weaver, [and] Pablo Ximenes the straw man.' The street is crowned by the island's church, 'a plain building,' which is roofed with the 20,000 Welsh slates that Sir Edward's uncle has brought out from Bristol.

Scanning the pews one Sunday, Edward is gratified to witness 'the devotion of all present, and the great good order and cleanliness of old and young, Protestants and Catholics, Spaniards, Germans, Dutch, English, whites, blacks, and mulattoes.' They are 'a motley group' of 'soldiers and sailors, artificers and husbandmen; yet one flock, under one shepherd.' Naturally, this microcosm of the Atlantic world is is entirely self-sufficient, and when a ship leaves for Jamaica, 'there was not an order for supplies of any kind.'

Word of the Seawards' island haven soon reaches the region's mariners, castaways and renegades, and over the coming months, several of them make their way to the island harbour. The first of the newcomers are Martin and Purdy, two black Bermudans 'of happy humour,' who Edward contracts for a period of seven years, 'after which it was understood their labours would be their own, and themselves to all intents and purposes free.' Among the other refugees to find their way to Seaward Island are 'a man and his wife of the name of Simmonds, who had kept school in Worcestershire.' Simmonds becomes the island's first schoolteacher, and bringer of the last of the

---

[i] At times, Jane Porter's shadowing of the original Puritan colony on Providence is uncanny, and leads one to wonder how she came to know so much about a drama that had been completely forgotten in England. Sir Edward relates that Simmonds was one of 'seventeen white families, amounting to fifty-three souls, [who] arrived here in the *Mary*, from Bristol, driven from England by the pressure of the times incident to the severe winter of 1739.' Was Porter aware of the *Mary* that had been captured by pirates on its way to Providence in 1639? Did she know about John Symons, the settler who ended his days languishing in a dungeon in Algiers?

three Cs: civilisation. His eager pupils learn how to read and write, but also how to make straw hats for export.[i]

The island's model school is complemented by its model doctor, who uses the latest advances in Western medicine to banish the last of the medieval killers. When the island is hit by an outbreak of smallpox, Dr Gordon, 'highly approving the inoculation plan introduced from Turkey by Lady Wortley Montagu,' vaccinates all the islanders against the virus, and there are no fatalities.[ii] The doctor is ever the humanist: when Francis Drake returns from the Miskito coast with 'two young negroes intended for Doctor Gordon,' he tells the governor that he is 'no friend to slavery,' and will only take them on as servants. 'And if you please, Sir Edward, we will call the man William Wallace, and the girl Joan of Arc,' says the good doctor. In no time, he has 'taught his man Wully to speak so much like himself that if it were not for his colour you might mistake him for a descendant of the patriot whose name he bore.'

Their island haven is a free port, and its governor welcomes all traders, but it attracts privateers as well as refugees. When a Dutch skipper arrives, Sir Edward tells him 'there were no harbour charges exacted here; that trade was free, excepting in spirits, wine, or beer, which could not be sold or landed without my permit.' But the sinful ways of the buccaneers cannot be avoided: after the Dutchman's crew get drunk on rum that they have illegally brought ashore, some of the settlers also succumb to temptation. They buy a case of gin from the Dutchman, and proceed to get blind drunk. When Sir Edward hears about their defiance of his law, he rows to Black Rock and smashes the remaining bottles. One of the 'debauchees' subsequently catches a fever and dies. It is the first death on the island, and one that the governor calls 'a punishment from a higher power.'

Shortly afterwards, he receives a letter from the governor of Jamaica warning him of 'very unfriendly, not to say hostile, proceeding on the

---

[ii] Lady Mary Wortley Montagu (1689–1762) was an English aristocrat, diarist and poet, and wife of the British ambassador to Turkey. She is chiefly remembered for her letters describing her travels around the Ottoman Empire, but she is also known for introducing smallpox inoculation to Britain. Her husband, Edward Wortley Montagu was the grandson of Edward Montagu, Earl of Sandwich, who was in turn a cousin of Edward Montagu, Earl of Manchester, a prominent Providence Island Company shareholder.

part of the Spaniards towards the commerce of England.' When several islanders are captured by the Spanish and held captive in the dungeon at Portobello, Captain Drake avenges the kidnap by seizing a Spanish merchant ship, which is found to be carrying a valuable cargo of indigo, cocoa, and 'Peruvian bark' (cinchona, long used by indigenous peoples as a treatment for malaria, and much in demand in British India). It fetches $80,000 at auction in Kingston.

Yet in spite of the latest war between England and Spain, Sir Edward stays true to his humanitarianism. When a ship of the *guardacosta* founders on the reef, he finds accommodation for the crew and tells Xavier to repair their vessel. But he finds it harder to accommodate the privateers. Although they spend some of their loot on George St, 'the profusion of money, the introduction of wine and spirits, and the presence of our profligate visitors' are 'a great nuisance to the place.' After 'frequent counsel with those I loved and esteemed,' Sir Edward closes the port to the privateers.

Edward and Eliza reflect on how life has changed in the eleven years since they first came ashore. Seaward Island is prosperous and has 'improved in all the arrangements of social life... Our laws were few, but wholesome; and we desired to make our holy religion the rule of our conduct. In consequence, the population was healthy, orderly, industrious, and contented.' Most of the black islanders are by now coming to the end of their seven-year indenture, and some are earning wages as free men. The Seawards' example has 'excited a salutary emulation for something beyond a hut, a garment, and a meal,' and the governor sees the yearning for self-improvement 'at every habitation within and without, and in the dress of the inhabitants.'

But as the community has grown more vigorous, its founders have become less so. The May rains bring fevers, and Eliza is among those to sicken. She only recovers 'slowly and imperfectly,' and is inclined to melancholia. 'The child is grown up,' she tells her husband. 'We may leave it to itself now.' They sail for England, and as the island recedes from view for the last time, she sighs at 'the recollection of the time when that land was to me an earthly paradise.' But her wistfulness soon passes; flush with the money they make from the sale of Henry Morgan's treasure, they buy a townhouse on Bruton St (high society having gravitated from Holborn to Mayfair in the century since the island was last governed from London).

The next 74 pages of the original manuscript of *Sir Edward Seaward's Narrative* are missing, but the last four pages have survived, and the story picks up just as Seaward Island is about to be surrendered to the King of Spain. Sir Edward tells the Secretary of State that he 'cannot suffer the people to be treated in this manner, abandoned like dogs,' but the minister insists that, 'the thing is done.' 'O, my love, it is too much,' he confides to Eliza, 'to see our people turned over to the Spaniards without security, or even stipulation.' Yet Eliza has become strangely indifferent to the island's future. 'They will soon find another home and be satisfied... Besides, it is God's will, my dear Edward, in the dispensations of his providence, that our islands should again become a desert.' Sir Edward resigns himself to the Spanish take-over, though not before telling the minister that he expects 'a proper settlement will be given, for such as may choose to go to the Mosquito shore.' The minister agrees, and makes arrangements for the evacuation of the islanders to Cape Gracias a Dios, where he will 'satisfy the Indians for six square miles of land, such as might be fixed on for their residence.' With this last gesture of enlightened beneficence, Seaward Island passes out of English hands for the last time.

Sir Edward Seaward's Narrative was a great sensation, and ran through several editions over the course of the nineteenth century. Part of its appeal lay in Jane Porter's artful blending of history and fantasy, which makes it a pioneering work of the genre that has since become known as 'historical fiction.' Even readers who had never heard of Providence speculated that the story might be true, so closely did it chime with their understanding of Britain's civilising role in the world. One journalist recalled that *Sir Edward Seaward's Narrative* 'was so like truth that – as I was told by one of the Admiralty clerks – three intelligent members of staff were employed for several days searching for evidence whether the island did or did not actually exist.'[3]

In truth, Jane Porter's book owed more to 1831, the year it was first published, than it did 1631. There was much talk of emancipation that year, and it ended with the Baptist War, the largest slave insurrection Jamaica had ever seen. Being unwilling to accept the implications of the revolt, loyal imperialists embraced Jane Porter's book, and its suggestion that the British were the Caribbean's enlightened benefactors. Intoxicated by the myth she had created, Porter insisted that the story was true, and that she had only edited a diary that she had been given by the writer's family. She did not divulge the diarist's name, but it was likely her eldest brother William Ogilvie Porter, a naval surgeon who had travelled widely before retiring to become a doctor in the Bristol area. While Jane Porter makes no mention of Providence, she clearly knew the island's history well, and was happy to rewrite it for a generation hungry for good news from Britain's Caribbean colonies.

Karl Marx's oft-cited maxim that history repeats itself first as tragedy and then as farce first appeared in *Scorpion and Felix*, a little-known novel that he wrote in 1837. 'Every giant ... presupposes a dwarf, every genius a hidebound philistine,' he wrote. 'The first are too great for this world, and so they are thrown out. But the latter strike root in it and remain.' Marx was thinking of the French Revolution, the Emperor Napoleon Bonaparte and Louis Philippe, 'the bourgeois king' who took his place, when he wrote those lines, but the same pattern can be seen in the history of Providence. The original story is that of the Providence Island Company; the tragedy that followed is the slave-driven factory that the British created in Jamaica; and the farce is *Sir Edward Seaward's Narrative*.

But perhaps the inclusion of a mere novel in Marx's schema is a cop-out. If so, there is another Providence-related farce to consider: the misguided attempt to build a British colony on the Miskito coast in 1822. By chance, this was the brainchild of another member of the MacGregor clan. Like his distant relative Jane Porter, Gregor MacGregor, was a creature of the age of nationalism. If she was intoxicated by Britain's civilising role in the world, he was no less obsessed by the patriotic rhetoric of Latin America's republican revolutionaries. She wanted to mythologise Britain's colonial history, and spurned uncomfortable facts for the sake of a palatable story. He wanted to turn his own life into a myth, and in the process, perpetrated one of the greatest frauds of all time.

During the wars for Latin American independence, Gregor MacGregor styled himself as a devoted servant of the patriot cause and carried 800 British veterans of the Napoleonic Wars from Liverpool to San Andrés, where they hoped to join Simón Bolívar's struggle to free Latin America from Spanish tyranny. He proved himself a valiant commander, but he was also an egomaniac, with a knack for fusing insurgent causes with his own. After the abject failure of his attack on Cartagena in 1815, which he only escaped with great difficulty, he sailed to Cape Gracias a Dios, where he met George Frederick Augustus, the king of the Miskitos.[4] The Miskito kingdom was by then under British protection, and King George Frederick Augustus was eager to please a hero of the struggle with imperial Spain. He granted MacGregor 8 million acres – an area the size of Wales – to build a colony at the old Black River settlement, which had been abandoned after the Treaties of Versailles in 1783. MacGregor told himself that when the war was over, he would become ruler of his own private fiefdom. With this vision of future grandeur to inspire him, he threw himself back into the fray.

By 1821, the Spanish had been defeated and MacGregor was flat broke. He sailed back to London, where he sold the title deeds to his fiefdom to a group of City merchants for £16,000. Excited by the prospect of building a colony of their own, but also by the lucre to be made in trade with the newly independent republics of Latin America, they set about raising the money they needed by issuing interest-bearing bonds, assuring their investors of fantastic returns. They rented an office in the City, which they called the Poyais Legation. In the interviews he granted to Fleet Street journalists, MacGregor let it be known that he was to be addressed as 'His Serene Highness Gregor, Prince of Poyais, Cazique of the Poyer Nation, and defender of the Indians.' He proceeded to concoct 'a grandiose, pretentious scheme to establish an overseas Arcadia for the surplus population of his native Scotland, while at the same time extending the hand of Calvin to backward pagan natives in some remote corner of the Caribbean.'[5]

MacGregor left the job of signing up would-be settlers to the Legation's loquacious agent, Thomas Strangeways, who assured interested parties that Poyais was the sovereign territory of 'an intelligent gentleman, who was many years senior Naval Officer in the Bay of Honduras.' The Prince of Poyais had already built a magnificent capital called St Joseph, a flourishing town of 20,000 citizens, who drove their carriages along wide, paved boulevards and supped rum punch in the shade of colonnaded mansions. Their money was protected by the Bank of Poyais, and their laws by the Poyaisian houses of parliament. There was a theatre, an opera house and a magnificent domed cathedral, where the people of Poyais regularly gathered to thank God for their good fortune.[6]

Now the Prince was looking for upright settlers to carry British values of commerce, Christianity and civilization to the surrounding wilderness. Thomas Strangeways told would-be migrants that

> on account of the richness of the soil, the luxuriance of the woods, the great salubrity of the air, [and] the remarkable excellence of its waters and provisions... Poyais is excelled by no country under the influence of British Dominion.

He offered them land at two shillings an acre – roughly equivalent to the daily wage of a London labourer. Plenty of punters were hooked by Strangeways' schpiel. Britain was still struggling to get out of the slump it had fallen into after the Napoleonic Wars. Unemployment was high, social unrest was rife, and government ministers fretted that a revolution like the French might sweep the country. Many demobbed soldiers were keen to emigrate, and the government backed them, in a policy later denounced as 'the shovelling out of paupers.'[7]

By early 1822, the Legation had raised £200,000, largely through the sale of land to 500 unwitting Scots, who invested their life savings in MacGregor's scheme. Among those to buy shares in the venture was George Wilson Bridges, a Church of England minister resident on Jamaica, who was typical of the pious hypocrites that passed for religious leaders on the island. Bridges made £1,000 a year conducting marriages, baptisms and funerals for slaves, and an additional £240 a year renting out his vicarage in Mandeville for use as a tavern. He spent much of what he earned on mounting a campaign against the island's missionaries and abolitionists. One might expect such a hard-headed man to have heeded the journalist who likened Poyais to the medieval utopia of Cockagne, a land so improbably blessed that 'roasted pigs run about with forks in their backs, crying "Come eat me!"' The same journalist also pointed out that Poyais had been Spanish territory since 1783, when Britain ceded its claim to the Miskito coast. Yet the cynicism that marked Bridges' career in Jamaica evaporated at the very thought of a new British colony in the Americas. Prince Gregor's realm was 'capable of producing, in the utmost perfection, whatever is peculiar to the tropics,' he wrote.[8]

Another to fall for MacGregor's schpiel was James Douglas, a Scottish doctor whose adventures on the Miskito coast began when he happened upon an open letter from the Government of Poyais, inviting 'a well-qualified surgeon to accompany a party of settlers to the Mosquito Shore.' Douglas got the job, stocked up with medical supplies, and made his way to Gravesend, where he boarded the *Honduras Packet* in November 1822. He and the other 76 passengers were delighted to meet Colonel Hector Hall, who had been appointed governor of the new settlement. They were also delighted to be able to exchange their savings for Bank of Poyais dollars, which MacGregor had commissioned from the Bank of Scotland's official printer.

After crossing the Atlantic, they put into Kingston for a few days. While he was there, Dr Douglas attended the trial of a group of pirates who had been brought before the Admiralty Court. 'They were of all colours, North and South Americans, British, negroes and mulattoes,' he wrote in his account of his adventures. 'I thought them the most savage, bloodthirsty, repulsive-looking wretches I had ever seen.' It seems likely that at least some of the men in the dock had spent time on Providence when the island was under the command of Louis-Michel Aury. Made redundant by the death of their leader and the triumph of the patriot cause, they had been reduced to common piracy. In Henry Morgan's day, seaway robbery had flourished only when it suited the governor of Jamaica; once the struggle to put the new colony on its feet was won, the buccaneers became a hindrance to legitimate trade, and had to be brought to book. Now that the wars of independence were over, the same process was in train again. Dr Douglas did not stick around to hear the judge pass sentence, but 'when passing Port Royal Point on my departure, I saw 21 of the gang hanging in chains.'

One morning in early February 1823, the *Honduras Packet* dropped anchor off the mouth of the Black River. The passengers scanned the forest canopy for the domed cathedral of St Joseph, but the trees swept down from the mountains to the water's edge in an unbroken green wave. The governor of the new settlement due to be built in the suburbs of the city, Colonel Hector Hall, was as bewildered as the rest of the passengers. He sent a scout inland, but he came back no less mystified. The captain of the *Honduras Packet*, Thomas Hitchcock, had seen enough: he hauled anchor and sailed away, claiming non-payment for services and supplies. He took the bulk of their supplies with him, and later sold them to the Miskitos at Cape Gracias a Dios.

The settlers' first days were spent clearing bush, pitching tents and collecting rainwater. It was an inauspicious beginning, but the locals soon came to their rescue. 'My Carib friends and I maintained a very good understanding during my stay on the coast,' wrote Dr Douglas. 'They supplied me with game, fish and fruit, in return for bleeding them, an operation of which they were very fond, and were never tired.' Dr Douglas convinced his new friends to build him a house, and on the afternoon he took possession of it, he

> felt prouder than under other circumstances to have owned the best house in Finsbury Square. I bought a small canoe of mahogany wood, which I could easily paddle by myself, and what with improving my house, shooting, fishing, reading, and my slight professional duties, I passed my time most pleasantly for several weeks.

For as long as the locals enjoyed the novelty of the white man's medical treatment, Dr Douglas could afford to be nonchalant.[iii] But they soon tired of being bled, and once they had drunk the last of the settlers' rum, and bartered for the last of their powder and shot, they left. The settlers' meagre supplies dwindled away, and men little accustomed to hunting or fishing soon grew weak from lack of food. Their spirits were temporarily revived by the arrival of the *Kennesly Castle*, which arrived from the Scottish port of Leith with another 160 settlers. But they were soon deflated again: the newcomers had brought no provisions, and no tents, assuming they would be able to buy both in St Joseph.

It rained heavily and incessantly in the following days. As the air turned sultry and oppressive, the newcomers came down with 'bilious remittent fever,' and within four days of their arrival, the first of them had died. Two weeks later, all but nine of the 220 settlers were sick with fever. 'One family of seven persons – father, mother, and five sons – were all ill,' wrote Dr Douglas. 'They lay on the ground on cane leaves. On visiting them this evening, I found the mother had been dead some hours, without the knowledge of the others.'

---

iii   Since the Caribs had been largely exterminated by the 1820s, the natives that James Douglas met were probably Garifuna. The Garifuna are mixed race descendants of the Africans who interbred with the native Carib and Arawak peoples of the region. They speak Garifuna and can be found along the coast of Belize, Guatemala, Honduras and Nicaragua.

The grisly farce began its inexorable descent. A man was killed by an alligator after his dory capsized in the river. A cobbler who had left his family in Edinburgh to take up a post as Official Shoemaker to the Princess of Poyais shot himself through the head. 'Not being able to get anyone to dig a grave, I collected some brushwood, which I piled in his hut, and set fire to it,' Dr Douglas wrote. James Hastie, a sawyer who had journeyed from Scotland with his wife and three children wrote, 'It seemed to be the will of providence that every circumstance should combine for our destruction.'[9]

Into this scene of devastation stepped the Miskito king, who was curious to see how his new neighbours were getting on. The arrival of George Frederick Augustus, accompanied by several of his ministers, was 'a perfect Godsend to us, as he caused his people to hunt and fish for us,' Dr Douglas recalled. The king 'spoke and read English remarkably well,' for he had been educated and crowned in Jamaica, under the watchful eye of the island's governor. Sir George Nugent's wife remembered 'his little savage majesty' as 'a plain, puny looking child,' who came to tea one day.

> He wore a crown of silver gilt, ornamented with mock stones, upon his head, of which he seemed very proud. He became quite savage in a short time. He cried, roared and yelled horribly, and began to pull off his clothes in the most violent manner, and was nearly naked before we could have him carried out of the room.[10]

But George was now 26, and raised in the ways of a Jamaican gentleman. Dr Douglas describes him as 'a tall and handsome-looking man, but a most debauched character,' who 'drank excessively, swore a good deal, and was excessively fond of playing at "All-Fours."'[iv]

While one of his ministers prepared a meal for the settlers, another told them the history of the Miskito coast, the highlight of which was the destruction of the settlement that the Spanish had built at Black River 30 years before. 'With diabolical glee,' he described how they had surrounded the main longhouse while its inhabitants slept, put the thatch

---

iv All Fours, also known as High-Low-Jack or Seven Up, is an English tavern trick-taking card game that was popular in English taverns as a gambling game until the end of the nineteenth century. It is still played in Trinidad and Tobago.

to the torch, and massacred them as they tried to escape. The king even showed Dr Douglas the site of the old settlement. Cutting through the bush with his machete, he uncovered the ruins of what had once been the Spaniards' church, and next to it, 'the remains of what had been a good stone house,' where the governor had lived. It was only then that Dr Douglas realised that the house his Garifuna friends had built for him stood on the site of the Spaniards' hospital, which 'accounted for my having found some square tiles and a lot of broken glass while levelling my floors.'

Dr Douglas was remarkably slow to catch the king's drift. He recalled that after they told him what they did to foreigners they took a dislike to, the king and his court 'rather suddenly, and in great or pretended wrath,' took to their dories and paddled away. Colonel Hall explained that the king had demanded that he take an oath of allegiance to the ruler of the Miskito coast. When he refused, the king told him that he had never granted Gregor MacGregor the title of prince, or the right to sell land; that MacGregor was a scoundrel; and that the new arrivals were trespassing on his territory.

Bereft once more, and still suffering for want of medical supplies, the settlers' fevers grew worse. Within a week, nine more had died, and more deaths would have followed had a schooner not arrived from British Honduras. Captain Marshall Bennett had been on his way from Belize to Cartagena, but 'having heard through the English papers of our settlement,' thought it prudent to stop by. The following day, he took 57 of the stricken settlers back to Belize. Dr Douglas was one of the hardy few that chose to remain at the site of the imaginary colony, but within days of Bennett's departure, he came down with a crippling headache. He was by then 'as thin as a whipping post, and as yellow as a guinea,' and would probably have died had the superintendant of Belize not sent out a second ship, which evacuated the last of the settlers.

In Belize, he was found lodgings with 'a very kind negress,' and spent the next four months languishing on the brink of death. One morning, he was pulled out of bed 'by a procession of sailors who carried me on board of a schooner in a hammock slung on an oar.' The ship spent a few days in Havana, and then sailed to Boston, where he made a full recovery and was discharged. Dr Douglas' adventure in colony building had almost killed him, yet he was remarkably sanguine about Gregor MacGregor's pie in the sky. 'As far as I could learn at the time, and have since learnt, the conduct of the directors was perfectly in good faith, and their objects perfectly legitimate. They signally failed from ignorance.'

The Prince of Poyais had his own ideas of where the blame lay: MacGregor accused Colonel Hall of mismanagement, and the merchants of Belize of deliberately sabotaging his colony out of jealousy. In August 1823, he sent a third party of settlers to Poyais. Finding nothing at Black River, they proceeded to Belize, where they were assigned a new site at Stann Creek, 40 miles north of the capital. But they were no better prepared for the rigours of colony building than their predecessors, and soon deserted the place. In the autumn, MacGregor sent out another five ships of settlers, but each was sent back by Royal Navy vessels.

Of the 300 Scots to be stranded on the Miskito coast, 200 had died, whether in accidents, of disease or by suicide. Just 45 made it back to Britain, where they fully publicised their terrible experiences. The Prince of Poyais fought back against 'the bare-faced calumnies of a hireling press,' and sued the *Morning Herald* for libel.[11] He lost the case, but that didn't stop him issuing a new prospectus for his chimerical colony. Undaunted by the howls of protest from emaciated settlers and bankrupted investors, he even took it upon himself to write and publish a constitution for the government of the Miskitos. Only when an anonymous handbill began circulating in the City of London, warning investors of 'Another Poyais Humbug,' did he flee to France, where he again tried to sell shares in his non-existent fiefdom.[12]

By this time, the Colombian government had got wind of the scam. In October 1824, General Francisco de Paula Santander, the acting president of Gran Colombia, issued a decree prohibiting 'any enterprise directed to establish foreign colonies or settlements along the Miskito coast.'[13] Gregor MacGregor appealed to Simón Bolívar, his former comrade-in-arms, but his plea met with little sympathy from *el Gran Libertador*. When his wife died in 1838, MacGregor gave up his ludicrous pretensions and left Scotland for Venezuela, where he was reinstated in his former military rank and given a military pension. He died in Caracas in 1845, and was buried with full military honours in the city's cathedral.

18
HOW THE LIGHT CAME IN

The reality of life in Poyais was a world away from Jane Porter's divinely protected fantasy of life on Seaward Island, but the ideal commonwealth that the Providence Island Company had envisaged was eventually realised. Over the course of the nineteenth century, the islanders discovered the commerce, Christianity and civilisation that were purportedly central to the British imperial mission, though the British played no part in their passage to the island. There was no prince or enlightened governor to fulfil the ideal, nor was it the work of a native despot. Instead, it was realised gradually, by the islanders themselves. This triumph, all the more remarkable for being completely overlooked by the outside world, was the culmination of a long struggle with what might be described, both literally and metaphorically, as the forces of darkness.

The British Parliament had outlawed the buying and selling of slaves in 1808, as part of a gradual turning away from mercantilism, the economic model that had provided much of the funding for the Industrial Revolution. Over the course of the nineteenth century, Whitehall turned its attention to India, southern Africa and Australia: new lands in which to grow cotton and wheat, raise cattle, and mine iron, copper and gold. But only in 1834 did Parliament pass the Slave Abolition Act, which abolished slavery throughout the British Empire.

The English-speaking settlements dotted around the western Caribbean were not British colonies, but they looked to the governor of Jamaica for guidance in matters of the law. Francis Archbold's daughter Mary, who had married the American sailor and merchant Philip Beekman Livingston, inherited a great deal of land and slaves on Providence. In March 1834, she decided that their 19-year-old son, Philip Beekman Livingston Jr should return to the island to liberate the family's slaves. Philip Jr had been born at home in Bottom House in 1814, and spent his early childhood wandering the family's cotton fields. But his parents wanted him to have some schooling, and since there was no school on the island, they moved to Jamaica when he turned 12, and bought a farm near Kingston, which they called Providence Plantation. Philip Jr left school at the age of 15, was apprenticed to a merchant ship, and spent the next five years carrying goods between Kingston and London.

A few months before he was due to complete his apprenticeship, his ship docked in Kingston, and Philip asked the captain's permission to pay a visit to his ageing mother. The captain refused, so on the night before they were due to sail for the ports of northern Jamaica, Philip jumped ship. The captain hurriedly took on a replacement, hauled anchor and set sail. A day out of port, the ship was wrecked on a reef in Annotto Bay, and the entire crew was eaten by sharks. For Philip Jr, who was already a God-fearing young man, this was no lucky escape, but 'one of the links in the chain of events in God's providence.'[1]

He thought the same of his mother's decision to give their slaves their freedom. Officially at least, the Colombian government had banned the trade in slaves in 1822, but nobody paid any attention to the new law on Providence. Slaves often died before their time, and most of the island's landowners regarded slave owning as both a necessity and a right. But the annual return on the price of a slave had been shrinking ever since world cotton prices peaked in 1790: when Francis Archbold sowed the first cottonseeds on Providence, a pound of raw cotton had fetched 36 cents in New Orleans but by 1830, the price had fallen to just eight cents per pound.[2]

Philip Jr left Jamaica for Providence, where he emancipated the family's slaves, divided their land between them and kept a share for himself. Many of the island's landowners followed his example, and freed their slaves voluntarily, giving each of them a small plot of land on which they could build a house and grow enough food to sustain themselves. But plenty of them refused, muttering that slaveholding was their birthright, and that by setting them free, Livingston would only make the blacks harder to dominate.

By 1846, when the island's magistrate prepared a report for the government in Bogotá, the population of Providence stood at 1,925, of whom just 137 were still enslaved. John James Davidson also found that whereas almost half of the male slaves were over 60, two thirds of the female slaves were under 40. This suggests that while most of the enslaved workforce had been emancipated, the island's white families were still not willing to free their domestic staff.[3] In 1851, Bogotá followed the British example, and abolished slavery throughout the republic, but plenty of slave owners were accustomed to ignoring the government's orders, and stubbornly held out against emancipation. Only in 1853, when Philip Jr wrote to the British consul in Bogotá, who raised the matter with the Colombian president, did government agents visit the island to tell the last of its slave owners that the game was up.

When the news that they were to be freed reached the shacks that had grown up around Bottom House, their inhabitants erupted in celebrations that lasted for a month. The same happened in Freetown, the settlement built by the island's free men on the ribbon of flat ground between Town and Old Town (the name given to the village that had once been called New Westminster). But the last of the island's slaves were not free yet: their owners insisted that they would only give them the land they needed to support themselves after they had given them another three years unpaid work. The black population had advanced, but only to the status of indentured servants. Full emancipation, and the precious title deeds to a plot of land, only came in 1856. Even after becoming property owners, many former slaves couldn't afford to keep the plots they were given, and sold them back to their former owners in return for enough money to build a house.

Until the late 1700s, the enslaved population of the Caribbean had known nothing of Christianity, and the Church of England showed no interest in proselytising among them. Consequently, the religious life of Providence's slaves was governed by the beliefs passed down by the first arrivals from West Africa. While divided by language and culture, all the slaves came from societies that practised some form of witchcraft. In the Caribbean, it came to be known as obeah.

Obeah was used to communicate with the dead, who were believed to hold power over the living. In 1929, an old Jamaican woman told the folklorist Martha Beckwith that the dead lived on in a person's shadow, which was identified with the tricky spirit. 'It's not the soul [that makes the duppy], for the soul goes to heaven. And it's not the body, for we know that goes away into the earth. It's the shadow,' she said.[4] The only person who could communicate with the dead was the obeah man, who was synonymous with shadow catcher. The obeah man could kill by catching a person's shadow, thereby holding him spellbound.

When the Baptist preacher and abolitionist James Phillippo arrived in Jamaica in 1823, slaves were prohibited by law from practising any form of religion, and he was among the first white men to preach to them. Phillippo spoke to an obeah man, one of 150 on the island, and through him made a study of obeah, which he called 'a species of witch-craft employed to avenge injuries or a protection against theft.'[5] But the obeah man was also a doctor, for ailments that couldn't be treated with bush medicine were held to be the work of malicious spirits, summoned by malicious neighbours. As a result of this conflation of spirit and body, the parts of doctor and priest were usually played by the same person, and the obeah man was the most powerful man in the community.

Obeah was an art held to be a science. When an epidemic broke out, the community wanted to know why, and this sparked endless specula-tion and invective (the same hysteria was seen in New England at the height of the witch trials in the 1690s). The accusing finger was usually pointed at whoever was deemed to have offended the spirits of their ancestors. This could be anyone regarded as solitary, proud or generally uncooperative, but the accusation was usually levelled at the sick, the disabled, the elderly or anyone encumbered by memories of Africa, for the motherland was both cause and cure of the slaves' woes.

At the end of the eighteenth century, there was a religious revival in Britain, and this coincided with the rise of the abolitionist movement. The Baptist church took the task of enlightening the heathen masses se-riously, and sent its first missionaries to the Caribbean in 1792. In 1815, Parliament responded to the campaign to abolish slavery by passing an act that compelled the Church of England to appoint curates to spread the Gospel among the slaves. Slave owners were expected to provide 'proper places besides the church' for their slaves, 'where divine service might be performed on Sundays and holidays.'[6] Slave owners liked the propaganda effect of the act, for it suggested that they were becoming more attentive to the spiritual needs of their heathen charges. But even after the Church dropped the fee for baptising a slave to two shillings and sixpence, they refused to give their workforce the time they needed to go to church or learn to read. Religious faith and literacy were direct challenges to their power, and most Church of England curates were no less cynical about their new duties. In 1826, a slave owner described watching a curate assemble 100 slaves and baptise them en masse, pocketing two shillings and sixpence a head.

The opposition that the Baptists encountered in Jamaica only grew more bitter as the number of baptised slaves grew. The Colonial Union, which mobilised the island's lower class whites against emancipation, took to burning down Baptist and Methodist chapels, and missionaries often found themselves tarred and feathered by angry mobs. In 1831, matters came to a head when the Baptist convert Samuel Sharpe roused 50,000 of his fellow slaves to rise up against the planters. In the aftermath of the revolt, 1,000 slaves were hanged and fourteen Baptist chapels were burned to the ground.

The revival of religious conviction was also apparent in the United States, where it came to be known as the 'Great Awakening.' It spawned countless sects and competing denominations, of which several became vehicles for abolitionism and black redemption. By the 1840s, there were three million black Baptists in the United States, gathered in churches such as the Six Principles Baptists and the Baptists of the Spirit of the Two Predestined Seeds. Philip Livingston Jr had heard about this revival when he was living in Kingston, and in the autumn of 1844, he made a trip to Oberlin, Ohio, where he listened to many Baptist sermons and decided to join the Baptist church. He was baptised in Lake Erie, and on New Year's Day 1845, he was granted his preacher's license.

Philip Jr returned to Providence and married his childhood sweetheart, Ann Eliza. But she missed her family on San Andrés, so they decided to set up home on the bigger island. It was just 40 miles from Providence, and movement between the two brother islands was easy and frequent. Although Philip had yet to graduate from his correspondence course in medicine, he set himself up as a general practitioner, and used the little he knew to treat a population with only the dimmest conception of medical science. A photograph taken shortly after his return shows a short, slender, and rather gloomy looking man, with blue eyes expressive of something between fear and reproach, a resolute mouth and a thick, carefully trimmed beard.

In addition to his work as a GP, Philip worked as a missionary of the American Baptist Home Mission Society of New York City, for which he received an annual salary of $125. The Baptists taught that the first church in any community should spring from its first school, so he began teaching a group of free blacks how to read, write and do basic arithmetic. His students built a thatch-roofed shelter at Mount May, under the tamarind tree that crowned the highest point on the island. Despite the abolition of slavery, most of the black population of San Andrés still had to work in the fields during the day, so Philip taught them at night.

At first, they were reluctant to give up their Sundays for prayers, as it was their only free day. But once they learned how to read for themselves, the stories Philip had read to them from the Bible took on new meaning, as did the Sabbath day. A Sunday congregation meeting was soon up and running, and in 1849, Philip performed his first baptism. His first initiate was his wife, Ann Eliza. Dressed in white, and accompanied by his students, the Livingstons walked down to a pool of water on the edge of San Andrés Bay, where they sang *Amazing Grace* and offered up prayers for the light that was about to enter their hearts. Philip and Ann Eliza took off their shoes and waded into the water until it reached their waists. He pulled his wife's head under the water and raised her up again, in imitation of the resurrection of Christ. Then he went to one house and his wife to another, where they changed into dry clothes.

Three years later, Philip's congregation adopted the Baptist covenant. Aside from the spiritual bond that it created, the covenant was akin to a constitution, specifying the duties that members of the congregation were expected to perform, and the protection they could expect in return. In swearing to abide by article 20, which stated that 'the brethren will be mutual to each other as iron sharpens iron,' they effectively established a mutual aid society, an act of community building that would have been unthinkable under slavery. As slaves, Philip's congregation had been kept in a state of obligatory, impoverished equality. Following their emancipation, they had each been given a plot of land, however small, and they had quickly become proud and possessive landowners. In recognition of the independence they had gained in becoming property owners, article 25 of the covenant insisted that Baptists were only to sell land to their fellow Baptists.

Provision was made for the sick and the aged, to be paid for from the dues they paid to the church every month, and Philip drew up a programme of education. Reading, writing and mathematics were the priorities, but his curriculum also had a strong moral purpose. Among the vices he prohibited was alcohol: they were not to drink it, and wherever possible, they were not to carry it as cargo in their boats. He also warned them about the dangers inherent in 'going to the billiard halls, participating in ball games and horse races on Sundays, and buying lottery tickets.'

The congregation was now ready to build a church. Coral rock and shells were gathered from the beach and carted up to Mount May for the foundations. A wooden church was erected, with four columns supporting a porch that ran the length of one side, and a tower was built for the belfry, where a bell was suspended. Since termites were a perennial problem, the entire structure was then doused with gallons of paint prepared with turpentine, arsenic, potash and mercury. A tall front door with a burnished spring lock was fitted, and the three high windows were glazed and hung with muslin curtains.

The First Baptist Church of San Andrés was consecrated on 16 October 1853. The carpenters in the congregation had made pews to rent to individual families, but before long, they had all been taken, so they built a gallery for another 80 people. As their numbers increased, so did their monthly dues, and Philip was able to buy the necessary accoutrements: a hand bell, which he bought for $5, and four kerosene lamps, for $4 each. By 1857, the church at Mount May was doing so well that its minister felt able to invest $50 in that most essential of modern devices: a wall clock.

The plantation owners of Jamaica did not welcome the news that their slaves had become workers, who expected to be paid for their labour. But what brought them to ruin was not the wages bill they now had to pay, but their workforce's retreat from the plantations. As soon as they were able, free men bought plots of land for themselves, and turned their backs on the plantations for good. The plantation owners grew so exasperated that they resorted to cutting down the free men's fruit trees, in an effort to drive them back to work. It was in vain: by 1852, most of Jamaica's landowners had thrown up their hands in surrender to ruin, and over 240 estates had been abandoned.[7]

Plantation owners on the other Caribbean islands fared better. Being smaller, there was less virgin land to which a freed slave could resort, and the black population had no choice but continue working in the cotton and cane fields that had made the white population rich. But they charged for the work they did, and only worked until noon, for they were determined to spend the rest of the day tending their own plots. Some of them also began growing cash crops, and were soon competing with their former masters to supply the local market. As wages became the plantation owners' principal outgoing, their cotton became more expensive, and they soon found themselves being undercut by competitors from the Indian subcontinent.

The wealthiest landowners on San Andrés began casting around for less labour-intensive crops to grow, and in 1850, half a dozen of them got together to plant coconut palms. The island's free men followed suit, planting coconuts on their plots, in the hills, and wherever else they would take root. This didn't suit the white landowners at all, for they weren't accustomed to competition, and slavery had made them eminently unsuited to the life of a smallholder. After 70 years of instructing, inspecting and punishing, they were now obliged to turn their hands to manual labour. Coconuts didn't require year-round tending, but come harvest time somebody had to climb the palm's trunk, and as Philip Livingston put it, 'bone and sinue is the capital to bring in wealth here.' The island's free men were flush with the taste of freedom and eager to enjoy the fruits of their labour. 'Thrift was soon manifested among the emancipated part of the population,' Philip wrote in his diary.

> Lands were purchased and cleared, timbers felled and coconut planted, and by the time 1856 had dawned upon San Andrés, it had become a coconut country. Two schooners under the English flag – white washed Yankees – are regular traders, and others under the same flag come to fill up or load for the Costa Rica Railroad Company, who have established a large store here.

But while black islanders were growing coconuts on their own land, the white merchants still dominated the trade with the Americans, and they did their best to maintain the exploitative relationship they had grown up with. They refused to pay the growers more than $7 per thousand coconuts, and the growers had no way of circumventing them. So Philip established a cooperative, which consolidated the collective power of the smallholders and undercut the prices the merchants were offering the Americans.

At first, the cooperative simply bartered their crop for the clothing, building materials and tools that its members needed. But the switch to cash was quick, as was the sale of kitchen stoves, sewing machines, and bolts of cloth. For the first time in their lives, the island's black population had money to furnish a household, and because the larger, white landowners were not part of the cooperative, 'they had to beg and wait, as well as pay, to get their coconuts prepared for shipment.'

Philip watched as demand for the island's coconuts continued to outstrip supply. 'Rather unusually, the price of the article kept pace with the increase of the article,' he wrote, 'the price advancing first to $10, then to $12, until by the year 1857 it was commanding $16 per thousand.' San Andrés was by then exporting 150,000 coconuts every month, and the cooperative was making $2,400 a month.[8] Thanks to the demand for coconuts in the United States, which only increased in the second half of the nineteenth century, San Andrés was probably the only island in the Caribbean where emancipated slaves flourished after emancipation.

> Money is plentiful, and the persons who in 1850 would have bowed to the earth to pick up a five cent piece, and were wont to utter their plaintive "Ha de massa" with naught but tatters to don on any occasion, are now to be seen in broadcloth, muslins, and costly fashionable hats.

Handsome new houses were built with timber imported from New Orleans, the windows were glazed and hung with drapes to keep out prying eyes, and black people were finally able to enjoy the pleasures that come with privacy.

By 1869, American ships were coming to San Andrés in such numbers that the Department of State set up a consulate on the island. They appointed Philip to run it, and sent him a Stars and Stripes, which he would run up the flagpole in his front garden every morning. The consul was responsible for collecting taxes due on cargo going to the US, clearing vessels, granting visas, reporting shipwrecks, caring for castaways, settling disputes between captains and crew and defending any American citizen who fell foul of the Colombian authorities. By 1873, Philip Livingston was the most important man on the archipelago, respected by the powerful, and loved by the powerless, who called him 'Papa Massa.'

The American flag was soon flying in other parts of the island, for there were now twelve agents for the coconut companies living there.

San Andrés' only connection with Colombia was the monthly mail boat, yet the *New York Times* reached the island just a few days after rolling off the presses. The islanders' children spent their weekends playing baseball and drinking soda, which they bought with US dollars, and the more prosperous among them even went to high school in the States. When a hurricane destroyed just about every house on the island in 1877, the *intendente* cabled the president of the United States before he notified Bogotá. San Andrés might have been part of the sixth canton of Cartagena, but as the *intendente* pointed out in his annual report, the islanders 'paid more attention to what the captains of the American ships say than they do to any established authority.'[9]

King Coconut reigned in San Andrés, and his rule looked to be a benevolent one. 'What change in a quarter century,' Philip marvelled. 'Almighty God must surely have turned the wheel of destiny in that time.'[10] Religion and profit jumped together on San Andrés, just as they had in New England 200 years before. The transformation was apparent not only in the new streets laid out around the wharf, but in the islanders' frame of mind. Life no longer appeared governed by blind chance; instead, it was directed by a merciful God. This was the breakthrough that Hope Sherrard, the Puritan colony's minister, had spent his time trying to effect, and it took place not on the English colony on Providence, but the (practically) American colony on San Andrés. Two hundred and fifty years had passed since Lord Saye wrote to the governor of Massachusetts to convince him that God meant his chosen people to settle in Central, not North America. The extraordinary rise to power of the United States had proved his Lordship wrong. For the people of San Andrés, freedom, prosperity and the United States rose together, and they regarded all three as gifts from a merciful God. 'Those States first founded by thy firm decree, will by thy power achieve their destiny,' Philip declared.

But the American consul was quick to spot new vices among his congregation. When the coconut boom began, 'the people, viewing it as a great favour from God, were thankful and quite satisfied with the price, not expecting or anticipating any increase in that department.' But by 1870, they had grown accustomed to their prosperity, and 'would complain that coconuts were bringing nothing if they fell to $15 per thousand.' By its very nature, the coconut business encouraged the islanders to do nothing, for the palms require little tending. Their new-found wealth combined with their idleness to make them greedy, and Philip was dismayed to see 'the usual increase in covetousness with the increase of prosperity.' Although their houses were 'much nicer and more expensive than their [former] owners' houses,' the black population's thirst for recognition made them imitative of the whites. 'They know of no distinction whatever among the whole race of men on the earth, and will not hire themselves to be cooks or helps, lest it derogate from their gentleman or ladyship.' Their vanity even blinded them to the contempt with which the American ships' captains treated them. 'Whilst the captains call these people "nigger" or "orang-utan" in their absence, they are highly flattered by them in their presence, which makes them conceive themselves to be of as much importance as emperors or Kaisers.'[11]

Philip first took the Word of God to Providence in 1851. Preaching in a makeshift church to illiterate islanders with no knowledge of the Bible, he made sure that his first Sunday service was a dramatic affair. He had brimstone sent to the island from Kingston, which his assistant burned in a cauldron behind the pulpit to simulate the rank fumes that awaited the unrepentant sinner in hell. Only when all present were struggling for breath did Philip begin to preach. In the absence of God, sin had crept into their hearts, he thundered. Whatever the outward signs of peaceful contentedness, they were lost souls, akin to the hundreds of shipwrecked mariners to have died on the cays. Their only hope of salvation from the tide of sin threatening to overwhelm them lay with their celestial captain, Jesus Christ. As Philip succumbed to the terrible smoke pouring from the mouth of hell, his assistant threw him a lifebuoy and dragged him into the sunlight outside, closely followed by his awestruck congregation.

The islanders had every reason to believe Papa Massa, for he was a highly respected man, and few could resist the power of his message. Four years after preaching his first sermon on Providence, the East Side Baptist Church opened its doors, and within a generation, almost all the islanders had been baptised into his church. At sunrise every Sunday morning, they emerged from their isolated farmsteads in their finest clothes, the women in wide-brimmed hats or bonnets; the men in suits and straw hats. The wealthier, whiter families arrived on horseback, while their poorer, darker-skinned neighbours came barefoot. The state of their finances held no interest for the Lord, Philip assured them. Come the day of reckoning, it was their hearts, not their wallets that would be in the balance.

Christianity gave rich and poor alike a common language. It tempered the stubborn individualism that their isolation had fostered, and challenged the simple dichotomy between white goodness and black malignity that they had grown up with. It also gave Philip enormous control over what the British naval officer, C.F. Collett, called their 'moral character.' The values he preached were the brotherhood of all believers, the importance of co-operation, and the perennial value of education. Until Philip began preaching, the white islanders' only understanding of discipline was the punishment they dished out to their slaves. He taught them to turn their watchfulness inward, for a good Christian had to exercise self-discipline if he was to cleanse his soul of its diabolical accretions. He had to strive to be good: sober, straight talking and honest in his business dealings, and respectful to his neighbours. And he should avoid dancing, drunkenness and loose women, for sexual promiscuity was also a sin.

Until the arrival of Baptism, marriage had been an entirely secular ceremony on Providence, reserved for the island's biggest landowners and performed by the *intendente* on San Andrés or the captain of any American or British ship that happened to be on the dock. Now the islanders had a church minister to join them in holy matrimony. By article 27 of the Baptist covenant, the men agreed not to marry non-believers, and to find a partner among the congregation. If a man was productive, he would become prosperous, and this would allow him to keep his wife at home, where she would reflect her husband's unstained conscience by keeping her household neat and tidy.

Philip's acolytes brought their children to be baptised. Some gave them Old Testament names like Isaac, Israel or Lemuel (which would surely have brought a smile to Hope Sherrard's face). Others chose one of the plain names that their fathers had heard sailing around the region's English-speaking ports: Alexander, James or John. There were also Spanish names, like those given to Mario and Antonio Rankin. Yet the names in the island's register of births, deaths and marriages show them to have been anything but predictable. Multiple fragments washed up on the island's shores, as seen in the names given to Plutarco Robinson, and Abdulrahim Wong. As for Eudosia, Lorehema and Rovine Robinson, and their cousins Zulli, Zenon and Zaldoa, their names can only have been conjured up by the island's remoter poets.

Philip warned his congregation to keep their children, and particularly their daughters, in check. They were to show good manners when meeting the elders of the community, and to spend their mornings helping their parents. The boys should learn the rudiments of their fathers' trade: how to repair a lobster pot, read a sextant or deliver a calf. The girls should do chores around the house, in preparation for becoming good housewives. As there was no school on Providence, few children learned how to read or write. But a free Jamaican called Mr Watson came to the island to work as a private tutor to the children of the wealthier families, and he agreed to give classes to the poorer children as well. Not to be outdone by their own children, the adults also signed up for classes in reading, writing, arithmetic and geography. They attended class in the evening, and returned home on horseback, their schoolbooks in one hand, a lantern to light the crooked shoreline road in the other.

In 1871, the Colombian Congress made primary education free and compulsory throughout the republic, and stipulated that the school on Providence should be financed from the sale of guano. [i] By 1873, there was a school at Rocky Point, where Alejandro Archbold taught 25 students, and another in Town, where Cleveland Hawkins taught a further 40. Since the Colombian Ministry of Education had no idea how to educate English speakers, they devised their own curriculum. By the turn of the century, over 90 per cent of islanders could read and write. But education went no further than primary level, so anyone who could afford to sent their children to high school in Jamaica or the United States.

That meant the children of the island's upper class. Members of this elite band invariably owned upwards of five acres, as well as a cargo boat, and most of them were Robinsons, Archbolds or Newballs from Smooth Water Bay. Their determination to keep their family trees 'clear' of black blood had resulted in generations of inter-marriage between the Robinsons and the Archbolds – of the nine children Frederick Robinson had by Eugenia Archbold, four went on to marry other Robinsons. The most noticeable adverse effects were deafness and a mild form of mental retardation. Cordell Robinson, author of *The Genealogical History*

---

[i] The cays off Providence were covered in phosphate-rich bird droppings, which were much in demand among American fertiliser manufacturers. For a time, guano was the island's chief export.

of Providencia Island, claims that until recently, 'nearly every family on Providence included at least one relative who to some degree was afflicted.' Unsurprisingly, the 'simple' were not stigmatised as they were elsewhere. One visitor to the island recalled meeting 'Brother Montague,' who wandered the island humming hymns on request, and slept on the floor of whichever kitchen he happened upon. But he 'kept a smile upon his face, and laughed for joy just to meet a fellow man.'[12]

Members of Providence's lower class were invariably black, and lived in Bottom House, Southwest Bay and Freetown. Most of the men worked as labourers for the bigger landowners, and fed themselves with what they grew on their plots. But some of them joined the crews of the cargo ships that were plying the western Caribbean in growing numbers, and this gave them the chance to visit distant relatives in English-speaking ports like Greytown, Colón and Puerto Limón. Their material lives were not unlike those of their forefathers under slavery, but they were also members of the Baptist church, and their creed taught them that God had made all men equal. They relished the opportunity to better themselves, and by the close of the nineteenth century, the church had gone a long way towards cementing a new, moral hierarchy on the island, which vied for dominance with the race-based hierarchy ordained by slavery.

But the main factor working to undermine the colour bar was promiscuity. Many black women worked as domestics in Smooth Water Bay, and this brought them into daily contact with men like Frederick Robinson. The nine children Frederick Robinson had by Eugenia Archbold were not his only offspring, for he had 27 children in all, by ten different women. One of them, Roosevelt Robinson, followed his father's example and had 16 children by seven women. Monogamy might have been the ideal, but it was not the norm, and many a landowner's son made the nightly trek from Rocky Point, Lazy Hill and Smooth Water Bay in search of the pleasures to be had at the bottom of the island. Having lots of children by lots of women enhanced a man's self-esteem. It caused a lot of heartache for the mothers of his illegitimate children, but the women gained a measure of prestige, and perhaps some financial support from these illicit couplings too.

The island's minister fulminated at the philanderers from the pulpit, and several of the island's most powerful men were 'turned out of church' for their adulterous relationships. But there were limits to what Philip could do, and the respectability that he encouraged in his congregation was always at risk of being undermined by a man's desire for a reputation. The tension between respectability and reputation was ancestral, for just as the islanders owed their religion to the Puritans, they owed their social lives to the pirates that had unseated them. In belated recognition of the facts of island life, Philip baptised all newborns, though he chose to bring 'outside children' into the Christian fraternity in the privacy of the mother's home. Though it was never open acknowledged, it was only the philandering of men like Frederick Robinson that saved Providence's white families from a dwindling gene pool, and the likelihood that growing numbers of their children would be born with genetic abnormalities.

Ann Eliza Livingston had been ill since 1856. Philip had done his best to treat his wife with the medical resources at his disposal, but he knew that if she were to survive, she needed to be treated in the United States. The American Baptist Home Mission Society wired him the money for two return tickets to New York City aboard a coconut ship, and they set out on the long journey north. The operation went well, but Ann Eliza's health did not improve, and they returned to San Andrés prepared for the worst. 'God will do better for her than me,' Philip wrote in his diary. 'I can be of no more use.'[13]

Ann Eliza died in the summer of 1862. Following her death, Philip came to realise that whatever their outward show of Godliness, the islanders still depended on superstition to explain the world around them. While his wife's body was lying in its casket, they brought their babies to his house, in the belief that passing a newborn child over the casket would appease the dead woman's spirit. When the casket was carried to the cemetery, onlookers pulled their shutters closed for fear that Ann Eliza's spirit would enter their homes. And when it began to rain at her graveside, they said that it was because she was crying in heaven. Why was she crying, they asked one another? The speculation, insinuation and gossip seemed endless. Philip impressed upon them the importance of turning their backs on such heathenish leftovers. Funerals should be quiet, dignified affairs. Why wail and moan when Ann Eliza was bound for the glory of everlasting life? There was no room for 'duppies' in his church, nor the obeah men who claimed to talk with them.

But the past could not be erased with a sweep of the preacher's hand, as Philip was about to find out for himself. During her illness, Ann Eliza had been cared for by the family's housekeeper. When she died, Josephine Pomare stayed on to cook, clean and look after the motherless children. Three years later, Philip and Josephine went to the mayor's office and asked to be married. This caused a terrible scandal on both islands: the women said that it was too soon after Ann Eliza's death; the men muttered that a white man should not marry a black woman. This was rank hypocrisy, of course, because they all knew that prior to his marriage, Philip Jr had had two 'outside' children by a black woman. Ann Eliza had adopted both children, and the Livingstons had gone on to have two children of their own.

The following Sunday, Philip walked to the pulpit with his single shot 30-30 rifle in his hand. When the pews were full, and the door had been closed, he laid it across the lectern. He had married of his own free choice, he told the congregation, and it was none of their business who he had chosen to be his wife. After much preaching and many prayers, a conviction of their own sinfulness fell upon them. They admitted their shortcomings and asked their neighbours to forgive them. There had been no recorded baptisms in 1886; the following year, there were 196. This revival of religious conviction was Philip's crowning achievement, and was remembered by the islanders for years to come. He died in August 1891, at the age of 77.

PART FOUR

19
MODERN TIMES

I spent four months on Providence, and talked to many islanders about
the changes that had swept over the island since its golden years. They
were friendly, easy-going and willing to talk, but also careful to ensure
that I only spoke to the island's most reputable figures. I was a guest
from distant England, and it was important that I went home with the
right impressions.

This made me all the keener to talk to those perched on the lower branches of the island's family tree, of whom Ed was undoubtedly
one. I found him begging and sitting in the shade outside the bank in
Town, his crutches either side of him. He needed money for antibiot-
ics, he said, and lifted the dressing under his shirt to show me a deep
and festering wound on his hip. He showed me his *cédula* (ID card*)*,
as if it somehow validated his story. It was hard to read his face; like
many islanders, his predecessors could have been black, white or Miskito, though he also looked to have some Arab blood. Ed was well used
to the 'cutting of eyes' that people gave him as they waited to use the
island's only cash point. Since we were both outsiders, I made a point
of joining him on the pavement, if only to hear an island story before
I too made my excuses and left him to his worries.

One day Ed invited me to meet his stepfather. Baldwin was a Seventh-Day Adventist, and had a lot of unconventional beliefs that I might
find interesting, he told me. We found him eating ice cream with a dark-
skinned young man in the shade of his porch. I began by asking him why
Adventists didn't eat pork. 'When God cast out the Devil from Man, he
threw him into the heart of a pig,' he said. 'Swine have tiny worms that
get into your brain and drive you crazy.' Baldwin didn't eat crab, lobster
or conch either, for they too were scavenging animals.

'Isn't that right, pastor?' he asked the man in the neighbouring rocking
chair. The pastor hummed agreement, absorbed in the bottom of his tub

of ice cream. 'The Bible says that Sunday is the first day of the week. Right, pastor? The last day of the week is Saturday, which is why God intended it to be the Sabbath day. Right, pastor?' More quiet humming. The young pastor was clearly used to acting as Baldwin's sounding board.

Baldwin looked down at me from the porch. His eyelashes looked to have been singed, and I pictured him doing battle with sulphur-coated demons. The Bible had given him a programme, and espousing its unshakeable tenets increased his authority. Playing the part of judge in a courtroom of his own making, he could give vent to his nature, which was fastidious, unforgiving and probably cruel. But what I knew, although he didn't know that I knew it, was that Baldwin had prostate cancer. So I was taking dietary tips from a dying man. I also knew that Ed hadn't grown up in his stepfather's house, with his mother and many siblings, but in his grandfather's house further down the road, for Baldwin resented having to compete with another man's children for his wife's affections.

The Seventh-Day Adventists first came to Providence in 1905. Pastor Frank Hutchins and his wife arrived aboard the *Herald*, selling popular editions of the Bible. At nightfall, the residents of Old Town would row out to the Americans' yacht to listen to his sermons. His awestruck face illuminated by the gas lamps strung around its deck, they listened solemnly as Pastor Hutchins told them about the imminent Destruction of the World. The abundance of shooting stars in the night skies that year was a sign of the Second Coming of Christ, he said, and many credulous islanders believed him. Even the sceptics among them found it hard to resist the appeal of Dr John Eccles, the doctor-cum-dentist who had accompanied the Hutchins to the island. The following morning Dr Eccles set about pulling and filling their teeth, and fourteen islanders converted to Adventism there and then, some out of fear of the endless darkness that awaited the sinner after death; others out of gratitude to Dr Eccles for putting an end to a lifetime of toothache.

Accompanied by this emissary from the world of modern medicine, Pastor Hutchins and his wife spent the next month preaching and singing in the island's seven villages. The pastor went with his portable organ strapped to his back, the dentist with his Gladstone bag of basic medical supplies, while Mrs Hutchins urged them on with her psalm singing. They spent 28 consecutive nights preaching and singing, clambering over rocks on the shoreline to speak to the fishermen, and hiking into the hills to visit the most solitary huts.

Among the first to convert to Adventism were members of the Robinson, Archbold and Newball families of Smooth Water Bay. The Adventists were keen educationalists, and in 1911, they built the island's first Adventist school at Rocky Point. Its only teacher was Rudolph Newball, who had just graduated from an Adventist school in Alabama that provided vocational training for 'coloured' students from the Caribbean and Latin America. Newball taught classes in Bible studies, natural history, English, algebra, typewriting and the organ. He charged a peso a month, a fee which many of his pupils paid by catching and selling fish before they went to school. When 100 of them had signed up for classes at his one-room school, he had those in the higher grades teach what they had learned to those in the lower grades. His school became known for its order and discipline, as well as the mutual love and respect between teacher and pupils. In 1977, 95-year-old Rudolph Newball told his daughter that none of his pupils had ever disappointed him.[1]

The Americans' confidence in re-interpreting their sacred texts for the modern age increased in tandem with their country's international ambitions. Seventh-Day Adventism was just one of a plethora of Christian sects originating in the Great Awakening of the 1840s, and it is no coincidence that the term 'manifest destiny' was first heard in the United States in 1845. The term was coined by the journalist John O'Sullivan during the campaign for Spanish Texas to join the Union. He saw it as the 'manifest destiny' of the United States 'to overspread the continent allotted by providence for the free development of our yearly multiplying millions.'[2] Later that year, Texas became another of the United States.

Five years later, California followed suit, and news of the discovery of gold in its hills spread east. In the absence of a railway across their vast country, Americans wanting to join the gold rush had to sail down the east coast, through the Florida Straits, and across the Caribbean to Greytown in Nicaragua. From there, they could take a paddle steamer up the River San Juan and across Lake Nicaragua to Rivas, and join the mule train for the short journey down to the Pacific port of Brito, where they would find a third ship waiting to take them up the coast to San Francisco. This tortuous journey spurred on the builders of the Pacific Railroad, but it also convinced their political representatives of the need to build a canal through the isthmus of Central America. A canal would allow east coast ports to trade with the west coast, but its scope was ultimately global: by dividing Central America, the United States would unite the world.

In June 1902, Congress approved construction of the Panama Canal, and by November, the province of Panama had declared its independence from Colombia. The country was in the grip of the War of a Thousand Days, the last and most vicious of the fratricidal bouts that had been convulsing the country since its declaration of independence from Spain, and was in no position to challenge its breakaway province. By the Isthmian Canal Convention of 1904, Panama granted the United States a 10 mile-wide strip of land between the Caribbean and the Pacific 'in perpetuity.'[ii]

As American engineers set to work building the canal, workers poured in from all over the Caribbean, and the Canal Zone became the latest, and most powerful Anglo-sphere to spring up on the coast of Central America. For a time, there was even talk of building facilities on San Andrés or Providence to store the coal that passing steam ships would need. The USS *Nashville* came to San Andrés, and a State Department representative tried to persuade the islanders to join the Panamanians in seceding from Colombia. They refused, perhaps because several members of them were familiar with the United States' system of racial segregation, having been denied admission to American universities. In 1913, the US government gave Bogotá an indemnity of $25 million for the loss of Panama, its shipping lines switched from steam to diesel, and all talk of secession came to an end.

Although San Andrés and Providence remained Colombian territories, their ties to the Canal Zone only grew stronger after the canal opened in 1914. The Canal Zone was a prosperous haven, run by fellow English speakers with a familiar love of orderly calm, and the islanders found their feet quickly. So many of them went to Colón that it was said that there were more of them in the town than there were on the islands.

Others gravitated up the isthmus and found work building the railways in Costa Rica, which was fast becoming a major supplier of tropical

---

[ii] The Canal Zone was controlled by the United States between 1903 and 1979. It was under joint US–Panamanian control from 1979 until 1999, when it was restored to Panama.

fruit to the American market. The American palate had long baulked at tropical fruit, but in 1869, Captain Lorenzo Baker of Boston happened to buy some bananas while he was in Port Antonio, Jamaica. He took them back to New England, where the strange and exotic yellow fruit sold well. Returning to Jamaica, Baker bought a derelict sugar estate in Portland parish, and began growing bananas. But further expansion was hampered by the Jamaican planters, who dismissed banana cultivation as 'a backwoods nigger business.' The obvious solution was to build plantations in Central America, but as the Panama Canal's builders had discovered to their cost, yellow fever made the region a death trap for new arrivals.

Fortunately for Lorenzo Baker, a Cuban doctor was about to make the greatest advance in medical science since Edward Jenner's discovery of a vaccine for smallpox in 1796. Dr Carlos Finlay had spent 30 years trying to convince the authorities in Havana that yellow fever was carried by mosquitoes. They ridiculed his theory, but he persevered with his research, and by the turn of the century, he had hit upon the evidence he needed to prove it. The authorities backed his proposal to eradicate the mosquitoes' breeding grounds. In 1901 Havana was declared free of yellow fever.

Armed with acres of mosquito netting, Lorenzo Baker was now in a position to conquer the mosquito empire of Central America. Returning south, he began building banana plantations, and it was from this modest beginning that the mighty United Fruit Company emerged. Within a generation, the company's land holdings had grown so vast that it could bribe the region's politicians in lieu of paying taxes, and overthrow any government that questioned its dominance of the region. Thereafter, the economies of Central America and the Caribbean became entirely dependent on American capital.

Providence was also drawn further into the Yankee orbit. So many islanders left in search of work in Central America that when Dr Herman von Tietje first reached Providence in 1910, he thought he had come to an island of women. With so many men away working, the women had to till the fields and look after their broods of children by themselves. Dr von Tietje had come to the island from his native Austria, via Boston and Panama. Along with his library of medical textbooks, he brought everything he needed to build the first modern house on the island, and when it was finished, people came from all over the island to admire its concrete walls, tiled bathroom, and network of copper pipes. He also brought the medical equipment he needed to practise as a doctor and a dentist, which was just as well, for modern healthcare had sailed away from Providence with Dr Eccles five years before. The first issue of the *Searchlight*, the islands' first newspaper, rolled off the press in San Andrés in 1912, and it carried an advertisement for the Austrian's services. It boasted that Dr von Tietje had 'the best-equipped surgery in all Central America,' and could 'cure every case of haemorrhoids (piles) without the knife,' and 'all diseases of the male and female sexual organs.'[3]

In the nineteen years he spent tending to the islanders' medical complaints, a lot of women came to the doctor's surgery, and he had children with several of them. Herman von Tietje was an enigmatic figure; even his daughters didn't know why he had chosen to spend the last third of his life on an island that most of his countrymen had never even heard of. But he had a confidant in Ephriem Archbold, the captain of the ship that had brought him to the island from Colón, and when the doctor died in 1931, the captain divulged his friend's secret. Herman had fled to Providence because of the Mayerling Incident. The mystery surrounding the discovery of the lifeless bodies of Crown Prince Rudolf of Austria and Baroness Mary Vetsera at the imperial hunting lodge at Mayerling on the morning of 30 January 1889 was the greatest *cause célèbre* of its day. It was no secret that Rudolf and Mary had been lovers, and while the circumstances of their deaths have yet to be ascertained, they probably committed suicide after the imperial household forced Mary to have an abortion.

Dr von Tietje didn't tell Captain Archbold exactly how he came to be involved in the incident, but if he was the doctor who performed the operation, he had good reason to flee. Crown Prince Rudolf had been first in line to inherit the throne of the Austro-Hungarian Empire, and his suicide caused a dynastic crisis with consequences more devastating than anyone could have imagined. Since he had no offspring, the succession passed to Archduke Franz Ferdinand, who was opposed to the growing reconciliation between the Austrian and the Hungarian parts of the Empire. Matters came to a head when the Archduke was assassinated in Sarajevo in 1914; a month later, the troops were fighting the opening battle of the First World War.

Dr von Tietje had been determined to keep his secret. Shortly before he died, he set fire to his house. The only modern building on the island, the best-equipped surgery in Central America, and all of his possessions went up in flames. The suspicion that he had been trying to burn incriminating evidence only grew stronger after Captain Archbold fulfilled his friend's last request, and placed a death notice in the *Panama Star and Herald*, informing the general public that Herman von Tichenbach had just died.

Among Dr von Tietje's other friends on Providence was an English Catholic priest called Richard Turner. In the nineteenth century, the island had served as a refuge for Colombians driven into exile after getting involved in the internecine political conflicts raging in the country's rural districts. There was no one to minister to them until the turn of the century, when the first Catholic priests arrived from Baltimore. But Bogotá became suspicious of the Americans' intentions in the western Caribbean after the Panamanians voted to secede from Colombia, and drafted in Father Turner to replace them.

Conversions to Catholicism were few – just a handful of islanders from the better-connected families – but thanks to the $100 a month that the Colombian government allocated for the upkeep of the island's mission, a group of Capuchins were dispatched to the islands in 1926. The brothers and sisters on Providence were led by Father Carcagente, who followed the precedent set by the Baptists and Adventists by opening a school next to the capacious Catholic church in Freetown. Their arrival was part of Bogotá's attempt to 'colombianise' the islanders. Motivated largely by fear that Colombia might lose the islands to the United States, 'colombianisation' was remarkably similar to the process of *reducción* that the Spanish had used to subjugate the natives of South America during their *conquista* of the New World. As seen through Capuchin eyes, the world was divided into the civilised, the semi-savage, and the downright barbarian. Civilisation was synonymous with the Catholic faith and the Spanish language. As applied on Providence, that meant rote learning of Spanish expressions that none of the class understood, and the creation of a generation of cowed, semi-literate children who knew all about the *conquistadores*, and nothing about Francis Archbold, much less the Providence Island Company.

Until 1923, Colombia's national independence day had not been celebrated on the islands, but 20th July had become a public holiday thereafter. The islanders would don their Sunday best and ride their horses to the church for a commemorative service. Father Turner would lead them in singing 'Te Deum', and then the *intendente* led them from Freetown to the mayor's office in Town, where he delivered a speech reminding them of the loyalty they owed to the fatherland. The children were given a sandwich and a bottle of King Cola – a rare treat from the Canal Zone – and there was free rum for the men, who typically drank until they passed out.

But after the Capuchins arrived, Protestant schoolchildren were told to stay away on 20th July. Baptists were the Devil, said Father Carcagente, who even baptised some Baptist children into the Catholic faith without their parents' consent. Those that resisted were reminded that they were bastards, for parents who had married in a Baptist church were living in sin, and the children of such unions were illegitimate in the eyes of God. Colombia's Constitution was no less insistent on religious uniformity, and since the law did not recognise children born out of wedlock as legal heirs, the entire system of land ownership on Providence was suddenly thrown into question.

Not long after, the Colombian president declared that the island was at imminent risk of being invaded by the Nicaraguans, and ordered the Baptist high school closed down, on the specious grounds that the building was needed to house the 50 soldiers due to arrive from Cartagena. No soldiers came, but 'colombianisation' went on apace. Protestants were excluded from jobs in local government, and their children were barred from receiving scholarships to study on the mainland. Many of them responded by converting to Catholicism and signing up for Spanish classes, an act of surrender that led to their being branded 'job Catholics.'

One day in 1928, the nuns at San Luis School on San Andrés told the girls that they would be having a Bible study class the following day, and that each of them should bring the family Bible to class. This came as some surprise to their parents; while they didn't know much about the Church of Rome, it was common knowledge that the Catholic Church did not encourage its followers to read the Bible for themselves. But the girls did as they were told, and on arriving for class the next day, they were told to put their Bibles on a table at the back of the room. While one of the sisters distracted their attention with a lesson on the geography of the Amazon, the others carried the Bibles into the yard, doused them in kerosene and set them alight.

News of the sacrilege was quickly to spread across both islands. Within a few days, the coconut palm the Bibles had been burned under died, an act of divine retribution that was only compounded by the terrible blight that afflicted practically all the coconut palms on San Andrés over the following three years. The blight was an unmitigated disaster, for the island was supplying half the coconuts eaten in the United States at the time. The largest of the American importers, the Franklin Baker Company, had been sending its steamship from Hoboken, New Jersey to its wharf on San Andrés every three months. But it stopped coming once the blight took hold and and the company began importing coconuts from the Philippines instead.

The coconut trade, which had been paying for all the accoutrements of modern living since Emancipation, collapsed. Families on both islands were made destitute, for many Providence men had gone to San Andrés to work in the coconut groves. The smaller producers, most of whom were the grandchildren of slaves, sold their groves to the bigger landowners, most of whom were the descendants of slave-owners. For the first time since the 1630s, hunger stalked the islands, and hundreds of jobless men had no choice but to leave in search of work in Central America. But it was a bad time to go, for the Great Depression had brought mass unemployment to the entire region, and they found themselves competing with idle hands from all corners of the Caribbean. Many islanders considered the blight divine punishment for the burning of the Bibles, and railed at the Colombians and their religion. Whatever its cause, it was a rude awakening to the risks inherent in monoculture, and the vicissitudes of the modern world.[4]

I found Rodrigo Howard sitting with his friends on the short boardwalk that ran parallel to the road leading out of Town. A retired schoolteacher, he was still slim at the age of 80, with a head of close-cropped grey hair. He was going to do some weeding on the plot behind his house, he said, and invited me back to his house to talk. I followed him up a steep flight of wooden stairs that led from the road running past the Catholic church in Free Town to his single-storey wooden house, and we settled into armchairs that sighed under our weight.

Like the rest of the islanders, Mr Howard had sealed the wooden walls of his house with several layers of gloss paint to keep the termites out. But the passage of time had turned the magnolia sepia, and it had had a similar effect on the rest of his sparsely furnished front room. A TV stood on a Bakelite-topped cabinet, with legs that stuck out at angles, as things tended to in the 1950s. Inside the cabinet were some dog-eared LPs, though I couldn't see a record player. "All those records are brought from Colombia. Most is porro and so on," he told me. "Me and my wife were married here, but for my career, we went to a place in Sucre named Corasál. I was teaching there for eleven years, in a Roman school. My time over there, I got to know about religion, and owing to the fact that the Baptists derived from the Catholics..."

He looked at me bashfully, as if gauging my reaction to the revelation that he had become a 'job Catholic.' I gave him a blank look, which didn't help him. "Well, to me the Catholic have more what Jesus was preaching. But my family is all Baptist besides me, and they don't say that."

I asked him about the first settlers of Providence, and he hummed recognition. "Theodor Birelski was my great-great-great-great-grandfather," he said. Very slowly, Rodrigo Howard shuffled to the bookcase on the far side of the room. His back was straight but stiff, as if each bone in his spine had fused to its neighbour. He returned with a heavy tome with a dark blue leather cover, on which the word 'Howard' had been embossed in gold, and sank back into his chair. He didn't open the book, but placed both his hands on the cover, as if to warm them. "Simon Howard," he said with great deliberation. "I think he came here from..." There was a long pause. "... Boston."

Was that around the time of independence, I asked? "No, it was before." He repeated the last word, and it hung in the air, grave and vague. "He got married to a nurse that was here to attend a Spanish group of soldiers. They had several children, boys and girls, and they married from other families. So all the Howards around this area – Providence, San Andrés, Panama, the coast – are coming from that fellow."

So are there Howards in Panama as well? "No. Some went from here to Colón and didn't come back." Not for the first time, an islander had simultaneously confirmed and denied something I'd said. Maybe he hadn't understood me, but was too polite, or too embarassed to say so. "In a few hours, we can get to any of the Central American countries in launches. My father used to carry mango, orange and coconut to Colón and Limón as a sailor. When I was a boy, there was only one teacher on the island, Rafael Archbold Taylor, so my father taught me to read in English, and arithmetic. He used to bring back our clothes and books from Colón. In those days, hardly any more fruit was here, only orange and mango. But in 1940, there was a large hurricane and all the orange trees fall down."

Mr Howard pronounced orange as 'o-REENJ', one of several examples I'd heard of what an American linguist believed to be Scottish pronunciation of Elizabethan English.[5] The islanders pronounced turtle as 'turkl,' and middle as 'migl.' They also called a chicken a 'fowl', a pig a 'hog', and used 'vex' when Britons would say 'annoy.'

Were there still links with Central America, I wondered? 'These boats still go to Panama to bring cargo from there, but we don't have anything to export anymore. Most of the young people just didn't continue to farm. Some will go from here and meet them there, and talk with each other. But most only carry cocaine,' he said with a resigned, faintly embarassed smile.

Looking out of the open window, I could see a cargo ship being unloaded on the dock. I was reminded of the catamaran trip I had made from San Andrés several months before, and was struck by an unexpected feeling of isolation. The sight of the sea was no longer a novelty, but until that moment, I had had no sense of being surrounded by it. I had been under a comforting illusion that I was living at the tip of a peninsula, rather than an island 150 miles off the coast of Central America. By most reckonings, isolation and loneliness are practically synonymous, but I didn't feel alone. Providence might have been alone, but its people shared their separation with one another, and I was basking in some of the warmth they gave off.

"They are going to dredge out the harbour. Every day getting something new," he said with a sigh. "Supposed to have a good future. But changes are becoming…" I waited for him to finish his sentence, but that was all Rodrigo Howard had for me. He had ended as he had begun: vague and hesitant, as if peering through thick fog.

The blight of the coconut palms was a terrible blow to both islands, but the main driver of outward migration from Providence was not the collapse of the coconut trade, but the breakup of the handful of families that ruled the island. In the 1930s, its largest landowner was Frederick Robinson. He owed his wealth to the black workforce of Bottom House, which was bound to the old white man by a system of patronage that kept them in perpetual debt. When he died in 1936, he stipulated in his will that his land be divided between his 27 children. This created fields that were too small to sustain a family, so many of them sold their shares and left for Cartagena or Barranquilla. The old man's workers, who were now bereft of their principal source of credit, followed them, signing up as sailors and deckhands on the ships that ferried goods between the ports of the western Caribbean. The island's population went into a steep decline that wasn't reversed until the 1960s.

In the late 1930s, Bogotá began to show more interest in the islanders' welfare. Non-Catholics were still barred from public office, but students from Baptist and Adventist families were offered scholarships to high schools on the north coast, and some of them went on to university in Bogotá and Medellín. The first hospital was built on San Andrés, the first motorcar arrived at the dock, and a yard in North End became the venue of the Ritz Theatre, where the islanders were able to watch Hollywood films for the first time time (newsreels and cowboy films proved especially popular).

It was around this time that the teacher and Adventist minister Rudolph Newball brought the first motorbike to Providence – not that it served much purpose, for the only paved road ran no further than the hospital, a few hundred yards up the hill from the dock. The first electricity generating plant was built in 1937; it supplied electricity to the houses and shops in Town, but only between six and ten o'clock at night. The rest of the islanders continued to use kerosene lamps to keep the darkness at bay, and this 'dark pollution' ensured that they continued to be haunted by 'duppies' and the ghosts of dead pirates.

But thanks to a wind-up battery charger, the people of San Andrés were soon able to listen to radio broadcasts for the first time, and in September 1939, an American voice informed them of the outbreak of war in faraway Poland. In the opening stages of the Second World War, Colombia's distance from the main theatres of conflict allowed it to remain neutral. But the islands' proximity to the Panama Canal soon brought them to the attention of the Axis powers. Responding, American warplanes dotted the skies, the dock at North End became crowded with boats from the US coastguard base in the Canal Zone, and when work began on the fortification of the canal's defences, many islanders found work in Colón again.

They returned with new cars and rolls of crisp dollar bills, which they spent on the modern household goods on offer at Rignier's, the well-appointed new department store that opened in North End. There were now taxis to ferry them between North End, Mount May and San Luis, and trucks to carry their coconuts from the groves to the dock. By 1940, most of the groves were back in production; while it was too late to restore the trade with the United States, the growers found new markets for their produce in Cartagena, and began shipping copra, oil and bran, which the Colombians turned into soap.[iii]

Like the United States, San Andrés came out of the war flourishing. The Colombian economy was doing well too, and like many post-war governments, Bogotá expanded its remit to promote development and extend credit to the nation's farmers. The first bank opened its doors, and the National Institute of Food Supplies opened a branch on the island. For the first time, the poor could receive subsidised food, which lifted the burden of helping them from the church's shoulders. With prosperity, more islanders could afford to send their children to school on the mainland, and the number of bilingual islanders began to rise.

In spite of its proclivity to fratricide, Colombia is one of the few countries in Latin America not to have endured decades of dictatorship. But in June 1953, Lieutenant General Gustavo Rojas Pinilla deposed the democratically elected government and suspended Congress. His rule lasted six years, and was widely welcomed for giving the country some respite from *La Violencia*, the term used to describe the terrible wave of bloodletting that swept the Colombian countryside after the assassination of the populist Liberal leader, Jorge Eliécer Gaitán, in 1948. Determined to restore order to a country buckling under the weight of the fighting between Liberals and Conservatives, the general appointed a cabinet largely composed of military men, and set about reforming the country's constitution and revitalising its economy.

[iii] Copra is the dried kernel of the coconut.

Shortly after coming to office, President Rojas Pinilla visited San Andrés, the first Colombian president ever to do so. Bogotá was keen to put its relations with the islands on a new footing, he told the huge crowds that gathered to hear him speak. He made San Andrés a free port, where foreign imports could be landed without paying more than 10 per cent tax. The free port was a boon to the urbanites of Bogotá, Medellín and Barranquilla, who couldn't resist the opportunity to buy American stoves, washing machines and fridges at knockdown prices. So keen was he to entice them to San Andrés that Rojas Pinilla even offered free flights to anyone who booked accommodation on the island for more than five nights. It was a dramatic gesture, but hardly a practical one, for the island's only hotel was still just a blueprint. No matter, said the general; let them stay in the islanders' homes. It would give mainlanders a chance to get to know the most isolated citizens of the republic, and the island's women an extra source of income.

The Colombians came in their droves, for few of them had ever been on holiday before, and fewer still had ever left the mainland. They returned home with their precious white goods, and memories of the vicarious thrill that came with stepping back in time to the era when San Andrés was ruled by *piratas ingleses*.

The duty-free business was also a boon to Colombia's merchants, who rushed to the island to get a slice of the action. At the time, there was just one, short street in North End: 20th of July Avenue, which was lined with two-storey wooden houses whose owners had never heard of renting business premises. Few of them spoke more than the rudiments of Spanish, and most had grown up with the honourable business practises inculcated in the Baptists' covenant. By contrast, the mainlanders were quite unscrupulous, and hoodwinked their landlords into signing fraudulent rental agreements. In a rush of entrepreneurial innovation, the newcomers shipped in jacks to elevate the houses ten feet into the air, hastily erected concrete columns, and bricked up the space below. Within weeks of agreeing to rent his ground floor, the landlord found himself living over a shop with plate glass windows showing off all the appliances of the modern kitchen.

When he realised how naïve he'd been, he sought legal advice from the island's only lawyer. But Francis Newball Hooker only knew about contracts relating to the sale of coconuts, and besides, he had retired. His successor was his nephew, Paulson Newball, who had none of his uncle's scruples. Instead of coming to the aid of the beleaguered islanders, he connived with the newcomers, inserting devious clauses that ensured that the shopkeeper would assume ownership of the building at the end of his tenancy. His landlord could file a lawsuit against him, but that would cost him a great deal of money, which he invariably had to borrow. Once the case came to court, he found himself facing a continental lawyer, who was often on first name terms with the continental judge, who invariably sided with the continental merchant. Before he knew it, the landlord was both broke and homeless.

The same combination of native innocence and foreign guile was apparent in the government's development of San Andrés. General Rojas Pinilla ordered an expansion of the island's airport, which involved multiple compulsory purchase orders. In some cases, the landowners sold up willingly, but much of the land for the new runway was appropriated without any kind of compensation. The general also ordered a tarmac road built around the island. It would mean the loss of 100,000 coconut palms, but he assured the islanders that the rewards would outweigh the losses. The construction of the International Hotel proved no less destructive. In excavating the ground for its foundations, the bulldozers destroyed a cemetery, and the bones of generations of islanders were tipped into the sea.

The desecration of the islanders' heritage might have been easier to swallow if the free port had given them jobs. But they didn't have the skills or experience needed to work in the shops and hotels springing up around them, and the new employers preferred to bring in their own staff. Many of them were of Syrian or Lebanese descent, and they recruited their workforce through family networks and political patronage. They came to dominate the retail trade, and before long, the houses and warehouses on 20th of July Avenue had been muscled aside by the duty free shops of the *Avenida 20 de Julio*.

The development of the free port was a disaster, but it would be unfair to blame it entirely on the mainlanders. San Andrés' wealthiest families were no less captivated by the rush to modernise than the government in Bogotá, and plenty of them willingly sold land that had been passed down from generation to generation since it was first apportioned by Tomás O'Neille. Besides, the free port brought some benefits: new docks were built, and a chamber of commerce was established. Rising land prices brought wealth to some, and as the standard of living rose, some

311

migrant workers opted to return home from Colón and Cartagena. The men found work as taxi drivers and tour guides, while their wives got work as chambermaids and cooks, which gave them a measure of financial independence they had not known until then.

But for most islanders, the promise of the free port was quick to lose its lustre, and it was with the bitter taste of betrayal in their mouths that they cursed the 'panyaman.'[iv] The politicians and their underlings had no time for their complaints, so they took their frustration out on the unfamiliar faces crowding their streets. But men accustomed to fighting with their fists were no match for the mainlanders, many of whom carried knives. Come Monday morning, the little island courtroom would be crowded with defendants lamenting the drunken brawl they had got into on Friday night. A new police station was built, and the governor of the island's jail, which had been unoccupied for years, was soon complaining of overcrowding. The islanders had never felt the need to fit locks on their windows, or bolts on their doors, but now both were considered essential.

Paradise had lost none of its allure for the mainlanders. Whether as tourists, shopkeepers, labourers or salesmen, they came in their thousands, and newspapers on the mainland took to calling North End 'the Colombian Coney Island.' They were perplexed by the islanders' complaints. Wasn't development good for San Andrés? Wasn't the island finally being brought into the fold of national life? Only a separatist, or somebody with a perverse hatred for the fatherland could possibly object. When marches were organised to protest at the whittling away of the islands' native culture, the Colombian *intendente* dismissed them as the work of '*negros ignorantes*'.

In 1953, the population of San Andrés had stood at 3,705; over the ten years that followed General Rojas Pinilla's visit, it doubled (by 2014, it stood at over 70,000).[6] As the demand for food went up, abundant and cheap seafood became scarce and expensive, and the huge shoals of fish that had once swum in the shallow waters of San Andrés Bay disappeared. The tourists were keen to try turtle meat, so the island's fishermen caught them in ever-increasing numbers. When the number of

---

iv 'Panyaman' is a corruption of 'Spanish man.' The term became a common term of abuse in the 1970s, when the islanders began to assert their rights as members of what they called the 'raizal' population. Ironically, the word comes from the Spanish; it means 'roots.'

adult turtles went into decline, they caught young turtles; then they too disappeared. As the demand for water went up, the water table dropped, and the island's farmers noticed that their fruit trees were producing less fruit. So they sold their orchards to the developers, and abandoned the land for the town. The island's classrooms became overcrowded, and the standard of education began to fall. Classes in Manners and Ethics, Arts and Trades, and Agricultural Instructions were dropped. Then the schools stopped teaching English, and Spanish gradually became the lingua franca of San Andrés.

The islanders had rushed to embrace the modern world at breakneck speed, but they were blind to the environmental and cultural destruction that development brought in its wake. It was as if they only appreciated the vivid beauty of 'the sea of seven colours' when it was captured on a postcard; by then, the phrase had became a slogan for the island's tourist board, and it was too late. The same year, the office of the *intendente* was devastated by a fire. Bogotá had always opted for native Spanish speakers when there were positions vacant at the seat of island government, so few islanders mourned its destruction. But the *intendente*'s office had also housed the island's archives, and the fire sent practically every scrap of written history up in smoke. It was assumed to be arson, but no culprit was ever charged. The same might be said of the fate of the island formerly known as St Andrew's: it had gone, and with it went all trace of what would soon come to be known as 'the old Caribbean.'

Providence had always regarded itself as the older brother of San Andrés. There was a certainly a racial dimension to the islanders' haughty indifference to the modern world, perhaps on account of their island having once been an English colony. By 1953, however, the last white islander was on her deathbed, and Providence had become a largely mixed race island. But it was still lighter-skinned than San Andrés, and the persistence of racial thinking created a small-minded obsession with hierarchy. At one end of the scale was the lauded minority of 'white' islanders, with their 'clear' skin and 'good' hair, most of whom lived at the top of the island. At the other end was the black majority that still lived in Bottom House and Southwest Bay.

Whatever their complexion, the islanders were still able to feed themselves with what they grew in the hills. But farming and fishing were the only resources they could draw upon. For a time there was talk of Providence becoming one of the cruise ships' ports of call, but the island didn't have a wharf capable of handling the arrival of such behemoths. As the connections between the islands and Colombia grew stronger, its more ambitious sons and daughters left for the mainland. Some found work with the oil companies that had begun drilling in the Magdalena valley. Others sought education in the United States, and went on to find work as missionaries, doctors or teachers in the Baptist and Adventist colleges that were springing up across the Americas.

By 1953, the island's population had dropped to less than 2,000, the lowest it had been all century. For many families, the only reminder of their absent son or daughter was the graduation certificate from an American college hanging on the wall. The monthly remittance, sent from the Colombian mainland or a small town in the American Bible Belt, helped them to maintain a relatively high standard of living, but the process of osmosis that drew the young and restless away from the old and settled seemed unstoppable. The island's traditional wooden houses fell into disrepair, and the charm of a way of life that was disappearing elsewhere began to wear thin. In 1953, there were 870 horses on the island, but just one motor vehicle: an old jeep that Elrue Archbold had brought back from the United States. Since the road running around the island was still little more than a rutted track, he used it to power the sugar mill when the cane-cutting season came around.

The government offered the islanders some compensation for their estrangement from the modern world. Following the hurricane that destroyed 400 houses in 1940, they had had to rebuild their homes by themselves, but when Hurricane Hattie swept hundreds of houses into the sea in 1961, various government agencies stepped in to help. Like distant relatives remembering an ageing, and increasingly isolated neighbour, the mainlanders were prone to sudden outbursts of goodwill. Between disasters, however, they remained conspicuous by their absence.[7]

20
'MAYBE THEY DON'T KNOW WHAT IS AN ISLAND'

When I told Ed that I wanted to explore the island's hilly interior, he introduced me to his cousin Basha, who said that he would be more than happy to act as my guide. The following day, I walked up the path that led through his overgrown garden, past some discarded pallets mildewing in the long grass, to his shack. The place looked abandoned – just discarded food boxes and a pile of rumpled clothes on the rough wooden floor of a windowless hut.

Even islanders less rusticated than Basha made do with very little. Perhaps it was the beauty of their surroundings that allowed them to get away with so few belongings. They had no need of carpets, curtains, radiators, bathtubs or the other essentials of life in colder climes. Nor did they have much in the way of cultural artefacts: maybe a TV, if only to watch the soaps, but no books, magazines or newspapers. Even if they had wanted such things, there was nowhere to buy them. Few of them owned cars, and those that did had no need of a garage. What every house, apart from Basha's, *did* have was a tiled floor. The gleaming floor was a status symbol, and played the same role as the gleaming car does in the UK; it also made it easier to keep a place free of ants.

The old folks I spoke to often complained about the thieves of Freetown and Bottom House, but I couldn't see what a thief might have stolen, at least until the advent of the mobile phone. There were none of the accoutrements of success to excite a neighbour's envy: no flashy cars or designer clothes; no glossy magazines or 'good schools;' no charity events or garden parties. The lack of material goods meant that there was no shame in having – or doing – very little.

What grated was not the frugality of island life, but the terrible neglect and indifference that the islanders had fallen into. People still gave me their landline numbers, even though the phones had stopped working the previous April (since everyone had a mobile, I suppose the phone company couldn't see the point in repairing the network). I encountered similar problems when I rented a little cabin in Smooth Water Bay for the second half of my stay. Annie told me that she had had no mains water since the pipes that carried water from the dam on the other side of the island burst. That was six months ago, but she wasn't bothered. "Water will come with the rain," she said stoically, as she set a row of buckets under the eaves to collect the rainwater.

The chaos that characterised local government on Providence had its advantages, for nobody feels bound by rules that aren't enforced. The islanders didn't need a helmet, lights or a number plate to ride their scooters, and they used them to transport whatever they liked, be it an infant son, an ailing aunt or a bottle of propane gas. The younger ones would tear up the road pulling wheelies and nobody did anything to stop them, and the only traffic warnings on the island were the graves of teenage daredevils that I saw in the cemetery in Freshwater Bay.

I heard Basha calling my name, and walked back to the road to watch him bring his cows down to the field behind his shack. He went up into the hills twice a day, he said; once to take them up to feed, and later to bring them back down again. The herd's owner spent most of his time in Indianapolis, and only came back to the island from time to time. In the run-up to Christmas, he would be back to slaughter several head of cattle. Christmas coincided with the harvest festival, which meant baked beef, pork and chicken, lots of sponge cake, and lots of bush rum.

We started up the hill, following paths made muddy by the cows' hooves, through dense woods to the foot of a grassy hill, where the sun beat down mercilessly. Providence had become prosperous on the back of its fruit trees, but most of its orange and mango orchards had been cleared for cattle pasture. Breaching the first of the hills leading up to the Peak, we came to a lookout point and gazed across the reef to the electric blue water over the sand banks. The view was a balm, calming our minds and drying out our words. The volcanic rock of the Three Brothers cays was rendered black by the white light reflecting off the sea, and I could only make out the silhouettes of the man-of-war birds that glided in and out of the shadows. The grass around us, which was yellowing at its tips, was waving like a sheet in the onshore breeze. The dry season usually began in January, but there had been little rain that year, and despite the occasional shower, deep cracks had appeared in the ground. As the heat rose off the land, it alternated with the breeze in warming and then cooling my skin. Would I ever live as tranquil, or as frugal a life again, I wondered?

Hidden in the pasture were masses of delicate purple flowers that reminded me of the miniature blooms I'd seen on the cliffs of north Devon the previous summer. Basha said that they could be taken as a tea to bring down high blood pressure and treat diabetes. I pointed west, and told him about the green land on the other side of the sea, which also rose up through wooded valleys to open pasture. "A lotta sea to climb to get there," he said.

As a child, he had come this way to get from his home in Rocky Point to school in Old Town. In those days, there had been a well-worn path that zigzagged between carefully tended plots of gungo peas, melons, and sweet potatoes. Every plot sustained a family, and every family had one. It was their birthright and most precious possession, and had been passed down through the generations since Francis Archbold first came ashore. But in the years since Basha left school, most of his classmates had left the island to look for work elsewhere, and many of those who stayed behind had found jobs in local government. In the 1980s and '90s, Bogotá had renewed its efforts to integrate the island into national life. Money was poured into the island's public sector, and before long, a third of the islanders were employed courtesy of the mayor's office. Contracts were often reserved for allies, jobs for loyal voters, and farming started to look like a job for losers.

Left untended, the fruit trees died, the vegetable plots became overgrown with weeds, and the path between Rocky Point and Old Town was lost to the bush. By Basha's reckoning, only 20 of the 5,000 people on Providence still walked the paths that led into the heart of the island. He had cleared the one we were on just a week before, but it was already thick with cockspur saplings. The cockspur bush, aka the bullhorn acacia, had been brought to Providence from Central America to serve as a boundary marker. Its branches are covered in thick black thorns, which grow in pairs and resemble the horns of a bull. But that isn't the only weapon in the cockspur's arsenal; at the tip of each thorn is a tiny hole, which is the entrance to the nest of an exceptionally aggressive ant. En masse, associate ants will bite any animal that tries to climb, bore into or defoliate its host. In return for this service, they get a constant supply of the protein-rich sap inside each thorn.

For generations, the cockspur served as an emblem of the islanders' possessive love of the land. But when they turned their backs on farming, it began to run wild. It is a hardy and adaptable plant, and thanks to the mutual aid between bush and ant, it makes any walk into the island's hilly interior difficult and potentially dangerous. It is an appropriate end for an island that once served as the embodiment of the idea of divine protection. Far from returning to the benign state of nature that Daniel Elfrith found when he reached the island in 1629, the untended garden has become a grotesque parody of providence, the source of nothing more useful than a tropical crown of thorns for the islanders' heads.

Once we'd ducked under the barbed wire running along the crest of the hill, we were in the 'bare bush' at the head of Cedar Valley. There were the usual 'bad elements:' cockspur, pica-pica and the birch with copper-coloured bark that peels off in layers as thin as tracing paper – its sap is a delicate pistachio green that belies the harm it can do if it gets in your eye. But the other elements we found were all good: lignum vitae, the tree of life; the wild parsley that sends you right off to sleep when drunk as a tea; and 'stinking toe,' a long chocolate-coloured pod whose seeds reinvigorate the blood. When the breeze set the dry pods on another bush rattling, Basha reminisced about how they used to roast its seeds in a pan to make bush coffee. But who drank bush coffee nowadays, he wanted to know? The younger islanders had effectively become urbanites, albeit on an isolated island of seven villages, and they only wanted to drink Nescafé and Milo.

As we clambered down the slope into Cedar Valley, we came across a farmer who was clearing the undergrowth from the few plantains on his plot. He let his machete hang loose in his hand, and watched us approach. Somebody had been stealing his fruit, he grumbled. To take a mango or two was time-honoured practice, but these days, boys took them by the sack-full. A farmer was within his rights to kill such a thief, said Basha sympathetically. Although thievery seemed to preoccupy every islander over the age of 40, thefts were rare, and from what I could gather, there had only been two murders on the island since 1789. Nostalgia and righteous bluster, on the other hand, were commonplace.

Come the rainy season, the stream running through Cedar Valley would become a torrent, Basha told me. What he didn't say was that thanks to the grazing of his cows, it would carry much of the island's topsoil out to sea. The last of the cedars had been felled long ago, but there were still some magnificent cotton trees in the valley. They were wider than they were high, and their roots were huge arms that branched off the trunk as fins two metres before they reached the ground. Their trunks were perfectly round and straight, and were encased in smooth, grey bark and jagged thorns to keep fruit-eating iguanas at bay. A boat built of timber from a cotton tree was the fastest there was, said Basha wonderingly; he knew of one that had been caught by the wind and hadn't stopped running until it hit the Miskito coast.

We scrambled back up to the crest of the hill. In a hollow formed by the curious spires of volcanic rock was a small copse of lemon trees, where we found dozens of bright yellow lemons nestling in the grass. They were round like limes, and had a delicious scent made pungent by the brief shower of late morning; it was sharp yet creamy, as if the warmth of the sun had brought out their latent milkiness. We gathered armfuls of them, which Basha carried in his shirt, holding it in front of him like a bib. He was going to make lemonade, he said.

But not yet: we had worked up a thirst by the time we got back to Rocky Point, so I bought us a couple of cans of Old Milwaukee from the schoolgirl who ran the village shop. We drank them in the shade of the bus shelter opposite the church, and when the beer was gone, I went back for more. Getting drunk in the daytime was a good way to lose track of time. I could see why there were so many empty tins of Old Milwaukee rusting in the grass in front of Basha's shack.

Yet there were still fighters on the island. Luz Marina Livingston had spent the past year clearing the abandoned plot of land her family owned on a hill overlooking Manchineel Bay. Judging by the undergrowth we passed on the way up, it must have been a heck of a job. She already had an acre or two planted with lemon, sweet and bitter orange, banana, guava and papaya trees. She had had two big water tanks shipped over from San Andrés, and built a shelter for them and her makeshift bush kitchen. She'd spent last Christmas up there by herself, sleeping in a hammock strung between the wooden posts that supported the corrugated zinc roof.

I wondered what had driven her to work so hard, all alone on her hillside plot. She told me that she had studied radio and television production at university in Bogotá; and how her family had worried about her living on the mainland when Pablo Escobar was running rampant, and the threat of explosions and gunfights was ever-present. "I had a trust inside that it would be great," she said. "Bogotá has become for me like a public university of life. When you live in the city, wow, then you learn a lot, and you grow up. And if you want to keep advancing and get knowledge, then you keep going."

Luz Marina lived in Bogotá for eleven years, working first for the National Institute of Radio and Television, and then for one of Colombia's first mobile phone companies. "Sometimes on a Sunday, one o'clock in the morning, I would be in my office working. It was cool, you get the experience, but when I was 27 years, I said 'OK, I don't want to be closed up in an office. I want to be outside. My dad is getting old, and my parents want to see me.'"

"When I get back home, I just have enough time to share with my dad. To get to live the last part of him and live that spirit… I got it. My dad was really free-hearted, free-minded, free-handed – free everything. He was a little of everything. He was a musician, he was a fisherman and he was a farmer. On Saturday mornings, we would go on horse to his farm and take back home bananas and cassava and corn and watermelon. In those times, you could survive off what you have on your land. You could exchange with your people, and you didn't worry about having effective cash. We get back home and he would start to make a big share for people in the area. Say, 'OK, this is for this person, and this is for that lady down there.' The original people was so united. Everything was home-made, and people were self-sufficient. It was amazing."

"But things changing, and very fast, especially with the younger set of people," Luz Marina went on. "Now everybody wants to have the last iPhone. The new generation get over-ambitious for money. You can rip me off and you will do it. The consumer moral is changing everything. Old time, people could go with their eyes closed. You can still find people that are very honest in this place, but it's not like before. They lost this confidence in people. You miss that."

Until the 1980s, Providence had been something like a museum piece, preserving customs from an era before modern transport and technology. Cash had always been present on the island, but most of it stayed in the cash register at the island store and was only removed when a merchant ship stopped by with goods for sale. Electricity had come to Town in the late 1930s, but it was only when Bottom House was connected to the grid in the late '80s that the villagers were able to power televisions, electric ovens and washing machines. The arrival of electricity also brought light in abundance, which banished the malevolent spirits that had haunted the island since Francis Archbold's day, and finally brought the age of 'dark pollution' to an end.

"A couple months later, my dad died. I say to myself, 'the island give so much to me, it's time I give back something to the island.'" Luz Marina clubbed together with her friend Annie Chapman to produce a radio show, which went out every weekend. They'd talk about anything: shipwrecks, bush medicine, cruise ships, and the arrival of 'sweet thing,' the name the islanders gave to crack cocaine. But their favourite topic of conversation was politics: by the millennium, *el departamento de San Andrés y Providencia* was on the brink of bankruptcy, and Bogotá had to step in to take over the running of the islands. A series of interim governors resigned, aghast at the amount of money that had gone missing. The bank froze the local government's accounts, and seized what was left in the pot to recover what they were owed. On Providence for some time the mayor's employees went unpaid, and retirees couldn't get their pensions.

For the first time since the blight of the coconuts in the 1920s, families began to go hungry. Community marches were organised, and public employees went on strike, but this only resulted in a breakdown in the provision of public services. Even after the local government's finances were restored to some semblance of order, the islands' governor was unable to find a long-term solution to the crisis because the deputies in the islands' Legislative Assembly refused to approve the bills that would have restructured the administration. They had become entirely dependent on Bogotá and the annual grant it gave to the islands, and had nothing else to fall back on.

Amidst so much corruption and misgovernment, the islanders grew disillusioned, not only with their politicians, but with Colombia itself. An opinion poll found that, given the chance, 25 per cent of islanders would vote to become independent; a further 17 per cent wanted the islands to become British or American dependencies. But their feelings were mixed – just as many of them simply wanted Colombia to provide them with more jobs.[1]

On the Monday after her radio show went out, the mayor would shoot Luz Marina dirty looks in the street. He wasn't the only one: a third of the islanders worked for local government in one way or other. Many of them considered deference to authority part of the Baptist heritage, and didn't appreciate two women on the radio reminding them that they were living in a democracy, where politicians were supposed to serve the people.

Every time Ed saw me he let out a gargled laugh of pleasure, for I was his new best friend (though I couldn't help feeling that any one who gave him cigarettes, bought him packets of frankfurters, and gave him rides home on his scooter could have done the job as well as I did). This time, however, he wasn't smiling. "You didn't come to church yesterday," he said. The only reason I gave Ed money was so as not to see the face that he pulled: the one that told me that I was just another of the heartless people to wander in and out of his world. Only the day before I'd agreed to go to the Baptist church in Town with him, but maybe because I had found an internet connection, discovered that Liverpool had beaten Spurs 5-0 the previous Saturday, and gone to Roland's Bar on Manchineel beach to celebrate, I hadn't been able to face it.

I pulled a face of deep remorse, and we lapsed into silence. A police van pulled up, one of only two on the island, and a pair of mainlanders got out. I had often passed the other police van on my circuits of the island; it was on blocks over the mechanics' pit at the island's only garage, and judging by the thick layer of dust, had been for some time. The van in front of us had two big dents in its windscreen, and I asked Ed if he knew what had caused them. He screwed up his face in distaste at the memory. Three boys from Bottom House had taken delivery of a 300-kilo consignment of cocaine from San Andrés, he said. They were planning to take it to Costa Rica in a fast boat, but a *sapo* grassed them up.[i] The police raced down to Bottom House, raided their homes, and took them back to the station, where they set the electric probes on them. The next time the police van passed through the neighbourhood, the young men's friends let rocks do the talking for them.

Providence had been a mid-ocean fuelling station for the fast boats

---

[i] Colombians use the Spanish word for a toad to describe informers, because they can't help croaking.

since the Millennium, when Colombian traffickers stopped carrying cocaine across the Caribbean to Miami, and instead began running it into the myriad creeks of the Miskito coast. From there, the precious cargo was loaded onto trucks, which carried it along the overland route through Mexico to the border with the United States. Until then, the island's young sailors had been content to spend the first years of their careers saving up the million pesos [£3,000] they needed to get their mariner's license. There was healthy demand for their services throughout the western Caribbean, for they had grown up on the edge of the second largest coral reef in the Americas, and in learning how to navigate it, acquired an ability to read the sea that was second to none. They would spend the next 20 years working on cargo ships, and by the time they hit 40, they had enough money to come home, get married and build a house. But a young mariner could make the same money in two or three years working on a fast boat. As a result, there were thought to be 600 men from Providence and San Andrés languishing in the state penitentiary in Tampa, Florida on drugs trafficking charges.

It didn't take Ed long to brighten up. He wanted to introduce me to his brother, "the one I told you about, who lives in California." We found Manuel – "you can call me Manny" – painting his new house, which was the latest addition to the cluster of concrete houses around Ed's stepfather's place. Apart from the floors, which were still bare earth, the building work was complete. Manny had been painting the walls since eight that morning; it was now five, and he was tired. "Working hard, man. Unlike the people here," he said. Over an Old Milwaukee, Manny told me about the man who had cut most, but not all of the grass in front of his house. "He said he'd be back, but I never saw him again." I asked if he'd already paid him – he had. Manny had obviously been away for some time. In fact, he had been away for 23 years, working as a limousine driver in Santa Clara, while he saved up the money he needed to build his house.

Ed peeled one of the June plums that had fallen under a tree, and handed it to me, while the three of us watched a little plane come in to land at the landing strip behind the family's plot. Ed told me that he had spent his childhood watching pilots do battle with the headwind, and had worked at the airport as a teenager. One day, he had even tried to make off with a biplane, but had only got as far as the end of the runway before he was hauled out of the cockpit by its furious pilot.

"You're talking to a bad man," said Manny, pointing at his brother with a knowing smile. Ed shrugged nonchalantly, but my look of surprise begged an explanation. It had all started when he was caught carrying 300 kilos of cocaine from Medellín to Pereira in his wife's car, he said. The judge gave him eleven years, which he spent shuffling between prisons in Medellín, Montería and Valledupar. At first, he was content to serve his time working in the kitchens, preparing rice, beans and chicken for his fellow inmates. But incarceration began to get to him, and one day, he took a knife from the kitchen and stabbed one of the prison guards in the throat. When reinforcements arrived, he took the dead man's gun and shot two more of them. He managed to escape, but four months later he was stopped at an army checkpoint, and soon found himself back in court. This time the judge gave him 49 years. He got out in 22, which was four years ago.

Following his release, he flew back to San Andrés, where he found work as a moto-taxi driver. Not long after, a hit-and-run driver piled into him, killing his four passengers, and leaving him seriously injured. For the first time, I imagined Ed's life before his accident: slim and healthy, in freshly laundered clothes and new shoes, with a swagger he'd never have again. Ed had been one of those who never even considered fishing or farming for a living. Instead, he left for Medellín, where he latched on to the cocaine business, it being the only line of work for teenagers who try to steal biplanes. Once onboard, it was only a matter of time before he was thrown.

Partly as a result of his injuries, and partly his lack of skills, Ed was a beggar. He was redundant – and voluntarily so. Even confined to a chair, he could have been chopping up fish or sitting behind a desk, if any office would have had him, but he preferred to beg. And now he was boasting to his new best friend in his stepfather's yard: of how he had once been the *cacique* of the prison, didn't like people who were all mouth and no trousers, and was afraid of nobody. But I was more embarrassed than intimidated. It must be hard for a *cacique* not to be feared anymore.[ii]

When I asked Manny how the island had changed since he left for California, he said that these days every family has a relative involved

---

[ii] The word *cacique* was originally used to refer to to a native chieftain, but in this context, it means top dog, or boss.

in the cocaine business. Providence is too small for capos to hide out, so the big Colombian organisations – the *Paisas*, *Urabeños* and *Rastrojos* – came no further than San Andrés. Drive-by shootings have become commonplace there, he said. There are drug-related deaths on Providence too: when a bale goes missing, one of the fastboat's crew has to pay for the mistake. But those extracting payment were always careful to throw the body overboard a few miles out to sea, where it is sure to be eaten by sharks. If a young man ever dies on the island it was usually after trying to pull a high-speed wheelie on his scooter.

Having tried and failed to go to church with Ed in the weeks leading up to Christmas, I was determined to get there the following Sunday. But when I got to Rocky Point, I found myself dawdling outside the New Jerusalem Baptist Church, worried that I might ascend the steps to find the congregation sitting in a horseshoe around a chair reserved just for me. So I sat and watched the believers arrive for Sunday service on their scooters instead. The men came in their Sunday best, the women in high heels and hats, their rumps squeezed into dresses that fell just short of the knee, with an infant on their lap. Once inside, they sang hymns that sounded like power ballads, with names like 'I Am not my Own (I Belong to Jesus)'. The voices that carried through the open windows were all female, which only added to my suspicion that the men were only there to appease their partners, who were in turn only there to show off their babies, and have a good sing-song.

The music stopped and there was a reverent hush before a slick and assured voice made itself heard. The minister made a big effort to sound heartfelt, but the sermon he preached was so anodyne, I felt sure he only expected to be judged on his delivery. His performance was an expression of wholly temporal values: social standing, and a presumed right to judge who was respectable and who was not. His message echoed what I had heard from every islander over the age of 40: the island's youngsters regarded manners, morals and respect for one's elders as things of the past, and the rot would only stop when the congregation inculcated a culture of discipline in their children. I had tried talking to the younger islanders, to see how they responded to the charges being levelled at them, but without much luck, for most of them had inherited their parents' deference, if not their devotion. The few to proffer an opinion confirmed what I suspected: the age of self-sufficiency and unquestioning respect for authority was over; the world was a big place now, and they would be leaving for jobs on the mainland as soon as they were able.

The minister was addressing an echo chamber. Worse still, the rot that had crept through the political establishment had also found its way into the Baptist church. The island's politicians and clergymen had long kept up the pretence that right was on their side, and that the wrongdoers were always 'panyamen.' But there were those in the congregation who knew full well where the money to pay the church's new pews and embroidered cushions had come from. Plenty of the islanders had looked the cocaine business straight in the eye on the Sunday a stray bale washed up off Rocky Point. When the news reached the crowded pews, they dashed to the shore, eager to beat those rushing to the prize from all over the island. Among those seen racing home with a five-kilo brick of cocaine balanced on the petrol tank of their scooter were several middle-aged women in broken heels and lop-sided hair-dos. They were extreme variants of a type common to all communities where religious faith and conservative values collude: the 'one-day-a-week Christian.'

21

'STILL A LITTLE BEHIND TIME'

I spent Christmas at Posada Enilda, which floated on the unmarked border that separated Smooth Water Bay from Bottom House. Enilda Chamorro and her brother ran a tight operation, along the lines they'd learned working on the cruise ships, and hadn't lost the habit of dressing in white. Since building a house out of steel would have been impractical, they had done the next best thing and built it out of concrete. The islanders had embraced the stuff with gusto; it made for a rather barren built environment, but aridity was part and parcel of modernity in those parts, along with the gallons of room fresheners, deodorants and bleach used in the island's more respectable households.

My room at the Posada Enilda had air conditioning, which made a refreshing change, but brought problems of its own. To keep the room cool, the sun had to be kept out, so Enilda had covered the windows with sheets of adhesive black plastic and told me to keep the curtains drawn. It was a bit like living in a fridge, except that the light only came on when I closed the door.

Enilda was one of several islanders hoping to find recompense for the collapse of farming in the tourist trade. But their first experience of mass tourism had not been encouraging. A few years before, the captain of a cruise ship carrying 2,000 Americans decided to pay Providence a visit. Since his vessel was too large to dock at the wharf, he dropped anchor outside the harbour and ferried his passengers to the dock in longboats, 90 at a time. He had a soap dispenser and a vat of clean water installed on the dock, and instructed them to wash their hands before and after going ashore and not to touch, eat or drink anything, for his medical staff would not treat anyone who returned to the ship with an infection picked up on the island. By the time they left four hours later, the tourists had bought eight T-shirts, and ten pairs of earrings. Even the tourist brochures and raizal handicrafts had gone untouched. The island's guides, who had welcomed the visitors ashore with beaming smiles, glared at them sullenly as they clambered back into the longboats. It had been a humiliating experience, and one they saw no point in repeating.

On Christmas Eve, I scootered into Town and found a Christmas tree standing in the little square in front of the wharf. Except that it wasn't a tree, but a twenty feet-high wire cone wrapped in dark green tinsel. The lights on the pretend-tree, and the illuminations that had been strung up over the road leading out of Town, were Father Christmases, and candles had been replaced with seashells, seahorses and crabs. The Puritans would doubtless have approved of the islanders' keeping the religious component of the year-end festival in church.

The islanders were in church until midnight that night. Only then did the bands strike up, as they did on the three following nights. The compere introduced them as long lost members of the family, returned to their ancestral home. They came from Colón and Portobello in Panama, Cahuita, Bastimento and Bocas del Toro in Costa Rica, and were it not for Colombia's long-running dispute with Nicaragua, they would have come from Bluefields and the Corn Islands too. They sang in English, and like the local groups, they played calypso. Even their instruments were familiar: the guitar, violin and mandolin carried the melody, with the rhythm supplied by a single bass string set in a round metal tub, a clave and a horse's jaw, which was played with a stick to produce a sharp tap, or run along the teeth to make a sound like a snare drum.

The best-known of the groups from Providence was the Coral Group, whose front man was Willy B. Archbold. "The typical music that we play from my grandfather's time is from Jamaica," he told me over a post-gig drink. "We call one of the tune pasillo, one quadrille, one is jumping polka. Call one wals, call one schottis, call one mazorka. Look very pretty to see. We don't want this music to abolish, so we training so young one come to know it."

"Have you ever been to Jamaica?" I asked him. "Yeah. I been a cook on a small tanker carrying oil and we went to Jamaica plenty time. They have big tubes running under the earth, taking crude oil fifty miles off shore from the Gulf to Mexico. Hard work, man. But I got sick with my heart running brown sugar to Bahia Dulce, Guatemala, so when I reach home, they take me Medellín and put in a pacemaker. After that, all work was over."

I asked Willy what had happened to the English who first settled the island. "We never see them anymore. This Providence was given by England to Colombia, so we speak English. Then we was vexed because we said, 'Why the hell you did that? You should keep us.'"

But that was a long time ago, I said. "Yes, long time ago," he said in a whisper. "Bad people fi that, because Colombia treat us like dog. Spanish up in Bogotá take up all the money and put it in him pocket. If England could take it over back, I would rather that."

I had heard variants of the same story from several of the older islanders: Queen Victoria had given Providence to Colombia as a gift when the new republic won its independence from Spain, but on one condition: that if they ever gave the islanders cause for complaint, she would take it back. It was a nice story, but one that owed more to the fantastic Edward Seaward than the real Francis Archbold.

"Well, I will be soon out of this punishment," said Willy. "That's the last touch, because 76 years I have now." He asked me how long I'd been away from England. About three months, I told him. He thought for a moment. "England is by America?"

Yes, it had all been a long time ago. Yet England survived in unexpected places. Shortly after arriving on Providence, I had heard a strange song called 'The Ram Goat', by an island musician called Wycliffe Archbold. 'The eye of that old ram, it was really shine indeed/ It made a light as bright enough to shine all over the world,' he sang. The chorus went: 'I tell you that is the truth, for I would never have start to lie/ And if you go to Derbyshire, you know you might well as die.'

Since when had Derbyshire been such a hellhole, I wondered, and what did an old singer on Providence know about it? Thanks to the internet, I later discovered that 'The Derby Ram' is an old folk ballad, thought to date from 1760. The lyrics had evidently been warped in crossing the Atlantic, and the brilliance of the ram's eyes exaggerated, for the original version goes: 'The little boys of Derby, sir, they came to beg his eyes / To kick about the streets, sir, for they were football size.' The chorus was more innocuous too: 'And had you been to Derby sir, you'd have seen it as well as I.'[1] The bitter note of Wycliffe Archbold's version must have been adopted somewhere between England and the western Caribbean.

The next band to strike up was the best of the night: a young group from San Andrés called the Caribbean Style New Generation. It was an artless name, and one that belied the great sounds they produced. They marshalled two guitars and a mandolin, with all four players singing, not in English but Spanish. The sweat was soon pouring down their faces. This was the younger generation of islanders whose grandparents had told me not to bother talking to them. Their music spoke volumes: they were clearly untroubled by their dual Anglo-Hispanic heritage, determined to get the crowd dancing, and had no interest in copying the pretty, melancholy note that the older players struck.

The mayor, who was sitting with six other pale-faced old dignitaries at a trestle table at one side of the stage, watched them play impassively. I caught sight of his foot tapping in time with the music, but only for a couple of beats. The crowd seemed equally unmoved: the older ones had pulled up chairs and taken the weight off their feet; the younger ones seemed happy to watch the band and exchange greetings with friends, while their children darted around under the mayor's trestle table. I was mystified; the mood was more reminiscent of events at the parish hall in the Devon village where I grew up than any social event I had been to in Colombia, where any gathering without dancing was considered a flop.

But we were a long way from the mainland too. The islanders were never less than courteous and friendly, but they always seemed to be holding something in reserve. They were not open and demonstrative like the Colombians, but watchful, as if waiting for someone to mock or admonish them. Wasn't that part of the Puritan legacy? The culture of discipline the Puritans promoted had no time for the ribaldry and light-heartedness of the saints' days, when every country village in England came together to play sports and make music. As far as the Puritan conscience was concerned, leisure time was wasted time. Their censoriousness made their parishioners austere and frugal, but it also made them self-critical and socially awkward. The battle between merry and not-so-merry England has been raging ever since.

On my last Saturday on Providence, I went to a horse race on the beach at Southwest Bay. Horse racing flourished on the back of the trading circuit between the region's English-speaking communities. The older islanders had told me fondly about the days when they would sail to the Corn Islands and Bluefields with their horses to take part in races. But after the Sandinista Revolution of 1979, the Nicaraguan government discouraged communication with the islands, for fear that the Colombians' American allies would use them as conduits for their attempts to undermine the new government. Horse racing has never been popular in Colombia, and as the mainlanders exerted more influence on Providence and San Andrés, it had been largely eclipsed by baseball. Since the Millennium, the cocaine traffickers have begun plying the waters separating Providence from the Miskito coast, making them still more dangerous for islanders wanting to visit relatives in Central America. From my Spartan seaside cabin, I had watched the spotlights of anti-drugs police helicopters comb the mangrove swamps where the smugglers come to refuel their fast boats.

So a race day was a rare treat. I was hoping to run into Richard Hawkins, who was said to be one of the island's keenest horsemen. But he wasn't there – an old man told me that his wife had found out about his girlfriend and he'd had to leave the island until things cooled off. In the days before the slave traders came, Ghana had had a cavalry 100,000 horses strong, he told me. Many of the riders joined the Arabs when they invaded Spain, and later generations of riders came to the Americas as slaves, which explained the love of horse racing on the islands.

Horse racing was closely associated with obeah, the form of African witchcraft that had never quite gone away. Richard's late mother had been the island's principal practitioner of obeah, the old man told me, but she had died not long after electric light came to Bottom House. In his childhood, he had often tried to sneak a look at the horses before the race, but had always been chased away by their trainers, who were worried about strangers casting spells. The obeah men would try to put the jockey's soul in a bottle, the better to destroy him. How did they do it, I asked? "You have to read the black book, which only an obeah man has," he told me with a laugh. Nothing made him laugh harder than the imponderable workings of the obeah men, he said.

The day after my day at the races, Richard's girlfriend flew back to Switzerland, his wife cooled down, and he went back to 'Richard's Place,' the little bar where he sold cocktails to the odd tourist who made it to the end of the beach in Southwest Bay. I found him lounging in a hammock with a spliff and listening to Bob Marley with a friend. He must have been in his late fifties, but he was still strong, with no trace of the bloated gut common to most islanders of his age. He was wearing workman's boots, black jeans, a white shirt and a black waistcoat, and was one of the few island men with dreadlocks. He looked like a swashbuckling pirate, and a black swashbuckling pirate at that. I found him reserved, and a little intimidating. He gave me a quick look up and down, and went back to watching the horizon.

"See, the Haya given over 75,000 kilometres in square to Nicaragua just like that," he said in a deep baritone voice.[i] "And they already have business plan to do with China, which would be causing 42,000 million dollars. What the hell is that?"

The hell that was, was the Inter-Oceanic Canal, which the chairman of HKND, the Hong Kong-based construction company proposing to build it, was calling 'the biggest construction project in the history of humanity.' Like most Latin American countries, Nicaragua's biggest trading partner is no longer the United States, but China. In return for the right to build a new canal through Nicaraguan territory, the Chinese would pick up the £23 billion bill (four times the size of Nicaragua's annual GDP). HKND was confident of breaking ground on the project later that year and having it finished within five years.

The canal's proponents see it as essential, if the world is to handle ever-larger trade flows and the ever-larger cargo ships needed to carry them. Each of the new generation of cargo ships is capable of transporting a million flat-screen TVs, but they will be too large for the Panama Canal, even after its current expansion. Critics argue that the new canal will have a devastating impact on the Miskito coast, and HKND has no history of building canals, or anything else for that matter. Their suspicions have only been heightened by the veil of secrecy that the Nicaraguan government has thrown over its negotiations with the Chinese company.

"Nicaragua knows long time ago their *lindera* is 82 meridian down there on the west west, 270 on the compass," said Richard. "So don't let

---

[i] La Haya is the Spanish word for The Hague. In December 2007, the International Court of Justice recognized Colombia's sovereignty over San Andrés and Providence, but left open the question of the demarcation of the maritime boundary and sovereignty over the cays of Serranilla, Quitasueño, Serrana and Roncador. The ruling was very unpopular on Providence; the cays have always belonged to Colombia, but the islanders felt that Bogotá had not done enough to uphold their claim, thereby allowing Nicaragua to claim jurisdiction over them.

me catch you over the border! If treasure is here, if reef is here, if petroleum is here, you don't fucking business with that!" He petered out, muttering curses at the the Nicaraguans, the Chinese, and the Colombians' half-hearted defence of their territorial waters.

"It's a sad thing to see them giving over our sea what our generation from 1492 of existence of civilisation that done inhabit this island been surviving on," he said quietly. He looked up to catch my eye for the first time. "Those guys that say they're rich, they're not rich. They prefer to have some thousand billion bucks before having just the pleasure of your eyes to see that natural power and beauty. We ten thousand times more rich than them. Bill Gates is a ras to me." The CD started jumping. "But rich people have got better stereos," I said. Richard stared ahead forlornly.

"I feel like England should come back and take over and put his... scare into it. Because what Providence needs much more than anything is protection. This was a fruitful garden," and he listed the many varieties of mango that had grown on the island when he was a child: John Smith, Rachel, Number 11, Sally Tongue, Bull nut, kidney, Thai. "Twelve varieties of mango alone we used to grow. What! But we are making our own famine."

So why did everyone stop farming? I asked him. "Laziness and ignorance come in here because English move out and education fly away. And still Spaniard thinking that by black we still their slave."

Do you know when the English first came here? "They don't really have capacity to know definitely who the first set," he said even-handedly. "But the redskin Indian that come down through the United States was here first. Then the Spaniard come and kill them out and took their precious stone and riches. Twenty-seven civil wars. Then Henry Morgan come in and kill out the Spaniard dem."

So Morgan was the first Englishman on Providence? "Not really. Well, he was the first English pirate. He get that savaged that his mum sealed him out in a barrel from Jamaica to Trinidad, and then he come to St Andrews and get to know these places. So he went back and call up some of his friends and make bargain with them, and take three galleons and 480 slaves, and brought over here. Morgan sent Edward Mansveldt ashore to let Governor O'Neille know that he has two hours left to stay on this island. Mansveldt say, 'We come to take over, and we're going to kill out all you guys' (Richard said this with a lascivious slur). 'We take over and we let them go Cartagena."

"But Providence came first," I said. "The English were in Providence before they were in Jamaica, weren't they?"

"No," said Richard.

"Yes," said his friend Thomas, piping up from his hammock.

"No," said Richard. "Is afterwards that Morgan comes here. That's why they have so many civil wars, because everybody wants to be the owner of this island."

"So how long did Morgan stay on Providence?"

"About 16 years. He started giving names to the villages and give each one of the pirates in such a village orders to kill. The slaves was authorised to be like the soldiers now and kill out all the living Spaniards. Then Morgan killed himself, and the people them scatter and start to live on their own. That's why Providence is a big family disorganised, separated into villages. Spain come back in, and until now they still on us."[ii]

Here was Providence's creation myth. In the United States, it is is still widely believed that the Pilgrim Fathers arrived with God's blessing, and that this explains why America went on to become the most powerful nation on earth. But the only heavenly authority that Providence's pirates respected was tempestuous fate, and they were loyal to no master but the Admiral of the Brethren. After the death of Henry Morgan, they had fallen upon one another, and without unity, they had been unable to resist the encroaching Spanish.

"You have a little bit of harmony and unity but still there is something against us. You can't rebel against the system you alone, because then you become more crazy than normally crazy. And we like to stay normal crazy," Richard said with a malevolent chuckle.

There was a tantalising postscript to the island's creation myth, which kept the ghosts of the distant past ever present. "Through they get to find out they was killing all the Spaniard, the pirates dem leave. It was a bad weather, but they decide to risk it, and two of the three galleons get out the channel safe and took off. But the third one get bilge outside and sank there. That's the treasure – the third galleon. 8,600 million dollars – that is value of world history of treasure hunting."

"That is there," said Thomas authoritatively. "Seventy, eighty feet

---

[ii] Richard was right to highlight the role of the slaves in Morgan's fight with the Spanish, but he confused seventeenth-century figures like Henry Morgan with late eighteenth century figures like Tomás O'Neille.

maximum. A lot of people know about it, but they don't know where it is because I don't tell them."

"So why don't you go and get it?"

"You can't just get that shit like that!" said Richard savagely. "If you go out there, the barracuda with green eyes and blue tears that minding the treasure will drown you now. You have to go down there with a good invocation of spiritual and metaphysic part, to get that shit."

"What we really need from you is some good detector," said Thomas. "We need some money."

"They're not expensive," I replied evasively. Talk of sunken treasure was nothing new on the island. As long ago as 1877, the Colombian government had issued a decree banning the islanders from helping foreign treasure hunters. I had been warned that as soon as the islanders knew what you were looking for, you were at risk of being robbed.[2]

"There's a game going on," said Richard. "It's pretentious to be more smart." In spite of his volubility, I could see that he hadn't lost his initial reserve. He went back to watching the horizon, while I went back to my seaside cabin to pack my bags.

After three months on Providence, I was keen to see its hinterland: the English-speaking towns that dot the Caribbean coast of Central America between Portobello and Cape Gracias a Dios. Since it is no longer possible to make the crossing by sea, I had to take the catamaran back to San Andrés, and then catch a flight to Panama City. Four weeks later, I made it to Bluefields, where I caught a boat to the Corn Islands.

For as long as Antonio Escalona, the sea-fearing *intendente* of San Andrés, governed the Corn Islands, Colombian sovereignty had only ever been nominal. But in 1890, the Nicaraguans took possession of the islands, as part of their campaign to incorporate the Miskito coast into the rest of the nation. In 1894, the islanders petitioned the British government, in the hope that it would make the Corn Islands a protectorate. When that failed, they petitioned the governor in Cartagena, but Colombia had already given up its claim over the islands in return for Nicaragua's renunciation of its claim over Providence and San Andrés. The Corn Islands remain Nicaraguan territory to this day, and are of great strategic importance, for they stand at the gateway to the proposed Inter-Oceanic Canal.

I sailed on the *Captain D* (I think the '*D*' stood for *Dios*, since there was a picture of a robed Jesus, his arms outstretched, on the prow of the ship). The deck was crowded with drums of diesel, hessian sacks of plantains and watermelons and bags of cement. It was a day or two before *Semana Santa*, so there were also a lot of passengers, mainly locals, and some Nicaraguan tourists who had flown in from Managua. They occupied every last inch of space: on the poop deck around the captain's cabin, around the wheels of the minibus that took up much of the main deck, and atop the rusting freezers of meat on the deck closest to the prow.

Once we were at sea, I went in search of food. It took me a while to negotiate my way through the mass of bodies to the mess room. The older islanders had commandeered the dining tables, and were watching *The Last Temptation of Christ* on the TV. The queue slowly shuffled forwards through the heat, all eyes on Judas' betrayal of Jesus. In the canteen, a man I guessed to be of zambo descent was making instant noodles. How he took so long to make such a simple dish was beyond me. His wife was spreading jam over packaged bread with a teaspoon, and they were both flustered and unsmiling. I lost patience, and headed in to help myself to some hot water, but he was having none of it and chased me out of his kitchen.

Once I had been served my instant noodles I returned to the prow and fashioned a seat for myself in a pile of coiled ropes. The passengers around me were dozing on stacks of timber, or listening to *reggaetón* on their phones in the shade cast by a mountain of mattresses. The Miskito man next to me had his legs pulled up under his chin and a hooded rain jacket over his head. He was pathetically seasick, and was shivering from what I guessed to be exhaustion.

When the sun began to lose its strength, the ship's captain played country and western over the stereo, and I got up to watch flying fish skip across the water. The rhythm of the slide guitar was in sync with the ship as it pitched through the waves, and a melancholy voice, which alternated between English and Spanish, ebbed and flowed with the direction of the wind. Those who weren't dozing looked out over the sea in silence as low clouds diffused the last of the sunlight. Gradually the curtain fell on another day, and the stars came out one by one, until they dotted the entire sky.

Until 1999, only a handful of tourists made it to Little Corn. But the Americans had arrived in force since the island's inclusion in *1,000 Places to See Before You Die*, that tome of commandments for those with eyes on the horizon and leisure time to burn. By the time I got there, everyone on Little Corn was making money from them, whether by taking them on diving trips, cooking their meals, or cleaning their rooms. They had learned to make French toast and pancakes, and traditional dishes like *gallo pinto* and 'run-down' had become anachronisms.

I hadn't seen foreigners en masse for months, and watched them with fresh eyes. They invited looks, in their bikinis and board shorts, elaborate tattoos and T-shirts with important messages on the front. Fearing anonymity and craving recognition, they literally made spectacles of themselves, yet the looks they returned were often suspicious and watchful, and they seemed strangely brittle. While they prized both personality and physicality, the locals didn't seem to set much store by either. With so few meaningful choices to make, the locals spent a great deal of time ruminating on the nature of powers that would never be theirs. Weren't the Americans still blessed by providence? Weren't the islanders, like their piratical forebears, still more fearful and fatalistic?

Being on Little Corn, it was easy to forget that the island even had a history. The natives were there to keep the visitors from earthly cares, and the discretion with which they served them meant that it was all too easy to ignore them. So as not to disrupt the tourists' back to nature fantasies, they had tucked their homes in a dip in the dunes, and it was easy to believe that the world had been designed solely to please the five senses.

The beach huts at the smartest resort, which was run by a service-conscious American from Boston, were named after famous stowaways like Gulliver, Robinson and Napoleon. The guests were finding it hard to have nothing to do. They were always active, whether reading, checking the news on their phones or swapping stories with their friends. They flocked together for comfort, and on the rare occasions I saw them alone, staring out over the flat sea, they looked hopelessly forlorn.

Wherever I had been in the western Caribbean, I had had problems finding locals able to tell me about their history. The closest I had come to a relic was a solitary brick, in its own glass cabinet, in the Corn Islands' little museum. The teenage curator told me that it had arrived as ballast on an English ship in the seventeenth century. She suggested that I talk to Mr Otto, but a freshly painted wooden marker in the islands' cemetery told me that he had just died. I was directed to Miss Bridget, but she was was feeling shy and didn't want to talk, and Rasta Punch was at work.

Then the waitress at the restaurant where I had lunch mentioned Wanki, and had her daughter walk me to the little shack behind the restaurant where he lived. I found him sitting in his wheelchair outside his shack. Both his legs had been amputated half way down the thigh, and his chair looked home-made. It had a bicycle chain running between two sprockets, with handles instead of pedals, so he could power the wheels with his hands. I had found him on his eighty-fourth birthday, he told me. Although there was still life in his eyes and his fingers toyed absently with the frame of his chair, there was no strength left in his voice, and I had to crouch close to his wheelchair to hear him. He seemed to be giving a running commentary on the thoughts passing through his mind.

"I don't know where she gone. United States, somewhere around there. She gone long time. The doctor is what do this. Cut this one first. Then afterwards, cut this one."

Why did he cut them off? I asked. "This one was the sugar. This one never had no sugar, but still he cut it."

In the old times, did the pirates come to Little Corn? "I believe."

Like Henry Morgan? "Right by that mango tree over there. The swamp."

Did you ever go to Providence or San Andrés?

"No. If you got boat to load, go to Bluefields, Puerto Cabezas. The captain that I work with, him come and take lobster. Lobster! Used to catch lobster like sand. But now, no money in lobster. Hawksbill and loggerhead, all of them turkle used to come right there and lay eggs," and he pointed to the spot where an old woman was selling fizzy drinks from under a beach umbrella.

I tried running the names of the fishing banks by him – Quitasueño, Roncador, Serranilla – but he just groaned weakly, so we watched the tourists traipse across the sand for a while. In the neighbour's yard, a cock was crowing.

Were you a farmer? "Yeah. When we had plenty coconut we used to make the coconut oil by the drum. We send Managua to make soup."

Soap? Coconut soap? "Yeah. All kind of soup used to make Managua."

Did you learn Spanish and English at school?

"Yes. Spanish and English and Miskito. Three of them I speak. Them times, I don't know because I never born yet, but my grandfather was Miskito king."

This was an unexpected turn of events. What was your grandfather's name? I asked him.

"Andrew Henry Clarence," he said with a chuckle, as if at a dirty secret.

And Wanki is short for Juan Carlos?

"Wanki? That is the country where I come from. That is a big river. Rio Coco them call it, but the place them call it Wanki."

The River Wanks (or Wanki) was the old name for the River Coco. It started to sink in: I really had stumbled across the heir to the Miskito throne. One of my reasons for visiting Bluefields had been to follow up on a rumour that the heir was running a pool hall in the town. But the rumour was 40 years old, and I had found no trace of him.

"From ten year old I travelling. Before them kill me. Them wicked people. They want to kill everybody. From I was in Bluefields, 1979, one fella name Walder Hooker, lawman, he was going to send me to a place... England, because there is king too."

He sounded very pleased when I told him that I came from England. "Well, you know then."

But you didn't go? "No! People said if they carry me plane, they going to throw me out and kill me. So Walder Hooker tell me say, 'Best thing you go to little island.' That's how I come here. Not a soul knows that I is here now. Everybody think I dead. But I still living!"

So what happened to your mother and father? "I only one month old and my mother dead. And my father, them kill him good. Them study science business, so them kill you just so, without shooting you, without knifing you, without touching you."

Necromancy? "Yes. Them know about necromancy," he said with a chuckle. "When my grandfather dead, the president take him crown, the gold, half a million dollar, that too. Everything them take and sold."

I found myself making a dreamy hum of assent. My voice had slowed to a woozy trickle of words that threatened to come away from each other.

"But he was a king," Wanki said, as if to reassure himself that his memories weren't just part of a fantastic dream, and that once upon a time, the Miskitos really had ruled the coast. "That's why the England come and put the crown on him, because him win something." He chuckled, and his voice faded to a whisper. "All kind of history, it is. Well, I never born yet."

"When I come here, I was drinking rum. After a while, I see rum no good, so I give up the drinking and I baptised. I was studying from California Bible study. I promised that I would never touch that again, and God said, 'I will take care of you until I call you.'"

And your name is?

"Yeah." What's your full name Wanki? "I'll die here. I can't go home and I don't want to," and he chuckled again. He rolled up his trousers to reveal the stumps where his legs had once been.

"I never feel it, you know? Him inject it and him say, 'How you can't sleep?' I don't know. Just wide awake, didn't even feel it. Up to now, I don't got no pain out of this. Everything is excellent. Good."

It was time to go. I thanked the king of the Miskitos for his time, and he thanked me for keeping him company. Perhaps he hadn't heard me when I asked him his full name. Perhaps there were a few things he didn't want to tell me, or anyone else for that matter. Now I wonder, not why he didn't answer my question, but why he chose to tell me his secret at all. Perhaps I was the only person who had ever asked him about the history of the Miskito coast.

EPILOGUE

On my return from the Corn Islands, I spent the summer writing at my mum's house in Penzance. One day in August, the entire town showed up on the prom dressed as pirates. They were hoping to set the world record for 'most pirates ever assembled in a single place.' Strange, I thought, as I wandered through the crowds of buccaneers sporting eye-patches and three-cornered hats, a cardboard cutlass in one hand, a stick of candy floss in the other. Strange it is, that olde worlde criminals like Henry Morgan should be more popular than ever, yet their modern-day incarnations so completely overlooked. Who among this crowd of pirate lovers could even name a latter-day pirate? The trial of the Somali Abduwali Muse in February 2011 was the first case of piracy to come before an American court for 200 years, but it attracted considerably less attention than *Pirates of the Caribbean: The Curse of the Black Pearl*. Fiction is stranger than fact, but it is also more popular, and often considerably better paid. The latest instalment of the Johnny Depp franchise has grossed $654 million to date, a sum that dwarfs the $53 million that Somali pirates earned in 2011.[1]

Strange too, that an English town steeped in the small town politics of strivers vs. skivers, and still trying to sort worthy from unworthy poor should choose to dress up as pirates rather than Puritans. But perhaps I'm missing the point; perhaps it was all just play, and all the more appealing for being a bit silly. Given a choice between Puritan and pirate, who would you side with: the austere, moralising man in the frock coat, or the bawdy, fatalistic villain he has just condemned to the gibbet? The people of Penzance knew whose side they were on. Had I asked them what they thought of the real pirates of the Caribbean – the region's cocaine traffickers – I suspect that most of them would have shown themselves to be more Puritan than they'd care to admit. But perhaps not: per head of population, the people of the Southwest are the biggest consumers of illegal drugs in the UK, so perhaps they regard their drug smugglers as freedom fighters.

Turning history into a dressing-up box is all very well, but it can easily become a cover for indifference to the past. Perhaps it is precisely because the Atlantic World was created for Britain's benefit, that the British show so little interest in the modern Caribbean. It is too difficult for them; too bound up with the discomfort that they feel about the imperial mission their ancestors set for themselves.

The problem, it seems to me, is not post-colonial domination, but post-colonial neglect. After their former colonies won their independence, the British dropped them like hot potatoes. There is still a Commonwealth to remind them of the old club, but there seems to be little interest in the communities of the old empire, and those that were once on its margins, in places like Providence, San Andrés and the Miskito coast, have been entirely forgotten.

In a grizzly sort of way, Britain's post-colonial discomfort has been eased by what has become of the Caribbean in the last 30 years. The failure of the state to tackle poverty and inequality, the end of farming and the drift to the cities, the normalisation of mass unemployment and economic migration – the region's governments are wrestling with no end of problems. Tourism and remittances from relatives living in western countries seem to be the only things keeping their economies afloat. Without viable alternatives, the young are drawn into the cocaine trade, which has defied all attempts to stamp it out, weathered all recessions, and continues to offer good money to the daring.

On a recent trip to Jamaica, David Cameron acknowledged that the UK had neglected its relationship with the region, and promised an extra £400 million in aid. Although he made a point of ducking questions about the campaign to have Britain pay reparations for the harm caused by the slave trade, films like *12 Years a Slave* and *Django Unchained* show that there is more, rather than less, interest in the legacy of slavery today.

The time I spent on Providence led me to think about what the UK might do to acknowledge its legacy. In the internet age, an island as small as Providence should be prosperous. If the island were better known, it would be well placed to realise its potential as a destination for ecotourists, hikers and divers. But its young people need educational opportunities, scholarships and apprenticeships. Britain has the resources and opportunities they need.

Aside from helping Providence to navigate a course through the challenges of the twenty-first century, the UK would do well to re-assess its relations with the wider Caribbean. Recovery and recuperation from its imperial venture is ongoing, and will take a lot longer than most people think. All of the bigger islands are bedevilled by corruption, drugs and murder. Is the murder rate the result of poverty, the drugs trade, or is it part of the legacy of slavery? In fact, most of the murders committed in the Caribbean have little to do with drugs per se; nor is poverty what causes Caribbean men to pull triggers. Rather, their poverty only further undermines the fragile self-esteem of honour-bound men. I would venture that the murderousness that marks the Caribbean today has its roots in the honour codes of Elizabethan England, which were carried across the Atlantic by its adventurers, pirates and plantation owners to the West Indies. For as long as the church held sway, the piratical element was held at bay. But God, and the respect for authority He tends to bring with him, are conspicuous by their absence in the modern Caribbean.

The legacy of the English Puritans, gentlemen officers, common soldiers and pirates who came ashore almost 400 years ago goes far beyond the role they played in establishing the slave trade. That their legacy is so little discussed is a shame because the Puritans and pirates that set the stage for the drama on Providence also had a huge impact on the British. With their cardboard cutlasses, their penchant for naming and shaming, their witch-hunts and their booming trade in contraband, you could be forgiven for thinking the British never quite made it out of the 1630s.

ACKNOWLEDGEMENTS

In researching the early history of Providence, I referred to few primary sources, so I am grateful to Prof Karen Kupperman, who must have spent months deciphering the handwriting of William Jessop and the other contributors to the Providence Island Company's journal. My interest in Providence was first sparked by her *Providence Island 1630-1641: The Other Puritan Colony*, which covers the subject in depth.

I'd like to thank Jeremy Gibson of the Banbury Historical Society for the kindness and generosity he showed me on my visits to the birthplace of Henry Halhead, and Martin Fiennes at Broughton Castle for showing me around the ancestral home of Lord Saye and Sele. Dr Mark Jamieson illuminated me on the ways of the Miskitos.

I am grateful to Monica Orjuela at Patrimonio Natural, Patricia Enciso Dharmajyoti and Amparo Potón for helping me to find accommodation on Providence, and for introducing me to the islanders with the longest memories. For sharing their thoughts on the modern island, my thanks to Marcia Dittmann, Annie Chapman, Juan Ramírez Dawkins, Gabriella Domínguez, Ana Isabel Márquez Pérez and Harold Bush. Sam Cuming is a fellow student of the island's history, and he was often the only person I could talk to about the Puritan colony. Sam became my walking companion, as well as my drinking buddy and I owe him a big thank you.

This book would have been a much drier read without the insights into daily life I was given by the many islanders who agreed to be interviewed. Thanks are due to Amparo Taylor, Gloria Rapón, Josefina Huffington, Rodrigo Howard, Antonio Bryan, Wilberson Archbold, James Henry, Erminda Henry, Laura Newball, Narcissa Howard, Ingrid Robinson, Richard Hawkins, Victor Newball Abrahams, Henry Howard, Carol Robinson, Ed Forbes, Cecilia Davis Carr, Carmelina Newball and Hazel Robinson. I'd like to extend special thanks to Luz Marina Livingston, and the late Antonio Archbold, for the interest they showed in my project, and the good vibes. Thanks are also due to those who had little to say about the island's history, but were a pleasure to spend time with all the same: Marv Bryan, 'Pink Floyd,' Antonio 'Basha' Fernández, and yes, even you Ed ...

Providence is not the only English-speaking community in the western Caribbean to have become a bit player in a Spanish-speaking drama, so when it came to leave, it felt only natural to extend my trip to the Caribbean coast of Central America. The towns that I visited – Portobello, Colón, Bocas del Toro, Cahuita, Puerto Limón, San Juan del Norte (and the ruins of Greytown), Bluefields, and the Corn Islands – share much of their history with Providence, and have faced similar problems in modern times. My acknowledgement of the help and support I was offered on the coast is tinged with regret that there isn't more room in this book for the stories I heard there. Thanks, all the same, to Rolando Sankey at the Museum of Afro-Caribbean Life, and Walter 'the Calypsonian' Ferguson in Cahuita; Abraham Goldgewicht and Winfred Cross in Puerto Limón; Edgar 'Rasta' Coulson in Greytown; and Carmen Cash Joseph, Shirlainie Howard and Deborah Robb Taylor in Bluefields. Thanks too to Onix Wilson at the Culture House on Big Corn, and Wanki Clarence on Little Corn.

This book has taken longer to write than I thought it would, and would not have been possible without friends who were kind enough to lend me their holiday homes. Thank you Liam Craig Best, Prof Jonathan Rosenhead and Poppy Golding. Special thanks are due to my ever-supportive mum, Deirdre Feiling, for letting me stay in Penzance for as long as I did. In the last stage of the writing process, I received a fellowship from the Hawthornden International Retreat for Writers, and a John Heygate award for travel writing from the Authors' Foundation of the Society of Authors; my thanks to the trustees of both organisations for their generosity.

I was able to count on Michael Ryan, Sam Low, Pablo Conde and Richard Garner for valuable feedback on early drafts – my thanks to them. Thanks too to Richard McColl at Colombia Calling, and Giles Edwards and Bethany Sagar-Fenton at BBC Radio Four, for taking an interest in the story I had to tell. Last but not least, thanks to my agent, Broo Doherty at the DHH Literary Agency, for her support and encouragement, and Andrew Lockett at Explore Books, a patient publisher and sagacious editor who saw the story's potential when others did not.

345

REFERENCES

CHAPTER 1 – BUILDING NEW WESTMINSTER

1. William Sorsby, *Old Providence Island: Puritans, Pirates and Spaniards 1630-1670*, chapter 1, p. 7. Note that Sorsby's book is an unpublished, undated manuscript, with page numbers that revert to one at the beginning of each chapter, hence the unorthodox page reference.
2. Karen Ordahl Kupperman, *Providence Island 1630-1641: The Other Puritan Colony*, Cambridge, Cambridge University Press, 1993, p. 26.
3. Robert Edward Lee Strider, *Robert Greville, Lord Brooke*, Cambridge, MA, Harvard University Press, 1958, p. 18.
4. William Harrison, cited in Arthur Finlay Scott, *Every One a Witness: The Stuart Age*, New York, Apollo Editions, 1975, p. 35. Taprobane was most likely either Sri Lanka or Sumatra. According to Sir John Mandeville's *Travels*, the island's inhabitants had a single giant foot, which they used to protect themselves from the sun.
5. Conrad Russell, *Parliament and the King's Finances*, in Conrad Russell, (ed.), *The Origins of the English Civil War*, London, MacMillan, 1973, p. 95.
6. Cyril Hamshere, *The British in the Caribbean*, Cambridge, MA, Harvard University Press, 1972, p. 27. According to Wikipedia, the brothers 'John and Samuel Jeaffreson' [sic] also invested in St Kitts; the latter was 'the 3xgreat-grandfather of Thomas Jefferson, third President of the United States'.
7. Nicholas J. Allen, 'Business and Treason: The Broughton Plotters', *Cake and Cockhorse*, Banbury Historical Society, vol. 16, no. 5, 2005, p. 166.
8. Kupperman, *Providence Island 1630-1641*, p. 18.
9. Ibid., p. 209.
10. Descriptions of Charles are from sources cited in Scott, *Every One a Witness*, pp.1, 7.
11. William Hunt, *The Puritan Moment: the Coming of Revolution in an English County*, Cambridge, MA, Harvard University Press, 1983, p. 231.
12. See Pamela Neville-Sington and David Sington, *Paradise Dreamed: How Utopian Thinkers have Changed the Modern World*, London, Bloomsbury, 1993, p. 90. See too, Karl Offen, 'Puritan Bioprospecting in Central

America and the West Indies', *Itinerario*, vol. XXXV, no. 1, 2011, p. 36.

13. Kupperman, *Providence Island 1630-1641*, p. 61.
14. Ibid., p. 26.
15. S. L. Caiger, *British Honduras Past and Present*, London, Allen and Unwin, 1951, p. 27. Cited in Sorsby, *Old Providence Island*, chapter 2, p. 6.
16. In the 1680s, Sir Hans Sloane described how Bahaman fishermen would catch up to 100 monk seals a night. By 1880, they were practically extinct, although a few survive to this day in the Triangle Reefs in the Bay of Campeche, Mexico. Despite being prey for hungry men for the past 500 years, they remain quite tame. See Sir Hans Sloane, *A Voyage to the Islands Madera, Barbados, Nieves, S. Christophers and Jamaica*, London, 1707.
17. Kupperman, *Providence Island, 1630-1641*, p. 32.
18. Cited in Scott, *Every One a Witness*, p. 245.
19. Kupperman, *Providence Island, 1630-1641*, p. 86.

CHAPTER 2 – EDUCATING ESSEX

1. The description is of the Verney household in Claydon, Buckinghamshire. Taken from *Memoirs of the Verney Family During the Seventeenth Century*, and cited in Arthur Finlay Scott, *Every One a Witness: The Stuart Age*, New York, Apollo Editions, 1975, p. 52.
2. William Hunt, *The Puritan Moment: the Coming of Revolution in an English County*, Cambridge, MA, Harvard University Press, 1983, p. 163.
3. Ibid., p. 207.
4. Oliver Cromwell is said to have died of English malaria, which he contracted during his early life in East Anglia. See Karen Kupperman, 'The Puzzle of the American Climate in the Early Colonial Period', *The American Historical Review*, vol. 87, no. 5, 1982, pp. 1262–89.
5. Hunt, *The Puritan Moment*, p. 39.
6. He said this in 1636. Ibid., p. 246.
7. The quote is from 1622. Ibid., p. 160.
8. Ibid. p. 39.
9. Ibid., p. 169.
10. Robin Clifton, 'Fear of Popery', in Conrad Russell (ed.), *The Origins of the English Civil War*, London, MacMillan 1973, p. 147.
11. Hunt, *The Puritan Moment*, p. 165.
12. Ibid., p. 225.
13. Cited in Scott, *Every One a Witness*, p. 199.
14. Hunt, *The Puritan Moment*, p. 124.
15. Ibid., p. 81.
16. From the Harleian Miscellany, cited in Scott, *Every One a Witness*, p. 177.

17. This remark was made in 1607. Hunt, *The Puritan Moment*, p. 149.

18. 'Dark parishes' is a term used in Keith Wrightson and David Levine, *Poverty and Piety in an English Village: Terling 1525-1700*, 1979.

19. Hunt, *The Puritan Moment*, p. 152.

20. Ibid. p. 130.

21. Ibid. p. 95.

22. Cited in Scott, *Every One a Witness*, p. 229.

23. Alison Games, *Migration and the Origins of the English Atlantic World*, Cambridge, MA, Harvard University Press, 1999, p. 48.

24. Ibid., pp. 82–3.

25. Karen Ordahl Kupperman, *Providence Island 1630-1641: The Other Puritan Colony*, Cambridge, Cambridge University Press, 1993, p. 162. Also Games, *Migration and the Origins of the English Atlantic World*, pp. 90, 104.

26. Kupperman, *Providence Island 1630-1641*, p. 179.

27. Games, *Migration and the Origins of the English Atlantic World*, p. 215.

28. This is the victualing typical of an eighteenth-century ship. The details are taken from N.A.M. Rodger, *The Wooden World*, cited in Diana Souhami, *Selkirk's Island*, London, Weidenfeld & Nicolson, 2001, p. 48. I have also used the Puritan William Bradford's description of conditions aboard the *Seaflower's* sister ship, the *Mayflower*, cited in Nathaniel Philbrick, *Mayflower: a Story of Courage, Community and War*, London, Harper Collins, 2006, p. 23.

CHAPTER 3 – THE SEAFLOWER

1. Between the foundation of Virginia in 1607 and 1700; Carville Earle, 'Pioneers of Providence: The Anglo-American Experience 1492-1792', *Annals of the Association of American Geographers*, vol. 8, no. 3, pp. 478–99.

2. Figures are for England and Wales in 1600. Emmanuel LeRoy Ladurie, 'Motionless History', *Social Science History*, vol. 1, no. 2, 1977, pp. 115–36.

3. William Dalrymple, 'The East India Company: The Original Corporate Raiders', *Guardian*, 4 March 2015.

4. Nathaniel Philbrick, *Mayflower: A Story of Courage, Community and War*, London, Harper Collins, 2006, p. 27.

5. Cited in Arthur Finlay Scott, *Every One a Witness: the Stuart Age*, New York, Apollo Editions, 1975, p. 34. In 1635, London had a population of somewhere between 300,000 and 350,000; see Alison Games, *Migration and the Origins of the English Atlantic World*, Cambridge, MA, Harvard University Press, 1999, p. 14.

6. Cited in Scott, *Every One a Witness*, p. 15.
7. Cited in Ibid., p. 201.
8. Good health was believed to be dependent on keeping a balance between the body's four 'humours': blood, yellow bile, black bile, and phlegm.
9. Karen Ordahl Kupperman, 'The Puzzle of the American Climate in the Early Colonial Period', *American Historical Review*, vol. 87, 1982, p. 1266. The Thomas Morton quote is from Wikipedia/Thomas Morton.
10. Carville Earle, 'Pioneers of Providence: The Anglo-American Experience 1492–1792', *Annals of the Association of American Geographers*, vol. 8, no. 3, p. 479.
11. William Sorsby, *Old Providence Island: Puritans, Pirates and Spaniards 1630-1670*, chapter 2, p. 14.
12. Games, *Migration and the Origins of the English Atlantic World*, p. 96.
13. Kupperman, 'The Puzzle of the American Climate in the Early Colonial Period', pp. 1262–89.
14. Nothing came of the bushes or the silk. Sorsby, *Old Providence Island*, chapter 2, p. 24.
15. Wikipedia/ History of syphilis.
16. Ladurie, 'Motionless History', pp. 115–36.
17. The quote is from John Robinson's 'Observations', cited in Scott, *Every One a Witness*, p. 110.
18. Karen Ordahl Kupperman, *Providence Island 1630-1641: The Other Puritan Colony*, Cambridge, Cambridge University Press, 1993, p. 28.
19. Ibid., p. 194.
20. Ibid., p. 33.
21. Games, *Migration and the Origins of the English Atlantic World*, p. 96.
22. Kupperman, *Providence Island 1630-1641*, p. 233.
23. Karl Offen, 'Puritan Bioprospecting in Central America and the West Indies', *Itinerario*, vol. XXXV, no. 1, 2011, p. 25.
24. Kupperman, *Providence Island 1630-1641*, p. 36.
25. Sorsby, *Old Providence Island*, chapter 2, p. 17. Also Kupperman, *Providence Island 1630-1641*, pp. 36–7.
26. Kupperman, *Providence Island 1630-1641*, p. 93.
27. Alison Games, '"The Sanctuarye of our Rebell Negroes": The Atlantic Context of Local Resistance on Providence Island, 1630–41', *Slavery & Abolition: A Journal of Slave and Post-Slave Studies*, vol. 19, no. 3, 1998, pp. 1–21.
28. Kupperman, *Providence Island 1630-1641*, pp. 157–8.
29. According to John Woodall, who described its symptoms in 1617, and went on to become Surgeon-General of the East India Company. See Scott, *Every One a Witness*, p. 139.

30. Diana Souhami, *Selkirk's Island*, London, Weidenfeld & Nicolson, 2001, p. 62. The attribution of scurvy to a deficiency of vitamin C wouldn't be made for well over 100 years. Although a Scottish naval surgeon, James Lind, proved that scurvy could be treated with citrus fruit in experiments he described in his 1753 book *A Treatise of the Scurvy*, his advice would not be implemented by the Royal Navy for several decades.
31. Kupperman, *Providence Island 1630-1641*, pp. 158, 211.
32. Games, *Migration and the Origins of the English Atlantic World*, p. 92.
33. Kupperman, *Providence Island 1630-1641*, p. 86.

CHAPTER 4 – CAKE, ALE AND PAINFUL PREACHING: A BANBURY TALE

1. William Sorsby, *Old Providence Island: Puritans, Pirates and Spaniards 1630-1670*, chapter 2, p. 21.
2. Karen Ordahl Kupperman, *Providence Island 1630-1641: The Other Puritan Colony*, Cambridge, Cambridge University Press, 1993, p. 10.
3. Arthur Finlay Scott, *Every One a Witness: the Stuart Age*, New York, Apollo Editions, 1975, p. 160.
4. Earl of Clarendon, *History of the Rebellion: A New Selection*, Oxford, Oxford University Press, 2009, p. 57.
5. Scott, *Every One a Witness*, p. 270.
6. 'The Local Influence and Family Connections of the First Viscount Saye and Sele', *Cake and Cockhorse*, Banbury, Banbury Historical Society, 1977.
7. Kupperman, *Providence Island 1630-1641*, p. 148.
8. Alison Games, *Migration and the Origins of the English Atlantic World*, Cambridge, MA, Harvard University Press, 1999, pp. 19, 46. The order was initially enforced only for those bound for New England, but it would likely have been applied to anyone sailing to Providence as well.
9. All references to Rishworth are from Guy Dixon, 'Samuel Rishworth of Providence Island: Councillor, and Abolitionist', *Journal of the Society of Genealogists*, vol. 30, no. 11., 2012.
10. Kupperman, *Providence Island, 1630-1641*, p. 234.
11. Complaints were made against Captain Punt, and the following March, the Court of the Company cross-examined the crew of the *Charity*. Punt was eventually dismissed, but without fine or punishment. Sorsby, *Old Providence Island*, chapter 2, p. 15.
12. From Fox's *North-West Fox, or Fox from the North West Passage*, 1635; cited in Scott, *Every One a Witness* p. 283.

CHAPTER 5 – THE FIRST VOYAGE TO THE MISKITO COAST

1. Karen Ordahl Kupperman, *Providence Island 1630-1641: The Other Puritan Colony*, Cambridge, Cambridge University Press, 1993, p. 40.
2. Elfrith's early career is described in Stanley Pargellis and Ruth Lapham Butler, 'Daniell Ellffryth's Guide to the Caribbean 1631', *The William and Mary Quarterly*, Third Series, vol. 1, no. 3, 1944, pp. 273–316. I have rendered Elfrith's words into contemporary English spelling.
3. *Oxford Dictionary of National Biography*, entry for Daniel Elfrith.
4. Kupperman, *Providence Island 1630-1641*, p. 94.
5. Alison Games, '"The Sanctuarye of our Rebell Negroes": The Atlantic Context of Local Resistance on Providence Island, 1630–41', *Slavery & Abolition: A Journal of Slave and Post-Slave Studies*, vol. 19, no. 3, 1998, pp. 1–21.
6. Karl Offen, 'Puritan Bioprospecting in Central America and the West Indies', *Itinerario*, vol. XXXV, no. 1, 2011, p. 35.
7. My description of Miskito life is taken from Robert A. Naylor, *Penny Ante Imperialism: The Mosquito Shore and the Bay of Honduras 1600-1914*, Plainsboro, NJ, Associated University Presses, 1989, pp. 24–5.
8. Offen, 'Puritan Bioprospecting in Central America and the West Indies', p. 29.
9. Ibid., p. 33.
10. Kupperman, *Providence Island 1630-1641*, p. 104.
11. Ibid., p. 280.
12. See vol. I of John Masefield, (ed.) *Dampier's Voyages*. Cited in Diana Souhami, *Selkirk's Island*, London, Weidenfeld & Nicolson, 2001, p. 42.
13. Games, 'The Sanctuarye of our Rebell Negroes', pp. 1–21.
14. William Sorsby, *Old Providence Island: Puritans, Pirates and Spaniards 1630-1670*, chapter 2, p. 28.
15. Michael Olien, 'The Miskito Kings and the Line of Succession', *Journal of Anthropological Research*, vol. 39, no. 201, 1983.

CHAPTER 6 – THE PRIDE OF THE RIGHTEOUS

1. These details of a service are from a description of services in Virginia, and are taken from Babette M. Levy, 'Early Puritanism in the Southern and Island Colonies', in *Proceedings of the American Antiquarian Society*, vol. 70, Part 1, 1960, pp. 97–8.
2. Karen Ordahl Kupperman, *Providence Island 1630-1641: The Other Puritan Colony*, Cambridge, Cambridge University Press, 1993, p. 192.
3. Ibid., p. 235.
4. Alison Games, *Migration and the Origins of the English Atlantic World*, Cambridge, MA, Harvard University Press, 1999, p. 154. Also Kupperman, *Providence Island 1630-1641*, pp. 241–2.

5. William Sorsby, *Old Providence Island: Puritans, Pirates and Spaniards 1630-1670*, chapter 2, p. 19.
6. William Hunt, *The Puritan Moment: the Coming of Revolution in an English County*, Cambridge, MA, Harvard University Press, 1983, p. 257.
7. Nicholas Tyacke, 'Puritanism, Arminianism and Counter-Revolution', in *The Origins of the English Civil War*, Conrad Russell (ed.) London, Macmillan 1973, p. 136.
8. Hunt, *The Puritan Moment*, p. 225.
9. References to Henry Roote are from Kupperman, *Providence Island 1630-1641*, pp. 237, 131.
10. Karl Offen, 'Puritan Bioprospecting in Central America and the West Indies', *Itinerario*, vol. XXXV, no. 1, 2011, p. 34. Also Kupperman, *Providence Island 1630-1641*, p. 90.
11. Sorsby, *Old Providence Island*, p. 22.
12. Karen Ordahl Kupperman, 'Definitions of Liberty on the Eve of Civil War: Lord Saye and Sele, Lord Brooke, and the American Puritan Colonies', *The Historical Journal*, vol. 32, no. 1, 1989, p. 29.
13. Sorsby, *Old Providence Island*, p. 26.
14. Ibid., pp. 25–6.
15. Games, *Migration and the Origins of the English Atlantic World*, p. 77.
16. In the Chesapeake, there was a slow transition from indentured servitude to slavery spanning some six decades. On Barbados, the planters switched with alacrity to slavery as they transferred their agricultural production to sugar in the 1640s. Providence provides a different model. The colony on Providence distinguished itself from all other contemporary English Atlantic colonies in its rapid commitment to slavery, and in its simultaneous use of numbers of enslaved American Indians and English indentured servants. Alison Games, '"The Sanctuarye of our Rebell Negroes": The Atlantic Context of Local Resistance on Providence Island, 1630–41', *Slavery & Abolition: A Journal of Slave and Post-Slave Studies*, vol. 19, no. 3, 1998,.

CHAPTER 7 – THE AFRICANS, 'DURING THEIR STRANGENESS FROM CHRISTIANITY'

1. Francisco Biafara's account is from David Wheat, 'A Spanish Caribbean Captivity Narrative: African Sailors and Puritan Slavers, 1635', in *Afro-Latino Voices: Narratives from the Early Modern Ibero-Atlantic World, 1550-1812*, eds. Kathryn Joy McKnight and Leo J. Garofalo, Indianapolis, IN, Hackett, 2009.
2. Isseke is in Ihiala LGA, Anambra State, in the Niger delta. It is the closest possible origin of Olaudah based on the linguistic and ethnographic

evidence he left in his memoir. See http://www.nairaland.com/870908/igbo-1700s/4.

3. *A Voyage to the River Sierra-Leone on the Coast of Africa*, by John Matthews, was printed for B. White and Son in 1788. Cited in Marcus Rediker, *The Slave Ship: A Human History*, London, Penguin Books, 2008, p. 266.

4. J. H. Elliott, *Empires of the Atlantic World: Britain and Spain in America 1492-1830*, New Haven, CT, Yale University Press, 2006, p. 100.

5. Karen Ordahl Kupperman, *Providence Island 1630-1641: The Other Puritan Colony*, Cambridge, Cambridge University Press, 1993, p. 171.

6. Alison Games, '"The Sanctuarye of our Rebell Negroes": The Atlantic Context of Local Resistance on Providence Island, 1630–41', *Slavery & Abolition: A Journal of Slave and Post-Slave Studies*, vol. 19, no. 3, 1998, pp. 1–21.

7. P. W. Thomas, 'Court and Country under Charles I', in Conrad Russell, (ed.), *The Origins of the English Civil War*, London, MacMillan 1973, p. 180.

8. Games, 'The Sanctuarye of our Rebell Negroes', pp. 1-21.

CHAPTER 8 – 'A NEST OF THIEVES AND PIRATES'

1. This account of the Spanish attack is taken from A.P. Newton, *The Colonising Activities of the English Puritans: The Last Phase of the Elizabethan Struggle with Spain*, New Haven, CT, Yale University Press, 1914, pp. 196–7; and Karen Ordahl Kupperman, *Providence Island 1630-1641: The Other Puritan Colony*, Cambridge, Cambridge University Press, 1993, p. 198. Their accounts differ; Newton says that the fleet was commanded by the governor of Cartagena, Nicolas de Judice. Also see the Wikipedia entry for the governor of Cartagena, Francisco de Murga.

2. William Sorsby, *Old Providence Island: Puritans, Pirates and Spaniards 1630-1670*, chapter 2, pp. 37, 39.

3. Kupperman, *Providence Island 1630-1641*, 1993, p. 199.

4. Sorsby, *Old Providence Island*, chapter 3, p. 1.

5. Karen Kupperman, 'Errand to the Indies: Puritan Colonization from Providence Island through the Western Design', *The William and Mary Quarterly*, Third Series, vol. 45, no. 1, 1988, pp. 70–99.

6. Kupperman, *Providence Island, 1630-1641*, p. 198.

7. W. Frank Craven, 'The Earl of Warwick: A Speculator in Piracy', *The Hispanic American Historical Review*, vol. 10, no. 4, 1930, p. 459.

8. Ibid., p. 460.

9. Sorsby, *Old Providence Island*, chapter 3, pp. 4–6.

10. Kupperman, *Providence Island, 1630-1641*, p. 105.

11. Dudley Pope, *Harry Morgan's Way: The Biography of Sir Henry Morgan, 1635–84*, London, Martin Secker & Warburg, 1977, p. 27. See also

Lucía Méndez González, *La Visión de Inglaterra sobre América a través de Fray Thomas Gage*, Instituto de Investigaciones Históricas, Universidad Michoacana de San Nicolás de Hidalgo (UMSNH), and the Wikipedia biography of Thomas Gage.

12. W. Frank Craven, 'The Earl of Warwick', p. 469.

13. Sorsby, *Old Providence Island*, chapter 3, p. 3.

14. Alison Games, '"The Sanctuarye of our Rebell Negroes": The Atlantic Context of Local Resistance on Providence Island, 1630–41', *Slavery & Abolition: A Journal of Slave and Post-Slave Studies*, vol. 19, no. 3, 1998, pp. 1–21.

15. British Library Add. MS 6385B, p. 106. This is the decipherment of Add. MS 10615, which is a collection of letters from William Jessop to the islanders. Kupperman, *Providence Island 1630-1641*, p. 76.

16. Kupperman, *Providence Island 1630-1641*, p. 76.

17. See the entry for Daniel Elfrith in the Oxford Dictionary of National Biography. Neither his authority nor his land was restored to Elfrith until the company intervened to defend him and Bell from their enemies in March 1637. Sorsby, *Old Providence Island*, chapter 3, p. 14.

18. This is from Samuel Axe's letter to the company of March 1639. See Kupperman, *Providence Island 1630-1641*, p. 109.

19. William Hunt, *The Puritan Moment: the Coming of Revolution in an English County*, Cambridge, MA, Harvard University Press, 1983, p. 270.

20. Sorsby, *Old Providence Island*, chapter 3, p. 21.

21. According to Gregory King's Tables of 1688, there were 160 Temporal Lords in England, who each made an average of £3,200 a year. King's tables were published in Gregory King, *Two Tracts*, G. E. Barnett, (ed.), Baltimore, MD, Johns Hopkins Press, 1936. Cited in Arthur Finlay Scott, *Every One a Witness: the Stuart Age*, New York, Apollo Editions, 1975, p. 160.

CHAPTER 9 – 'RAW POTATOES AND TURTLE MEAT'

1. Karen Ordahl Kupperman, *Providence Island 1630-1641: The Other Puritan Colony*, Cambridge, Cambridge University Press, 1993, p. 204.

2. Karen Ordahl Kupperman, 'A Puritan Colony in the Tropics', in Ralph Bennett, *Settlements in the Americas: Cross-Cultural Perspectives*, Newark, DE, University of Delaware Press, 1993, p. 242. Unless indicated otherwise, all the following quotes from Nathaniel Butler's diary are taken from Sam Cuming, *A Short History of Providence and San Andres 1629-1901*, Bogotá, Banco de la República, 2015.

3. Kupperman, *Providence Island 1630-1641*, p. 259.

4. Alison Games, '"The Sanctuarye of our Rebell Negroes": The Atlantic

Context of Local Resistance on Providence Island, 1630–41', *Slavery & Abolition: A Journal of Slave and Post-Slave Studies*, vol. 19, no. 3, 1998, pp. 1-21.

5. William Sorsby, *Old Providence Island: Puritans, Pirates and Spaniards 1630-1670*, chapter 3, p. 17.
6. Games, 'The Sanctuarye of our Rebell Negroes', pp. 1-21.
7. See Guy Dixon, 'Samuel Rishworth of Providence Island: Councillor, and Abolitionist', *Journal of the Society of Genealogists*, vol. 30, no. 11., 2012.
8. Games, 'The Sanctuarye of our Rebell Negroes', pp. 1-21.
9. Loren C. Turnage, *Island Heritage: a Baptist View of the History of San Andres and Providencia*, Historical Commission of the Colombia Baptist Mission, 1977, p. 12.
10. Blair Worden, 'Providence and Politics in Cromwellian England', *Past and Present*, no. 109, 1985, p. 73.
11. Kupperman, *Providence Island 1630-1641*, p. 278.
12. James J. Parsons, *San Andrés and Providencia*, Oakland, CA, University of California, 1956, pp. 33–4.
13. Jeremy Gibson and David Fiennes, 'Henry Halhead and Providence Island', *Cake and Cockhorse*, Banbury Historical Society, 1978.
14. Sorsby, *Old Providence Island*, chapter 2, p. 26.
15. Gibson and Fiennes, 'Henry Halhead and Providence Island'.
16. According to William Jackson, who visited the islands during his cruise around the Caribbean sometime after 1641. Karl Offen, 'Puritan Bioprospecting in Central America and the West Indies', *Itinerario*, vol. XXXV, no. 1, 2011, fn p. 69.

Chapter 10 – The Last Days of Their Lordships' Isle

1. William Sorsby, *Old Providence Island: Puritans, Pirates and Spaniards 1630-1670*, chapter 3, p. 38.
2. Ibid., p. 26.
3. Ibid., p. 31.
4. Unless stated otherwise, my description of the attack of 1640 is taken from this letter, dated 17 June 1640, and cited in Alison Games, '"The Sanctuarye of our Rebell Negroes": The Atlantic Context of Local Resistance on Providence Island, 1630–41', *Slavery & Abolition: A Journal of Slave and Post-Slave Studies*, vol. 19, no. 3, 1998, pp. 1–21.
5. Sorsby, *Old Providence Island*, chapter 3, p. 31. Also Karen Ordahl Kupperman, *Providence Island 1630-1641: The Other Puritan Colony*, Cambridge, Cambridge University Press, 1993, p. 289.
6. Sorsby, *Old Providence Island*, chapter 3, p. 33.
7. Kupperman, *Providence Island 1630-1641*, p. 291.

8. Ibid., p. 294.

9. See http://doverhistorian.com/2013/12/03/hope-sherrard-of-sandwich. Also A.P. Newton, *The Colonising Activities of the English Puritans*, New Haven, CT, Yale University Press, 1914, p. 306.

10. Tristram Hunt, *The English Civil War at First Hand*, London, Penguin, 2011, p. 25.

11. Ibid., p. 43.

12. The MP was Sir Thomas Peyton. Hunt, *The English Civil War at First Hand*, p. 45.

13. Karen Ordahl Kupperman, 'Definitions of Liberty on the Eve of Civil War: Lord Saye and Sele, Lord Brooke, and the American Puritan Colonies', *The Historical Journal*, vol. 32, no. 1, 1989, p. 31.

14. Hunt, *The English Civil War at First Hand*, p. 46.

15. Ibid., p. 50.

16. Kupperman, *Providence Island 1630-1641*, p. 175.

17. Sorsby, *Old Providence Island*, chapter 3, p. 29.

18. Ibid., pp. 40–1. Also Karen Kupperman, 'Errand to the Indies: Puritan Colonization from Providence Island through the Western Design', *The William and Mary Quarterly*, Third Series, vol. 45, no. 1, 1988, pp. 70–99.

19. Karen Ordahl Kupperman, 'A Puritan Colony in the Tropics', Ralph Bennett, (ed.), *Settlements in the Americas: Cross-Cultural Perspectives*, Newark, DE, University of Delaware Press, 1993, p. 250.

20. Kupperman, *Providence Island 1630-1641*, p. 265.

21. Ibid., p. 323.

22. My account of the Spanish attack is taken from Sorsby, *Old Providence Island*, chapter 4, pp. 4–14 and Kupperman, *Providence Island 1630-1641*, pp. 336–9. An account of what happened after the Spanish retook the island can be found in Donald Rowland, 'Spanish Occupation of the Island of Old Providence 1641-1670', *Hispanic American Historical Review*, vol. 15, 1935, p. 298.

23. Kupperman, *Providence Island 1630-1641*, pp. 340–3.

CHAPTER 11 – 'LITTLE MORE THAN A SUMMIT OF A HILL'

1. Tristram Hunt, *The English Civil War at First Hand*, London, Penguin, 2011, p. 83.

2. Ibid., p. 85.

3. Taken from *Memoirs of Colonel Hutchinson* (1639-41), cited in Arthur Finlay Scott, *Every One a Witness: The Stuart Age*, New York, Apollo Editions, 1975, p. 272.

4. Broughton Castle official brochure.

5. Hunt, *The English Civil War at First Hand*, p. 139.

6. Christopher Hill, *God's Englishman: Oliver Cromwell and the English Revolution*, London, Penguin, 1972, pp. 64, 74.

7. Hunt, *The English Civil War at First Hand*, p. 151.

8. Blair Worden, 'Providence and Politics in Cromwellian England', *Past and Present*, no. 109, 1985, pp. 55–99.

9. The words are those of the Puritan soldier and Leveller, Edward Sexby; cited in Hunt, *The English Civil War at First Hand*, p. 171.

10. Hill, *God's Englishman*, p. 98.

11. Scott, *Every One a Witness*, p. 252.

12. William Sorsby, *Old Providence Island: Puritans, Pirates and Spaniards 1630-1670*, chapter 5, p. 3

13. Ibid., chapter 5, p. 1.

14. Ibid., chapter 6, p. 1.

15. Donald Rowlandson, 'Spanish Occupation of Old Providence, or Santa Catalina 1641-70', *Hispanic American Historical Review*, vol. 15, no. 3, 1935, p. 303.

16. Sorsby, *Old Providence Island*, chapter 5, p. 5.

17. The first hand descriptions of William Jackson's voyage that follow are taken from *A Brief Journal, or a succinct and true relation of the most remarkable passages observed in that voyage undertaken by Captain William Jackson to the Western Indies or continent of America*, 1642, Sloane MSS 793 or 894, pp. 2–30.

18. Karen Ordahl Kupperman, *Providence Island 1630-1641: The Other Puritan Colony*, Cambridge, Cambridge University Press, 1993, pp. 345–6. *Certain Inducements to Well Minded People* was likely written by one of the Providence Island Company's former shareholders, but there is no way of knowing, since all that remains of the scheme is a single, ragged pamphlet, and its title page is missing.

CHAPTER 12 – THE WESTERN DESIGN

1. Tristram Hunt, *The English Civil War at First Hand*, London, Penguin, 2011, p. 228.

2. Christopher Hill, *God's Englishman: Oliver Cromwell and the English Revolution*, London, Penguin, 1972, p. 126.

3. Karen Ordahl Kupperman, *Providence Island 1630-1641: The Other Puritan Colony*, Cambridge, Cambridge University Press, 1993, p. 141.

4. Alison Games, *Migration and the Origins of the English Atlantic World*, Cambridge, MA, Harvard University Press, 1999, p. 135.

5. Hill, *God's Englishman*, p. 74.

6. Clarence Henry Haring, *The Buccaneers in the West Indies in the Seventeenth Century*, London, 1910, p. 89. Also Kupperman, *Providence Island 1630-*

1641, p. 351.

7. Kupperman, 'Errand to the Indies:', pp. 70–99.

8. Games, *Migration and the Origins of the English Atlantic World*, p. 153; and Dudley Pope, *Harry Morgan's Way: The Biography of Sir Henry Morgan, 1635–84*, London, Martin Secker & Warburg, 1977, p. 15.

9. Pope, *Harry Morgan's Way*, p. 159.

10. Ibid., pp. 66–7.

11. Ibid., p. 158.

12. Ibid., pp. 67–8.

13. Kupperman, *Providence Island 1630-1641*, p. 353.

14. Kupperman, 'Errand to the Indies', pp. 70–99.

15. To put things in perspective, Providence covers 24 square miles, and Bermuda just 20 square miles, while Barbados has an area of 166 square miles, which makes it a little bigger than the Isle of Wight, which covers 146 square miles. Jamaica's area is 4,243 square miles, while Cuba's is 44,000 square miles. See Games, *Migration and the Origins of the English Atlantic World*, p. 121, and Pope, *Harry Morgan's Way*, p. 15.

16. A. P. Newton, *The Colonising Activities of the English Puritans: The Last Phase of the Elizabethan Struggle with Spain*, New Haven, CT, Yale University Press, 1914, p. 323.

17. William Sorsby, *Old Providence Island: Puritans, Pirates and Spaniards 1630-1670*, chapter 6, p. 3.

18. Ibid., chapter 6, p. 19.

19. Blair Worden, *God's Instruments: Political Conduct in the England of Oliver Cromwell*, Oxford, Oxford University Press, 2012, p. 56.

20. Austin Woolrych, *Commonwealth to Protectorate*, Oxford, Clarendon Press, 1982, pp. 165, 274.

21. Hill, *God's Englishman*, p. 175.

22. Ibid., p. 171.

23. Hunt, *The English Civil War at First Hand*, p. 274.

24. The quote is from the Scottish Presbyterian theologian Samuel Rutherford. See Hill, *God's Englishman*, p. 217.

25. Henry Parker, a nephew and close associate of Lord Saye, in his *Discourse on Puritans*, cited in Kupperman, *Providence Island 1630-1641*, p. 248.

26. Hill, *God's Englishman*, p. 256.

CHAPTER 13 – THE RISE OF PORT ROYAL AND THE RECAPTURE OF PROVIDENCE

1. Cyril Hamshere, *The British in the Caribbean*, Cambridge, MA, Harvard University Press, 1972, p. 63.

2. William Sorsby, *Old Providence Island: Puritans, Pirates and Spaniards*

1630-1670, chapter 6, p. 18.

3. 'America and West Indies: April 1662,' *Calendar of State Papers Colonial, America and West Indies*, vol. 5, 1661-1668, W Noel Sainsbury, (ed.), London, 1880, pp. 84–9.

4. Instruction to Thomas, Lord Windsor, cited in David Marley, *Wars of the Americas: A Chronology of Armed Conflict in the Western Hemisphere, 1492 to the Present*, vol. 2, Santa Barbara, CA, ABC-CLIO, 2008, p. 239.

5. In the words of a contemporary observer cited in Hamshere, *The British in the Caribbean*, p. 74.

6. Instructions to Thomas, Lord Windsor, cited in Sorsby, *Old Providence Island*, chapter 6, p. 16.

7. Citations from correspondence between Modyford and Charles II taken from Sorsby, *Old Providence Island*, chapter 7, p. 7.

8. A. P. Thornton, *West India Policy Under the Restoration*, Oxford, Clarendon Press, 1956, p. 37.

9. E. A. Cruickshank, *The Life of Sir Henry Morgan*, Toronto, Macmillan, 1935, p. 136.

10. Dudley Pope, *Harry Morgan's Way: The Biography of Sir Henry Morgan, 1635–84*, London, Martin Secker & Warburg, 1977, p. 252.

11. Ibid., p. 65.

12. Gabriel Kuhn, *Life under the Jolly Roger: Reflections on Golden Age Piracy*, Oakland, CA, PM Press, 2010, p. 43.

13. James Burney, *History of the Buccaneers of America*, Payne and Foss, 1816; Reissued online as *Project Gutenberg's History of the Buccaneers of America, by James Burney*, 2011, p. 45.

14. Ibid., p. 55.

15. Pope, *Harry Morgan's Way*, p. 125.

16. Cruickshank, *The Life of Sir Henry Morgan*, p. 20.

17. Sorsby, *Old Providence Island*, chapter 7, p. 13.

18. Ibid., chapter 8, p. 3.

19. Pope, *Harry Morgan's Way*, p. 130.

20. Sorsby, *Old Providence Island*, chapter 8, p. 6.

21. Pope, *Harry Morgan's Way*, p. 131.

22. Diana Souhami, *Selkirk's Island*, London, Weidenfeld & Nicolson, 2001, p. 101.

23. John Esquemeling and Henry Powell, *The Buccaneers of America: A True Account of the Most Remarkable Assaults Committed of Late Years Upon the Coasts of the West Indies by the Buccaneers of Jamaica and Tortuga*, Cambridge, Cambridge University Press, 2010, p. 191.

24. Sorsby, *Old Providence Island*, chapter 9, p. 3.

CHAPTER 14 – HENRY MORGAN, ADMIRAL OF THE BRETHREN

1. Patrick Leigh Fermor, *The Traveller's Tree: A Journey Through the Caribbean Islands*, London, Penguin Travel Library, 1950, pp 310–11.
2. Robert Guttman, 'Henry Morgan: The Pirate who Invaded Panama in 1671', *Military History Magazine*, 1991.
3. Dudley Pope, *Harry Morgan's Way: The Biography of Sir Henry Morgan, 1635–84*, London, Martin Secker & Warburg, 1977, p. 153.
4. Cyril Hamshere, *The British in the Caribbean*, Cambridge, MA, Harvard University Press, 1972, p. 84.
5. Cited in William Sorsby, *Old Providence Island: Puritans, Pirates and Spaniards 1630-1670*, chapter 9, p. 11.
6. A. O. Esquemelin (trans. Alexis Brown), *The Buccaneers of America*, London 1972), p. 145. Cited in Sorsby, *Old Providence Island*, chapter 9, p. 14.
7. Pope, *Harry Morgan's Way*, p. 242.
8. Hamshere, *The British in the Caribbean*, p. 85.
9. Cited in Sorsby, *Old Providence Island*, chapter 7, p. 17.
10. Sorsby, *Old Providence Island*, chapter 9, p. 15. The only eyewitness account of how Henry Morgan took Santa Catalina was written by the Dutch pirate-surgeon Alexander Esquemelin. His accuracy has always been suspect, but in recent years two other accounts have come to light that confirm his account. The young Spaniard Fernando Mercado Saavedra and the Indian simply known as Juan de la O were captured by Henry Morgan's deputy, Edward Collier, and taken to Santa Catalina to serve as guides. Their testimonies are in the *Escribania de Camara* of the Archives of the Indies in Seville.
11. Esquemelin *The Buccaneers of America*, p. 145. Cited in Sorsby, *Old Providence Island*, chapter 9, p. 14.
12. Unless otherwise stated, quotes from those who took Providence with Morgan are taken from Esquemelin, *The Buccaneers of America*, cited in Pope, *Harry Morgan's Way*, pp. 216–19.
13. Guttman, 'Henry Morgan: The Pirate who Invaded Panama in 1671'.
14. Pope, *Harry Morgan's Way*, p. 237.
15. Peter Earle, *The Sack of Panama*, New York, Viking Press, 1981, p. 244.
16. Sorsby, *Old Providence Island*, chapter 10, p. 12.
17. Hamshere, *The British in the Caribbean*, p. 87.
18. £237,000 would be worth £19.6 million in today's money, while £107,000 is the equivalent of £8.8 million today. Pope, *Harry Morgan's Way*, p. 249.
19. Karen Ordahl Kupperman, *Providence Island 1630-1641: The Other Puritan Colony*, Cambridge, Cambridge University Press, 1993, p. 355.
20. Sorsby, *Old Providence Island*, chapter 11, p. 4.
21. Ibid., chapter 11, p. 20.
22. *Dictionary of National Biography* entry for Sir Thomas Modyford. Cited in

Sorsby, *Old Providence Island*, chapter 11, p. 2.

23. Pope, *Harry Morgan' Way*, p. 264.

24. James Parsons, *San Andrés and Providencia*, Bogotá, Banco de la República, 1964, p. 39.

CHAPTER 15 – MARINERS, CASTAWAYS AND RENEGADES

1. 'Henry Halhead and Providence Island', *Cake and Cockhorse*, Banbury Historical Society, 1978.

2. James Burney, *History of the Buccaneers of America*, Payne and Foss, 1816; Reissued online as *Project Gutenberg's History of the Buccaneers of America, by James Burney*, 2011, p. 325.

3. Ibid., p. 326.

4. Dudley Pope, *Harry Morgan's Way: The Biography of Sir Henry Morgan, 1635–84*, London, Martin Secker & Warburg, 1977, p. 334.

5. Reference to Britain's income from its colonies is an estimate Pitt the Younger made in 1798. Isabel Clemente, *San Andres y Providencia: Tradiciones culturales y coyuntura politica*, Uniandes, 1989, p. 32.

6. Cyril Hamshere, *The British in the Caribbean*, Cambridge, MA, Harvard University Press, 1972, p. 128.

7. John Style was writing in 1670. See Orlando Patterson, *The Sociology of Slavery*, London, MacGibbon and Kee, 1967, p. 46.

8. The Royal Africa Company surrendered its monopoly over the traffic in slaves when the Stuarts were deposed at the Glorious Revolution of 1688. Ibid., p. 95.

9. Ibid., p. 43.

10. Stephen Kemble, the American commander of a British ship, described the stay he made on San Andrés in 1780 in *The Kemble Papers*. He found about twelve families living there. They had 100 head of cattle and raised a little cotton. See James Parsons, *San Andrés and Providencia*, Bogotá, Banco de la República, 1964, p. 40.

11. Ibid., p. 35.

12. According to a report that the government inspector, José del Río, prepared for his superiors in Cartagena in 1793.

13. We also know that Coromantis survived the middle passage in greater numbers than did other tribes, which is why the elements of West African culture that survived the voyage to the New World tended to be Coromanti. The Ibo and other Nigerian slaves were considered 'the lowest and most wretched of all the nations of Africa,' with a marked tendency to commit suicide once in chains. The culture of the Congolese and Angolan slaves disintegrated under the pressure of enslavement. Bryan Edwards, pp. 88–9. Cited in Patterson, *The Sociology of Slavery*, p. 137.

14. James Parsons, *San Andrés and Providencia*, Bogotá, Banco de la República, 1964, p. 42.
15. Ibid., p. 44.
16. This is the explanation favoured by J. Cordell Robinson in *The Genealogical History of Providencia Island*, San Bernandino, CA, Borgo Press, 1996, pp. 8, 101.
17. Ibid, p. 8
18. Orlando Patterson, *The Sociology of Slavery*, London, MacGibbon and Kee, 1967, p. 49.

Chapter 16 – The Last Englishman

1. In referring to 'Curracoa natives,' Jacob Dunham must have meant visitors from the Dutch colony of Curaçao, although this is the only mention I have seen of their presence on Providence. Quotes from Dunham's journal are from Project Gutenberg's eBook of Jacob Dunham, *Journal of Voyages, Containing an Account of the Author's being Twice Captured by the English and Once by Gibbs the Pirate*, New York, 1850, p. 116. Available at http://www.gutenberg.org/files/33835/33835-h/33835-h.htm
2. *Memorias de Agustín Codazzi*, Marisa Vannini Gerulewicz (ed.), Caracas, Universidad Central de Venezuela, 1970, p. 334.
3. James Parsons, *San Andrés and Providencia*, Bogotá, Banco de la República, 1964, p. 50.
4. Ibid.
5. *Memorias de Agustín Codazzi*, p. 465.
6. The government of colonial America was modelled on that of Spain, which was divided into 32 provinces, each headed by a Treasury official known as an *intendente*, and 14 military regions, each headed by a viceroy, captain-general or *commandante general*. In 1888, the islands became part of the department of Bolívar. The capital of the island intendencia was only transferred to San Andrés in 1912. Parsons, *San Andrés and Providencia*, p. 164.
7. Ibid. C. F. Collett says that 'criminals are transported here and to St. Andrews, for which purpose these islands appear to have been used by the Spaniards previous to their being taken possession of by the buccaneers.'
8. C. F. Collett, 'On the Island of Old Providence', *Journal of the Royal Geographical Society of London*, vol. 7, 1837, pp. 203–10.
9. The Colombian peso was worth 80 US cents in 1830 (see Frank Safford, *The Ideal of the Practical: Colombia's Struggle to Form a Technical Elite*, Austin, TX, University of Texas Press, 2014, p. xi). The dollar was worth £4.76 that year (see Victor Bulmer-Thomas, *The Economic History of the Caribbean Since the Napoleonic Wars*, Cambridge, Cambridge University

Press, 2012, p. 496), which means that 113 Colombian pesos would have been worth £433 in 1830, the equivalent of £21,429 today.

10. According to a Colombian government report of 1835, cited in Adolfo Meisel Roca, 'La estructura economica de San Andrés y Providencia en 1846', *Cuadernos de Historia Económica y Empresarial*, Banco de la República, no. 24, 2009.

11. Described in 1912 by John Albert, one of two brothers who came to Providence as Catholic missionaries from Baltimore. See J. Cordell Robinson, *The Genealogical History of Providencia Island*, San Bernandino, CA, Borgo Press, 1996, p. 16, fn. p. 46. A catboat, or a cat-rigged sailboat, is a sailing vessel characterized by a single mast carried well forward, usually near its bow.

12. Charles Leslie, *A New History of Jamaica: From the Earliest Accounts to the Taking of Porto Bello by Vice-Admiral Vernon*, London, 1740, p. 36, cited in Orlando Patterson, *The Sociology of Slavery*, London, MacGibbon and Kee, 1967, p. 39.

13. Patterson, *The Sociology of Slavery*, p. 40.

14. Ibid., p. 39.

15. Charles Corbett, *Essay Concerning Slavery*, London, 1746. Cited in Patterson, *The Sociology of Slavery*, p. 50.

16. Cyril Hamshere, *The British in the Caribbean*, Cambridge, MA, Harvard University Press, 1972, p. 131.

17. Parsons, *San Andrés and Providencia*, p. 45.

18. Information on the origins of Providence's black population is taken from *A History of Old Providence*, an anonymous testimony given to anthropologist Bill Washabaugh in 1980. The most likely source of this information is the island's late, unofficial historian Oscar Bryan, who is the subject of Peter J. Wilson's *Oscar: An Enquiry into the Nature of Sanity*, Long Grove, IL, Waveland Press, 1974. Orlando Patterson says that in Jamaica the Mongala were called 'Mungolas' or 'Munguelas.' See Patterson, *The Sociology of Slavery*, p. 140.

19. Patterson, *The Sociology of Slavery*, p. 105.

CHAPTER 17 – 'A SORT OF LYING THAT MAKES A GREAT HOLE IN THE HEART'

1. Cited in Paul Theroux, *Sir Vidia's Shadow: A Friendship Across Five Continents*, London, Penguin, 1998, p. 353.

2. All quotes are from Lady Jane Porter and William Ogilvie Porter, *Sir Edward Seaward's Narrative, of his Shipwreck and Subsequent Discovery of Certain Islands in the Caribbean Sea*, London, Longman Brown Green and

Longmans, 1841, 2 vols.

3. Samuel Carter Hall, *Dictionary of National Biography*, entry for Jane Porter.
4. At some point between 1634, when the Miskito headman Jeremy allowed his son Oldman to journey to England, and 1823, the tribe's chief became a king. Whether this was an organic process, mimicry of the English, or foisted upon the Miskitos by the governor of Jamaica is open to conjecture. See Michael Olien, 'The Miskito Kings and the Line of Succession', *Journal of Anthropological Research*, vol. 39, no. 201, 1983.
5. Robert A. Naylor, *Penny Ante Imperialism: The Mosquito Shore and the Bay of Honduras 1600-1914*, Plainsboro, NJ, Associated University Presses, 1989, p. 79.
6. For details of Poyais, see David Sinclair, *The Land That Never Was: Sir Gregor MacGregor and the Most Audacious Fraud in History*, Cambridge, MA, Da Capo Press, 2004, p. 15.
7. Naylor, *Penny Ante Imperialism*, p. 79.
8. George Wilson Bridges, *The Annals of Jamaica*, 1828 (reprint), London, John Murray, vol. 2, 1968, p. 143. Cited in Karl H. Offen, 'British Logwood Extraction from the Mosquitia: The Origin of a Myth', *Hispanic American Historical Review*, vol. 80, no. 1, 2000.
9. Sinclair, *The Land That Never Was*, p. 98.
10. *Lady Nugent's Journal of Her Residence in Jamaica from 1801 to 1805*, Philip Wright (ed.), Institute of Jamaica 1966, p. 211.
11. Sinclair, *The Land That Never Was*, p. 261.
12. Ibid., p. 294.
13. Walwin G. Peterson, *The Province of Providence*, Pueblo Viejo, Christian University of San Andres, 2001, p. 58.

CHAPTER 18 – HOW THE LIGHT CAME IN

1. Loren C. Turnage, *Island Heritage: a Baptist View of the History of San Andrés and Providencia*, Cali, Historical Commission of the Colombia Baptist Mission, 1977, p. 19.
2. Adolfo Meisel Roca, *La estructura economica de San Andrés y Providencia en 1846*, Cuadernos de Historia Economica y Empresarial, Banco de la República, no. 24, 2009.
3. Ibid.
4. Martha Beckwith, *Black Roadways: A Study of Jamaican Folk Life*, Chapel Hill, NC, University of North Carolina Press, 1929, p. 89. Cited in Orlando Patterson, *The Sociology of Slavery*, London, MacGibbon and Kee, 1967, p. 203.
5. James Phillippo, *Jamaica: Its Past and Present State*, J. Snow, 1843, cited in Patterson, *The Sociology of Slavery*, p. 185.

6. G. W. Bridges, *The Annals of Jamaica*, vol. I, London, 1827, p. 555.
7. Cyril Hamshere, *The British in the Caribbean*, Cambridge, MA, Harvard University Press, 1972, p. 157.
8. Turnage, *Island Heritage*, p. 25.
9. James J. Parsons, *San Andrés and Providencia*, Oakland, CA, University of California, 1956, p. 70.
10. A report prepared by Philip Beekman Kivingston, SS Commercial Agent, San Andrés, 31 December 1873.
11. *The Cultivation of Coconut on San Andrés Island*, a short description written by Philip Beekman Livingston Jr in 1873; unpublished.
12. In 1953, there were 25 deaf-mutes on Providence. The rate of deafness was running at 12.5 per thousand people, which was considerably higher than the global average of 1.6 per thousand. J. Cordell Robinson, *The Genealogical History of Providencia Island*, San Bernandino, CA, Borgo Press, 1996, pp. 65, 70.
13. Turnage, *Island Heritage*, p. 26.

CHAPTER 19 – MODERN TIMES

1. J. Cordell Robinson, *The Genealogical History of Providencia Island*, San Bernandino, CA, Borgo Press, 1996, pp. 52, 80.
2. Cited in Thomas R. Hietala, *Manifest Design: American Exceptionalism and Empire*, Ithaca, NY, Cornell University Press, 2003, p. 255.
3. Robinson, *The Genealogical History of Providencia Island*, p. 16. There are more details in the footnotes on p. 27.
4. For more details, see James J. Parsons, *San Andrés and Providencia*, Oakland, CA, University of California, 1956, p. 69. Not all of the islanders fell back on an angry God to explain the crisis. Worldlier heads knew that the same blight had also wiped out the coconut groves on the mainland. In 1929, the islands had responded to the protectionism in vogue among Central American governments by opening trade with Cartagena and Barranquilla. The mainlanders often wrapped their goods in the fronds of the coconut palm, and the blight had travelled with them.
5. Jay Edwards, *Social Linguistics on San Andrés and Providencia*, Tulane University (unpublished Ph.D dissertation) 1970.
6. The quotes are from Parsons, *San Andrés and Providencia*, p. 94. The first statistic is from p. 87. The second is from Wikipedia/San Andrés.
7. Facts and figures relating to life on Providence in the 1950s and 1960s are taken from Parsons, *San Andrés and Providencia*, p. 12; pp.100-3.

Chapter 20 – 'Maybe They Don't Know What an Island Is'

1. The poll was conducted by Harold Bush in 1988. Isabel Clemente, *San Andres y Providencia: Tradiciones culturales y coyuntura politica*, Uniandes, 1989, p. 243.

Chapter 21 – 'Still a Little Behind Time'

1. See http://www.folkplay.info/Texts/86sk--lj.htm. Also https://en.wikipedia.org/wiki/The_Derby_Ram.
2. James J. Parsons, *San Andrés and Providencia*, Oakland, CA, University of California, 1956, p. 75.

Epilogue

1. 'Empire Strikes Back,' *New Internationalist*, 2013.

Index

Providence Island *cont.*
  Britain, becomes strategically
    insignificant to 249
  church, absence of 254
  christianity, attitudes to on 289
  creation by volcano 214
  creation myth of 334
  crime on 318
  crops and food sources 15, 17, 34, 39,
    41, 68, 77, 92, 99 223, 243, 250,
    316, 333
  as 'Eden' 16, 38
  education established on 290, 299
  empire building, and 158
  first Europeans on 5
  major families of 215
  independence within state of
    Colombia 246
  independence, islanders' views on
    246, 321
  *Intendencia de Providencia y
    San Andrés* ix, 246–8, 362
  labour shortage on 78
  land mass 358
  maps of the world, not on 222
  modern amenities arrive 308
  names of islanders on 289
  politics of modern Providence 321
  population of 215, 238, 279, 308,
    314
  present day journey to 212
  privateering centre of 93, 97, 187,
    245
  racial hierarchy on 313
  religious revival in nineteenth
    century 288
  servants, use of 42
  slavery, end of 281
  slaves, possible survival of 207
  slaves, fear of growth of 108
  Spanish take control 189
  Spanish language imposed 303
  treasure, rumours of 217, 252, 333,
    334–5
  Western Design, and 166, 176

Providence Island Company, the ix,
    10–14, 16–19, 25, 30, 34, 39–41,
    43–5, 57–9, 63–7, 74–7, 85, 87–
    9, 92–6, 98, 100–9, 113, 115–16,
    122, 124–7, 129–31, 135, 137–8,
    145, 156, 158, 160, 162, 170, 172,
    211, 259–60, 270, 303, 357
  monarchy, as focus of opposition to
    101
  ideals realised? 278
  loss of island, reaction to 137–8
  rebuff Puritan proposals 76
Providence, Rhode Island ix, 258
Providence, the 102
Prynne, William 89
Puerto Rico 155
Punt, Captain Thomas 54–5, 350
Purchas, his Pilgrimage 35
Purchas, Samuel 35
Puritans and Puritanism ix-xi, 7, 23–7
    74–5, 144–8, 148, 172–4, 341
  attitudes to Charles II 170
  attitudes to God 24, 29, 54, 71–2,
    111–2
  grandees 10–13, 41, 75
  idea of America 29–30
  impact on world of finance 171–2
  legacy of 171–3, 330, 341–3
  psyche 25–6, 171–2
  self-belief in English Civil War 147
  sports and games and 26–7, 68, 73,
    330
  version of imperialism and ideas
    about 127, 158
  way of life 19, 24–7
Pym, John 7, 11, 12, 13, 19, 40, 44–6,
    52, 94, 96, 100, 104, 124–9,
    143–4, 156, 158, 160

R

radio 321–2
Raleigh, Sir Walter 57, 94–5, 206
Reformation, the 8–9, 24, 47, 72
religious revival of late eighteenth
    century 281–2

T

tallow 16, 102, 130

Tanner, Captain John 30–1, 36, 40, 50, 53

Teach, Edward 'Blackbeard' 205

Tempest, The 1

Texas 299

y Texeda, Antonio Maldonado 119, 132–3

theocracy, rule by 77

Thirty Years' War, the 9, 60

Thompson, Maurice 10, 162

Three Brothers Cays 214, 316

von Tietje, Dr Herman 301–3

tobacco 5, 10, 17–18, 30, 35, 40–2, 44, 50, 68, 76, 79, 81–2, 84, 88, 92, 95, 102, 130, 131, 149, 161, 228, 233, 235, 243, 265

Tobago 92, 101, 129, 136, 276

Tolú 135, 154

Tortuga 178, 180, 182, 186, 219

tourism x, 312, 327–9, 342

Town 213, 222, 253, 280, 297, 328

Treasure Island (1883) vii

Treasurer, the 58, 107

Treaties of Versailles 230, 234, 240, 242, 271

Treaty of Madrid, the 196–7, 205

Trinidad 101, 136, 276

Trujillo 113, 114, 151, 153, 244

Turner, Richard 303–5

turtles 16, 60, 61 64, 111, 233, 251, 255–6, 314–5

U

United Fruit Company 301

United States of America (USA) 4, 10–11, 17, 35, 58, 66, 74, 107, 180 , 211, 221–2, 230, 236, 248, 254, 282, 287–8, 290, 292, 299–301, 303, 305, 309, 314, 323, 332–4,

USS *Nashville* 300

V

Valentine, the 152

Venables, General Robert 163–5

Venezuela 241, 247, 277

Veracruz 57, 96, 238

Vetsera, Baroness Mary 302

Victoria, Queen 329

La Violencia 309

Virginia 1, 7, 11, 17, 28–30, 32, 34–5, 38, 46, 50, 66, 68, 73, 78–9, 107

  tobacco crops 17

Virginia Company, the 35

W

Wallace, Captain 136

Wallace, William 259, 267

Wanki 338–40 (see also Miskito King, the)

Warner, Thomas 10

War of a Thousand Days, the 300

wars of independence in Latin America, the 241, 248

Wars of Religion, the 21–2, 52, 100

Warwick, Earl of (Robert Rich) 2, 6–7, 9, 11, 13, 17, 19, 24–5, 28, 58, 66, 75, 100–1, 103–5, 126–7, 129, 136, 144, 151, 155–6, 160–1, 170

  appointed Governor-in-Chief of the Colonies 155

  death of 170

Warwick, Sir Philip 12

Warwick, the 102

Wentworth, Thomas (Earl of Stafford) 128

Western Design, the 160–8, 173, 175–6, 179,

  failure of 165

Whetstone, Sir Thomas 186–7, 189–90, 192–3

whip, use of as punishment 255

Winslow, Edward 11

Winthrop, John 10, 17, 71, 130–1, 161

witchcraft 23, 176 (see also obeah)

Wormeley, Christopher 87

X

Y

Z